Studia Fennica
Linguistica 18

THE FINNISH LITERATURE SOCIETY (SKS) was founded in 1831 and has, from the very beginning, engaged in publishing operations. It nowadays publishes literature in the fields of ethnology and folkloristics, linguistics, literary research and cultural history.

The first volume of the Studia Fennica series appeared in 1933. Since 1992, the series has been divided into three thematic subseries: Ethnologica, Folkloristica and Linguistica. Two additional subseries were formed in 2002, Historica and Litteraria. The subseries Anthropologica was formed in 2007.

In addition to its publishing activities, the Finnish Literature Society maintains research activities and infrastructures, an archive containing folklore and literary collections, a research library and promotes Finnish literature abroad.

STUDIA FENNICA EDITORIAL BOARD

Pasi Ihalainen, professor, University of Jyväskylä, Finland
Timo Kaartinen, docent, lecturer, University of Helsinki, Finland
Taru Nordlund, docent, lecturer, University of Helsinki, Finland
Riikka Rossi, docent, researcher, University of Helsinki, Finland
Katriina Siivonen, substitute professor, University of Helsinki, Finland
Lotte Tarkka, professor, University of Helsinki, Finland
Tuomas M. S. Lehtonen, Dr. Phil., Secretary General, Finnish Literature Society, Finland
Tero Norkola, Publishing Director, Finnish Literature Society, Finland
Kati Romppanen, Secretary of the Board, Finnish Literature Society, Finland

Editorial Office
SKS
P.O. Box 259
FI-00171 Helsinki
www.finlit.fi

Registers of Communication

Edited by
Asif Agha & Frog

Finnish Literature Society • SKS • Helsinki

Studia Fennica Linguistica 18

The publication has undergone a peer review.

VERTAISARVIOITU
KOLLEGIALT GRANSKAD
PEER-REVIEWED
www.tsv.fi/tunnus

The open access publication of this volume has received part funding via
a Jane and Aatos Erkko Foundation grant.

© 2015 Asif Agha, Frog and SKS
License CC-BY-NC-ND 4.0 International

A digital edition of a printed book first published in 2015 by the Finnish Literature Society.
Cover Design: Timo Numminen
EPUB: eLibris Media Oy

ISBN 978-951-858-017-4 (Print)
ISBN 978-952-222-798-0 (PDF)
ISBN 978-952-222-799-7 (EPUB)

ISSN 0085-6835 (Studia Fennica)
ISSN 1235-1938 (Studia Fennica Linguistica)

DOI: http://dx.doi.org/10.21435/sflin.18

This work is licensed under a Creative Commons CC-BY-NC-ND 4.0 International License.
To view a copy of the license, please visit http://creativecommons.org/licenses/by-nc-nd/4.0/

A free open access version of the book is available at
http://dx.doi.org/10.21435/sflin.18 or by scanning this
QR code with your mobile device.

Bod – Books on Demand, Norderstedt, Germany 2018

Contents

Preface   7
Acknowledgements   9

Introduction

    Asif Agha and Frog
    An Introduction to Registers of Communication   13

I. Approaching Register Phenomena

    Asif Agha
1. Enregisterment and Communication in Social History   27

    Susanna Shore
2. Register in Systemic Functional Linguistics   54

    Frog
3. Registers of Oral Poetry   77

II. Between Language and Register

    Janus Spindler Møller
4. The Enregisterment of Minority Languages in a Danish Classroom   107

    Lian Malai Madsen
5. Investigating a Register Label
Integrated Speech in Copenhagen   124

    Kapitolina Fedorova
6. Foreigner Talk
A Register or Registers?   138

    Alejandro I. Paz
7. Stranger Sociality in the Home
Israeli Hebrew as Register in Latino Domestic Interaction   150

III. Registers in Transition

TIMO KAARTINEN
8. The Registers and Persuasive Powers of an Indonesian Village Chronicle   165

JAMES M. WILCE AND JANINA FENIGSEN
9. Mourning and Honor
Register in Karelian Lament   187

DOROTHY NOYES
10. Inimitable Examples
School Texts and the Classical Register in Contemporary French Politics   210

IV. Corpus and Performance

WILLIAM LAMB
11. Verbal Formulas in Gaelic Traditional Narrative
Some Aspects of Their Form and Function   225

MARGARET BENDER
12. Shifting Linguistic Registers and the Nature of the Sacred in Cherokee   247

EILA STEPANOVA
13. The Register of Karelian Lamenters   258

V. Performance and Poetics

14. "On Traditional Register in Oral Poetry" (pp. 277–306), comprised of previously published selections of John Miles Foley's works, is not included in the open access publication for reasons of copyright.

LAURI HARVILAHTI
15. Register in Oral Traditional Phraseology   307

KATI KALLIO
16. Multimodal Register and Performance Arena in Ingrian Oral Poetry   322

Contributors   336
Index   337

Preface

The present volume is the result of a multi-year initiative to bring together scholars from both sides of the Atlantic into an interdisciplinary dialogue on register phenomena. These efforts culminated in two Register Colloquia at the University of Helsinki. The first one, titled "Register: Intersections of Language, Context and Communication", met during 23–25 May 2012. The second one, titled "Register II: Emergence, Change and Obsolescence", met during 22–24 May 2013. The articles collected here are drawn from materials presented at these colloquia, including papers by keynote speakers and invited contributions from additional participants.

The Helsinki Register Colloquia were organized by the Department of Folklore Studies of the University of Helsinki and by the Academy of Finland research project "Oral and Literary Culture in the Medieval and Early Modern Baltic Sea Region: Cultural Transfer, Linguistic Registers and Communicative Networks" (2011–2014) of the Finnish Literature Society.

These colloquia brought together scholars from three continents and many fields for a series of rich and fruitful discussions that worked to span many disciplinary divides. Of course, our coming together as scholars was only a first step. Opening up a cross-disciplinary conversation – or any conversation – depends on language, and on frameworks within which that language is used. The Helsinki Colloquia offered a venue in which many frameworks and perspectives could be engaged and negotiated in a multidisciplinary fashion. The success of these conversations nonetheless depended on our recognition that all relevant terminologies and analytic frameworks are not always fully shared by all participants. In other words, rather than concern over a language-barrier in the conventional sense, we were concerned with overcoming the register-barriers that have developed between traditions of scholarship. This involved recognizing that register contrasts involved not just differences in lexicons or grammars, but were bound up with differences in larger frameworks for thinking about conduct and communication – theories, ideologies and valuations – which might also require "translation" or elucidation if communication was going to succeed. The challenge posed by communication also had another, positive side. The process of "translating" from the terminologies and frames of reference of one discipline into those of another necessarily involved bridging distinct perspectives, and this process itself produced *new* perspectives on the ideas, concepts and data being "translated", leading in turn to the development of new understandings and new knowledge.

The editors have worked actively with all contributors to improve the multidisciplinary accessibility of individual articles and to increase dialogue between them. Our multidisciplinary conversations have enabled the negotiation of new understandings of "register" both as a term and a concept, and these ideas have been carried forward from the Helsinki Register Colloquia into the articles that constitute this volume. It is our hope that a continuing dialogue with the perspectives of our readers may take this multidisciplinary conversation even further.

Acknowledgements

For their support in holding the Helsinki Register Colloquia during 2012 and 2013, we would like to thank: the Finnish Cultural Foundation; the Federation of Finnish Learned Societies; the Academy of Finland research project "Oral and Literary Culture in the Medieval and Early Modern Baltic Sea Region: Cultural Transfer, Linguistic Registers and Communicative Networks" (2011–2014) of the Finnish Literature Society; the Academy of Finland research project "Oral Poetry, Mythic Knowledge, and Vernacular Imagination: Interfaces of Individual Expression and Collective Traditions in Pre-Modern Northeast Europe" (2012–2016) of Folklore Studies, University of Helsinki; and the Research Community "Cultural Meanings and Vernacular Genres (CMVG)" of Folklore Studies, University of Helsinki.

We would also like to thank David Elmer, Lauri Harvilahti and John Zemke for their help in organizing a suitable contribution by the late John Miles Foley, and Pennsylvania State University Press and Indiana University Press for their kind permission to reproduce relevant passages from Foley's published work.

Finally, we would like to thank all of the many participants of the Helsinki Register Colloquia for the discussions and insights that are in the background of this collection and the work it presents.

Introduction

Asif Agha and Frog

An Introduction to Registers of Communication

It may not be an exaggeration to say that our understanding of linguistic and other forms of human communication has advanced more during the 20th century than in any preceding period. Yet these changes did not occur all at once. Instead, different levels of organization within communicative conduct became focal objects of scholarly attention at different times. Earlier in the 20th century, research paradigms in many disciplines were dominated by approaches that favored abstract models of homogenous sign systems underlying the complexities of situated communication. A transformative shift began after the middle of the century, when scholarship began to turn from abstractable models to contextual and perspectival variation, from an exclusive focus on *langue*, defined as the object of linguistics by Ferdinand de Saussure (1857–1913), to the organization of *parole* into forms of situated language use within social practices. Attention to situated practices soon revealed that many features of *parole* rely on the tendency of language users to adapt the resources of *langue* in heterogeneous ways within specific varieties of communicative conduct. "Register" originated as a term to designate these varieties.

In recent decades, approaches to register phenomena have become central to many disciplines in Europe and North America. The present volume brings together work by anthropologists, folklorists, linguists, and philologists. The sixteen articles collected here represent approaches that have developed on both sides of the Atlantic. Many authors discuss the development of register studies in their own fields and employ analytic techniques developed within distinct disciplinary traditions. They focus on the register organization of a range of semiotic devices – whether grammatical units or prosody, whether lexical items or melodic contours, whether verbal signs or kinesic behaviors, whether spoken as utterances or circulated through script-artifacts. They describe models of communicative conduct in a variety of social practices and historical locales, and the range of phenomena they describe is far wider than those studied in early approaches to registers.

The epistemological limits of earlier approaches were shaped by the circumstances in which they emerged: as they began to explore situated discursive practices towards the middle of the 20th century, scholars continued, ironically enough, to rely on *langue*-centric criteria for identifying registers, even as they tried to move beyond them. For instance, in an early use of the term "register" as a label for speech varieties, T. B. W. Reid identified differences in registers of speech and writing mainly by appeal to lexical or grammatical criteria, as if variation in language use involved nothing else, as if these dimensions of variation sufficed as criteria for reasoning about complex social practices; and although he linked observable facts of discursive variation to what – as he put it – may "roughly" be called "different social situations" (Reid 1956: 32), he lacked explicit criteria on how such "social situations" are distinguished from each other, or how utterances become linked to them, or for whom they do so, or when, or why. Other writers who took up aspects of Reid's definition continued to link facts of discursive variation to "different situations" (Halliday, McIntosh & Stevens 1964: 87) or to "types of situation" (Hymes 1974: 440), but lacked explicit criteria on either identifying or characterizing such "types", or specifying why only some differences among them mattered to speech variation while others did not. And so it was that early definitions of the term "register" were felt by contemporaries to lack "any precise and clear sense" (Hervey 1992: 191), and the lack of explicit criteria seemed to them to constitute "problems inherent" to its use in empirical research (Ferguson 1981: 10), so that many of them avoided the term altogether.

It is hardly surprising, however, that, in the intervening half-century, studies of register phenomena have moved well beyond the limitations of early work. The authors of the accompanying articles rely on a great many developments that differentiate the contemporary study of situated discourse from earlier efforts, and describe the developments on which they rely in their own articles. They describe a great variety of communicative signs (whether verbal or non-verbal, whether audible or visible) that are brought together into locale-specific models of communicative conduct, or *registers of communication*, whose signs are performed and construed in relatively symmetrical ways by persons acquainted with them, and enable them to interact with each other in specific social-interpersonal practices.

These articles are grouped into five thematically organized sections. The opening section brings together a few perspectives on these developments and orients the reader to the main issues that underlie recent developments.

Approaching Register Phenomena

Although any perceivable behavior communicates something to someone who perceives it, not all such behaviors are organized as socio-centric models of communicative conduct, or as register models whose signs are performed and construed in comparable ways by a group of communicators. When such social-semiotic regularities do exist, they are identifiable only in the practices of those who treat them *as* a distinct register, and thereby comprise the social domain of its users. When semiotic registers are approached as locale-specific models of communication and as models-for specific social domains of users, as in the accompanying articles, the initial point of departure for identifying them, and for differentiating them from other behaviors, is always the set of reflexive practices through which varied semiotic devices (such as the ones noted earlier or described below) are grouped together into models of significant conduct by those whose behaviors these are, where explicit ethnographic attention to *who* these persons are (as a group differentiable from others) also identifies the social categories of persons in whose lives the register enables a distinctive set of social practices. The identification of such models relies on a broad range of metasemiotic data that typify the form and significance of the behaviors they model. Such typifications explicitly or implicitly group specific behaviors together as comparable in indexical effects (and hence identifiable as repertoires of *that* register, and not of some other), and also clarify the indexical significance they have (such as the specific roles and relationships they clarify) for those who recognize and deploy these signs during communicative conduct.

These themes are taken up in the initial article in this section, where Asif Agha dialogically engages the articles collected together in this volume to show that despite the enormous variety of socio-historical locales in which these authors examine register formations – and whether the practices they study are the practices of Danish schoolchildren or Gaelic storytellers or Karelian lamenters or Latino migrants or Russian traders or any of the other social categories discussed in this volume – each one of these studies relies on specific forms of metasemiotic data as criteria that distinguish specific register partials from other behaviors, and clarify the indexical significance they have for communicators. Agha employs the term "enregisterment" to describe the reflexive process through which register formations are differentiated from each other and emerge as apparently bounded sociohistorical formations for their users. He offers a comparative discussion of how features of so-called "languages" and "genres" are unitized as signs of a register by the reflexive practices of their users. And he offers a comparative discussion of the metasemiotic criteria that make the sign-types of any given register segmentable from the totality of discursive and non-discursive behaviors that co-occur with register partials in any routine instance of performance.

In her lucid review of Halliday's Systemic-Functional approach to register formations, Susanna Shore describes some of the developments that led to this early account of register formations. As Shore's discussion makes clear, the Systemic-Functional approach remained focused (like other early approaches) on a grammar-centric conception of register variation, locating registers within what is described as a "Language System". Halliday's approach tended to rely on intuitive criteria for identifying registers, and to assume that registers identified by these criteria were bounded and stable phenomena. The Systemic-Functional approach nonetheless enabled scholars to conduct a number of early studies of register phenomena. Shore's elegant description thus enables the reader to compare that approach with the other approaches employed by authors in this volume.

The section closes with Frog's discussion of registers of oral poetry. The article describes how elements of a poetic register comprise indexically significant units of different degrees of size and complexity. Frog illustrates how the form and indexical significance of signs of a poetic register tend to be genre-dependent. When verbal units become conventionally linked to indexing a particular symbolic element, their indexical values inform the meaning of the verbal unit. These devices are then used in combination with other devices to realize more complex units of communication in poetry, such as an epic story-pattern, in the same way that combinations of verbal material make a visual symbol recognizable.

Together, these three articles provide the reader with a good background for evaluating the themes and discoveries explored in later chapters.

Between Language and Register

It has long been understood that the folk-term "language" does not denote a unitary phenomenon but encompasses a number of distinct kinds of semiotic regularities, such as the phonological and morphosyntactic organization of speech tokens, deictic systems that anchor utterances to occasions of use, varied types of contrasts that occur within a language (whether of dialect, genre or style), as well as ideas and ideologies that link a language as a whole to an imagined "language community" to which speakers feel they belong as social persons, often as members of sociopolitical formations like nation-states.

The articles in the second section of this volume, *Language Contact*, address the social construction and functions of register formations in multilingual environments. As we have already noted, early approaches to register phenomena tended to focus exclusively on the grammatical organization of communicative conduct, and thus on abstract "systems" (akin to Saussure's *langue*) through which the organization of communicative conduct could be imagined. The question of how other features of a language (such as the ones just described) become linked to register contrasts that differentiate persons and practices from each other was not explicitly theorized or empirically studied in earlier approaches.

Contemporary approaches to register formations view abstract "systems" as obscuring the diversity of significant behaviors that are manifest during language use, and find that actually occurring forms of utterance contribute a far more diverse set of semiotic partials to register formations than abstract systems allow us to imagine. All of the articles in this section therefore begin with utterances as perceivable behaviors that occur in observable participation frameworks of embodied communication, and attempt to clarify the kinds of semiotic processes through which different aspects of the thing called "language" are organized or reorganized into specific register formations. They explore the ways in which discursive behaviors draw resources from each other. They examine the ways in which reflexive processes regroup some of the behaviors on which they draw into identifiable register models in communication. They explicitly describe the (sometimes implicit) metasemiotic practices that formulate features of utterance-acts as social indexicals for their users. Janus Spindler Møller's article introduces J. Normann Jørgensen's concept of "languaging" to describe how speakers draw on features of different languages as complementary and contrastive register partials in a multilingual environment. Møller focuses on the contrastive valorization of specific linguistic resources by children in a schoolroom setting, where register contrasts and their underlying valuations are negotiated in an emergent social process. Lian Malai Madsen's article then proceeds to clarify a distinct metasemiotic process that organizes speech behaviors and social relations in multilingual settings in Denmark. She shows that metapragmatic descriptions of minorities, such as Danish discourses about the "integration" of minorities, are taken up in highly distinct ways in the behaviors of these minorities, and formulate new contrasts among speech registers for them. She also shows that when minority schoolchildren evaluate speech differences, their metapragmatic practices invest speech forms with stereotypical indexical values that contribute to broader processes of sociolinguistic change, which, in turn, further differentiate relationships among registers and their users. The article by Alejandro I. Paz explores the contrastive case of uses of Israeli Hebrew by Latino immigrants in Israel, where they constitute a marginalized, bilingual migrant group. Paz describes how Hebrew and Spanish function as registers that indexically differentiate social relations among Latinos in Israel, and how contrastive registers are strategically employed and manipulated in the domestic practices of their users. Kapitolina Fedorova's article examines the characteristic ways in which Russian speakers communicate with foreign tourists in St. Petersburg on the one hand and with speakers of Chinese in a Chinese–Russian border zone on the other. Her discussion highlights the social-interpersonal organization of register formations, how they are informed by evaluative ideologies of the characteristics of persons in interlocutor roles, and how these ideologies constitute metapragmatic frameworks that differentiate distinct Russian registers of foreigner talk from each other.

These four articles make explicit themes that are implicit in other articles in this volume. The cases they explore – where distinct languages or language varieties function as distinct registers for their users – are highly transparent both to researchers and to the language users who formulate metapragmatic accounts of their own practices. Hence, through these articles, the processes through which registers emerge and the ways they index the social characteristics of persons become readily accessible to the reader, providing a background for approaching articles in later sections where these issues may not be as readily apparent.

Registers in Transition

Since registers are sociohistorical formations that invariably undergo changes in form and significance through the practices in which they are deployed, all registers are to some degree "in transition" between seemingly discrete models of communicative practice. But such changes do not occur everywhere or all at once, do not proceed at the same pace, and are not symmetrical for all users. For register formations like "standard" languages, whose characteristics are regulated by entrenched institutions, the rate of discernible change tends to be slower than for ones that are regulated to lesser degrees. Nonetheless, from the standpoint of enregisterment, any empirically describable register is a sociohistorical snapshot of larger processes of change, even if the relevant dimensions of change are not always of the same kind, or rapidity, or social consequence.

The articles in the third section of this volume thematically focus on the ways in which transformations in registers intersect with adaptations by social actors to distinct cultural circumstances and historical contexts. They focus in particular on register formations in political and religious practices, where processes of syncretism and change become directly observable whenever earlier practices are compared with more recent ones, and where the comparison shows the latter to be discernibly reorganized by newer ideologies. Whereas articles in the preceding section concentrated on registers of spoken discourse, Timo Kaartinen turns our attention to the incorporation of both oral and written registers in a document produced by a local political agent in Indonesia, who capitalizes on indexicals of authority and authenticity associated with them. The article reveals the complexity with which an individual can incorporate a wide spectrum of register partials within a single script-artifact, and, by bringing them together, pursue highly specific or singular political agendas, even as processes of cultural change decrease the number of persons capable of recognizing traditional registers across generational time. In their article on Karelian lament, James M. Wilce and Janina Fenigsen examine the practices of lament revivalists, who draw on a traditional register of oral-poetic discourse that marks deference and intimacy towards transcendent beings, and who, through access to archival materials, attempt to revive traditional lament rituals in transformed ways in order to introduce them into modern practices. The article by Dorothy Noyes then carries the discussion into the broader domain of semiotic registers that rely on the enactment and manipulation of emotionally charged public symbols in political life, and discusses the negotiation of their indexical values from different politically positioned perspectives. Noyes offers a nuanced perspective on how the activities of politicians are construed in the light of existing registers of French political conduct by media coverage of politicians' activities, and how in these forms of metapragmatic commentary in the public sphere, the registers of an earlier tradition are reanalyzed within an ongoing processes of enregisterment.

Together, these three articles offer complementary perspectives on the adaptability of register models to changing historical settings and on the consequences of these changes for the social lives of their users.

Corpus and Performance

The analysis of register formations can rely on all sorts of materials and often relies on complementary types of data. Different types of data reveal different aspects of register-mediated social processes to varying degrees.

The chapters in the second and third parts of this volume build especially on fieldwork observation, questionnaires, interviews, the media and public discourse. These varieties of data are particularly suited to investigating register models of the significance of performed behaviors, including the significance of deviations from established models, and their reanalysis into distinct models by identifiable groups in society. This is because information about social attitudes, understandings and situations of register use tend to be in sharpest focus in these types of data. The chapters of the fourth and final sections of this volume examine entextualized script-artefacts that exhibit the usage of particular registers. This type of data brings the devices that comprise a register's repertoires into sharper focus, making it better suited to answering particular types of research questions. And yet the two types of data are complementary. Although they once tended to be used exclusively or in isolation from each other, they are today generally recognized as two sides of the same coin that can be reciprocally informative, and more useful together than in isolation.

This data of register usage in script-artefacts is often constructed as a delimited corpus (whether by systematic criteria or due to limited data) as a methodological condition for the critical assessment of features of the register and their conventions as social phenomena. Theories and methods associated with corpora have advanced considerably in recent decades, but conceptions of "corpus" tend to remain discipline-dependent: we are more likely to be familiar with the findings of other disciplines than with the criteria that organize their underlying data. The importance of corpora in register studies therefore warrants some comments here.

Delimiting a corpus is a methodological strategy that establishes a frame for approaching data. This constructs a corpus as a tool that can be used in different ways in order to answer a variety of questions. The data of a corpus are not necessarily limited to text transcripts of only the verbal aspect of behaviour, even if many corpora are limited to such transcripts for methodological or historical reasons. The potential range of information available even in historically limited corpora is highlighted by Kati Kallio's chapter on singing traditions in Ingria, where her corpus includes data on melodies, situations and associated practices. The questions that a corpus can be used to answer remain dependent on the data comprising it, and the types of data in a corpus remain dependent on the technologies (and interests) of the period that produced it.

Corpus-based research allows an adjustable focus on items in the data. At one extreme, the focus is on the corpus as a whole to produce general information about the relative frequency of patterns or items without differentiating their relative value, as is characteristic of corpus linguistics. It can also be used to target elements of the lexicon and units of utterance, as in William Lamb's development of a typology of oral formulae in Gaelic storytelling in this volume, or it can provide a more general frame for establishing the conventionality of such elements as in Lauri Harvilahti's illustration of milieu-specific adaptations of formulaic language in Finnish and Estonian oral poetries (cf. also Foley, this volume). Qualitative assessment of individual items in the data can also be integrated into the approach, calibrating them with relative rather than uniform values. Methodologically, this involves a shift to assessing items in a dialectic relation to a corpus, as Eila Stepanova has elegantly done in her discussion of individual, social and situational variation in the register of Karelian lament. Advancing to the far extreme, this sort of calibration brings a single item of the data into focus, in relationship to which the corpus becomes a context reflecting social practice, and against which the item and its variation may be critically assessed even when that item is otherwise merely an element of a text transcript. A corpus can thus provide a versatile tool for register research.

Approaching a register through a corpus of entextualized transcripts of use is not exclusive to considerations of its formal aspects and of the devices or elements that comprise its repertoires. For example, Lamb analyzes the formalization and social markedness of the Gaelic storytelling register by considering how the prestige attributed to the register conferred prestige on those competent in its use. Stepanova draws a corresponding conclusion that the Karelian lament register indexes gender from within her corpus, where it is evident that the register is used exclusively by women. In her own article, Margaret Bender builds an argument of larger historical scope, revealing historical changes in conceptions of gods and even of the structuring of the cosmos through the analysis especially of deixis in a limited corpus of three Cherokee religious texts from different periods. Such approaches can thus offer valuable information and insights even when their data appear limited when compared to ethnographic data.

Performance and Poetics

There is a deep-rooted tendency in Western scholarship to draw a clear distinction between "poetry" and "prose" (and, by implication, "poetic" versus "non-poetic" texts), which is unambiguously reflected in modern editorial practices. Like many such binary oppositions, this poetry–prose distinction breaks down under scrutiny. The division has most effectively been collapsed and displaced by ethnopoetics. Nevertheless, this way of thinking about poetry remains pervasive in many disciplines. It thereby presents an obstacle to how many scholars approach traditional poetry and its relevance to registers studies. The poetry–prose division seems to go back to the Classical distinction of poetry from other types of verbal behaviour as language in a predictable, formal meter. Today, modern editorial practice clearly indexes poetry as a category distinct from other forms of linguistic behaviour (whether or not it is formally metered). In addition, poetry tends to be conceived of in terms of its modern forms, which can draw more or less freely on any and all linguistic resources available rather than being as tightly organized and socially recognizable as the poetic registers discussed in this volume. These factors have left oral poetries largely outside the purview of most disciplinary approaches to registers, although they are no less historically structured through social practices, and hence register studies concentrating on oral poetry have developed somewhat independently in folklore studies and philology.

In addition to being significant for the development of register studies in linguistic anthropology, Dell Hymes' seminal work on "The Ethnography of Speaking" (1962) led to what is now known as ethnopoetics (e.g. Hymes 1981). This work shattered the popular poetry–prose divide by demonstrating that so-called prose narrative registers exhibited hierarchical structuring of units of utterance corresponding to what Hymes referred to as *lines*, *stanzas*, *scenes* and *acts*. This approach concentrated on the structures and poetics of discourse irrespective of whether it had a formal meter. Such units can be marked and organized with, for example, lexical, syntactic, poetic and rhetorical devices in addition to formalized metrical structures. This approach thereby reconverged with ideas about rhythm and structure well known to Classical rhetoricians, who would not have seen, for example, the Karelian laments as "poetry" because they lack meter (cf. Stepanova, this volume). In the present context, ethnopoetics provides a frame for adapting tools and perspectives developed with metered poetry to other types of discourse, as Lamb has done in his adaptation of Oral-Formulaic Theory to analyse the register of Gaelic story-telling which would otherwise be editorially rendered as prose. Rather than being fundamentally different, work in ethnopoetics has emphasized that poetic features and structures penetrate all forms of discourse to varying degrees. A register that is socially distinguished as poetry in a particular culture will exhibit culture-dependent densities of particular poetic features (some more than others), normally within a broader semiotic register of performance, that index the register as an elevated way of speaking of a particular type.

The conventionalized formal constraints of oral poetry provide a fruitful environment for exploring different aspects of units of composition. Although today we tend to think of words in terms of the units we find listed in a dictionary, John Miles Foley's chapter in this volume offers a rich discussion of vernacular conceptions of what constitutes a "word" of oral poetry, what he calls an "integer" of the register (see also Harvilahti, this volume). These integers correlate with distinguishable meaningful units of the way of speaking. Foley describes these as "metonymic" in the sense that their use within the frame of the register allows them to import a package of indexical associations, valuations and interpretations according to the patterns of use of that integer of the register – i.e. the unit of the register is meaningful through all of its uses, of which a particular use is a single instantiation and metonym. This process is not unique to poetry, it just becomes more easily observable because of how formal constraints of meter and limits on how the register is used can condition lexical choices. These same conditions provide a site for considering the historical development of a register's distinctive lexicon, semantics and relationships among devices of a register during usage (Frog, this volume). The lexicon and its conventions of use can clarify role relations and positionings (Wilce & Fenigsen, this volume), ideologies and conceptual models (Bender, this volume; Stepanova, this volume). In his chapter, Harvilahti carries the discussion still further to the insights oral poetry can offer to an understanding of the cognitive implications of poetic forms. The insights enabled by a register strongly conditioned by poetic formal constraints can then be taken and compared to registers where the corresponding phenomenon may not be as easily noticed.

Speech registers may constitute only one component of a semiotic register of performance. This is highlighted by Stepanova in her discussion of the Karelian lament register through which the performer ritually embodies grief in the community. The embodied enactment of a register of performance enables that register to be recognizable even if its verbal aspect may not diverge profoundly from forms of discourse in informal contexts. Richard Bauman's work on performance (e.g. Bauman 1977) has been tremendously influential on register studies, especially in moving beyond verbal devices alone to interpersonal patterns of their dynamic enactment – which involve a register model of situated behaviour. With his emphasis on verbal art, Bauman describes performance as a situation in which the enactment of the register entails responsibility for the quality and appropriateness of performance. However, when registers are generally viewed in terms of semiotic models for behaviour and interaction, their enactment along with co-occurring signs constitutes the frame of performance, which includes potential vulnerability to criticism from others. As in the case of poetics, performance cannot be approached as a simple binary of "performance" versus "not performance". Instead, the question is one of relative degrees of formalization and institutionalization. Just as formal conventions of oral poetry foreground certain aspects of language and units of utterance, the social markedness of performance traditions highlights the position of the performer in relation to the situation, interactants and audience of performance, thus foregrounding links between the register and the roles and relationship performed through it (e.g. Stepanova, this volume). The strategic performance of registers by youths to their parents may be no less marked (Paz, this volume), and the performance of Danish urban "street" behaviour on a television comedy program is more marked than is its performance by youths in schools (cf. Madsen, this volume). Processes that make specific phenomena visible can enable fruitful comparison with processes of other kinds. The potential dynamic flexibility of the use and construal of a register's devices should also not be underestimated. Even where the integers of a tradition are distinctively marked or the speech register is quite formalized, its relationship to performance may not be simple and invariable. Kallio shows that elements of the same poetic performance (such as melody and dance) may become linked to different situations, whether in occasion-specific or routinized ways, thereby differentiating performances in indexically specific ways. The salience of oral-poetic discourse and of formalized performance behaviours thus reveal a range of social phenomena during performance, and the insights they offer can then be used as a foundation for examining other registers of quite distinct types.

Perspectives

The articles in this volume turn away from an image of language as a unified system to language as a plurality of registers. They consider both the discursive and non-discursive signs used in interpersonal communication and their organization into register models of communicative conduct. Their authors reflect a diversity of voices from perspectives developed in several disciplines, which often work with distinct types of materials. Reading these articles sequentially will carry a reader from an understanding of approaches to register phenomena to the register organization of languages in multilingual communities, to discussions of how registers are transformed in changing ideological environments, to elucidations of their treatment in corpus-based studies, and finally to discussions of the use of registers in oral performance and verbal art. This diversity of topics, questions and perspectives is itself key to bringing register phenomena into focus as features of social life in the lived experience of people in societies around the world.

References

Bauman, Richard 1977. *Verbal Art as Performance*. Prospect Heights, IL: Waveland Press.

Ferguson, Charles 1981. 'Foreigner Talk' as the Name of a Simplified Register. *International Journal of the Sociology of Language* 28: 9–18.

Halliday, M. A. K., Angus McIntosh & Peter Strevens 1964. The Users and Uses of Language. In *The Linguistic Sciences and Language Teaching*. Bloomington: Indiana University Press. Pp. 76–110.

Hervey, Sándor 1992. Registering Registers. *Lingua* 86: 189–206.

Hymes, Dell 1962. The Ethnography of Speaking. In *Anthropology and Human Behaviour*. Ed. T. Gladwin & W. C. Sturtevant. Washington, DC: Anthropology Society of Washington. Pp. 13–53.

Hymes, Dell 1974. Ways of Speaking. In *Explorations in the Ethnography of Speaking*. Ed. Richard Bauman & Joel Sherzer. Cambridge: Cambridge University Press. Pp. 433–451.

Hymes, Dell 1981. *"In Vain I Tried to Tell You": Essays in Native American Ethnopoetics*. Philadelphia: University of Pennsylvania Press.

Reid, T. B. W. 1956. Linguistics, Structuralism and Philology. *Archivum Linguisticum* 8(1): 28–37.

Approaching Register Phenomena

I

Asif Agha

1. Enregisterment and Communication in Social History

In previous work, I have characterized enregisterment as a social process whereby "diverse behavioral signs (whether linguistic, non-linguistic, or both) are functionally reanalyzed as cultural models of action, as behaviors capable of indexing stereotypic characteristics of incumbents of particular interactional roles, and of relations among them" (Agha 2007a: 55). The capacity of speech and accompanying behaviors to acquire stereotypic indexical values, and thus to be treated as semiotic registers differentiable from each other, has consequences for how interpersonal roles and relationships are communicated in every known society. Yet since these models are unevenly distributed and variably centered in social practices, their empirical study requires attention to the processes and practices whereby performable signs become recognized (and regrouped) as belonging to distinct, differentially valorized semiotic registers by a population, and once formulated as models of conduct, undergo forms of further regrouping and reanalysis within social history, thereby yielding fractionally congruent variant models, often for distinct populations.

To speak of "registers" is to speak of a sociohistorical snapshot of a process of enregisterment, and thus to consider particular phases or segments of social history from the standpoint of sociocentric models of significant conduct. The case of "speech registers" is the special case where the behaviors at issue include speech behaviors (or, where utterances occur as part of these behaviors), and thus a case where performable actor personae may be understood as speaker personae, and models of conduct as "ways of speaking" (Hymes 1974). To understand how such models of conduct emerge, for whom they do so, or how they appear to persist in certain times and places requires attention to the metapragmatic activities through which criterial behaviors are distinguished from others, are typified as indexicals of act or actor, and, through social regularities of typification and dissemination, acquire stereotypic indexical values for those acquainted with them.

The articles in this volume consider register models associated with a great many forms of interpersonal behavior, and, in each case, identify cultural models of communicative conduct that are expressed through these behaviors. Whichever ones of these cases we consider – whether the carefully timed deployment of speech, melody and gesture by Karelian lamenters; or of Arabic and Danish lexemic partials in utterances by Copenhagen schoolchildren; or of speech, gesture, bearing and dress by politicians in France; or of Spanish or Hebrew utterances by Latino bilinguals in Israel; or, indeed, if we consider any of the other cases discussed in this volume – we are considering activity routines in which the deployment of speech and non-speech behaviors is organized into cultural models of significant conduct, whose semiotic partials are typically recycled from behaviors otherwise known to current interactants (often under fractionally distinct models of performance or construal) and, through a dialectic of norm and trope (Agha 2007a: 5–10), are reanalyzed and renormalized into models distinctive to particular social groups and their practices, whence they become ethnographically observable and amenable to study by anthropologists, linguists and others.

Each such model is located in a particular time and place in social-demographic history; none of them is intelligible to all who perceive the behaviors that express it; and some among them are subject to competing valorizations by those who have stakes in such models. Any register model is minimally a three-dimensional object of study, that is to say, is empirically identifiable only at the intersection of three distinct variables, whose values shape its organization and change (Agha 2007a: 167–170): it is expressed or made manifest through criterial behaviors (its *repertoires*), which have stereotypic indexical values (its *social range*) for persons who recognize or perform such signs in their practices (its *social domain*). For any such model, the values of these variables are identified by researchers through attention to the reflexive activities that formulate its felt discreteness in acts of performance and construal by users, and thus furnish evidence for its social-interpersonal existence at some given time, and, across a series of observations, furnish evidence for change. When the behaviors that express a register model are grouped into partly non-overlapping repertoires by distinct populations, or become subject to competing valorizations, fractionally distinct variants may effectively co-exist with each other, thereby differentiating persons and groups from each other, and, through the reanalysis of repertoires and their stereotypic indexicality over time, may result in subsequent changes in group-relative identities and relationships within social history.

Language Contact

Several accompanying papers explore forms of enregisterment in situations of language contact that emerge from wage-labor migration or trade, and thus explore situations where more than one "language" – in the sense of a phono-lexico-grammatical system; hereafter, a PLG system – is available in discursive interaction, and where distinct social categories of persons formulate distinct models of the stereotypic indexical effects of utterances sourced from one or the other PLG system (see Agha 2007b for a discussion of "language", and Agha 2009 for a discussion of bilingualism). Before we turn to questions of how perceivable behaviors, including speech behaviors, may be treated as stereotypic indexicals belonging to registers of conduct, or how metapragmatic typifications provide data on such models, it is worth observing that a PLG unitization of speech tokens (into phonemic or morphemic unit-types, for example) does not by itself suffice to identify units of social indexicality. Indeed, the speech tokens that are treated as stereotypic social indexicals in some community need not be sourced from any one PLG system, but may exhibit fractional fidelity-to-type in relation to units of more than one such system. Although this form of hybridity is common in register formations of many kinds, it becomes especially salient under conditions of language contact. An example from Copenhagen youth speech is described in the passage quoted below (where the italicized comments in square brackets are my own interpolations):

> In the exchange in example 2, Michael asks for glue or paste. Esen answers with the construction "eine limesteife". The word "eine" is associated with German, and this is quite straightforward. However, the word "limesteife" [*pronounced as li:mestajfe; understood as 'gluestick'*] is not associated with any language or variety (that we know of). The element "lim" pronounced with a long high front vowel ([i:]) equals the Danish-associated word for "glue", and the middle -e- may also be associated with Danish, as many compounds associated with Danish have an -e attached to the first element as a compound marker. This is not the case of the word "lim", however. In addition, the element "steife" is not associated with Danish, and neither with German in any sense that would give an immediately accessible meaning here. It may sound like a German word to the Danish ear, but not to the German ear [*i.e., may differ in perceived fidelity to PLG type for distinct social domains of speaker*]. This feature does not lend itself to being [*uniquely*] categorized in any [*one*] "language" [*by all speakers*]. The word "limesteife" indexes "German" to a Danish person. It would be a possible member of the set of features which a Dane could construct as "German". However, it is highly unlikely to be designated as a member of a set of features constructed by a German as "the German language". It is nonetheless possible to analyze it, to find a meaning in the context precisely because we analyze at the level of features. (Jørgensen, Karrebaek, Madsen and Møller 2011: 25.)

The expression "eine limesteife" is uttered as a speech token by Esen in response to Michael's query, and is intelligible in relation to it. Yet the speech token does not exhibit unambiguous fidelity-to-type with respect to word-types from either Danish or German: Esen's utterance is fractionally congruent with both Danish and German along distinct dimensions of phonological or morphoysntactic organization, and thus comprises a blend of two distinct PLG systems. I have argued elsewhere (Agha 2009) that bilingualism is a social practice that involves the transposition of speech tokens across geographic or social settings in ways that alter their "type"-level construal, both at the level of grammar and social indexicality: bilinguals reanalyze PLG blends not only as grammatical types but also as stereotypic indexicals of role and relationship (and hence reanalyze the register models used to interpret them) in in-group encounters. When bilinguals form an immigrant minority in a destination locale, their in-group metapragmatic treatment of their own practices comes into contact with out-group metapragmatic frameworks employed by monolinguals native to that locale, yielding forms of social differentiation not anticipated in either framework.

In contemporary Copenhagen youth speech, several features of speech behavior are grouped together as isopragmatic indexical repertoires (i.e., are treated as having comparable indexical values), and two such repertoires are shown in the columns of Table 1. Each repertoire is emblematic of a distinct youth identity, the contrast between them differentiating a register boundary.[1]

Table 1. Enregistered emblems of "Integrated" vs. "Street" persona

	"Integrated" demeanors	"Street" demeanors
repertoires	creaky voice syllables	absence of creaky voice
	stress-timed prosody	syllable-timed prosody
	longer vowels	shorter vowels
	standard word order, gender	non-standard word order and noun gender
	Danish PLG sourcing	non-Danish PLG sourcing ("polylingual" lexemes)
	polite phrases	swearing, slang
	high pitch	affricated-palatal /t/, fronted /s/, voiceless uvular /r/
stereotypic social indexicality	higher class (wealth)	toughness
	sophistication, authority	masculinity
	academic skill	academic non-prestige
	self-possession	absence of politeness
	Danishness	panethnic "street" persona

Source: Madsen 2013, Quist 2008.

Contrasts between "integrated" and "street" behaviors involve multiple dimensions of PLG organization, including phonology, lexis and morphosyntax: contrasts of pronunciation include presence versus absence of creaky voice, stress-timed versus syllable-timed prosody, longer versus shorter vowels (except before syllables with schwa). Morphosyntactically, "street" utterances can have SVO word order in environments where "integrated" utterances exhibit VSO inversion, and "common" gender marking where the latter exhibit neuter gender forms. Perhaps the most salient features of "street" repertoires are lexical items sourced from languages other than Danish and tropically altered in significance, including cases where word-forms sourced from PLG systems like Turkish, Arabic, Kurdish or Serbian acquire features of word-sense or stereotypic indexicality wholly or partly reanalyzed when they occur in Danish utterances.[2]

Any repertoire-centric conception of registers – and, in particular, any reductionist attempt to equate register formations with just their repertoires – readily deconstructs itself because it cannot account for the principle of selection whereby speech behaviors are grouped into repertoires: How are the behaviors that comprise these repertoires differentiated from all other behaviors? Why do the ones grouped into repertoires in Table 1 have comparable social indexical values? (For instance, why do palatalized /t/ and polylingual lexemes both index "street" demeanors?) Answering these questions requires attention to the metapragmatic activities through which social persons differentially respond to and typify speech behaviors, whether implicitly or explicitly, and through such treatment differentiate repertoires from each other and formulate their stereotypic indexical values (Agha 2007a: 147–157).[3]

Møller (this volume) uses the term "languaging" to describe acts of sourcing units of a PLG system in utterances. Cases where units of more than one PLG system are sourced in a single utterance (as in the "eine limesteife" example above) may be termed "polylanguaging." The practice of drawing on multiple PLG systems is common not only in the "street" register of Danish but in youth registers all over the world – the United States (Eble 1996), Japan (Gagne 2008), Indonesia (Smith-Hefner 2007, Boellstorf 2004), Africa (Newell 2009, Samper 2002, Githinji 2006) – and, in all cases, attention to the metapragmatic practices of users clarifies the social range of indexical values, including the social personae (youth, social class, sexuality, cosmopolitanism, and others), indexed by their use.

In multilingual settings, the differential enregisterment of speech varieties need not, of course, be limited to phonemic or lexemic segments of PLG systems but may extend to the use or non-use of entire PLG systems, whether viewed as "dialects", "sociolects" or "languages" (Agha 2007a: 132–142). The ratified use (or non-ratified use, or avoidance) of one or another such "language" in specific interactional settings itself constitutes metapragmatic data on speech valorization, data on the degree of "fit" or indexical congruence (Agha 2007a: 24) of utterances with the construable settings in which they are performed. In the multilingual classroom setting discussed by Møller, where the official language of instruction is Danish, students who are asked to recite versions of a Danish poem in their home languages exhibit avoidance of these languages, but only in specific co-textual scenarios: Israh resists using Arabic "as part of a presentation in front of teachers, classmates and researchers" but freely uses Arabic (including Arabic curses) when addressing peers *sotto voce* in the same classroom. Similarly, Fartun resists reciting the Somali version of the same Danish poem when she is asked to give an "onstage" presentation to the entire class. By contrast, both students had been perfectly willing earlier on to include their Arabic and Somali versions of the poem in digital sound files to be played impersonally in a collective class performance. It is only when these sound files are misplaced, and students are asked by teachers to recite their poems orally and individually before their classmates, that they exhibit a sustained pattern of avoidance. Thus, neither Israh nor Fartun appear negatively to valorize the "social voices" associated with Arabic and Somali performances, but do negatively valorize performances that link these languages to their own biographic identities or "individual voices" (Agha 2005b: 39–45) in Danish-dominant public settings, where such performances would make Israh and Fartun appear less "integrated".

Madsen (this volume) shows that even the metapragmatic expression *integreret* ['integrated'] has a prior social history of dissemination through which it becomes known to Copenhagen youth, and, once it enters their usage, is converted into a register name through a process of lexemic revalorization. The word-form *integreret* has been used for some time in official State discourses (formerly by the Danish Ministry of Integration, nowadays by the Ministries of Law and of Social Affairs), but not with the same sense, and thus not as the same lexeme. In its bureaucratic usage, which reflects the mediatized projects of a State bureaucracy (cf. Agha 2012), the term denotes a population (not a speech variety) that stands in a specific relationship to the State: it names a minority immigrant population that the State seeks to assimilate into a mainstream national culture. From a bureaucratic standpoint, such a minority population is "integrated" to the degree that it has adapted its practices to those of majority Danish society, often in response to policy efforts by the Ministry that is tasked with bringing about this type of accommodation. The integration of a minority by a Ministry is, of course, a large-scale metapragmatic project, a social engineering task that, given the continuous in-flow of new immigrants, can never be wholly completed once and for all. Hence the effective integration of populations is, in practice, a degree notion, and distinct minority populations (as well as distinct generations within a minority population) may appear by Ministry criteria to be integrated to different degrees within Danish society. Any such mediatized project of assimilation thus yields society-internal criteria of group differentiation.

In the metapragmatic discourses of minority schoolchildren, the term "integrated" undergoes several transformations. First, whereas in Ministry discourses the term "integrated" denotes a culturally assimilated population, in youth discourses it denotes the performed demeanors of individual students, including their speech behaviors. Second, the framework of social differentiation implied by Ministry discourses is fleshed out in youth discourses as a contrast between enregistered emblems, as in Table 1, where the behavioral routines that express "integrated" vs. "street" demeanors are grouped into distinct repertoires (shown in the top half of the table) and each is associated with contrastive indexical stereotypes (shown in bottom half). Third, these emblems are indexically selective for specific activity routines and participation frameworks: "integrated" speech is said to be appropriate in addressing teachers, or addressing elderly Danes to whom one wishes to show respect, but not in talking to one's own relatives (with whom one speaks "normal Arabic"), nor with friends within peer groups with whom "street" language is more appropriate (Madsen 2013). These emblems are thus deployed through a reading or construal of the current interactional scenario that forms a multi-modal context (now treated as an emergent semiotic co-text) for acts of speaking; they are indexically selective for distinct co-textual scenarios in this sense. Fourth, since these emblems are expressed through multiple indexical cues, which may be deployed in a gradiently congruent manner, it is possible to inhabit "integrated" and "street" personae to different degrees in social interaction, as is the case with enregistered emblems in any society (see Agha 2007a: 265–267). Finally, the term "integrated" has been tropically generalized among Copenhagen youth as an expression usable ironically to formulate metapragmatic commentary on the very idea of a Standard, so that schoolchildren now use the term not only to speak of varieties of Danish but also of "integrated" (vs. normal) Arabic, where varieties of a distinct language become enregistered in ways analogous to Danish; or describe Urdu as "integrated Punjabi", a formulation where two distinct languages are ironically ranked on a cline of social indexicality, but where the mutually unintelligibility of their PLG systems becomes irrelevant.

It would be a mistake to imagine that the recycling and reanalysis of metapragmatic models from mediatized discourses (such as State discourses about integrated populations) into everyday discourses (such as youth discourses about integrated speech) is a unidirectional process, or to imagine that here the story of register differentiation comes to a halt. We have simply examined two historical phases of a social process, and identified two distinct models of personhood, which, although indexically linked to each other (the latter is produced by immigrants, which the former classifies), are not models for the same social actors. In a third metasemiotic formulation of register contrasts, the speech of Copenhagen youth is further recycled and differentially revalorized in mediatized artifacts disseminated to national target markets that extend well beyond, but also include, the very children whose speech these artifacts incorporate: on the Danish national TV channel DR2, a comedy sketch show, *Det Slører Stadig* ['It Still Veils'], deploys scripted activity routines for characters that partly recycle and partly transform the diacritics shown in Table 1. For instance, the character of Latifah, a female student, deploys the audible partials of "street" language along with visible diacritics of a "gangster" persona (track suit bottoms, hooded sweatshirts, gold chains, large earrings, heavy make-up) thus extending both the semiotic range of the register formation (from audible to visible signs) and the social domain of its circulation (from school settings to national television), thus transforming the register even if its speech repertoires remain the same.

The incorporation of street and integrated registers within a TV show, which is both a mediatized artifact and a televisual commodity, formulates them as commodity registers designed for a national target market (for a discussion of other cases, see Agha 2011: 44–46). The indexical selectivity of youth registers for co-textual scenarios of appropriate use is also preserved, but is now rendered salient for TV audiences through hyperbolic exaggeration in comedic routines: when Latifah discusses nuclear physics with a blond (and visibly non-minority) fellow student, she speaks fluent "integrated" speech; but when she answers her cell phone, and speaks to a presumed fellow "gangster", she switches back to "street" in a seamless and thus comedic change of footing. Finally, in episodes where Latifah interviews adult non-minority persons of higher social status than herself (such as professors and politicians), her explicit use of metapragmatic descriptions (like "ordinary" versus "integrated") for differences in speech behaviors between herself and her interlocutors makes the register boundary salient for those Danes who neither live in Copenhagen nor happen to be schoolchildren, thus expanding the social domain of those able to recognize the register contrast to a potentially nationwide audience.

Fedorova (this volume) shows that when monolinguals adapt their speech to the co-presence of bilingual others, the indexical selectivity of speech for social category of interlocutor can shape the speech repertoires understood as appropriate in interacting with them. When Russians interact with foreigners, the variety of Russian they speak does not constitute a single register of "foreigner talk", as earlier writers supposed (Ferguson 1981),[4] but tends to be differentiated through indexical selectivity for the kinds of persons they imagine their interlocutors to be. Fedorova compares the speech varieties Russians use in interactions with two kinds of foreign others: one data set involves interactions with ethnic Chinese along the Russian–Chinese border, the other involves interactions with foreigners primarily from Western countries in St Petersburg. In both cases, the variety of Russian used for foreigners differs from speech patterns used among Russian native speakers, but involves distinct speech patterns for the two kinds of foreigners.

Table 2. Enregistered styles of foreigner talk in Russian

	Chinese interlocutors	Western interlocutors
Repertoires:	impolite pronouns	minimal ellipsis, diminutive avoidance,
	imperative mood	slower speech rate, Russian glossed,
	pejorative other-voicing	"helpful" other-voicing
Participation frameworks:	S A	S A
	Russian Chinese	Russian Westerner

Note: S = Speaker, A = Addressee. Source: Fedorova 2013, and this volume

Russian speakers appear to have derogatory stereotypes about ethnic Chinese along the Russian–Chinese border (Fedorova 2013). The variety of Russian they use in speaking to Chinese interlocutors (shown on the left in Table 2) is deformed along dimensions of PLG organization that are consistent with pejorative stereotypes: the pronominal contrast between second person polite and impolite forms is neutralized in favor of impolite forms; distinctions of tense and mood tend to be neutralized in favor of imperative verb forms; and a distinctive lexical repertoire, which simulates Chinese mispronunciations of Russian words, is common in talking to Chinese interlocutors in a pattern of pejoratively other-voiced speech.

By contrast, in the St. Petersburg data (shown on the right), where foreign interlocutors are primarily Westerners (often foreign students or guests), Russian speakers exhibit speech patterns that selectively deform everyday Russian along quite distinct dimensions: at the level of PLG organization, they tend to use "more formal, grammatically correct forms of speech"; their utterances tend to minimize ellipsis of copulas and inter-clause conjunctions (which are common in speaking to native speakers), and to avoid diminutives (which imply intimacy), thus deploying a grammatically hypercorrect and lexically formal register of Russian; their speech also has a slower speech rate, includes metalinguistic glosses of Russian words, and is sometimes voiced as the speech of their Western interlocutors, as if designed to help them with their Russian.

In each case, cultural models of "kinds of persons" shape the speech varieties felt to be appropriate in interacting with them. Each variety involves a co-occurrence style (Ervin-Tripp 1986), in which a number of features occur together in a distinctive way (thus comprising its diacritics, Agha 2007a: 248), and constitutes an enregistered style (Agha 2007a: 185–188) insofar as it is indexically selective for a distinct interactional scenario: when Russians talk to Chinese interlocutors their speech contains impolite pronouns, direct commands and pejorative other-voicing; when they speak to Westerners their speech tends to be grammatically hypercorrect, lexically formal, and includes "helpful" other-voicing. The difference cannot be explained as a regional dialect difference "between Western and Eastern Russia" because Russians who use the first pattern for Chinese interlocutors in Chita (a town on the Eastern border with China) switch to "the same hypercorrect strategies" found in St. Petersburg when they talk to European visitors to Chita (Fedorova 2013: 78, n. 9). Each pattern of PLG deformation and other-voicing constitutes an enregistered style that is indexically selective for, or appropriate to, a particular scenario of interpersonal conduct, where it formulates images of self and other in ways intelligible to its users. And since each enregistered style is expressed through multiple co-occurring cues, it is always possible to inhabit these roles and relationships to gradient degrees, just as in the Danish case discussed above.

In discussing Latino migrants in Israel, Paz (this volume) also describes a case where the activity routines of bilinguals are indexically selective for categories of interlocutor, but the cultural models through which these routines are construed, which Paz calls "domestic intimacy" and "stranger sociality", are very different from the ones discussed above. These models emerge for Latino immigrants in Israel not merely through contact between the Spanish and Hebrew languages, nor merely between their speakers, but also through "contact" between cultural models for construing speech and speakers, between models these immigrants bring from the home country and those they encounter in Israel. Latino migrants experience a sharp contrast between cultural norms of *educación* ['refinement, cultivation'] to which they were socialized in Latin America and the relative directness of Israeli interactional norms, which they contrastively associate with rudeness or aggression. In Israel, where Latinos encounter both norms, *educación* is associated with in-group domestic interactions among their friends and kin, participation frameworks in which Spanish is also appropriate. By contrast, Israeli interactional styles (of both speech and non-speech behavior) are perceived as lacking *educación*, as direct and sometimes rude. Since Latinos use Hebrew in out-group settings with Israeli citizens, they come to associate PLG units of the Hebrew language with indexical stereotypes of aggression, and their own use of Hebrew with social distance and out-group forms of "stranger sociality". This situation is complicated by the fact that Latino children are socialized to Israeli norms of directness while growing up in Israel, and deploy them along with Hebrew utterances in interactions with parents. In such situations, parents perceive their children as performing stranger sociality within the home, and Hebrew as a register of social distance in in-group settings. This contrastive valorization of PLG units of distinct languages – with Spanish as stereotypically indexical of greater politeness, and Hebrew of greater directness and aggression – has a relatively small social domain within Israeli society, namely the Latino migrant community itself.

Despite obvious differences, the Danish, Russian and Israeli registers exhibit some common features: although all three cases involve co-textual arrays in which PLG tokens occur, the principle of register differentiation is not a PLG system but the treatment of otherwise diverse signs – whether differing in sense along dimensions such as presence vs. absence of propositional content (lexical items vs. prosodic contours), or differing in signal-scope as localizable vs. configurative signs (morphemes vs. their constituent-order), or differing in sensory channel as audible vs. visible signs (allophones vs. apparel) – as stereotypic indexicals of comparable activities or personae, as evidenced in the metapragmatic practices of their users. Diverse behaviors are likened to each other, or unitized as signs of the "same" register, by the comparability of their stereotypic indexical values for users, which enables the analyst to group them into repertoires. Their grouping into repertoires, their stereotypic indexical values, and their users (who formulate the model) are correlative dimensions of any such register, providing criteria on the identifiability of the register formation and of its semiotic partials, and on their differentiability from those belonging to other models of conduct. And insofar as unitized items of a repertoire appropriately co-occur with each other, they form enregistered styles, which are indexically selective for specific co-textual scenarios, in which they express images of actor or activity type that may be inhabited to gradient degrees. Similar processes are at work in the cases to which I now turn.

Enregisterment within and across Genres

The term "genre" has been used in a great variety of ways to describe enregistered styles of varying degrees of complexity and indexical selectivity for interlocutors and settings. When distinctive devices recur within a genre, each indexes the fact that the genre's performance is now under way, thereby "keying" its performance (Bauman 1977). Bauman lists a series of devices that are distinctive to many performance genres, and function as diacritics distinguishing a genre's performance from other discursive behaviors, but observes that any such list is of "limited utility" because such devices exhibit enormous variability across traditions, and the empirical task is always to identify "the culture-specific constellations of communicative means that serve to key performance in particular communities" (Bauman 1977: 22), or, in my terms, to identify the register models of conduct that are distinctive to a genre's performance,[5] and which, in turn, enable participants to recognize its distinctive devices and infer from their performance that it (and not some other activity) is now under way, or who is doing it, or what they are doing through it, or to whom.

The term "register" has become influential in studies of oral performance through the elegant work of John Miles Foley, who drew on a broad literature in linguistic anthropology,[6] including Bauman's own seminal work on performance, to answer questions initially posed in Milman Parry's and Albert Lord's work on Yugoslav epic (and on its implications for Homeric epic), to which their Oral-Formulaic Theory was proposed as a candidate answer. These questions began as a puzzle: what is the "special technique of composition" which allows the Yugoslav bard, who "has not memorized his song" but "is composing as he sings," to produce novel songs at an extraordinarily rapid speed? (Lord 1960: 17). Does this ability rely on familiarity with some special units that enable larger wholes to be composed during performance? How are such units to be identified? When asked about this ability, the bards themselves replied by describing their familiarity with each *reč* ['word'] of the song, and by expressing confidence in their own ability to repeat a song *reč za reč* ['word for word'] across instances of performance. Yet the metalinguistic term *reč* does not only denote a word (in the sense of a "lexical item") in a PLG system. It also denotes verbal units of more varied kinds, including a ten-syllable poetic line, a combination of such lines, a speech, a scene, and others. The metalinguistic term *reč* thereby unitizes performance, segmenting performed utterance into significant partials, but in a way Parry and Lord found puzzling.[7] Parry proposed the term "formula" (for a metrically configured group of words) to describe one such type of unit, and Lord proposed that a "formula pattern" (involving prosodic, metrical and morphosyntactic templates) is "the fundamental element in constructing lines" (Lord 1960: 17). Although this proposal has proved highly influential in subsequent work, it does not provide criteria for identifying all "culture-specific" units for all known genres of performance, and thus does not enable their comparative study. Moving beyond Parry and Lord, Foley interprets "the *reč* as an integer" and, citing Bauman's observation that units of performance tend to be culture-specific (see Foley 1995: 11, n. 21), observes that "each culture and language and genre will establish its poetic "lexicon" of integers more or less differently" (Foley 1995: 23), thus incorporating Bauman's criterion into his own highly synthetic and insightful approach to the study of registers of oral poetic performance. Foley uses the terms "expressive integers" or "structural integers" for the unitized co-textual arrays (of varied signal scope) that comprise the register's expressive repertoires; the term "metonymic significance" for their indexical significance, which differs from their localizable-propositional content, and appears "metonymic" because it enables audiences to anticipate unfolding motifs developed later in performance, of which these indexically valued utterance-partials appear to be *pars pro toto* segments and proleptic signals (Foley 1995, 2002b); and "performance arena" for the setting in which these indexical signs are appropriately and effectively performed, which includes the characteristic activities or situations during which the register is typically performed, as well as "a suitably prepared performer" and "a suitably prepared audience", that is, includes speech participants who are acquainted with the register (or belong to its social domain), and whose presence in the current participation framework enables its effective performance and construal.[8]

Thus although Foley's proposals constitute a genuinely original and synthetic approach to oral poetic registers, they are entirely compatible with approaches to register formations of other kinds in contemporary linguistic anthropology, not least because they share common intellectual roots.

I noted earlier that when the behaviors that express a register model are re-grouped into partly non-overlapping repertoires by distinct populations, or are treated as appropriate to distinct settings or activities, and thus as having distinct indexical values, fractionally distinct register models effectively co-exist with each other, and such differences indexically differentiate the social groups whose practices these are. We have so far been focusing on cases where the reanalysis of PLG units across register boundaries (and their grouping with other features, such as prosody, speech rate, or interlocutor-origo voicing) differentiates groups and practices from each other. When partials of a recognized genre are regrouped or re-bundled in performance, or are performed appropriately in distinct contexts, they exhibit the same kind of register differentiation, a feature obscured by the classification of the performance (as an undifferentiated whole) into one genre or another.

Genre taxonomies have proved to be handy ways of describing verbal practices in folklore because they allow scholars to classify performances (often in the form of recorded or transcribed text-artifacts of performances), and to sort them within archives, corpora and compendia. They continue to remain useful for this purpose even if the criteria that are used to differentiate genres from each other are enormously varied in the literature,[9] perhaps because they reflect the varied interests and concerns of the scholarly projects that rely on them. Moreover, since the term "genre" is used in different ways in distinct disciplines (e.g., literary criticism vs. folklore), and in schools of thought within them, it is worth noting that, in folklore, recent approaches view genres not as idealized categories but as open frameworks for the entextualization of expressions in social situations. As Frog points out in his article in this volume, a focus on the genre characteristics of performance attends more to the placement of verbal devices within performable wholes rather than on the social indexical values of the devices themselves. Since a focus on the genre characteristics of performance by no means precludes an interest in its register characteristics, these two distinct spheres of analytic concern can complement each other in several ways, as they often do in contemporary folklore research. In order to approach their complementarity, however, it is useful to begin by noting a difference between genre taxonomies and register models: insofar as genre taxonomies rely on external criteria of classification, they do not permit access to the principles by which speech behavior is organized into register models of conduct by those whose behavior it is.

Kallio (this volume) discusses a corpus of Ingrian oral poetry, which was collected by more than twenty scholars between 1853 and 1938, and contains a large number of items (5,500 poems, 500 musical notations, and 170 short sound recordings). Each item is a record of a performance, and the size of the corpus captures a broad stretch of the social history of performances. In working through the corpus, Kallio notes that observable features of style in poetic performance vary quite substantially within the corpus itself, so that most poems contain features of more than one genre. Whereas genre taxonomies do not make this variation tractable, an approach that treats elements of performance as semiotic partials of register models, and hence as social indexicals, shows that "even the most problematic Ingrian recordings are amenable to analysis as natural results of the use of specific registers in atypical contexts, resulting in fractionally distinct variants, which are often adopted as typical for distinct performance situations by distinct users" (Kallio, this volume).

Kallio's analysis relies on viewing stylistic features not as isolable devices in performance, but as indexically motivated elements of enregistered styles. Viewed as separate items, the stylistic devices that occur in this corpus (specific poetic themes, melodies, rhythms, vocal styles, opening formulas, forms of repetition, speech rate, kinesic accompaniments) appear enormously heterogeneous in form and isolable significance (as do the Russian and Danish ones discussed above), and many aspects of their significance are obscured when they are inspected in isolation: the significance of devices that lack propositional content (speech rate, melodies, kinesic behaviors) becomes difficult or impossible to describe; and devices that do have isolable propositional content (formulas, song lyrics) also have non-propositional indexical values in performance, which such a treatment obscures. However, when these devices are evaluated as segments of multi-channel sign-configurations in which they exhibit recurrent forms of co-variation with each other, and with identifiable features of setting (actors, activities, participation frameworks), observable patterns of their recurrent and ratified co-deployment across time and place themselves constitute a kind of implicit metapragmatic data on stereotypic indexicality. In ratifying their recurrent co-deployment, audiences recognize that they typically go or "fit" together, i.e., are indexically congruent with each other. In some cases, metapragmatic descriptions are also available, which furnish explicit evidence. In a few cases, atypical usages are construable as meaningful tropes whose construal appears to presuppose the stereotypic values from which they depart, thus confirming the analysis.

One type of regularity of recurrent patterning is the co-deployment of linguistic and non-linguistic signs in the same activity routines. Thus when a characteristic four-beat melody regularly occurs in a large number of Ingrian wedding songs (identified by thematic content), the melody appears stereotypically to index the activity routines that accompany it over a large number of ratified performances. And in "atypical" usages when performers explicitly say that with the "same wedding melody [we] sing to children" (Kallio, this volume), their reports provide explicit metapragmatic data of two kinds: the performer's explicitly calling it a "wedding melody" confirms its stereotypic indexicality qua musical phrase, and the predicate describes the appropriateness of the melody (but not of the thematic content of wedding songs) to acts in which "[we] sing to children," thus specifying the indexical selectivity of the melody qua extractable sign-fraction for a distinct participation framework for at least this social group, the referents of "we". Entirely distinct melodies recur in songs recited at calendric rituals of "swinging" on a large swing (large enough to seat 10 or more people) at the beginning of summer. In one case, where two singers are performing a "swinging song" but do so with a 5-beat melody typical of lullabies, the ethnographer records that a young girl was present at the time. The 5-beat melody is atypical for swinging songs, but used here because it is indexically selective for the child. Similarly, formulas and melodies from "the most formal and ritualistic registers of wedding song" – where their formality mediates relations between the bride's and groom's families, who are strangers to each other at the wedding – are also used to bid welcome to strangers of other kinds, including "foreigners, such as scholars, fieldworkers or even presidents" (Kallio, this volume), and are thus treated as extractable fractions of wedding songs that are now unitized as indexicals of formal greetings of more varied kinds.

In other cases, patterns of the recurrent linear placement of elements in a song provide implicit metapragmatic data. Kallio notes that distinctive verbal formulas and melodies typically occur at the beginning of *Kokkovirsi*, the bonfire song, where young maidens sing and dance together at seasonal festive bonfires. The recurrent song-initial placement of these devices formulates them as diacritics of the *Kokkovirsi* song genre, as keying its performance, but also as stereotypic indexicals of the life stage and activities of the young maidens who sing these songs. By contrast, wedding songs, which begin with distinct melodies and formulas, mark a life cycle transition for the bride as she prepares to leave her friends and natal family. When *Kokkovirsi* formulas and melodies occur in wedding songs sung by the bride's friends, they occur in the middle of the song, and in these non-initial song segments index the co-membership of bride and singers in a past community of young maidens, even as the rest of the song laments the bride's immanent departure from it.

It will be evident that the treatment of genre partials as stereotypic indexical signs of a register requires attention to a wide range metapragmatic data (which are not available for many performances recorded long ago, as Kallio's observes). When such data are indeed available they permit the formulation of specific empirical hypotheses about the way in which unitized indexical signs in many channels of performance clarify the significance of these performances for informed audiences, that is for speech participants who belong to the register's social domain (but not, of course, for others who may also be present during performance.) And such hypotheses can be tested or improved upon by considering additional data within the limits of empirical access.

In all such cases, register models tend to involve both discursive and non-discursive signs. For instance, performances of Serbian *bajanje* ['magical charms'] include a range of "linguistic, paralinguistic and non-linguistic" expressive integers (Foley 1995: 127) – including the conjurer's leaning over and whispering the charm in the patient's ear, speaking softly and very rapidly, using an archaic lexicon, distinctive neologisms, an octosyllabic poetic line, and characteristic patterns of rhyme, parataxis, and parallelism – and which, despite their apparent heterogeneity (to outsiders) as behaviors of phenomenally distinct types, are grouped together under a scheme of metasemiotic construal whose elements indexically imply each other in appropriate use, and thus appear unified (to members of its social domain) as indexically congruent sign-partials of a register's repertoires. Such "cross-modal icons" are commonplace and well described for register formations around the world (Agha 2007a: 179–185).

Similarly, the enregistered styles of Karelian lament involve a variety of discursive and non-discursive signs – including prosodic features, such as pharyngeal constriction and "cry breaks" (Urban 1988); melodic contours (Tolbert 1990); metrical patterning of PLG types, as in alliteration; kinesic routines, such as swaying or rocking the body (Honko 1974); and a distinctive lexical repertoire (Leino 1974) – whose routinized co-occurrence yields multi-channel sign-configurations traditionally performed in specific rituals (such as funerary or wedding ceremonies) but also on other occasions. Although most of the same features recur across performances, distinct co-occurrence styles were apparently normalized as appropriate to distinct rituals or to distinct segments of ritual cycles.

Stepanova (this volume) shows that whereas these enregistered styles exhibit features common to a variety of lament traditions in the region (including Karelian, Ižorian, Votic, Vepsian and Seto laments), and thus comprise what she terms a "pan-regional semiotic register" of lament, differences among lament registers indexically differentiate locale-specific lament traditions and the social identities of their practitioners. Since lamenters are traditionally women, each lament style stereotypically indexes the female gender of performer, a pan-regional feature. However, the lexical register of lament is differentiated in each such lament tradition into a core lexicon (terms for kin, divine beings, and self) and a situation-specific lexicon (terms for things only occasionally relevant to lament performance), but the difference is handled differently across traditions, thus differentiating traditions and practitioners from each other. And since the core lexicon is more widely known by lamenters in each tradition, variable degrees of familiarity with the situation-specific lexicon indexically differentiates specific types of lamenters *within* each tradition.

Tolbert describes varied atypical situations where laments were said to occur in everyday life. In such situations, lamenters evidently conformed to norms to gradient degrees, as in cases where a person could start to "almost lament" on the phone simply by "sprinkling" her speech with its distinctive lexicon and heightened intonation (Tolbert 1988: 114). This suggests that register partials of the lament genre could be variably sourced from the more elaborate enregistered styles and deployed with gradient fidelity to norm, thus permitting occasion specific interactional tropes, as with any other register of conduct.

The above cases also show that the register organization of devices used in any performance genre may be diverse not only in phenomenal characteristics (such as audibility or visibility) but also in the degree to which they constitute localizable vs. configurative signs. Frog (this volume) discusses the latter issue for poetic utterances, where unitized signs of a register may be highly localizable (such as lexical items) or highly configurative (such as poetic lines, or arrays of lines), and thus appear to constitute small or large "orders of signifiers". They are unitized as signs of a register by social regularities of reflexive treatment – whether through implicit regularities of ratified construal or through explicit metapragmatic descriptions, as discussed above – which also formulate the significance they have for informed audiences.

On the other hand, when such signs are examined in isolation from the metapragmatic practices that formulate them as signs, differences of perceivable channel or signal scope appear to constitute a puzzle, as they did in earlier approaches (see n. 4).

Issues of signal scope do not pertain only to the discursive devices that are treated as the register's signs but also to the span of discourse that separates them from the discursive devices whose co-occurrence they index, which often occur later (and are thus indexed in a proleptic fashion) within performance, so that the register's devices appear to be (metonymic) parts of larger wholes. For instance, Foley observes that South Slavic phrases of the form "He/she spoke" (where the verbum dicendi need not be "speak", but some more specific hyponym) constitute a class of utterances that introduce reported speech frames. However in the repertoires of poetic register, members of this class function in much more indexically specific ways:

> On the other hand, a verbal phrase of precisely the same metrical extent, "He cried out," when delivered at or near the beginning of a performance, has deep and telling reverberations, signifying *the lament of the prisoner-protagonist in the Return Song*, a particular brand of shrieking loud and persistent enough to *move the captor and his wife to bargain for the prisoner's release* and leading eventually to his Ithaka-like arrival, disguised as a beggar, to compete against a gathering of suitors and attempt to *reclaim his South Slavic Penelope and his home*. (Foley 1995: 96; italics mine.)

Foley observes that in South Slavic epic, performance initial utterances like "He cried out" index (to an informed audience) that a variety of specific episodes are likely to unfold later in performance, an effect which Bauman 1992a calls "building a structure of anticipation," and which Foley terms their metonymic indexicality. In the above quote, Foley describes these episodes in capsule summaries (which I indicate approximately by italics). Within the performance, however, they unfold as the activities of characters in subsequent "episodes" of the performance. Thus performance-initial localizable expressions of the type "He cried out" stereotypically index the subsequent co-occurrence of more extended thematic episodes, but only for audiences acquainted with the poetic register and its tradition. And for audiences also familiar with the Odyssey, for instance, they also liken the final episodes of the Slavic epic to the return of Odysseus to Ithaka, and to his wife, Penelope, as Foley suggests in the above quotation.

At the same time, it is worth noting that the unitized signs of a register's repertoires (of whatever signal scope) are only experienced in events of performance under conditions of further contextualization by other signs, which occur as emergent co-textual arrays (as is the case with all indexicals; for deictics, see Agha 2007a: 48–50), and which "fill in" aspects of significance additional to any significance that is stereotypically associated with the register's signs themselves. The formula "he cried out" is a formulaic template, which includes many variants (like *i pocmili* ['and he cried out'] and *sužanj cmili* ['the prisoner cried out']). The invariant features of the template qua register partial involve only some (and not all) phrase-internal features of its PLG organization. Hence some of its variant features inevitably occur *within* the same phrase token where the template occurs.

Lamb (this volume) discusses this issue for the case of formulas in Gaelic prose narratives. He observes that, for each of the formulaic templates he discusses, a large number of instances recur in the narratives of storytellers separated from each other in time and place. When these templates recur across many performances – or are "consistent across many users", sometimes across a span of centuries (Lamb, this volume) – their recurrence across locales provide evidence for a sociological regularity, namely that these patterned templates are comparably enregistered for (or recognizable to) a wide social domain of speakers within Gaelic traditions of storytelling. Some of the templates he discusses are illustrated below in English translation:

NP_i raised music and vanquished (NP_i's own) sadness
NP_i was far from NP_j's friends and near NP_j's foes
NP_i saw/thought that NP_i was far from NP_j's friends and near NP_j's foes
NP_i put the binding of the three narrows on NP_j firmly and painfully/tightly

But what exactly recurs? Which among the PLG features of these templates are recurrent partials of a register of performance? Certain features of PLG organization, such as their organization as noun phrases or adverbial phrases, and much of the non-deictic lexical material that fills these phrasal slots, appear fixed across the instances that Lamb analyzes (and this material is indicated here by underlining). But constituents that have deictic features, whether involving NP level deixis (pronouns and anaphors) or clause-level deictic contrasts (active vs. passive voice), vary readily across instances (and these lexical segments are not underlined). The following attested examples of the last formulaic template above (along with narrators' name) exemplify some of these issues:

(a) [He$_i$] put [the binding of the three narrows] [on him$_j$] [firmly and painfully] (MacGilvray)

(b) [He$_i$] put [the binding of the three narrows] [on them$_j$] [firmly and painfully] (Gillies)

(c) [The binding of the three narrows] was put [on them$_j$] [firmly and tightly] (MacLennan)

Although the repertoires of this register of storytelling involve relatively invariant PLG templates (often of multi-clausal signal-scope), only devices that convey context-independent propositional content appear to be invariant in form across acts of using them. Devices such as deictics vary across instances because they anchor referents to some here-and-now of performance, an issue entirely independent of the register consistency of phrase tokens, or of their fidelity to the register's sign-types. Items of the register thus co-occur with other items within the same phrase tokens in discontinuous intercalation. And although the register's devices are context-independent from the standpoint of the propositional content of the phrases in which they occur, they readily function as stereotypic social indexicals at the level of the narrative as a whole, where, in each instance of performance, they formulate the narrative as traditional storytelling, the narrator as a proficient exemplar of its tradition, and formulate the phrase token itself as a proleptic signal metonymically indexing features of performance yet to come during that very telling, but do so effectively only for an informed audience, namely for participants who belong to the social domain of the register.

Wilce and Fenigsen (this volume) focus on the lexical partials of lament performances, in both Karelian laments and their adpatations in laments of contemporary Finnish lament revivalists, which the revivalists call *itkukieli* ['lament language'], and which Wilce and Fennigsen call "lament register". This discussion illustrates a process common to many register systems, where the effects of extended semiotic arrays tend to be associated with some of their partials. Although Karelian laments involve multiple semiotic cues that comprise an enregistered style (as noted above), the lexical repertoires distinctive to lament are the most readily extractable sign-fractions of the performance, and hence susceptible to varied forms of metapragmatic commentary and reanalysis. The presence of these lexical items within funerary laments was traditionally assigned a specific significance: Stepanova (this volume) points out that the dead were believed to no longer be able to understand colloquial speech and the lexical register of Karelian laments was regarded as a special language that they could understand, culturally ratifying it for communication with supernatural powers.

Yet these lexical items do not establish social relations among specific persons by themselves, but only through a voicing structure formulated by co-occurring signs. The voicing structure of funerary lament enacts relationships between the bereaved who are co-present and the deceased addressed by the lament. When the lamenter addresses the deceased in the presence of bereaved living relatives, the latter are formulated as its ratified overhearers (Wilce and Fenigsen, this volume). The lamenter may perform her own personal grief but also the grief of the deceased's living relatives. The lamenter was understood "as a mediator, in whose laments emerges not only her own voice, but also the voices of the living community, the deceased and [the community of] the dead" (Stepanova 2011: 138). The living and the deceased could thus both be understood as the principals of the message animated and delivered by the lamenter on their behalf. The expressions that comprise the lexical repertoires of lament include deverbal noun phrases – as in the example cited by Wilce and Fenigsen (this volume), *O šie miun armahane n-ihalane n-imettäjäzeni* ['Oh, you$_i$ dear gentle one who suckled me$_j$'] – whose referents, persons i and j (indicated by subscripts in the gloss), are identified by deictic reference transposed through this voicing structure and situation: the referent of me$_j$ (person j) could be understood as the lamenter, who animates it, a co-present relative, the overhearer-principal, or even the deceased; and the referent of you$_i$ (person i) as the one who gave birth (not to the lamenter but) to person j, whoever that may be in relation to the circumstances of utterance. The lamenter is thus globally formulated throughout the performance as an intermediary between the living and the dead in one or the other of these ways.

As expressions that occur in more local stretches of utterance, the lexical items of lament register "fill in" additional features of role and relationship. They identify referents through matrilineal tropes for kin-reference[10] and person tropes for self-reference. They index deferential avoidance and intimacy: avoidance/deference is marked by acts of referring to deceased persons through elaborate circumlocutions (rather than personal proper names),[11] and intimacy by diminutive suffixes. The individuals (living and dead) among whom relations of deference and intimacy are being performed by the lamenter are understood, once again, through the voicing structure of the lament. And since the same lexical item may be used for more than one type of kin, the referent of any expression "is clear both to the reciter and to the listeners" (Leino 1974: 116) only under conditions of entextualized performance where co-occurring signs enable reference maintenance (as in other honorific registers, Agha 2007a: 323–324) through co-textual arrays of signs that are less transparent to native speakers than are lexical items, and thus less readily discussed as extractabilia from performance.

Thus although lament performances mark social relations among identifiable persons through a multi-channel array of signs, the lexical register of lament is more readily discussed out of context than is the enregistered style of which it is an element. Native speakers thus reanalyze an enregistered style as a lexical register of forms that possess an indexical force that actually derives from the semiotic array as a whole (for similar forms of misrecognition in other languages, see Agha 2007a: 286–293, 322–332).

The reanalysis of register partials can take a variety of other forms too. The derived composite need not constitute a distinct register in the sense of a social-semiotic regularity comparably recognized and used by many persons. In some cases it constitutes an emblem of a highly distinctive persona associated with just a few people, or even a single individual, as some of the other authors in this volume show.

Singular Personae

Kaartinen (this volume) discusses a chronicle from Eastern Indonesia whose author, Kende, draws on a range of devices from registers of writing and verbal art to fashion a document that depicts his community's political history. The chronicle neither belongs to an established genre nor signals conventional expectations in a reader. Rather it employs devices sourced from several distinct registers (and of varied signal-scope and stereotypic indexicality), whose very juxtaposition signals the document's genre hybridity and singularity, even as its register partials formulate a composite sketch of who it attempts to reach, what it seeks to convey, and how it derives its own authority.

The chronicle is only recognizable as a form of political communication to someone acquainted with local models of doing politics. In the village of Banda Eli, political authority is vested in two kinds of chiefly offices, the *Ratu* and the *Kapitan*, each associated with a distinct participation framework of chiefly communication: the *Ratu*'s "inside speech" is understood as an appropriate response to disputes that have arisen within households and intra-familial networks, where it seeks to bring about reconciliation, and where the Bandanese language is appropriately used as a register of in-group intimacy. The "outside speech" in which the *Kapitan* is expected to be proficient presents the unity of his community to outsiders, its stereotypic addressees, where the national language Malay/Indonesian is appropriately used as a register of out-group communication.

Since Kende holds the office of *Kapitan*, and since his chronicle is composed in Malay, it is formulated as a form of political communication addressed to outsiders. But it is written in *Jawi*, a register of writing that employs Arabic script for Malay, thus imposing some further indexical selectivity on its addressees/readers. Since the Latin alphabet has replaced *Jawi* in Banda Eli and other regions, many members of Kende's own community (and from elsewhere) cannot easily read it. The chronicle is indexically selective for outsiders who have a certain kind of traditional cultivation, a feature marked globally by the use of *Jawi* script throughout the document.

Other devices that recur within the chronicle are of more limited signal-scope and more varied in indexical effects. Although the document describes historical developments in Kende's community to outsiders, it does not do so as a "history" that depicts chronologically sequential events leading up to the present but as a "chronicle" of bounded episodes serially involving specific characters from the past, each story providing a charter for some specific set of present-day relationships. These episodes depict encounters between Kende's community and various historical others, such as colonizing Europeans, other indigenous chiefs, Muslims elsewhere in the Islamic world, and functionaries of the modern Indonesian State. In each narrative episode, these outsiders interact with local incumbents of the chiefly office held by Kende's ancestors in the past and by Kende at the time of writing, thus highlighting his positional authority within his community in a "heroic I" addressed to his readers. When Kende's ancestors encounter ethnolinguistic others, the utterances assigned to these others are sometimes presented as songs within direct reported speech frames – whether songs depicting dialogues between ancestors, or songs of lament at losses in war – where the laments and narrated dialogue belong to traditional registers of verbal art, and where the voicing of songs as reported speech imply that these utterances are reproduced verbatim in the chronicle, and thus citable as "proof" of its accuracy and veracity within the chronicle itself. The protagonists of several episodes are enumerated in finite lists, a device used in ceremonial registers to recite ancestral names, titles and place names, where the recitation formulates society as an orderly whole, a formulation now incorporated in Kende's written account of his own community's historical past. The use of Arabic titles for subsections of the chronicle formulates it as belonging to a literary register of writing, and the specific titles Kende uses for its sections – *muqqadimah* ['introduction'], *bab* ['part'], *pasal* ['chapter'] – likens the episodes they describe to portions of traditionally larger literary works, as if excerpted from them.

The juxtaposition of devices sourced from distinct public registers into the chronicle formulates a composite indexical sketch of the characteristics of its author and his addresses that is recoverable neither from the denotational content of its PLG units, nor from its ambiguous genre characteristics. And although the registers on which it draws are social regularities, their juxtaposition in the chronicle constitutes a highly singular, potentially unique, performance. Kende's wide register range is emblematic of his singularity, and formulates the chronicle he composes through it as a "monument" of a tradition that is perhaps disappearing. But the performance doesn't end with the act of composing the chronicle. The fact that Kende chooses to have his writings divided among faraway kin after his death suggests that, through their access to his achievement, others may yet be able to grasp and potentially to continue the chiefly tradition of which he is an exemplary member.

Noyes (this volume) discusses a case where the "classical" register of French political conduct, whose last exemplar was Charles de Gaulle, and which had since come to be seen as a "dead letter" or as emblematic of a bygone era, is suddenly brought back to life in public sphere media discourses, which treat the suicide of a Prime Minister, Pierre Bérégovoy, as a sign of the register's rebirth. Registers of political conduct appear inscrutable to outsiders because they draw selectively on the semiotic resources of a particular tradition. Within France, the "classical" register has involved a mode of presentation of a politician's public persona through a mastery of "linguistic, kinesic and visual forms" and the "material signs and stages that sustain it," which emerged as an enregistered model for bourgeois elites (in contrast to aristocrats) after the French Revolution, and grew in social domain after post-1880s educational reforms, when national schooling made its symbolic goods available to a lager public. But although the register became more widely recognized through schooling, the competence effectively to perform its emblematic ease and self-possession remained restricted to those born in "high bourgeois" circles, as was de Gaulle. By contrast, Bérégovoy, who was of working class origins, and never attended an elite school, was caricatured in political cartoons as lacking elegance as he rose through the ranks of the Socialist party. Yet after his nomination as Prime Minister and his naïve involvement in a scandal that cost the Socialist party an election, his apparent suicide was construed in the national press as indicating an "honorable" and "honest" politician who takes responsibility where others don't, and as "thus superior to all of us". This metapragmatic construal does not liken Bérégovoy's conduct as displaying de Gaulle's ease and self possession, but as "dignified" because it signals a commitment to the integrity of an office and a responsibility to those who elect him to it. In being reanimated, the register is partly re-interpreted. And the exemplary sample of the new emblem is a singular individual, Bérégovoy. However, once it re-enters public sphere discourses, the emblem remains available in evaluations of subsequent leaders, like Nikolas Sarkozy, as Noyes shows in her discussion. Whether or not it will come to constitute a widely enregistered new model of "classical" political conduct, and will consistently count as a new standard remains to be seen, of course, as is always the case at seemingly incipient moments of register change.

Cultural Models of Conduct in History

The enregisterment of performable signs as indexicals of actor or activity type, and thus as cultural models of conduct, is an ongoing semiotic process in social history, a process mediated by the reflexive treatment of differences in behavior as indexicals of distinct actor personae or interpersonal activities, and thus as signs capable of differentiating roles and relationships in interaction. Various disciplines that study features of communication – whether its "language" or its "genre" – encounter such systems of social indexicals in their data, and thus encounter the register organization of communicative conduct, a type of social-semiotic organization that requires distinct methods for its study.

The accompanying articles show that register formations are germane to varieties of speech and conduct in any sociohistorical milieu. And through the extraordinary care with which they describe the workings of register phenomena in their data – a few aspects of which I have attempted to bring together in comparative terms here – these articles show that attention to the register organization of behavior reveals aspects of meaning-in-conduct that remain opaque unless we attend to the reflexive processes through which features of interpersonal conduct are modeled as significant by those whose conduct it is.

These studies also make clear that the register organization of discursive behavior cross-cuts its PLG organization or any "genre" classification it may be given. I noted earlier that a PLG unitization of sentence-internal speech tokens does not suffice to identify stereotypic social indexicals of actor or activity type, nor their social-demographic organization as models-for particular users. The register organization of communicative behavior is orthogonal to, or cross-cuts, its grammatical organization, even if both forms of semiotic organization intersect in audible samples of speech behavior. Similarly, the genre organization of discourse into taxonomic text-types (by whatever criteria) is orthogonal to *both* its PLG organization *and* its register organization, even if all three types of organization are routinely evidenced in the same apparently continuous stretches of speech behavior. Nor do all three forms of semiotic organization have the same social domain: a speaker of some language who can routinely construe the PLG organization of its utterances is typically familiar only with a few genres of verbal art, and with only a few of its speech registers.

Whether the reanalysis of speech behaviors into distinct register models of conduct involves the reanalysis of PLG units or of genre partials or of both, whether these are sourced from one locale or from many, whether non-discursive signs are also involved or not involved, the reanalysis yields a register model insofar as otherwise diverse behaviors are grouped together into repertoires with a characteristic (and characterizable) range of stereotypic indexical values for some social domain of users, and is empirically identifiable only by attention to their reflexive practices. Indeed, all of the specific kinds of sign-types discussed above (lexical registers, enregistered emblems, enregistered styles, etc.), which are characteristic of register formations in societies around the world, are formulated as register partials through the reflexive practices of users, and change through them.

Effective competence in a register includes knowing when not to use it. Although individuals differ in their register range (the number and kinds of registers they effectively command), acts of deploying any one of them are susceptible to evaluations of appropriateness to setting both by the one deploying them and by other members of the current participation framework, and hence are interpersonally effective only when current interactants have a symmetric grasp of the register model and of the indexical selectivity of register partials for contextual variables. Indexically non-congruent displays – the use of hyper-polite speech in intimate settings, of women's speech by men, of slang in job interviews, etc. – are often avoided by persons acquainted with stereotypic indexical values; and, when they are actually enacted, are understood as tropic enactments that have some interaction-specific significance, but only by those acquainted with the register models on which they trope. And some among these tropic enactments are reanalyzed into fractionally congruent contrastive models, which differentiate persons and groups from each other, and thus make intelligible socially organized forms of semiotically expressible sameness or difference.

As we approach the study of register phenomena in different times and places around the world, we are able, in any given instance, to observe only a few of the features that processes of enregisterment make palpable to those who live with each other through them. But the set of phenomena that a collective project (such as this volume) brings to light is of course much wider than what any of us can individually glimpse or seek to describe. And if these efforts are successful, other issues, which we have not yet imagined, can also be explored, simply because other persons have imagined them and are enacting them through models of conduct elsewhere, together and on their own.

Notes

1   I have observed elsewhere that: "From the standpoint of its persona-indexing effects, any register constitutes a class of enregistered emblems [... which] convey stereotypic images of persons [...] We distinguish such formations from each other as distinct 'registers' when we approach them from the standpoint of repertoires; but if we approach them from the standpoint of personae, we are distinguishing enregistered emblems from each other" (Agha 2007a: 236). To this we may add the observation that when we distinguish these formations from the standpoint of social domain, we are distinguishing the socially organized cultural practices of identifiable populations.

2   The case of American youth slang – where word-forms are sourced from Spanish, Yiddish or African American Vernacular, and distinctly enregistered in the speech of college students – is perfectly analogous (see Eble 1996: 74–97). So also are a very

wide variety of forms of repertoire sourcing and reanalysis in adult speech from registers around the world, as in the case of Chinese elements in polite Japanese, Arabic in Persian, Sanskrit in Thai or Tibetan, Latin in English, and so on.

3 The details of how such metapragmatic data may be studied, how forms of typification formulate the significance of what they typify, how metapragmatic models differ in institutional authority or social dissemination, or enable forms of footing and alignment in social life, may be found in Agha 2007a (chapters 3–5) and Agha 2005b. I highlight a few issues in the discussion below.

4 In early work (such as Ferguson 1981), the word-form *register* is believed to name "one of the most promising tools of discourse analysis" even though the "problems inherent" to its empirical use are identified in questions like "How is a register identified? What constitutes a register? Do registers overlap?" (Ferguson 1981: 10), which writers in this period appear unable to answer. The general trend, instead, is to use the word-form *register* to describe variation in the use of PLG systems without explicit criteria for identifying either variants or their social significance. The reliance on intuitive criteria and a PLG-centric focus on something called a "language system" (as discussed in Susanna Shore's paper in this volume) impose severe limitations on early approaches (as discussed in Agha 2007a: 167–168 and Agha 1998: 154). Although the word-form *register* occurs both in earlier static approaches and in more recent reflexive approaches such as mine, it does not have the same word-sense, and is thus not the same lexeme. Hervey 1992 describes the older lexeme as follows: "It must also be said that, in spite of its place in systemic linguistics (Halliday and Fawcett 1987) this term remains one of the vaguest, fuzziest and least sharply defined in the repertoires of linguists and laymen, both of whom use it without any precise and clear sense of what they mean by it" (Hervey 1992: 189), a lack of clarity whose result is that many authors of this period "shy away from using the term "register" altogether", while others use it inconsistently (Hervey 1992: 191).

5 The italicized interpolations below highlight the approximate correspondence or overlap between Bauman's terminology and my own: Bauman is proposing that the comparative study of genres requires that the analyst be able to identify "the culture-specific constellations of communicative means [*repertoires and styles*] that serve to key [*stereotypically to index*] performance [*or genres of performance*] in particular communities [i.e., *for a social domains of users*]," and is thus urging that the analyst be able to identify registers models presupposed in use. Since any performance in which a register's tokens occur also has entirely distinct characteristics, including some that are entirely emergent within that performance (as discussed later in this article), the study of performance relies on many other analytic techniques too, the ability to identify register partials being one among them.

6 Foley 1995 relies upon and cites a wide range of studies in linguistic anthropology, including work by James Fox on Rotinese ritual language, Keith Basso on Apache place names, Ellen Basso on Kalapalo storytelling, Dell Hymes on Chinookan rarratives, Paul Friedrich on Homeric formulas, Dennis Tedlock on Zuni and Quiché Maya, Joel Sherzer on Kuna speech styles, Greg Urban on Amerindian ritual wailing, Steve Feld on Kaluli lament, Tony Woodbury on Yupik Eskimo texts, Jane Hill on Mexicano women's narratives, and a great many others.

7 The field methods employed by Parry and Lord for identifying types of *reč* include two types of metasemantic queries (both discussed in Agha 2007a: 119–122) – namely, requests for denotational glosses of the term *reč* ("This *reč* in a song, what is it?"), and requests for the identification of referential samples ("Is this a *reč*?", "Is this also a *reč*?) – and thus rely on the reflexive abilities of native performers to identify units of performance (see Foley 2002a: 12–15 for examples of their queries, and the data they elicit through them). However, Parry and Lord relied on very limited types of reflexive data, namely explicit metasemantic queries, and seemed unable

to interpret the answers they elicited from singers ("When asked what a word is, he will reply he does not know, or he will give a sound group which may vary in length from what we call a word to an entire line of poetry, or even an entire song"; Lord 1960: 25), sometimes treating these answers as evidence of ignorance or confusion ("As I have said, singers do not know what words and lines are"; Lord 1960: 28).

8   In defining the "performance arena" of a register, Foley makes clear that although the term "arena" relies on a "spatial metaphor," it is not intended to describe "any geographically or temporally defined place" (Foley 1995: 47) but is meant instead to describe, for any given register, the setting (participants, activities and situations) to which its use is indexically appropriate, and which, when its performance is ritually recurrent, links the register to an interdiscursively identifiable "tradition" of performance, so that it is experienced as belonging not simply to one semiotic encounter but to a semiotic chain that links many encounters to each other (Agha 2005a).

9   Richard Bauman observes that the term "genre" has been defined in a variety of ways in the folkloristic literature, "ultimately taking in everything that people have considered significant about folklore: form, function of effect, content, orientation to the world and the cosmos, truth value, tone, social distribution, and manner or context of use" (Bauman 1992b: 54).

10 Leino 1974 shows that nominal expressions are (1) possessive phrases that denote mother or father through kinship tropes that transpose the zero-point of referential reckoning to a matrilineal kin, whether to the referent's mother (when referring to father) or to the speaker's own mother (when referring to her), where (2) the possessum is a deverbal noun derived from verb stems denoting nurturing or maternal activities, so that both features identify deceased kin through tropic centering within a matrilineal framework of social relations.

11 Registers of avoidance have been described for many other societies, including cases where avoidance marks deference to kin (Dixon 1971), often through activities involving intermediaries (Haviland 1979), or both to kin and non-kin (Irvine and Gal 2000: 39–47), or cases where avoidance vocabularies are associated not with deference but with rites of passage such as male initiation (Hale 1971). Some registers of affinal avoidance are performed through both discursive behaviors (a special lexicon) as well non-discursive behaviors: "Tabooed relatives did not look one another in the eye, did not stand face to face, and did not sit in each other's presence with legs parted" (Haviland 1979: 376). In the Karelian case, the taboo vocabulary is part of a specialized enregistered style in the case of funerary laments – involves intermediaries and voiced deference to deceased kin in a rite of passage where they transition into a category of supernatural beings – but the lexicon does not subserve all of these functions in its other uses, nor does it appear to be invariant as a lexicon across all uses.

References

Agha, Asif 1998. Stereotypes and Registers of Honorific Language. *Language in Society* 27: 151–93.

Agha, Asif 2005a. Introduction: Semiosis across Encounters. *Journal of Linguistic Anthropology* 15(1): 1–5.

Agha, Asif 2005b. Voice, Footing, Enregisterment. *Journal of Linguistic Anthropology* 15(1): 38–59.

Agha, Asif 2007a. *Language and Social Relations.* Cambridge: Cambridge University Press.

Agha, Asif 2007b. The Object Called "Language" and the Subject of Linguistics. *Journal of English Linguistics* 35(1): 217–235.

Agha, Asif 2009. What Do Bilinguals Do? A Commentary. In *Beyond Yellow English: Toward a Linguistic Anthropology of Asian Pacific America*. Ed. Angela Reyes & Adrienne Lo. New York: Oxford University Press. Pp. 253–258.

Agha, Asif 2011. Commodity Registers. *Journal of Linguistic Anthropology* 21(1): 22–53.

Agha, Asif 2012. Mediatized Projects at State Peripheries. *Language and Communication* 32: 98–101.

Bauman, Richard 1977. *Verbal Art as Performance*. Prospect Heights, IL: Waveland Press.

Bauman, Richard 1992a. Contextualization, Tradition, and the Dialogue of Genres: Icelandic Legends of the *kraftaskáld*. In: *Rethinking Context: Language as an Interactive Phenomenon*. Ed. A. Duranti & C. Goodwin. Cambridge: Cambridge University Press. Pp. 127–145.

Bauman, Richard 1992b. *Folklore, Cultural Performances, and Popular Entertainments: A Communications-Centered Handbook*. New York: Oxford University Press.

Boellstorf, Tom 2004. Gay Language and Indonesia: Registering Belonging. *Journal of Linguistic Anthropology* 14(2): 248–268.

Dixon, R. M. W. 1971. A Method of Semantic Description. In *Semantics: An Interdisciplinary Reader in Philosophy, Linguistics and Psychology*. Ed. D. D. Steinberg & L. A. Jakobovitz. Cambridge: Cambridge University Press. Pp. 436–471.

Ervin-Tripp, Susan 1986. On Sociolinguistic Rules: Alternation and Co-occurrence. In *Directions in Sociolinguistics: The Ethnography of Communication*. Ed. John Gumperz & Dell Hymes. New York: Blackwell. Pp. 213–250

Eble, Connie 1996. *Slang and Sociability: In Group Language Among College Students*. Chapel Hill: University of North Carolina Press.

Fedorova, Kapitolina 2013. Speaking with and about Chinese: Language Attitudes, Ethnic Stereotypes and Discourse Strategies in Interethnic Communication on the Russian–Chinese Border. *Civlisations* 62(1/2): 71–89.

Ferguson, Charle. 1981. 'Foreigner Talk' as the Name of a Simplified Register. *International Journal of the Sociology of Language* 28: 9–18.

Foley, John Miles 1995. *The Singer of Tales in Performance*. Bloomington: Indiana University Press.

Foley, John Miles 2002a. *How To Read an Oral Poem*. Urbana: University of Illinois Press.

Foley, John Miles 2002b. Selection as *pars pro toto*: The Role of Metonymy in Epic Performances and Traditions. In *The Kalevala and the World's Traditional Epics*. Ed. Lauri Honko. Helsinki: Finnish Literature Society. Pp. 106–127.

Gagné, Isaac 2008. Urban Princesses: Performance and "Women's Language" in Japan's Gothic/Lolita Subculture. *Journal of Linguistic Anthropology* 18(1): 130–150.

Githinji, Peter 2006. Bazes and Their Shibboleths: Lexical Variation and Sheng Speakers Identity in Narobi. *Nordic Journal of African Studies* 15(4): 443–472.

Hale, Kenneth 1971. A Note on a Walbiri Tradition of Antonymy. In: *Semantics: An Interdisciplinary Reader in Philosophy, Linguistics and Psychology*. Ed. D. D. Steinberg & L. A. Jakobovitz. Cambridge: Cambridge University Press. Pp. 472–482.

Haviland, John B. 1979. Guugu-Yimidhirr Brother-in-Law Language. *Language in Society* 8: 365–393.

Hervey, Sándor 1992. Registering Registers. *Lingua* 86: 189–206.

Honko, Lauri 1974. Balto-Finnic Lament Poetry. *Studia Fennica* 17: 9–61.

Hymes, Dell 1974. Ways of Speaking. In *Explorations in the Ethnography of Speaking*. Ed. Richard Bauman & Joel Sherzer. Cambridge: Cambridge University Press. Pp. 433–451.

Irvine, Judith T. & Susan Gal 2000. Language Ideology and Linguistic Differentiation. In *Regimes of Language: Ideologies, Polities, and Identities*. Ed. Paul V. Kroskrity. Santa Fe: School of American Research. Pp. 35–83.

Jørgensen, J. N., M. S. Karrebaek, L. M. Madsen & J. S. Møller 2011. Polylnguaging in Superdiversity. *Diversities* 13(2): 23–37

Leino, Pentti 1974. The Language of Lament: The Role of Phonological and Semantic Features in Word Choice. *Studia Fennica* 17: 92–131.

Lord, Albert B. 1960. *The Singer of Tales*. Cambridge, MA: Harvard University Press

Madsen, Lian Malai 2013. "High" and "Low" in Urban Danish Speech Styles. *Language in Society* 42: 115–138.

Newell, Sasha 2009. Enregistering Modernity, Bluffing, Criminality: How Nouchi Speech Reinvented (and Fractured) the Nation. *Journal of Linguistic Anthropology* 19(2): 157–184.

Quist, Pia 2008. Sociolinguistic Approaches to Multiethnolect: Language Variety and Stylistic Practice. *International Journal of Bilingualism* 12(1/2): 43–61.

Samper, David A. 2002. Talking Sheng: The Role of a Hybrid Language in the Construction of Identity and Youth Culture in Nairobi, Kenya. Unpublished Ph.D. dissertation, University of Pennsylvania.

Smith-Hefner, Nancy J. 2007. Youth Language, *Gaul* Sociability, and the New Indonesian Middle Class. *Journal of Linguistic Anthropology* 17(2): 130–150.

Stepanova, Eila 2011. Reflections of Belief Systems in Karelian and Lithuanian Laments: Shared Systems of Traditional Referentiality? *Archaeologia Baltica* 15: 128–143.

Tolbert, Elizabeth 1988. The Musical Means of Sorrow: The Karelian Lament Tradition. Unpublished Ph.D. dissertation, University of California, Los Angeles.

Tolbert, Elizabeth 1990. Women Cry with Words: Symbolization of Affect in the Karelian Lament. *Yearbook of Traditional Music* 22: 80–105.

Urban, Greg 1988. Ritual Wailing in Amerindian Brazil. *American Anthropologist* 90(2): 385–400.

Susanna Shore

2. Register in Systemic Functional Linguistics

The notion of register has been an integral part of theorizing about language in systemic functional (henceforth: SF) theory, as developed by the linguist Michael Halliday and his colleagues and students since the 1960s. Register is intermediary in the dialectic between the language system (as a meaning potential) and the actualized meanings in countless spoken and written texts. From the perspective of the language system, a register is a sub-potential of the meaning potential of language; from the perspective of actual texts, a register is a text-type. Register is also important in SF theory because SF linguists have always been interested in the applications of linguistic theory, e.g. in first and second language teaching and critical discourse analysis. SF theory, however, is considered to be "appliable linguistics" rather than applied linguistics (e.g. Halliday 2010: 14).

The purpose of this article is to give some background to SF theory and to discuss the term *register* in relation to its theoretical context. The article is organised as follows. In the next section, I shall give some background to SF linguistics, discussing briefly the contributions of the linguist J. R. Firth and of the anthropologist Bronislaw Malinowski. I shall then turn to the work of Michael Halliday: first discussing general aspects of his theory and then focussing on how Halliday approaches registers and variation in language use. This will be followed by a discussion of developments of Halliday's work by Ruqaiya Hasan and James Martin. The focus in these sections will be on larger patterns (or schematic structures) in spoken and written texts and on the redefinition of register in Martin's approach. I shall conclude with my own synthesis of the SF approaches discussed in this article.

Background to Systemic Functional Theory: Firth and Malinowski

Michael Halliday's teacher was J. R. Firth (1890–1960), the first professor of general linguistics in the United Kingdom. At a time when the American linguist Leonard Bloomfield was saying that he wanted to study language without having to make "statements of meaning" (e.g. Bloomfield 1933: 140, 247), in an obvious intertextual link to Bloomfield, Firth repeatedly insisted that that object of linguistic analysis is precisely "to make statements of meaning so that we may see how we use language to live" (e.g. Firth 1957: 190; 1968: 192).

Firth's own approach was influenced by the Polish-British anthropologist Bronislaw Malinowski (1884–1942), with whom Firth collaborated. In Malinowski's (1946) view, language is "a form of living" (rather than the "counter-sign of thought"), and as a form of living it is inextricably bound up with culture. Prior to Wittgenstein, Malinowski (1946 [1923]) was saying that the meaning of words and expressions is their function in situational contexts.

Firth borrowed the term "context of situation" from Malinowski but redefined it in more abstract terms. Whereas Malinowski's context of situation refers to the ordering and arrangement of physical things and events, Firth's (e.g. 1957: 181–182; 1968: 16, 200) context of situation is a "schematic construct" abstracted from the flux of experience and from concrete instances of language use. The context of situation, the basis of linguistic analysis for Firth, is a dynamic and creative "patterned process" involving relations between (a) the participants, (b) the relevant characteristics of the participants, (c) their verbal and non-verbal actions, (d) relevant objects and other relevant events and (e) the effects of the verbal action (Firth 1957: 182; 1968: 177–178).

Firth extended Malinowski's "function in context" approach to meaning to linguistic levels of description: meaning is created not only in the situational context, but also in lexical, grammatical, phonological and phonetic contexts:

> To make statements of meaning in terms of linguistics, we may accept the language event as a whole and then deal with it at various levels, sometimes in a descending order, beginning with social context and proceeding through syntax and vocabulary to phonology and even phonetics, and at other times in the opposite order ... (Firth 1957: 192).

Firth's approach to meaning is best understood in terms of meaning-making or as the construal of meaning (cf. Shore 2010). Meaning-making is extremely complex, so in Firth's view, in order to get a handle on it, we need to break it down into the resources that are available at each level of description. Firth often used the metaphor of a prism to refer to his approach: the analysis of meaning is rather like breaking white light into its component colours using a prism (see e.g. Firth 1968 [written in the 1950s]: 108).

A precursor of the notion of register in Firth's approach is what Firth referred to as a restricted language. A *restricted language* is a delimited sub-language within the general language; it provides data that is already "fenced off" for the linguist (Firth 1968: 29–30, 87; Shore 2010). The way in which a language is restricted does not seem to be important for Firth: it is any form of speech or writing with "specialized vocabulary, grammar and style" (1968: 112, 87, 106). Examples given include the language used by Japanese pilots in combat, the language of modern Arabic headlines, the language of politics, science or meteorology, the language of personal address, the language of a particular text (e.g. the American Declaration of Independence) and the lyrics of a particular poet (Firth 1968: 29, 87, 98, 106, 112, 118–119).

The analytical tools used by Firth to describe textual data are *systems* and *structures*. A system is made up of the options or choices available at any level of analysis: for example, the system of prosodies in the intonation group, the syntactical system of declarative, interrogative or imperative and the lexical system of colour terms in English. The term *structure* refers to the elements chosen and their combinations and inter-relations at any level. Firth's structure might more aptly be referred to as patterning, and indeed Firth frequently refers to "patterns" and "patterning" in his writing as a synonym for (social and linguistic) structures (e.g. 1957: 136, 200). Firth's term *system*, thus, does not apply to a language as a whole. Firth (1957: 121) rejected the structuralist idea of an all-encompassing language system. His approach was, instead, "polysystemic" and multi-structural (1968: 186; Shore 2010).

Firth's ideas about language were ahead of his time, and his approach to meaning was sadly misunderstood in the United States, where linguistics was dominated by structuralism. Firth's ideas, however, were influential in the United Kingdom and his legacy can be seen in SF linguistics in a number of ways. Important from the point of view of register is the multifaceted approach to meaning and theorising about situational contexts and how they can be related to language in use.

Halliday and Systemic Functional Linguistics

The central figure in systemic functional linguistics is the British-born linguist, Michael Halliday (1925-). Halliday held various positions in the United Kingdom and the United States, before moving to Australia in 1976. He was professor of linguistics at the University of Sydney until his retirement in 1987. During his academic career, Halliday - together with his colleagues and students - developed a theory of language that eventually became known as SF theory.

The term *systemic* in the name of the theory is based on Firth's notion of a system. The use of language involves meaning-making *options* (i.e. choices): any instance of language use is seen as the realization of a number of simultaneous options on various levels (or, to use the contemporary SF term, *strata*) in a particular situation. Unlike Firth, Halliday also refers to the language system, but as a (fictitious) whole. A language is a meaning potential - or to put it more precisely - a *semogenetic* (i.e. *meaning-making*) *potential*; and any spoken or written text is the actualization of this potential (e.g. Halliday 1978: 109).

A language system is a system of systems, a complex and dynamic system comprised of a number of simultaneous and interconnected subsystems. An important aspect of a systemic approach is that categories are not presented as isolates but in relation to other categories in the (sub)system. The downside of a systemic approach is that options are modelled as system networks, which tend to get complicated (and are off-putting to a humanist). Moreover, system networks necessarily present all linguistic phenomena as discrete (cf. Halliday 2009: 68). Halliday's early work seems to approach categories in terms of prototypes:

> Language is patterned activity. [....] the patterns take the form of repetition of like events. Likeness, at whatever degree of abstraction, is of course a cline, ranging from 'having everything in common' to 'having nothing in common' [...] no two events are ever identical [... nevertheless] identity is a necessary hypothesis. (Halliday 2002a [1961]: 42, 46.)

These two perspectives – language described in terms of discrete categories and systemic options versus language described in terms of prototypes and clines – have more recently been referred to as a distinction between "typological" and "topological" approaches in SF linguistics (e.g. Martin & Matthiessen 1991; Lemke 1999; Rose & Martin 2012: 83).

The term *functional* is used in the name of the theory because the theory is "a theory of how language works" (Halliday 2002a [1961]: 38).

> A functional approach to language means, first of all, investigating how language is used: trying to find out what are the purposes that language serves for us, and how we are able to achieve these purposes through speaking and listening, reading and writing. But it also means more than this. It means seeking to explain the nature of language in functional terms: seeing whether language itself has been shaped by use, and if so, in what ways – how the form [SS: i.e. the organisation] of language has been determined by the functions it has evolved to serve. (Halliday 1973: 7.)

This approach led to the postulation of a number of basic, abstract functions (umbrella or superordinate functions) of language in its social and ecological environment, so-called *metafunctions*: the ideational, interpersonal and textual metafunctions (e.g. Halliday 1978; Halliday & Matthiessen 2014: 30–31).

The *ideational* (or representational) *metafunction* is concerned with how we use language to make sense of the world around us and the world of our imagination. The ideational metafunction is further subdivided into the experiential and the logical metafunctions. The *experiential metafunction* is concerned with how language is used to construe the things and the happenings in the world around us and in the world of our imagination. The word *construe* is used because a language is not regarded as simply providing names or labels for things that are already there, that have already been delineated in the world of our experience. Instead, the language that we speak is regarded as playing an active part in the semogenetic process. This is not to say that a language is a straightjacket, but it predisposes us to see and talk about the world in the ways provided by the language that we speak.

The focus of the experiential metafunction is, firstly, on how words (lexical items) are used to construe and classify the phenomena of our experience. Thus, in English, we have words to distinguish between walking, strolling, plodding, trundling, striding, rambling, hiking etc., and the verb *ramble* can also be used to refer to unorganized speech. Secondly, as isolated words are not in themselves sufficient to talk about the world, more important from an experiential point of view is how clauses (as process types) are used to configure words into meaning-creating patterns. (The term *sentence* is not used in systemic functional theory as a grammatical term; a sentence is an orthographic unit, which is typically realized as a clause or clause complex.)

The fact that the grammatical patterns of clauses are meaning-making can be illustrated with Lewis Carroll's (1965: 126) nonsense poem:

> 'Twas brillig, and the slithy toves
> Did gyre and gimble in the wabe:
> All mimsy were the borogoves,
> And the mome raths outgrabe.

While the lexical (content) words are nonsense, the poem is nevertheless meaningful, because the grammatical (or function) words like *and* and *the* as well as the patterns in the clauses are meaningful. The first clause construes an ambient process (*'twas brillig*, cf. *it was dusk/hot*), the second (*the slithy toves did gyre and gimble in the wabe*) is an intransitive material process (cf. *the slimy snakes did slither and slide in the cave*), the third (*all mimsy were the borogoves*) is a relational process (cf. *so miserable were the parakeets*). The last clause (*the mome raths outgrabe*) is syntactically ambiguous, but it could be seen as a transitive material process with *the mome* as the subject and *raths* as the object (cf. *the gazelle leopards outran*).

The other subfunction of the ideational metafunction, the *logical metafunction*, does not refer to logic as such but to the way in which we use language to join words, phrases or clauses into larger coordinating or subordinating complexes using conjunctions like *and*, *but*, *because* and *when*. In Carroll's poem, for example, the first conjunction *and* in the clause complex *'Twas brillig, and the slithy toves did gyre and gimble in the wabe* expresses a simple continuing relationship between the clauses. The meaning relationship between the clauses would be different if Carroll had used other options, such as *but* or *when*. The former would have construed some kind of adversative relationship, the latter a temporal relationship between the clauses.

The *interpersonal metafunction* is concerned with how we use language to enact diverse interpersonal relations and to expresses personal assessments, judgments and attitudes. The interpersonal metafunction is reflected in the grammatical options that we use to create roles for ourselves and for others: whether we are informing, questioning, offering etc. This kind of meaning is made in the grammar of English (and many other languages), above all, in the interpersonal clause types declarative, interrogative and imperative (*the toves gimbled, did the toves gimble? Gimble or else!*). Important from an interpersonal point of view are also the prosodies in an intonation group, for example, the difference between asking *are you going to the pub* with rising or falling intonation in English. Rising intonation might, for example, be followed by *I'll join you*, whereas falling intonation is likely to be an indicator of disapproval or a criticism. (See further Halliday & Matthiessen 2014; Halliday & Greaves 2008; Luukka 1995; Lauranto 2015; Shore 2012a; 2012b.)

Included in the interpersonal metafunction is *modality* (very broadly understood). The first type of modality usually distinguished in SF theory has to do with degrees of validity in the exchange of meanings: we use language to assess the *probability* of something said (e.g. *the borogroves were ~ must have been ~ may have been ~ certainly weren't ... mimsy*) and to assess the *usuality* of what is said (*the borogroves were often ~ sometimes ~ never ... mimsy*). The second kind of modality generally recognised in SF theory has to do with degrees of desirability in impending actions expressed in exchanges. We use language to express degrees of *obligation* (*The toves must ~ need to ~ are expected to ~ should ... gimble*) and degrees of *inclination* (*The toves are determined ~ keen ~ willing ... to gimble*). (Halliday & Matthiessen 2014; Shore 2012a; 2012b.)

From the point of view of the interpersonal metafunction there are, thus, two complementary perspectives on enacting social relationships: the personal (or subjective) and the interpersonal (or intersubjective). Modal assessments are not assessments that are made in someone's head, in a social vacuum, they are directed at another. If someone says or writes *Turku is the capital of Finland*, then he or she assumes an authoritarian role or regards the statement as unproblematic; the interpersonal meaning is marked as negotiable if other choices are made (e.g. *Turku must ~ could be the capital of Finland; Is Turku the capital of Finland?*).

The third metafunction, the *textual* (or *discoursal*) *metafunction*, reflects the fact that language has not just evolved to produce ideational and interpersonal meanings in isolated clauses or clause complexes realized as a single sentence in writing or as a single turn in a conversation. Language is also used to build up larger sequences of text and talk through the meaning-making options that we use to create cohesion and to organize the flow of discourse. So for example, we can connect longer stretches using connectives (*on the other hand, yeah but, next, however, by the way, and so* etc.). Instead of repeating nouns, we use pronouns, for example:

> Alice was beginning to get very tired of sitting by her sister on the bank, and of having nothing to do: once or twice she had peeped into the book her sister was reading, but it had no pictures or conversations in it. (Carroll 1965: 24.)

We can presuppose what was said through ellipsis:

> "Did you say 'What a pity!'?" the Rabbit asked. "No, I didn't," said Alice. (Carroll 1965: 78.)

There are other resources that are used to build up larger stretches of discourse, but connectives, pronominalisation and ellipsis are, perhaps, the most transparent. Of course, the lack of one of the resources just mentioned is a textually meaningful option. For example, Alice could have said: *No, I did not say "What a pity"*, which would bring added emphasis to her response. (See further Halliday & Matthiessen 2014; Shore 2012a; 2012b.)

While it is necessary for a grammarian to pinpoint the different kinds of metafunctional resources that can be used in the creation of meaning, investigating the meanings in a spoken or written text is not a question of picking out ideational and or interpersonal meanings. To borrow the metaphor of Firth above, the meanings in the text can be compared to white light; in order to understand them (and to talk about them in a systematic way) we need to disperse them, but at the same time we need to look the whole text from the simultaneous metafunctional perspectives to see how each perspective contributes to the interpretation of the text and how the meanings in a text reinforce or contradict each (Halliday 1989: 23; Halliday & Matthiessen 2014: 601–602, 731).

SF linguists talk about lexicogrammar (rather than about the lexicon and grammar as two separate phenomena). This is because grammatical items and patterns (e.g. the pronoun *she*, the article *the*, the pattern SUBJECT + VERB + OBJECT + CIRCUMSTANCE) and lexical items (e.g. *child, jump, ball, pond*) are considered to form a continuum of semogenetic resources going from the least delicate to the most delicate (or from the most to the least abstract on a scale of abstraction). For example, the English clause pattern SUBJECT + VERB + OBJECT + CIRCUMSTANCE is at the least delicate (most abstract) end of the continuum. The pattern itself is meaningful: 'someone (/some animate being) does (/did) something to someone/something in some place/time'. The pattern in itself is a choice (there are other clause patterns in English), but if this pattern is chosen, then more delicate (less abstract) lexical options are available: *Mother duck took her ducklings to the pond, the president led a very divided nation into the Great War*. Even metaphorical expressions are based on these resources: *My mother has been driving me round the bend*.

Diatypic Variation and the Metafunctional Hypothesis

From the 1970s, Halliday (e.g. 1978; 1989) started to theorise about variation in language in terms of dialectal and diatypic variation. *Dialectal variation* is variation according to who you are (or who you choose to be) in relation to a regional or social community. Dialectal variation covers not only the standard dialect and regional dialects but also various kinds of social dialects, for example, the variation that is associated with the way in which language is used by members of different social classes, different generations, different genders, different age or ethnic groups etc.

Diatypic variation is variation according to what you are doing, reflecting the different kinds of social and institutional activities that people commonly engage in. It is in relation to diatypic variation that Halliday talks about a *register* as a functional variety of a language (e.g. Halliday 1978; 1989). The term register was borrowed from Reid (1956: 32; Halliday 1978: 110), and Halliday and his colleagues set out to approach diatypic variation in a more principled way than Firth had done in his approach to restricted languages.

The difference between dialectal and diatypic variation is not always clear-cut, and dialectal variation can be associated with diatypic variation, for example, if one uses a standard dialect in formal situations and a neighbourhood dialect in informal ones (Halliday 1978: 34, 217). In a similar vein to Labov's (1972: 271) approach to sociolinguistic variables, Halliday (e.g. 1978: 35) characterises dialects as different ways of saying more or less the same thing. This is, of course, an oversimplification, and Halliday (like Labov) points out that dialectal differences carry social meanings and dialects involve different modes of meaning (and indeed different modes of being) (Halliday 1978: 35, 161, 184; cf. Labov 1972).

The focus in the study of registers in Halliday's approach is on how different meanings are made and how different meaning-making resources are deployed in different registers associated with different situations, for example, in a service encounter or in a school science class. As meanings are *realized* as lexicogrammatical choices, this also means investigating lexicogrammatical options.

The theoretical concept *realization* is used in SF theory to refer to the "(meta)redundant" relationship between linguistic meaning (content) and expression: there is not one without the other (Halliday 2002b; 2003a; 2003b). Unlike simple semiotic systems, where there is a simple redundant relation between meaning and expression (e.g. the colour red = 'stop' in traffic lights), language is a far more complex and stratified (multilevelled) system involving a number of metaredunancies. This means that meaning in SF theory covers both semantics and lexicogrammar, since the lexicogrammatical stratum makes meaning-making in language possible. Expression covers both phonology and phonetics, since actual sounds and prosodies (investigated in phonetics) are organized (and this organization is investigated in phonology).

The realization of the relationship between the strata is generally diagrammatically represented using concentric circles or using internal bracketing. A downward-pointing arrow is used to symbolize realization, as in Figure 1:

[semantics (MEANING) ↘ [lexicogrammar (MEANING) ↘
[phonology (EXPRESSION) ↘ [phonetics (EXPRESSION)]]]

Figure 1. Stratification and realization

The bracketing attempts to capture "a Russian doll" type of relationship, where one doll contains the rest of the dolls. Thus, semantics is realized by the realizations of all the subsequent strata, lexicogrammar is realised by the realization of all the subsequent strata and phonology is realized in phonetics. (Halliday & Matthiessen 2014: 25–26; Halliday 2002b; 2003a; 2003b; Matthiessen 2007, 534–535; 2009.)[1]

To talk about registers and to give them labels ("service encounter", "weather report") is not to imply that they are static or homogeneous (Halliday & Martin 1993: 59). Like dialects, they are "useful fictions" (e.g. Halliday 2003d: 362–363). We need to assume the relative stability of registers in order to be able to talk about them and, for example, to teach them to schoolchildren learning a first or a second language or to model them in human–computer interaction. As with dialects, there is also differential access to registers in any society, which is one of the reasons why Halliday and other systemic functional linguists have been concerned with the applications of linguistics in educational contexts (Halliday 1978; Martin 1989; 1992: 495; Christie & Maton 2011; Shore & Rapatti 2014).

Registers are often referred to as the (ideational, interpersonal and textual) "meanings at risk" (i.e. likely to occur), and as SF theory assumes that linguistic meanings are realized by their expression in language, registers can, at the same time, be regarded as the ideational, interpersonal and textual lexicogrammatical choices at risk. Another way of putting it is to say that registers are recognisable, recurrent patterns of lexicogrammatically realized meanings. So, for example, the future tense is likely to occur in a weather forecast in English; the past tense is likely to occur in a narrative. If the future tense does occur in a narrative, it is likely to occur in the quoted speech of a character. (Halliday 1978: 185; Halliday & Matthiessen 2014: 24-34.)

In more recent work, Halliday has discussed register from the point of the cline of *instantiation*. At one end of the cline is a language as a (dynamic and open) system, at the other end of the cline is an instance of the use of this language, i.e. an actualized (spoken or written) text. Halliday (e.g. 2002b: 359) has compared system and instance to the relationship between the climate (e.g. the climate in southern Finland) and the weather (on a particular day in Helsinki). There is not one without the other; they are two perspectives on a single phenomenon. Similarly, a language system makes it possible to produce meaningful texts in the language, but each text, in turn, affects the system (even if this effect is minute). The fact that this happens is evidenced by language change. All of this happens, of course, in interaction with the socio-cultural environment with its concomitant changes.

However, a language is not instantiated in a vague mass of spoken and written texts occurring in an amorphous socio-cultural environment. Intermediate between a language system and a (spoken or written) text is register (and the corresponding notion of a situation type in its social and institutional setting). Halliday approaches the notion of register from dual (and complementary) perspectives. From the point of view of language as a potential, a register is a subpotential. From the point of view of instances, actualized texts, a register is a (spoken or written) text type. This is diagrammatically represented in Figure 2 (based on Halliday & Matthiessen 2014: 28):

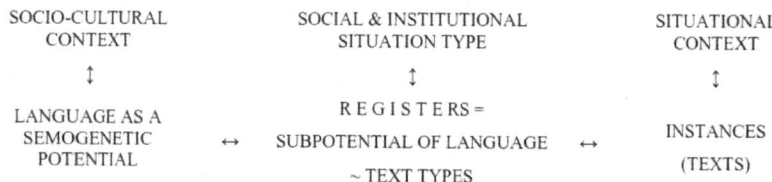

Figure 2. The cline of instantiation

The double-headed arrows are used to indicate the ongoing dialectic between language as a system and instances of language use. [2]

I pointed out earlier that categories in Halliday's theory are based on prototypes. This also applies to registers as text types. Distinguishing a type is not a clear-cut matter and, in practice, the way in which text types are distinguished by SF linguists vary. Halliday is, in essence, a grammarian and he distinguishes text types on an intuitive basis relying on everyday labels for texts such as recipe, public lecture, advertisement and bedtime story (e.g. Halliday 1978: 226; Halliday & Matthiessen 2014: 29).

To account for variation within and across registers, Halliday proposes a small number of relevant variables in the situational context of a text: the field of discourse "what is going on", the tenor of discourse "the relationships between the interactants", and the mode of discourse "the role being played by language" (Halliday 1978; 1989; see also Gregory 1967; Gregory & Carroll 1978). (Discourse is used in this connection simply as a cover term for spoken and written text.) Field, tenor and mode are, thus, umbrella categories, and while they are intuitively graspable, it is not always easy to understand how or why a particular feature in the situation is subsumed under one particular variable by Halliday. In the following, I shall explicate my understanding of Halliday's field, tenor and mode variables (henceforth: FTM-variables) with examples.

The *field of discourse* refers both to the nature of the socio-semiotic activity in which the text is playing a part and to the meanings that are maintained and shaped in the activity. Halliday distinguishes between *first* and *second order field*: (1) the activity itself and (2) the kinds of (experiential) meaning that are involved. For example, lecturing and telling stories are socially recognizable activities. The second order field in both these activities can vary: a lecture can be about business ethics, quantum physics, gardening or recent trends in sociolinguistics; a story can be about events and characters in a fairy-tale world, in the business world or in prehistoric times.

The *tenor of discourse* refers to the relevant participants and their roles and statuses: for example, whether the roles are symmetrical or not, whether one participant has an institutional role, how long the participants have known each other. These are not seen as determining but rather as potentially relevant factors. As with field, a further distinction is made between *first* and *second order tenor*. First order tenor refers to the social roles, e.g. interviewer and interviewee in an interview, seller and buyer in a service encounter, speaker and audience in a lecture. Second order tenor refers to the linguistic roles, e.g. questioner and answerer. Tenor can also be extended to include the roles used in narratology research to distinguish between the participants in a narrative communication situation: between real authors and readers and constructs in the text such as implied author and implied reader (e.g. Rimmon-Kenan 1983: 87–106).

The third variable, *mode of discourse*, refers to how language functions in the situations in which it is used. At the basis of mode is the *medium* of interaction and the primary distinction between speech and writing: whether the interaction is based on speech being articulated and heard or on writing on a paper (or screen) being read or on hybrid forms of these (e.g. written to be read aloud, transcribed spoken). The distinction between speech and writing brings with it a host of other distinctions. For example, spoken interaction may be face-to-face or it may be mediated in various ways (mobile phone, Skype), written interaction may simply involve the reading of a text (e.g. a novel) or it may be online chat that involves the real-time transmission of text messages among the participants. Mode also includes other factors such as whether turn-taking is frequent or infrequent, whether language is constitutive (e.g. a discussion about a game of football) or ancillary (e.g. an actual game in which there is very little talk).[3] In more recent studies, mode also includes how language interacts with other semiotic systems in the discourse (see e.g. O'Halloran 2004).

With reference to later developments discussed in this article, it is important to note at this point that mode also covers what Halliday (e.g. 1978: 144–145) refers to as the rhetorical mode. This refers to whether the discourse is argumentative, didactic, entertaining etc. This is one point of divergence with Martin's approach, to be discussed later on. Another difference is in the use of the term *genre*. Halliday seldom uses the term *genre* in his discussions of register variation. When it is briefly mentioned, it seems to be restricted to refer to literary or a stylised genres, for example, ballads, sonnets, prayers or fables (Halliday 1978: 133–134, 145). It is only later that SF linguists started to use the term *genre* to refer to "speech genres" in the Bakhtinian sense (Bakhtin 1985). The term *generic structure*, however, is used by Halliday not only to refer to the patterning of literary genres like ballads but also to the overall, larger patterning of everyday genres, including the organisation of turn-taking in conversation as analysed by Sacks et al. (1974; Halliday 1978: 133–134, 140). Generic structure is, according to Halliday (1978: 134), beyond the linguistic system: "it is language as the projection of a higher-level semiotic structure". (I shall return to this point in the section on Ruqaiya Hasan.)

When put together, Halliday's metafunctions and the FTM-variables constitute what is generally referred to as the metafunctional hypothesis: each of the FTM-variables is typically realized in language as a particular metafunction. (The metafunctions and the FTM-variables are, of course, in themselves hypothetical.) Because there is a realizational relationship between semantics and lexicogrammar, the FTM-variables are thus typically realized in certain kinds of lexicogrammatical options, as in indicated in Figure 3 (based on Halliday & Hasan 1989: 26):

VARIABLES IN THE CONTEXT OF SITUATION	typically realized by	DISCOURSE (ANALYSED METAFUNCTIONALLY)
field of discourse (the social activity)		ideational metafunction: ideational clause types (e.g. transitive, intransitive, relational etc.), lexical choices etc.
tenor of discourse (participant relationships)		interpersonal metafunction: interpersonal clause types (e.g. declarative, interrogative, imperative), modal verbs and adverbs, person etc.
mode of discourse (the part played by language)		textual metafunction: thematic progression, flow of information, cohesive ties (e.g. pronouns, connectives, ellipses) etc.

Figure 3. The metafunctional hypothesis

This hypothesis seems to be based on something that feels "intuitively right". For example, lexical choices as well as clause types distinguish the fields of cooking and mathematics (cf. *whisk together egg yolks, eggs, and sugar in a bowl* vs *2 to the fourth power is 16*). The tenor of discourse is likely to be reflected in interpersonal clause types. For example, the choice of clause type and the use of modality are likely to be different if the roles are symmetrical and familiar or asymmetrical and unfamiliar: *Don't be ridiculous, you can't do that!* vs *Do you think it would be worth considering other options?* The mode of discourse, for example, the actual presence of another in face-to-face interaction, is likely to be reflected in the use of pronouns. One can say, for example, *Would you like this one or that one?* in a face-to-face service encounter, without explicating the ones that are being referred to; this lack of explication would be unlikely in a telephone conversation.

As in figure 3 above, the relationship between the FTM-variables and the metafunctions is generally presented in terms of typicality, allowing for the fact that the untypical and unpredictable can occur (e.g. Halliday 1978: 31–35, 189, 225–227). However, in line with Gregory (1987: 103–104), it seems to me that the hypothesis appears "over-neat": in the empirical analysis of registers, there is likely to be mismatching between the contextual variables and the metafunctions. Nevertheless, the metafunctional hypothesis can be used as an *organising and investigative framework* in the analysis of discourse (cf. Gregory 1987: 104). If we do not have a framework like Figure 3, then the likely result is that each researcher makes individual observations unrelated in any systematic way to the observations of other researchers.

Registers can be seen as a continuum, with fairly restricted registers, such as weather reports, at one end, and fairly open registers, such as informal discussion among friends, at the other end. Intermediate between these are institutional registers, such as doctor–patient talk or classroom interaction. One of the slightly confusing aspects of Halliday's approach, however, is that at times he talks about registers as quite specific categories and other times as very general categories. Usually the examples given indicate that, from the point of view of instantiation, a register is seen as a text type (see Figure 2). Examples given in a recent publication include service encounters, weather forecasts, walking tours in a guidebook, bedtime stories, rental agreements, media interviews, advertisements, recipes and stockmarket reports (Halliday & Matthiessen 2014: 29).

However, this same list of examples includes e-mail messages; and in other publications Halliday refers to mathematical English as a register (Halliday 1978: 195; 1988: 163). It is difficult, for example, to see e-mail in terms of the "meanings at risk", since all kinds of text types can be sent by e-mail (advertisements, personal letters, minutes of a meeting etc.). Nevertheless, the use of the term *register* to refer to e-mail or mathematical English suggests that the metafunctional hypothesis can also be used as a very flexible framework to group texts together from the perspective of one of the FTM-variables, in the case of e-mail from the perspective of mode and in the case of mathematics from the perspective of field. Thus, registers can be distinguished broadly or narrowly: we can take a broad approach and home in on only one FTMvariable as in the case of mathematics as a register or we can home in on all three variables, for example, a mathematical explanation in a textbook written for primary school children. Halliday (e.g. 1978: 228) has used the term *delicacy of focus* to refer to whether registers as broadly or narrowly defined.

Ruqaiya Hasan's CC, GSP and AGS

Before discussing Ruqaiya Hasan (1931–2015), it is important to note that there has been a change in terminology in Hasan's work. In an early book *Language, Context, and Text*, co-written with Michael Halliday, the term *register* is used by Halliday (1989 [1985]) in part A of the book, whereas Hasan (1989 [1985]) uses the term *genre* in a roughly synonymous way in part B of the book. Hasan seems to avoid the use of the term *genre* in her later work, and instead of talking about "generic structure", she refers to the "general structure" of registers (e.g. Hasan 2009: 186). In the following, I shall use Hasan's more recent terminology even in the discussion of her earlier work.

Hasan introduced the term *contextual configuration* (CC) to refer to a certain configuration of field, tenor and mode associated with the situational context of a particular register. Thus, to simplify somewhat, a bedtime story can be characterized in terms of its field as story-telling that is a sharing and relationship consolidating activity, its tenor can be characterised from parent to child, and its mode is written to be spoken. The FTM-variables and particular contextual configurations (CCs) are abstractions that allow us to make generalizations across similar texts (and show how they differ from other texts) and to make correlations between variation in the situational context and lexicogrammatical choices in language.

In contrast to a context of situation with a particular CC is the *material (situational) setting* (Hasan 1973; 1996; 2009). This term is used to refer to the spatiotemporal aspects of an instance of language use: the physical objects and the actual people involved. Aspects of the material setting may impinge on the text, but they are unlikely to affect the FTM-variables unless they are repeated and become a feature of the context of situation.

Hasan also worked on the general structure (= Halliday's generic structure) of texts, but rather than talk about structure, Hasan (2009: 186) talks about the *general structure potential* (GSP) of a register, as opposed to the *actual global structure* (AGS) of a particular text. The term *general structure potential* is used by Hasan to refer to the stages that are characteristic of a particular register and realized by the typical linguistic feature of texts associated with a register.

Hasan distinguishes between *obligatory stages* (or, as she refers to them, "elements"), which are defined as those found in all complete instances of a register and thus are register-defining, and *optional stages*, which may occur but are not register-defining. The terms *obligatory* and *defining* are problematic in Hasan's discussions of GSP. By obligatory, Hasan means that without a particular stage, the text would not be considered to belong to a particular register. For example, a senile elderly person could go into a doctor's surgery and talk about the weather and various other things that come to his or her mind, but unless there is a stage that deals with talking about symptoms and attempting to give a diagnosis, the interaction would not be considered an instance of doctor-patient interaction in a surgery. Talk about symptoms and an attempt to give a diagnosis would, on the other hand, be "register-defining". It seems to me, however, that rather than talk about obligatory stages, it would be better to talk about prototypical or core stages.

Figure 4 indicates the GSP for a nursery tale (based on Hasan 1996 [1984]), but with slightly simpler and more transparent notation. (Small capitals are used for the stages.)

[(PLACEMENT)→ INITIATING EVENT] + SEQUENT EVENT(S) + FINAL EVENT + [(FINALE) ~ (MORAL)]

Figure 4. The general structure potential (GSP) of a nursery tale (Hasan 1984)

The optional stages are in round brackets; in other words, the obligatory stages are an INITIATING EVENT, SEQUENT EVENT(S) and a FINAL EVENT. These are the stages that occurred in all of the tales in Hasan's data. The first set of square brackets and the arrow indicate that in Hasan's data the PLACEMENT (corresponding more or less to the *orientation* in Labov's (1972) narrative schema) is either at the beginning of the tale or it is dispersed throughout the INITIATING EVENT. The brackets, thus, indicate how far the PLACEMENT extends. This is followed by one or more SEQUENT EVENTS and a FINAL EVENT (corresponding more or less to the *complication* and *resolution* in Labov's schema). The optional stages at the end are in square brackets and linked by a tilde to indicate that if both occur the order is not fixed: either FINALE + MORAL or MORAL + FINALE. The *actual global structure* is the structure in a particular text: e.g. PLACEMENT + INITIATING EVENT + SEQUENT EVENT + FINAL EVENT. (Hasan 1996 [1984]; 2009; cf. Labov 1972.)

The general structure potential is an integrated aspect of register in the sense that it is realized in typical semantic selections, which in turn are realized as lexicogrammatical options (cf. Figure 1). For example, the PLACEMENT is likely to be realized by static verbs (*was, lived*) and phrases with a head that refers to a location in time or space (*long, long ago; in a faraway country*). In the INITIATING and SEQUENT EVENTS, on the other hand, there are more likely to be active subjects and dynamic verbs (*the dragon grabbed the princess, the prince jumped to her rescue* etc.).

While the global structuring of spoken and written texts is realized by linguistic features in a text, it is not, however, tied to meaningful options in the linguistic system (e.g. choosing between a transitive or intransitive clause or between lexical options such as *last week* or *last year*). As I mentioned earlier, Halliday (1978: 134, 138) suggests that generic structure (= Hasan's general structure) is a higher-level semiotic structure projected in language. Neither Halliday nor Hasan discuss exactly what is meant by a higher-level semiotic structure, but as I understand it, this refers to the context of culture in which textual interaction takes place. As forms of interaction and ways of doing things, texts go beyond language (as a meaning potential) to the context of culture (as what Halliday refers to as a "behaviour potential") (cf. Halliday 1978: 39, 139–140).

James Martin and the Sydney School

James Martin is considered to be the leading figure in what has come to be known as the Sydney School. Together with his students and colleagues he has developed "genre and register theory", which has been particularly influential in research done with pedagogical applications in mind and well as in critical discourse analysis.

Martin began to use the term *genre* in the 1980s: he describes genres as "how things get done, when language is used to accomplish them" and as "linguistically realized activity types which comprise so much of our culture" (Martin 1984: 25; 1985: 250). The staging involved in genres is emphasised by Martin: a genre is a "staged goal-oriented purposeful activity", "we also recognise a text's genre by the sequence of functionally distinct stages or steps through which it unfolds" (Martin 1984: 25; Eggins & Martin 1997: 236).

The reference to goal-orientation and purpose in the quotes above points to the centrality of the global social purpose of texts in Martin's approach, and this can be seen as being roughly equivalent to what Halliday refers to as the rhetorical mode (i.e. whether the discourse is argumentative, didactic, entertaining etc.). Thus, rhetorical mode is no longer considered to be part of mode in Martin's model but rather as an overarching or controlling factor that is reflected in all of the linguistic features in a text. As the controlling factor, social purpose is reflected in the FTM-variables, and, in turn, in the ideational, interpersonal and textual meanings in a text.

Thus, part of a higher-level (or higher-order) semiotic in Martin's model is not only generic structure, the staging of genres, but also the social purpose of a genre. Although texts and genres typically have many social purposes (e.g. a news story can be used to inform and engage at the same time), Martin generally talks about purpose in the singular because it is the central purpose that is reflected in the staging of a genre.

Staging is tied to social purpose because in order to achieve a purpose in discourse, a text or sections of a text typically go through at least two stages (e.g. THESIS + ARGUMENTS, ORIENTATION + COMPLICATION + RESOLUTION). The staging is not necessarily linear, there are other kinds of global patterning: for example, White (2000) discusses what he refers to as the orbital structure of a news story: the NUCLEUS (the news in a nutshell) is at the beginning, followed by a variable number of SATELLITES (perspectives on the nucleus), ordered according to what are considered to be their significance (for cultural or ideological reasons). The structure is referred to as orbital because the satellites are cohesively linked to the nucleus rather than to each other. Linguists in the Sydney School generally make a further distinction between stages and phases: stages are obligatory, phases are optional and more variable (Rose & Martin 2012: 54; cf. Hasan distinction discussed in the previous section.)

The stages identified in the schematic structure of genres are not necessarily clearly delineated "blocks". In relation to Hasan's work, it was noted that the PLACEMENT of a nursery tale can either be at the beginning or scattered throughout the initial event. Similarly EVALUATION, which is central to many genres (e.g. critiques) need not necessarily be confined to a certain place in the text, it can be dispersed throughout the text (Martin & White 2005; cf. Labov 1972). Moreover, stages representing different genres, can be combined in a text representing what Martin refers to as a macrogenre, as discussed in more detail below.

Another significant change in Martin's approach is that he uses the term *register* to refer to the FTM-variables (e.g. Martin 1992: 495–496; Martin & Rose 2008: 11; Rose & Martin 2012: 22). This was originally based on Martin's misunderstanding of Halliday, according to a message that Martin sent to the Sysfling mailing list (9.11.2009). This use of the term, however, has been passed on to Martin's students, and it is used in this way by many scholars associated with the Sydney School.

In a similar way to Halliday's model of the linguistic system (see Figure 1), Martin and linguists in the Sydney School (e.g. Martin 2009; Rose & Martin 2012: 23) propose a stratified model of genre. This is usually presented diagrammatically as a series of concentric circles, where the idea is that one sphere encloses all of the remaining spheres, as in Figure 5 (based on Martin 2009: 12):

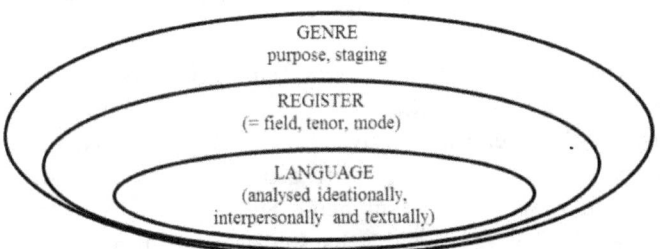

Figure 5. Genre and register in Martin's model

Representations like Figure 5, however, can be slightly confusing. Not only are the FTM-variables referred to by the term *register*, the term *genre* is often used as if it is synonymous with the notion of social purpose. In some places, this is even stated explicitly: "Beyond register [SS: the FTM-variables] is the global social purpose of a text, its genre" (Rose & Martin 2012: 22). There seems to have been a subtle move from talking about genres as linguistically realized, staged and goal-oriented purposeful social activities (i.e. all of the concentric spheres above) to using the term *genre* to refer to the outmost stratum. Another possible point of confusion is that the term *language* in Figure 5 does not refer to the language system (cf. Figure 2) but to the use of language associated with a particular genre.

Another problem with Martin's model is that his use of the term *register* seems to collapse the social and linguistic (e.g. Hasan 1995: 283). Figure 5 gives the impression that FTM-variables are realized only in language. The variables seem to be positioned between social purpose and linguistic choices in Figure 5 because they can vary from one stage to the next. For example, at the beginning of a service encounter, there is likely to be talk about the goods or services to be purchased (field) and it is the customer who asks for the goods and the salesperson who responds (tenor). Towards the end of the encounter, the talk is likely to focus on the exchange of money or payment (field) and it is the salesperson who indicates what has to be paid and the customer who responds (tenor). When paying for the goods, language is likely to have a more ancillary role than when the interactants are negotiating about the goods. (Ventola 1987; 2006.) Nevertheless, the fact remains that the entire activity can be identified as a service encounter, the social roles (salesperson and customer) are likely to be preserved during the encounter and the entire encounter is likely to remain mostly spoken and face-to-face (mode).

Two important terms used in Sydney School SF linguistics are *macrogenres* and *genre families* (e.g. Martin & Rose 2008: 218; Rose & Martin 2012: 128, 178, 331). The term *macrogenre* seems to correspond to what Bakhtin refers to as a secondary or complex genre:

> Secondary (complex) speech genres – novels, dramas, all kinds of scientific research, major genres of commentary, and so forth – arise in more complex and comparatively highly developed and organized cultural communication (primarily written) that is artistic, scientific, socio-political, and so on. During the process of their formation, they absorb and digest various primary (simple) genres that have taken form in unmediated speech communion. (Bakhtin 1986: 62.)

Examples given by Martin and Rose (2008) include textbooks: a history textbook, for example, may include sections that are biographical, explanatory or descriptive. Another example given by Martin (2009) is Nelson Mandela's autobiography, which starts as a "report" generalizing the cost of freedom and then turns into a "story" (cf. Mäntynen & Shore 2014).

Genre families are sets of genres that share some features but differ in others. Rose and Martin (2012: 128-132) identify three central social purposes in the genres that are relevant in reading and writing across the school curriculum: engaging genres (various kinds of stories), informing genres (historical recounts, explanations, reports, procedures) and evaluating genres (arguments and critiques). As umbrella categories, genre families are best seen as fuzzy categories with its members connected by family resemblances in the Wittgensteinian (1953) sense. While Martin stresses the importance of staging in defining genres, the staging in genre families can vary considerably. Informing genres include sequential explanations (e.g. of the water cycle), which typically consist of a PHENOMENON and its EXPLANATION (as a sequence of causes and effects) and procedures (e.g. an experiment or a recipe), which typically consists of the AIM, EQUIPMENT/INGREDIENTS NEEDED and STEPS.

The genre families outlined by Rose and Martin (2012) give further insight into the way in which Sydney School linguists conceive genre. A few of the genres identified by Rose and Martin correspond more or less to what would be referred to as a genre in everyday usage, for example, "a news story". Some of the genres identified, however, are cover terms subsuming various everyday genres: the term "procedure", for example, is used as a cover term for genres such as recipes, experiments and algorithms. Some of the genres are typically realized as part of a macrogenre: examples include sequential explanations (e.g. of the water cycle) and descriptive reports (e.g. of an animal, its appearance, its habitat etc.), although these could occur in educational contexts as independent texts (e.g. a response to an exam question or as a homework assignment).[4] All of this means that the relation between genres and texts in Martin's approach is not based on the relationship between text type and instance, as in Halliday's approach – or, at least, the issue is far more complex.

Synthesis and Concluding Remarks

The use of the terms *genre* and *register* in the Sydney School SF linguistics not only differs from Halliday's approach, it also differs from the way the terms are used in other approaches in linguistics, literary and cultural studies. This is unfortunate because there is a lot of important and pedagogically relevant research that has been carried out by Sydney School linguists. An easy solution would be to drop the terms genre and register as names for the strata, and use the term *genre* to refer to all of the strata, i.e. as follows (using bracketing instead of circles): [purpose & staging [FTM-variables [language/linguistic features (in a text)]]].

While it is not easy to chart the similarities and differences, the approaches of Halliday, Hasan and Martin could be combined if one accepts Martin's view that the main or global social purpose is a controlling factor, so that both purpose as well as core staging – or alternatively generic structure (potential) – are part of a higher-order semiotic. A tentative synthesis of SF approaches is given in Figure 6:

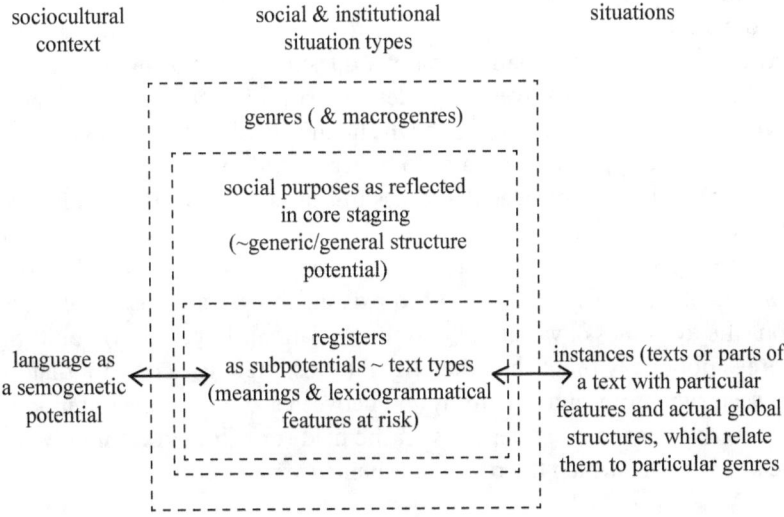

Figure 6. *A synthesis of SF approaches to genre and register*

As indicated earlier, the double-headed arrows are used to underscore the dialectical relationship underlying instantiation.

The squares inside Figure 6 are meant to represent different orders of patterning: with registers in the inner box the focus is on how instances of language use, i.e. texts, can be related to the linguistic system on the cline of instantiation. With genres (and macrogenres) in the outer box, the focus is on how registers are related to the social and institutional situation types that are characteristic of a particular culture. Within genres, the main social purpose is reflected in the core stages of a genre (or its structure potential). With macrogenres, there are several social purposes, which are reflected in sequential or overlapping sets of staging in texts.

More problematic is determining how to combine the different approaches to the FTM-variables. As intimated in the discussion of Martin's approach above, it may be useful to clearly separate 1st and 2nd order field and tenor. I have not included the FTM-variables in Figure 6 because it may be misleading to do so: the variables as well as the metafunctions postulated in SF theory provide a framework for looking at the relations between the language system and texts and between the cultural and situational context and texts. It seems to me that it would be odd to locate them in any one place in the diagram.

This article has focussed on language and on the relative stability of registers. The focus on language is because SF theory is a theory of language that links the systematicies in lexicogrammar via register to spoken and written texts. However, an SF approach can also provide a framework for analysing other semiotic systems as well as for analysing the interaction between language and other semiotic systems in spoken and written texts, as evidenced by recent SF research (e.g. O'Halloran 2004; Kress & van Leeuwen 2006; Baldry & Thibault 2006; Unsworth 2008; Ventola & Moya 2009; Painter et al. 2013).

The focus has been on the stability of registers because most SF linguists are interested in the applications of the theory. However, an SF approach can provide a principled but flexible framework for looking at variability and the dynamics of discourse (e.g. Hasan 1999; 2000). As I see it, the debate between stability and dynamics is not a question of opposing but rather of *complementary* perspectives. Complementarities in the study of language were problematized a century ago by the linguist Ferdinand de Saussure (1983 [1916]), whose approach was later to be trivialized in American structuralism. It seems to me, however, that Saussure's discussion of language in terms of synchrony and diachrony is also of relevance to the discussion of register. Saussure (1983 [1916]: 79–80) discussed these notions in terms of the axis of simultaneity (the relative stability of co-existing things) and the axis of succession (the dynamics of variation in time). As Saussure (1983: 8–9) points out, there is not one without the other. In SF terms, there is a constant dialectic between synchrony and diachrony and between stability and variability. The perspective chosen often depends on the field (or sub-field) of inquiry and the purposes for which the research is being carried out.

Notes

1. The focus on language in Halliday's linguistic theory does not preclude the contribution of other semiotic systems to meaning-making (Halliday 2003c: 2; cf. Firth's characterization of the context of situation discussed earlier and the references at the end of the final section of this article).
2. As the focus is on register, dialects (dialectal varieties) are ignored in Figure 2 and subsequent diagrams. The way in which dialects affect texts (spoken or written interaction) is beyond the scope of this article. For some early discussion, see Halliday 1978: 60–107.
3. There is no distinction between 1st and 2nd order in mode; the complexity in mode comes from the different combinations such as written to be spoken, transcribed spoken etc.
4. Once again, one also has to pay attention to the terms used in Martin's approach. For example, Rose and Martin's (2012) family of engaging genres (i.e. stories) includes an "anecdote". Thus is not an amusing account of an incident but a narrative without a resolution (corresponding more of less to what is called an *open narrative* in literary studies). (Cf. Shore 2014.)

References

Bakhtin, Mikhail 1984. *Problems of Dostoevsky's Poetics*. Ed. & trans. Caryl Emerson. Minneapolis: University of Minnesota Press.
Bakhtin, Mikhail 1986 [1953]. The Problem of Speech Genres. In *Speech Genres and Other Late Essays*. Ed. Caryl Emerson & Michael Holquist. Trans. Vern W. McGee. Austin: University of Texas Press. Pp. 60–102.
Baldry, Anthony, & Paul Thibault 2006. *Multimodal Transcription and Text Analysis*. London: Equinox.
Bloomfield, Leonard 1933. *Language*. New York: Henry Holt.
Carroll, Lewis 1965. *The Works of Lewis Carroll*. Feltham, Middlesex: Hamlyn.
Christie, Frances, & Karl Maton (eds.) 2011. *Disciplinarity: Functional Linguistic and Sociological Perspectives*. London: Continuum.
Eggins, Suzanne, & J. R. Martin 1997. Genres and Registers of Discourse. In *Discourse as Structure and Process: Discourse Studies: A Multidisciplinary Introduction*. Vol. 1. Ed. Teun A. van Dijk. London: Sage. Pp. 230–256.
Firth, J. R. 1957. *Papers in Linguistics 1934–1951*. London: Oxford University Press.
Firth, J. R. 1968. *Selected Papers of J. R. Firth 1952–59*. Ed. F. Palmer. London: Longman.
Gregory, Michael 1967. Aspects of Varieties Differentiation. *Journal of Linguistics* 3: 177–198.
Gregory, Michael 1987. Meta-Functions: Aspects of their Development, Status and Use in Systemic Linguistics. In *New Developments in Systemic Linguistics I: Theory and Description*. Ed. M. A. K. Halliday & Robin P. Fawcett. London: Frances Pinter. Pp. 94–106.
Gregory, Michael, & Susanne Carroll 1978. *Language and Situation: Language Varieties in their Social Contexts*. London: Routledge & Kegan Paul.
Halliday, M. A. K. 1973. *Explorations in the Functions of Language*. London: Edward Arnold.
Halliday, M. A. K. 1978. *Language as Social Semiotic: The Social Interpretation of Language and Meaning*. London: Edward Arnold.

Halliday, M. A. K. 1988. On the Language of Physical Science. In *Registers of Written English: Situational Factors and Linguistic Features*. Ed. Mohsen Ghadessy. London: Pinter. Pp. 162–178.

Halliday, M. A. K. 1989. Part A. In Halliday & Hasan 1989: 3–49.

Halliday, M. A. K. 2002a [1961]. Categories of the Theory of Grammar. In *On Grammar*. Collected Works of M. A. K. Halliday 1. Ed. Jonathan J. Webster. London: Continuum. Pp. 37–94.

Halliday, M. A. K. 2002b [1992]. How Do You Mean? In *On Grammar*. Collected Works of M. A. K. Halliday 1. Ed. Jonathan J. Webster. London: Continuum. Pp. 352–9368.

Halliday, M. A. K. 2003a [1990]. New Ways of Meaning: The Challenge to Applied Linguistics. In *On Language and Linguistics*. Collected Works of M. A. K. Halliday 3. Ed. Jonathan J. Webster. London: Continuum. Pp. 139–174.

Halliday, M. A. K. 2003b [1992]. The Act of Meaning. In *On Language and Linguistics*. Collected Works of M. A. K. Halliday 3. Ed. Jonathan J. Webster. London: Continuum. Pp. 375–389.

Halliday, M. A. K. 2003c. On the "Architecture" of Human Language. In *On Language and Linguistics*. Collected Works of M. A. K. Halliday 3. Ed. Jonathan J. Webster. London: Continuum. Pp. 1–29.

Halliday, M. A. K. 2003d [1992]. The History of a Sentence. In M. A. K. Halliday, *On Language and Linguistics*. Collected Works of M. A. K. Halliday 3. Ed. Jonathan J. Webster. London: Continuum. Pp. 355–374.

Halliday, M. A. K. 2009. Methods – Techniques – Problems. In *Continuum Companion to Systemic Functional Linguistics*. Ed. M. A. K. Halliday & Jonathan Webster. London: Continuum. Pp. 59–86.

Halliday, M. A. K., 2010. Pinpointing the Choice. In *Appliable Linguistics*. Ed. Ahmar Mahboob & Naomi Knight. London: Continuum. Pp. 13–24.

Halliday, M. A. K., & William S. Greaves 2008. *Intonation in the Grammar of English*. London: Equinox.

Halliday, M. A. K., & Ruqaiya Hasan 1989. *Language, Context, and Text: Aspects of Language in a Social-Semiotic Perspective*. Oxford: Oxford University Press. (Identical edition: Deakin University Press, Victoria, Australia 1985.)

Halliday, M. A. K., & J. R. Martin 1993. *Writing Science: Literary and Discursive Power*. London: Falmer.

Halliday, M. A. K., & Christian M. I. M. Matthiessen 2014. *An Introduction to Functional Grammar*. 4th edn. (1st edn by Halliday, 1985). London: Edward Arnold.

Hasan, Ruqaiya 1973. Code, Register and Social Dialect. In *Class, Codes and Control II: Applied Studies towards a Sociology of Language*. Ed. B. Bernstein. London: Routledge & Kegan Paul. Pp. 253–292.

Hasan, Ruqaiya 1989. Part B. In Halliday & Hasan 1989: 52–118.

Hasan, Ruqaiya 1995. The Conception of Context in Text. In *Discourse in Society: Systemic Functional Perspectives: Meaning and Choice in Language: Studies for Michael Halliday*. Ed. P. H. Fries & M. J. Gregory. Advances in Discourse Processes 1. Norwood, NJ: Ablex. Pp. 183–283.

Hasan, Ruqaiya 1996 [1984]. The Nursery Tale as a Genre. In *Ways of Saying: Ways of Meaning: Selected Papers of Ruqaiya Hasan*. Ed. Carmel Cloran, David Butt & Geoffrey Williams. London: Casell. Pp. 51–72. [First published *Linguistic Circular* 1984(13): 71–102.]

Hasan, Ruqaiya. 1999. Speaking in Reference to Context. In *Text and Context in Functional Linguistics*. Ed. Mohan Ghadessy. Amsterdam: Benjamins. Pp. 219–328.

Hasan, Ruqaiya 2000. The Uses of Talk. In *Discourse and Social Life*. Ed. Srikant Sarangi & Malcolm Coulthard. Harlow, England: Pearson. Pp. 28–47.

Hasan, Ruqaiya 2009. The Place of Context in a Systemic Functional Model. In *Continuum Companion to Systemic Functional Linguistics*. Ed. M. A. K. Halliday & J. Webster. London: Continuum. Pp. 166–189.

Kress, Gunther, & Theo van Leeuwen 2006. *Reading Images: The Grammar of Visual Design*. 2nd edn. London: Routledge.

Labov, William 1972. *Language in the Inner City: Studies in the Black English Vernacular*. Oxford: Basil Blackwell.

Lauranto, Yrjö 2015. *Direktiivisyyden rajoja: Suomen kielen vaihtokauppasyntaksia* ['Defining Directivity: Interactional Syntax in Finnish']. Doctoral dissertation, Department of Finnish, Finno-Ugrian and Scandinavian Studies, University of Helsinki. Available at: https://ethesis.helsinki.fi/.

Lemke, J. L. 1999. Typological and Topological Meaning in Diagnostic Discourse. *Discourse Processes* 27(2): 173–185.

Luukka, Minna-Riitta 1995. *Puhuttua ja kirjoitettua tiedettä: Funktionaalinen ja yhteisöllinen näkökulma tieteen kielen interpersonaalisiin piirteisiin* ['Spoken and Written Science: A Functional and Discourse Community Perspective of the Interpersonal Features of the Language of Science']. Jyväskylä Studies in Communication 4. Jyväskylä: University of Jyväskylä.

Malinowski, Bronislaw 1946 [1923]. The Problem of Meaning in Primitive Languages. In *The Meaning of Meaning: A Study of the Influence of Language upon Thought and of Science of Symbolism: With Supplementary Essays by B. Malinowski & F. G. Crookshank*. 8th edn. London: Kegan Paul, Trench, Trubner & Co. Pp. 296–336.

Mäntynen, Anne, & Susanna Shore 2014. What Is Meant by Hybridity? – An Investigation of Hybridity and Related Terms in Genre Studies. *Text & Talk* 34 (6): 737–758.

Martin, J. R. 1984. Language, Register and Genre. In *Children Writing*. Ed. F. Christie. Geelong: Deakin University Press. Pp. 21–29.

Martin, J. R. 1985. Process and Text: Two Aspects of Human Semiosis. In *Systemic Perspectives on Discourse I: Selected Theoretical Papers from the 9th International Systemic Workshop*. Ed. J. D. Benson & W. Greaves. Norwood, NJ: Ablex. Pp. 248–274.

Martin, J. R. 1992. *English Text: System and Structure*. Amsterdam: Benjamins.

Martin, J. R. 2009. Genre and Language Learning: A Social Semiotic Perspective. *Linguistics and Education* 20: 10–21.

Martin, J. R., & Christian Matthiessen 1991. Systemic Typology and Topology. In *Literacy in Social Processes*. Darwin: Centre for Studies in Language in Education, Northern Territory University. Pp. 345–383.

Martin, J. R. & David Rose 2007. *Working with Discourse: Meaning beyond the Clause*. 2nd edn. London: Continuum.

Martin, J. R. & David Rose 2008. *Genre Relations: Mapping Culture*. London: Equinox.

Martin, J. & White, P. 2005. *The Language of Evaluation: Appraisal in English*. London: Palgrave Macmillan.

Matthiessen, Christian M. I. M. 2007. The "Architecture" of Language According to Systemic Functional Theory: Developments since the 1970s. In *Continuing Discourse on Language*. Ed. R. Hasan, C. Matthiessen & J. Webster. London: Equinox. Vol. 2. Pp. 505–561.

Matthiessen, Christian M. I. M. 2009. Ideas and New Directions. In *Continuum Companion to Systemic Functional Linguistics*. Ed. M. A. K. Halliday & J. Webster. London: Continuum. Pp. 12–58.

O'Halloran, Kay (ed.) 2004. *Multimodal Discourse Analysis: Systemic functional Perspectives*. London: Continuum.

Painter, Claire, James Martin & Len Unsworth 2013. *Reading Visual Narratives: Image Analysis of Children's Picture Books*. London: Equinox.

Reid, T. B. W. 1956. Linguistics, Structuralism and Philology. *Archivum Linguisticum* 8: 28–37.

Rose, David, & James Martin 2012. *Learning to Write, Reading to Learn: Genre, Knowledge and Pedagogy in the Sydney School*. Sheffield: Equinox.

Sacks, Harvey, Emanuel Schegloff & Gail Jefferson 1974. A Simplest Systematics for the Organisation of Turn-Taking for Conversation. *Language* 50(4): 696–735.

Saussure, Ferdinand de 1983 [1916]. *Course in General Linguistics*. Trans. Roy Harris. London: Duckworth.

Shore, Susanna 1996. Process Types in Finnish: Implicate Order, Covert Categories, and Prototypes. In *Functional Descriptions: Language Form and Linguistic Theory*. Ed. R. Hasan, D. Butt & C. Cloran. Amsterdam: John Benjamins. Pp. 237–263.

Shore, Susanna 2010. J. R. Firth. In *Handbook of Pragmatics*. Ed. J. Verschueren & J.-O. Östman. Amsterdam: John Benjamins.

Shore, Susanna 2012a. Kieli, kielenkäyttö ja kielenkäytön lajit systeemis-funktionaalisessa teoriassa ['Language, Discourse and Genre in Systemic Functional Theory']. In *Genreanalyysi: Tekstilajitutkimuksen käsikirja*. Ed. V. Heikkinen, E. Voutilainen, P. Lauerma, U. Tiililä & M. Lounela. Helsinki: Gaudeamus. Pp. 131–157.

Shore, Susanna 2012b. Systeemis-funktionaalinen teoria tekstien tutkimisessa ['Systemic Functional Theory in Text Analysis']. In *Genreanalyysi: Tekstilajitutkimuksen käsikirja*. Ed. V. Heikkinen, E. Voutilainen, P. Lauerma, U. Tiililä & M. Lounela. Helsinki: Gaudeamus. Pp. 159–185.

Shore, Susanna 2014. Reading to Learn -genrepedagogiikan kielitieteellinen perusta ['The Linguistic Foundation of Reading to Learn Genre Pedagogy']. In *Tekstilajitaidot: Lukemisen ja kirjoittamisen opetus koulussa*. Ed. S. Shore & K. Rapatti. Äidinkielen opettajain liiton vuosikirja 2014. Helsinki: Äidinkielen opettajain liitto. Pp. 37–64.

Shore, Susanna, & Katriina Rapatti 2014. Johdanto ['Introduction']. In *Tekstilajitaidot: Lukemisen ja kirjoittamisen opetus koulussa*. Ed. S. Shore & K. Rapatti. Äidinkielen opettajain liiton vuosikirja 2014. Helsinki: Äidinkielen opettajain liitto. Pp. 5–20.

Unsworth, Len (ed.) 2008. *New Literacies and the English Curriculum: Multimodal Perspectives*. London: Continuum.

Ventola, Eija 1987. *The Structure of Interaction: A Systemic Approach to the Semiotics of Service Encounters*. London: Frances Pinter

Ventola, Eija 2006. Genre systeemis-funtionaalisessa kielitieteessä ['Genre in Systemic Functional Linguistics']. In *Genre - tekstilaji*. Ed. A. Mäntynen, S. Shore & A. Solin. Helsinki: Suomalaisen Kirjallisuuden Seura. Pp. 96–121.

Ventola, Eija, & A. Jesús Moya Guijarro (eds.) 2009. *The World Told and The World Shown: Multisemiotic Issues*. London: Palgrave Macmillan.

White, Peter R. R. 2000. Media Objectivity and the Rhetoric of News Story Structure. In *Discourse and Community: Doing Functional Linguistics*. Ed. Eija Ventola. Tübingen: Gunter Narr Verlag. Pp. 379–397.

Wittgenstein, Ludwig 1953. *Philosophical Investigations*. Ed. G. E. M. Anscombe & R. Rhees. Trans. G. E. M. Anscombe. Oxford: Blackwell.

3. Registers of Oral Poetry

Oral poetry has only relatively recently received concentrated address in term of "register". "Oral poetry" is here used to designate conventions of expressions that are aesthetically marked and unambiguously differentiated from conversational speech within a community. Such aesthetically marked discourse is approached as a form of living language that functions and develops like other varieties of language although it is subject to conventional constraints that condition how it functions and develops. As a form of verbal art, oral poetry has often been viewed through the lens of modern literature (e.g. Jakobson 1960), which easily produces a misconception. When "art" is correlated with novelty, as might be expected of poetry today, register may be subordinated to the art of expression rather than the expression being subordinate to a register of verbal art (cf. Hasan 1989: 97; cf. also Coleman 1999: 55–56). However, such novelty becomes unlikely in oral poetry insofar as it may threaten the success and effectiveness of the communication (Abrahams 1969: 194), as will become apparent in the discussion of the development of linguistic registers of oral poetry toward the end of this article. Sharp distinctions between "poetry" and "prose" in modern cultures (and especially in editorial practice) also produce inclinations to separate oral "poetry" as belonging to a wholly different category than "prose" discourses. However, so-called "prose" discourses, from formal narration to casual conversation, are also structured and marked by metrical and phonic poetic features.[1] Such features and their conventions are engaged on broad spectrums of manner and degree rather than as "poetic" in binary opposition to "prose". Oral poetry as discussed here is merely at the end of one or both of these spectrums. As John Miles Foley puts it: *"oral poetry works like language, only more so"* (2002: xiii, original emphasis). In practical terms, the formal conventions and constraints of an oral-poetic tradition can significantly narrow and condition choices in generative expression. As a consequence, certain aspects of variation and semiosis can be more easily recognized and observed as foregrounded by those constraints. Observing these phenomena in registers of oral poetry can then produce new research questions for addressing other varieties of linguistic behaviours where the same phenomena may be taken for granted.

The adoption of register as a tool for addressing oral poetries has exhibited a range of variation in how this term and concept is applied. The present article looks at the background of the diversity of what such uses include and exclude, ranging from lexicon, syntax and phonology to images, motifs and other elements mediated through language at higher orders of signification, and from para-linguistic features to the metasemiotic entity of a register as a model of and for a performative behaviour that indexes users and patterns of situational usage. This diversity uses of register links to discussions of genre. Following a discussion of linguistic registers of oral poetry, genre will be introduced as an essential frame of reference for elaborating variations in uses of register that are more broadly inclusive in various ways and the implications of those variations for research. Attention will also be given to relationships and interfaces between elements at different orders of signification, including abstract systems of images and metaphors against which language is produced and interpreted. Although this article is focused on oral poetry, it hopes to bring forward several issues that may be of more general interest. Above all, it sets out to raise awareness of the potential implications of more inclusive or exclusive definitions of register and awareness of aspects of categories of expressive resources that might easily be taken for granted.

"Register" is addressed here first and foremost as a tool developed by scholarship for discussion and analysis. Register is a construct, and as such, definitions of register cannot be correct or incorrect unless another definition is given precedence. To borrow Tzvetan Todorov's (1977: 248) words about "genre", use of the term "register" within any one discourse "must be interpreted at the level of the investigation and not of its object." "Register" is approached here as a flexible tool that centrally designates socially recognizable resources for expression associated with particular situations or strategies. The inclusion or exclusion of elements designated by this tool is then calibrated (whether by the individual researcher or following a "school" of research) for the address of particular research materials to answer specific research questions as perceived through the lens of a methodology (inclusive of theoretical frameworks). According to this model, a definition of "register" will not be "right" or "wrong"; instead, it will be more or less effective for a particular investigation.

The Penetration of Register into Academic Discourse Surrounding Oral Poetry

The term "register" was quite slow to filter into the discourse surrounding oral poetry and it arrived from different directions. When this term began to be formalized in the vocabulary of linguistics in the second half of the 20th century (cf. Shore, this volume), folklorists and philologists had vocabularies that were already established. They were accustomed to working with genres, and concern for variation between registers rarely extended beyond distinguishing "poetic" from "non-poetic" or "prose" diction. As a research object, folklore was addressed in terms of an abstract and ideal inherited resource or system of resources (cf. Krohn 1926). This was symptomatic of the era (cf. Irvine 1989), paralleling Saussure's (1967 [1916]) *langue*, or "language" as an abstract system, and also Bakhtinian "speech genres" (Vološinov 1930 [1929]), which were no less idealized even if they are reinterpreted through modern understandings today. Especially in the 1970s and 1980s (even if the roots go deeper), folklore research underwent a transformative shift in paradigm (see e.g. Honko 2000: 7–15). This turned attention from abstracted resources to how these were used and varied in contexts of living practice. This was the folklore equivalent of shifting research from Saussure's *langue* to his *parole*, or "speech" as language in practice (registers). Saussure himself proposed that *langue* and *parole* were so different that a single scientific discipline could only develop around one or the other of them (Suassure 1967 [1916]: 36–39). At the time, this turn from the *langue* to the *parole* of folklore was, however, not perceived as a turn to a different object of research. Instead, it was seen as a struggle over what was reasonable, methodologically viable, and scientifically relevant to study, and in what ways; as a consequence, this turn was nothing less than a revolutionary movement that redefined the discipline in terms of the *parole* over the *langue* of folklore (see Frog 2013b: 19–23).

Part of this battle over the study of folklore involved a debate over "genres", seen variously as ideal (etic) text-type categories advanced by scholarship or as emic categories emergent in local social practices (see e.g. Ben Amos 1976; Honko 1989; Bauman 1992; 1999; Shuman & Hasan-Rokem 2012; Koski et al. 2016). The emerging concerns remained rooted in the history of the discipline: text-type categories ("genres") remained the focus, but attention turned to situational variation in text-type products and (gradually) to meaning-generation in the use of folklore resources in the situational production and reproduction of text – i.e. how they mean things in particular contexts and situations. In sociolinguistics, the study of registers was similarly a turn from language as a monolithic Saussurian *langue* in order to attend to varieties of language as resource-types. This turn gave attention to the relationship of the situation to the choice of resource-type in producing texts, and attention to variation between resource-types. An important point of difference is that research on folklore materials had been built on the study of resource-types ("genres") already distinguishable from a monolithic *langue*. Whereas "register" emerged as a tool in sociolinguistics to discus typological variation of language in relation to contextual and situational factors, research on folklore was concerned with outcomes producing a particular type ("genre") of text. The correlation of certain situations with distinguishable varieties of linguistic behaviour was already long established. Moreover, these types were often formally marked and/or sufficiently conservative to a degree that they could also be elicited outside of conventional contexts. "Genres" tended to be distinguished from one another centrally in terms of formal features (e.g. lyric poetry) and/or the social significance of what the genre was used to represent or communicate (e.g. myth, belief legend). These linguistic behaviours could be realized across situations and thus situations were not seen as primary determinants in the selection of the resource-type. Although the developments in the different fields can be seen as reflexes of a cross-disciplinary shift in attention from the monolithic and abstract *langue* of resources to their *parole* of practice, the research history of disciplines and materials studied led this shift to be realized in different ways. Research on folklore materials became concerned with variation of the type ("genre") in relation to different situational determinants rather than variation *between* types ("registers") according to context or situation. This difference in research interest was perhaps the most significant factor in inhibiting the assimilation of the term "register" into folklore studies: it was a tool for addressing different questions.

The conditions that made research on oral poetry less receptive to the term "register" made it more receptive to the competing model of Bakhtinian "speech genre", which describes a type of language use like a register, although more vaguely and intuitively defined (Vološinov 1930 [1929]; Bakhtin 1986 [1952–1953]). However, rather than being concerned with contextual factors producing conventional variation in language, "speech genre" was centrally a tool to attended to the impact of conventionalization for the meaningfulness of expressions and types of expression (cf. Briggs & Bauman 1992; Bauman 1999; Seitel 2012). The term "speech genre" also connected to the familiar term "genre", facilitating its participation in redefining the latter concept in folklore studies and other disciplines. The turn toward meaning-production in uses of folklore further enhanced the appeal of this model because it also interfaced with Bakhtinian dialogism or Julia Kristeva's "intertextuality" (Kristeva 1980 [1969]; Bakhtin 1981; cf. e.g. Zumthor 1990 [1983]; Tarkka 1993: 89–90). As "register" became increasingly established in linguistics, the term also began to crop up in discussions of oral poetry, but it was neither a prominent tool nor framed the object of research (cf. e.g. Foley 1991: 193; Vleck & Eileen 1991: 23, 199–200; Doane 1994: 421; Reynolds 1995: 7); "genre" remained the fundamental term in the vocabulary.

John Miles Foley (1992; 1995) made "register" interesting and relevant to research on oral poetry by formalizing the term in conjunction with his theory of *word-power*. This theory provided a framework in which register designated the signifying elements characteristic of a particular tradition and their associated conventions of use. However, it was oriented to approaching the meanings of those elements and of a register as such. This use was consistent with interests in research on oral poetries in a way that consideration of an oral-poetic register in relation to other registers had not been. For oral poetry research, Foley's framework was innovative and offered a platform for approaching a number of phenomena that were already recognized or intuitively felt. Word-power was primarily concerned with the indexicality of traditional elements – i.e. the process by which regular patterns of use enabled them to develop associations, implications, valuations and conventional interpretations (cf. Peirce 1940: 98–119; Sebeok 1994: 31–33). This was in part a response to Kristeva's intertextuality and to the multivocality of Bakhtinian speech genres. Whereas the latter approaches both situate meaningfulness of expression as distributed through a network of relationships between texts or utterances independent of users (cf. Foley 1992: 275–276), indexicality recentralizes meaningfulness in the signifying elements as these are internalized by users who then use and interpret them according to subjective understandings. As with Kristeva's intertextuality and Bakhtinian speech genres, Foley extends indexicality to qualities of signification including rhetorical force and emotional investment, paralleling what Robert Jay Lifton (1961: 429–430) describes as "loading the language". "Word-power" was made a term for designating the package or load itself (N.B. "intertextuality" and "speech genre" refer to the relational indexicality of elements as a phenomenon rather than to their significance *per se*). Importantly, Foley's approach highlighted that indexical and also propositional significance and functioning of words or other elements was register-dependent. In other words, the register itself had to become recognizable as a context for expression and then those familiar with a register could access the packages of word-power associated with it. Foley therefore described performance as an "enabling event" and tradition as an "enabling referent" (Foley 1992: 278).

Although it was possible to adopt word-power without the term "register" (e.g. Niles 1999), Foley's model illustrated the potential for approaching oral poetry through register. Controversy and debate surrounding "genre" as a primary category for approaching oral traditions had burdened the research discourses surrounding oral poetry. Register circumvented that debate as a term designating the resources employed in text production whereas genre remained focused on categories of products. Thus a register could potentially be associated with multiple genres and also be used meaningfully and strategically independent of generic contexts. Of course, the impact of this approach was not immediate but gradual, and there were also independent, parallel adaptations, for example in philology (e.g. Coleman 1999). Nevertheless, Foley's formalized adaptation has had increasing impact especially across the past decade.[2] It has emerged as the nexus of this discourse, referred to in reviews of scholarship even where register is not a prominent tool (e.g. Thorvaldsen 2006), and Foley's work not infrequently seems to be somewhere in the background where register is elevated as a central term and tool that can be taken for granted without formalized introduction (e.g. Kitts 2005; Missuno 2012). Register has penetrated the discourse surrounding oral poetry and increasingly appears where previously expressions like "poetic diction", "language of poetry", etc. would have been used. Foley played a key role in this development much as Milman Parry and Albert Lord played for the term "formula" (on which see e.g. Foley 1988). This does not mean that Foley was the only scholar involved in this process or that his model of register was embraced without adaptation. Nevertheless, the central position of Foley's model has had consequences for the way that register has been used and further developed.

Foley adapted register as a tool at a time when there was no established model for its application to poetry. This was done in his synthesis of Oral-Formulaic Theory (esp. Lord 1960) with Richard Bauman's (e.g. 1984) theoretical approach to performance (Foley 1995). He took the linguistic term from Dell Hymes' (1989: 440) definition of registers as "major speech styles associated with recurrent types of situations." Although Foley (1995: 50) acknowledges Halliday's *mode*, *field* and *tenor* of discourse as contextual variables influencing register (on which see further Shore, this volume), he never applied and developed these. Hymes' definition allowed great flexibility as an inclusive term, and Foley treated register as inclusive of the full range of features explicated through Hymes' ethnopoetics. This included Hymes' *verse*, *stanza*, *scene* and *act* as structural units in realizing narration (Foley 1995: 2–27, 51; cf. Hymes 1981: 164–175). However, Foley used the elements or *integers* of tradition developed in Oral-Formulaic Theory research. Although these could be seen as equivalent at the levels of poetic formula and metrical lines, Oral-Formulaic Theory's *theme* and *story-pattern* described units narrated rather than formal units in which narrative was structured as verbalized text (cf. Lord 1960: 68–123; Foley 1988; 1999: 83–88). Register was thus treated as broadly inclusive of all elements or integers of a tradition with a capacity to signify and conventions for their combination. These integers were characterized by their ability to function as signs in the representation of *different* songs, stories or other identity-bearing texts (a point returned to below). It was also inclusive of metrics, stylistic devices and rhetorical structures, as well as embracing the multimodality of performance practice (cf. Kallio, this volume). The breadth of inclusion is in part connected to the units customarily analysed in (especially narrative) oral poetry traditions as opposed to in registers of aesthetically unmarked discourse. This breadth has not been consistent in adaptations of Foley's model and in fact is even easily overlooked by scholars who begin by approaching register narrowly in terms of language. All scholars who employ register as a tool in addressing oral poetry consider the language of *verbalization* (to adapt the term of Hasan 1989) to be a constituent of register. The verbal aspect of performative practices also remains at the center for almost all scholars handling register as a tool, however flexibly defined (Koski 2011: 322–324; but cf. Koski 2015).

Register at the Level of Verbalization

Verbal art will inevitably be associated with conventional users, uses, manners and situations of use, and also with co-occurrent non-verbal symbols and behaviours (cf. Kallio, this volume; Stepanova, this volume). These may evolve multiple conventional constellations where the oral poetry tradition is multifunctional, each of which may be more or less flexible. The users, uses, situations, co-occurrent behaviours and so forth nevertheless remain socially constructed rather than freely variable. Different traditions of oral poetry may vary widely in the flexibility with which they are used, from formalizing a situationally specific communication or address (cf. Stepanova, this volume; Wilce & Fenigsen, this volume) or ritualized dialogues between parties (cf. Bloch 1989; Sherzer 1999) to representing conventional content such as an epic narrative (cf. Foley 1999; Harvilahti, this volume) or even producing and maintaining poems as textual entities which circulate socially in rather fixed form (cf. Johnson 2002; Clunies Ross et al. 2012; Frog 2014b). The linguistic register of poetry might be relatively close to conversational speech or, at the opposite extreme, potentially incomprehensible for someone unfamiliar with the idiom (cf. Lamb, this volume; Stepanova, this volume). Poetic syntax (as well as morphology and even grammar) may vary markedly from that of other poetries or even appear completely free (cf. below) while meters and rhythmic-melodic phrases produce formal constraints on the length of linguistic phrases and clauses (cf. Harvilahti, this volume; but see also Stepanova, this volume). An oral-poetic register may also be cross-linguistic, as was the register of (several genres of) kalevalaic poetry used across Finnish and Karelian language areas (cf. Saarinen 2013: 37), and to a lesser degree with Ižorian language areas, where the registral lexicon exhibited greater variation yet also preserved morphology that dropped out of aesthetically unmarked discourse (Nikolaev 2011).

The interface of verbal art with cultural practices makes many uses predictable as culturally necessitated outcomes of particular circumstances (e.g. ritualized greetings) or as outcomes of incited activities (e.g. epic narration, accompaniment to dance). In some cases, oral poetry may provide one of multiple possible registral resources or means for accomplishing the same basic communication. As an illustrative example, we can begin with an extreme of compositional complexity, the so-called skaldic poetry in the *dróttkvætt* meter, which characterized the prestigious court poetry of the Scandinavian Viking Age. Skaldic poets were the oral publicists and propagandists of political authorities (cf. Frank 1978; Abram 2011). Once composed, a verse or longer poem could enter into social circulation with a remarkable degree of fixity in transmission – as a stable "text" – and this text could then circulate as a core of a package of associated information about, for example, the author, patron, circumstances of composition or performance, the events which the text describes or to which it refers, and so forth (cf. Kuhn 1983; Gade 1995). From a modern perspective, this may sound more like "literary poetry" than "oral poetry". Nevertheless, the composition is unambiguously rooted in highly conventionalized patterns of language use, and one reason for beginning with this example is precisely to break down those perspectives by drawing attention to some of the traditoinalized features of this register. For example, a skaldic poet, following a battle, could say to his patron the Old Norse equivalent of, *A truly mighty battle was conducted this day*, or *That was an impressive job, my lord*, or just *Wow, man, you really kicked some butt!* Of course if he did so, the poet then might not have a patron for very much longer. He could also formulate his sentiment in *dróttkvætt* verse (metrical alliteration in bold italic and metrical rhyme underlined), saying something like:

(1) Há*ð*i *g*ramr, þar's *g*nú*ð*u,
   *g*eira hr*e*gg við s*e*ggi,
   – rau*ð* fnýstu *b*en *b*ló*ð*i –
   *b*eng*o*gl at dyn Sk*o*glar.
        (Faulkes 1998: 66, v.219 / Þhorn *Gldr* 5.)

Wage-PAST.SG prince-SG.NOM, there, where roar-PAST.PL
spear-PL.GEN storm-SG.ACC against man-PL.DAT
– red-PL.NOM spew-PAST.PL wound-PL.NOM blood-SG.DAT –
wound-gosling-PL.NOM in din-SG.DAT Skǫgul-SG.GEN

> A prince waged storm of spears (BATTLE) against men where roared – red wounds spewed blood – wound-goslings (ARROWS) in Skǫgul's din (BATTLE).

Dróttkvætt is exceptionally demanding among the traditional poetries of Europe and thus, metrically, this half-stanza is dazzlingly complex. In each six-syllable line, the penultimate syllable should rhyme with a preceding syllable, alternating between whether the rhyme should exclude the vowel (odd lines) or include the vowel (even lines), while two syllables in odd lines should alliterate with the onset of the following even line, forming a couplet (not to mention rules governing syllabic quantity). This presents 14 phonic requirements (six of which have fixed positions) for 24 syllables. Of the 24 syllables of this half-stanza, only 14 positions *can* carry alliteration and/or rhyme because 10 are filled by an inflectional ending, preposition or pronoun. Meters such as *dróttkvætt* may be abstracted in analysis, but it is necessary to keep in mind that, in an oral arena, these exist only through their realizations as rhythms and phonic patterning in language. Similarly, the syntax appears scrambled, distributed across the four-line half-stanza, with a separate clause embedded in line 3. Like meter, however, syntax was necessarily internalized in conjunction with the poetry tradition as patterned language use. Whereas some poetries may have conventions governing enjambment (i.e. extending a phrase beyond a line; cf. Foley 1999: 70–72), syntax in *dróttkvætt* was constrained to the four-line half-stanza. To us, the word order might look free and even crazy from the perspective of aesthetically unmarked discourse, but it was nevertheless governed by syntax conventional to the register (Kuhn 1983; Gade 1995). Similarly, the language is rich with metaphors and poetic vocabulary such as *bengǫgl* ['wound-goslings'] for ARROWS, which would be semantically impenetrable without knowledge of the register. However, these expressions are "based on traditional paraphrasing patterns, and [are] not primarily the product of individual poetic inspiration" (Clunies Ross et al. 2012: lxxiii) – i.e. they are the naturalized way of speaking for the register. As John Miles Foley (1999: 74–75) has stressed, a register of oral poetry is merely one among many, each of which is accompanied by a frame of reference for norms of language practice; unmarked conversational discourse looks no less strange and artificial from the perspective of an oral-poetic register than the reverse. In this case, the dazzle-factor of the meter and dance of the lexicon makes it easy to overlook the conventional patterns of language use and the fact that the thematic content is so highly stereotypical (RULER WAGES WAR) that it renders almost no information (cf. Clunies Ross 2005: 74). As the publicists of kings, skaldic poets leaned heavily on the fact that their verses would be carried with packages of information through which they could be interpreted: "Although he is a professional user of language, he has in fact little he needs to say" (Fidjestøl 1997: 41).

Language is internalized as an integrated aspect of oral poetry through which meter and poetics are maintained and communicated. Formal structuring features such as meter and parallelism are thus in a symbiotic relationship with language (Foley 1990; Fox 2014: 374–383). The scrambled syntax of *dróttkvætt* verse accommodates the demands of the meter as does the rich poetic vocabulary of this tradition, which is remarkable for its generative system of the circumlocutions called *kennings*. A kenning is formed of a noun (or noun phrase NP_1) complemented by a second noun (or noun phrase NP_2) in the genitive or forming a compound to refer to a third nominal (NP_2-GEN NP_1 or NP_2-NP_1 = NP_3). The generative aspect was enabled by "paradigmatic substitution" (Clunies Ross et al. 2012: lxxi) within an extensive vocabulary of terms called *heiti* functioning as poetic equivalents. Thus, Rudolf Meissner (1921), in his classic survey, lists 39 poetic equivalents for 'fire' and 64 equivalents for water in *attested* examples of the kenning FIRE OF WATER = GOLD: these alone offer 39 × 64 = 2496 potential combinations to realize this single semantic unit (Fidjestøl 1997: 31). Although individual terms had the potential to be selected with intentions of producing subtle meanings, associations or semantic patterns within a text, they also more generally functioned as allomorphs in pragmatic variation for realizing the semantic formula (e.g. FIRE OF WATER) within the metrical and phonic environment of composition (Frog 2014b; 2015a). The potential for variation is dramatically increased when paradigmatic substitution in functional equivalence realizing the kenning may extend across multiple categories of semantic equivalence of *heiti*. Thus kennings for BATTLE could be produced from a base noun meaning SOUND (cf. *dynr* ['din'], line 4), WEATHER (cf. *hregg* ['storm and rain'], line 3), MEETING, etc., complemented by any *heiti* for WEAPON (cf. *geirr* ['spear']), ARMOUR, or AGENT OF BATTLE (cf. the valkyrie-name *Skǫgul*). Thus *geira hregg* ['storm of spears'] and *Skǫglar dynr* ['din of a valkyrie'] are produced by the same linguistic equation. In addition, other *heiti*, such as *gramr* ['prince'] (line 1) could be used independent of a kenning. The systems of images and metaphors also extended to use of other parts of speech, such as the use of the verb *gnýja* (*gnúðu*) ['roar']. Within the half-stanza above, the embedded clause in line 3 is lexically close to aesthetically unmarked discourse, while all rhyme and alliteration in other lines is carried by poetic terms with the exception of the opening verb *heyja* ['to hold, perform, wage']. When it is first met, the verbal virtuosity enabled by this idiom is as dazzling as the complexity of the meter itself. This was indeed a specialized register, but it is necessary to remember that competence in the register involved the internalization of these verbal systems, naturalizing them to normal functions of variation within that register.

Although the surface texture of verbalization exhibits remarkable variation so that no two stanzas are exactly identical, the patterns of language use are bound up quite intimately with the meter: language and meter appear interfaced in the internalization of the register. A pilot study of 340 battle-kennings in their metrical contexts revealed that the distribution of kenning elements was highly conventionalized. More than 70% of the examples were realizations of or variations on only 10 metric-structural "basic types" (defined according to metrical positions; see Frog 2015a). In the example above, the three kennings are all conventional metric-structural types:

(2a) *geira hregg*: line-onset two-syllable NP$_2$-GEN monosyllable NP$_1$

(b) *bengǫgl*: line-onset two-syllable NP$_2$-NP$_1$

(c) *dynr Skǫglar*: line-end monosyllable NP$_1$-ø two-syllable NP$_2$-GEN

The degree of metrical conditioning and what I have described as *metrical entanglement* (Frog 2015a) of language use can be highlighted by drawing attention to three features associated with example (2c). First, the valkyrie-name *Skǫglar* ['Skǫgul-GEN'] was the only term in the registral lexicon capable of both forming a battle-kenning and rhyming in -*ǫgl*-. Its use in realizing the formulaic expression here, rather than a more common NP$_2$-GEN familiar to this type such as *geira* ['spear-PL.GEN'] or *hjalma* ['helmet-PL.GEN'], is unambiguously associated with the phonic environment (Frog 2014b: 129). Second, the noun *dynr* ['din'] was a normal word outside of poetry, but in *dróttkvætt* composition, its use was surprisingly conventionalized. When *dynr* was not used in compounds in this meter, it was only used to form battle-kennings and was particularly linked to this metrical position rather than being used freely even in generative use of battle-kennings in other positions where it would be metrically appropriate (Frog 2009: 233–236). Third, this formulaic construction could occur in either odd or even lines. Although the base-word in the formula (e.g. *dynr*) never participated in rhyme, use in odd lines placed alliteration on (only) the two elements of the kenning (attested alliterations in /b/, /d/, /f/, /g/, /r/, /sv/ and /th/; Frog 2014b). Formula use thus included a convention of how phonic requirements of the meter were realized. This example highlights that meter was not simply learned through its realization in language but that the register was internalized with its interfaces with the meter and conventions of how language realized the appropriate poetics.

Language as used in a tradition of oral poetry is socially and historically constructed in relation to formal aspects of the poetic system, such as meter (Foley 1990: 52–239) and stylistic devices like parallelism (Fox 2014: 374–379). Of course, conventions of a poetic system vary from tradition to tradition. Nevertheless, "the ongoing symbiosis between prosody and phraseology" (Foley 1999: 78) inevitably involves realizing language in phonic, syllabic and semantic environments that motivate contextual variation in lexical choices. This produces a functional need for vocabulary capable of realizing semantically appropriate expressions in relation to, for example, the alliteration, rhyme and syllabic constraints in example (1), or the verbal variation motivated by parallelism in kalevalaic poetry in example (3) below, and also in Karelian laments (Stepanova, this volume; see further Roper 2012; Fox 2014). The lexicon evolves accordingly, potentially maintaining a rich diversity of dialectal vocabulary, loan-words and archaisms (including parallel morphological forms) as well as a formulaic lexicon (Foley, this volume; Coleman 1999; cf. Stepanova, this volume). Poetries with formalized meters constrain how expressions are realized by limiting possibilities for variation. This frequently evolves a rich lexicon of formulaic sequences as crystallized resources for expressing a certain idea while realizing metrically well-formed lines, as has been extensively explored in Oral-Formulaic Theory research (see e.g. Parry 1928a; 1928b; Lord 1960; Foley 1988; Foley & Ramey 2012). The system of kennings, *heiti* and metaphorical language of skaldic poetry above characterizes only one form of oral-poetic register – an extreme case related to how that poetry was used in composition and transmission. Kalevalaic epic was, in contrast, at an opposite extreme, with a predilection for the crystallization of full-line formulaic units and tight systems of such units.[3] Each such formula or prefab can be regarded as obtaining a dedicated entry in the mental lexicon of competent users (Wray 2002; cf. traditional "words" as integers of tradition in Foley, this volume). As such, each develops a specific package of word-power according to its regular patterns of use in the register. The lexicon of an oral-poetic register could potentially be vast. However, the role of conventions of use cannot be underestimated here. Metrical constraints facilitate conservatism in the production and reproduction of poetry, but individuals choose whether to aspire to conservatism or to capitalize on potential for variation (Harvilahti 1992) within a broader framework of social conventions (Frog 2010b: 99–100; 2011a: 48–50).

The semantics of a lexical item may also undergo levelling where it appears in pragmatic variation for maintaining "the same essential meaning" in relation to the "acoustical context" (Lord 1960: 53; cf. Foley 1999: 291n.14), where it is linked to another term through canonical semantic parallelism (Fox 2014: 51–60), or where use is shaped in relation to other conventions of a poetic system (see also Roper 2012). The language of kennings and *heiti* introduced above presents an extreme case where individual lexical items can act as semantic or functional allomorphs, especially in formulaic constructions. However, the phenomenon is much more general and, in practice, such patterns of generative language use may evolve contrasts with referential practice in other contexts (not to mention with a researcher's intuition). These patterns are internalized with the register, and some narrow patterns in the use of the registral lexicon may only become visible under statistical surveys, as was the case with *dynr* or conventions of alliteration in use of the formula in example (2c) above.

In addition to meter, a registral lexicon develops in relation to a number of other factors. Many of these are practical social realities of what is, or historically was, present or prominent in the cultural arena – e.g. socially central livelihoods, technologies, the ecological environment, as well as social networks and cultural contacts that could enable the assimilation of dialectal and loan-word vocabularies. More significant are conventions of use: a registral lexicon builds up vocabulary and flexibility in relation to what it is used to address or communicate (cf. Roper 2012; Stepanova, this volume). This renders it well-equipped to handle conventional subjects but not necessarily others (cf. Lord 1991: 77). For example, the kenning system introduced above was generative, enabling remarkable verbal variation, yet the corpus of several thousand stanzas preserves kennings for only slightly more than 100 referents.[4] The skald's lexicon was richly developed for the subject domains of war, women, wealth, patronage and poetry (see Meissner 1921) – i.e. the things that skaldic poets talked about – whereas the corresponding system of circumlocutions in Karelian laments was developed around familial relations, associated social roles, and the life-cycle transitions of marriage and death (Stepanova A. 2012; see also Stepanova, this volume) – i.e. the things that lamenters talked about. Neither of these registers would be well equipped for use in the place of the other.

Conventions of practice are frequently characterized by participant relations and evaluative positioning in relation to addressees, audiences, interactants and/or what the poetry is used to represent. Characteristic positioning may be conventional to a broad range of registers, but it can become particularly pronounced in oral-poetic discourse. This is especially apparent in the referential frameworks of poetic circumlocutions and their conventions of use. For example, in the register of Old Norse skaldic poetry, lords are referred to in terms of prowess in and enthusiasm for battle, their distribution of wealth and control of land; battle is positively indexed and the poetic ego is proud and deserving of reward (cf. Meissner 1921). In Karelian laments, the poetic ego is humble and self-effacing, the dead are positive, maidenhood is idyllic while a groom is threatening, and so forth (Stepanova A. 2012; Stepanova E. 2014 and this volume). Such positioning may also be indexed in other aspects of language, as when Karelian lamenters address inhabitants of the otherworld with the interrogative mood where Karelian specialists using the incantation tradition use the imperative mood (Stepanova E. 2012: 276; on honorific features of Karelian lament, see also Wilce & Fenigsen, this volume). Within the register, such positioning is unmarked – it is the norm, and there is nothing striking about it. Similarly, the oral-poetry will become interfaced with ideological frameworks and function in relation to these. For example, the system of skaldic diction constructs and conveys an embedded ideology of warfare and qualities characteristic of kingship. Moreover, kennings like *dynr Skǫglar* ['din of a valkyrie'] and *Viðris veðr* ['weather of (the god) Odin'] are interfaced with conceptual models of supernatural agents. Names of mythic beings were integrated compositional resources of the poetic system (cf. *Skǫgul* – -*ǫgl*- rhyme above; see further Frog 2014b). When Odin was the god of battle, poetry and kingship – subject domains richly developed in the skaldic register – and very frequently referred to in kenning constructions, it comes as no surprise that there are more than 150 attested Odin-names capable of meeting a full spectrum of alliterations and rhymes (Falk 1928; Price 2002: 100–107). Thus a register not only becomes better equipped for expressing certain things over others, but may also conventionally address those things from a characteristic perspective, with conventional positioning and associated evaluative stance, and even be interfaced with a potentially broad ideological framework.

Before leaving the linguistic register of an oral poetry, it is necessary to acknowledge that the preceding observations have suggested homogeneity or uniformity of a register and its range of uses within an oral-poetic system, and for some traditional poetries this may be the case. In other cases, the situation may prove far more complex, leading researchers to calibrate use of the term "register" in different ways in relation to the particular poetic system. For example, the Kalevala-meter was a historically dominant poetic form used for genres ranging from epic and incantation to lyric, wedding songs, proverbs, riddles and more (Kuusi 1994: 41; Frog & Stepanova 2011: 198–199). As mentioned above, the register was highly conservative, especially at the level of line-based formulae and larger verbal systems. These units or integers of the register can frequently be distinguished as associated with a particular genre. This makes it possible to discuss a register of a particular genre within the broader poetic system (cf. also Eila Stepanova's distinction between a *situation-specific lexicon* and a *core lexicon* of a register elsewhere in this volume). On the other hand, these generic registers were interpenetrating and transposable, with certain areas of a register able to be shared by multiple genres and linking together the broader poetic system (cf. Tarkka 2013).[5] It may therefore become meaningful and relevant to discuss the register of the kalevalaic poetic system as a whole. Zooming out to view the broad register of such an extensive and varied system is similar to expanding a view from individual written registers identifiable with academic articles, newspaper columns and magazine editorials to consider a broader register of "written prose".

A corresponding but quite a different issue is posed by Old Norse skaldic poetry and the so-called eddic poetry associated with genres of epic, riddles, charms and traditional knowledge. Here, the poetic system was characterized by a number of meters and different meters could be used within the same genre as well as across a wide range of different poetries, creating a much more complex set of interrelations. As in kalevalaic poetry and its genres, it is possible to talk about a "skaldic register" and more narrowly about "generic registers" (although the distinctions might be quite fluid), or more broadly of an "eddic and skaldic register" encompassing a spectrum genres marked by male-centered heroic ideology. However, the registral lexicon and its formulae are also historically shaped through their symbiotic relation to individual meters and provide resources for realizing those meters whether in skaldic practice or eddic genres. It is thus possible to talk about a register (or subregister) linked specifically to a particular meter such as *dróttkvætt* that may exist within the broader skaldic register or more generally within the still broader skaldic and eddic poetic system. (Frog 2014b: 107–109.) It remains necessary to observe that the broader the field of inclusion to which register is calibrated, the more likely that it will refer first and foremost to the systems of signifiers constitutive of that register. The frameworks of particular genres may affect conventions governing the combination of these resources (e.g. syntax or parallelism). They may also produce shifts in the value or signification of registral integers, whether owing to conventional generic patterns of contextual use (cf. Frog 2013a), or because the generic framework interfaces the linguistic register with systems of images and metaphors that may not be activated in other contexts, as in Old Norse skaldic poetry (discussed further below).

Register and Genre

The distinction between register and genre has in general not been consistently defined (cf. Biber 1995: 9–10). Although discussions of genre were significant in the background of the introduction of register into research on oral poetry, register was nevertheless introduced without defining the relationship between them (cf. Foley 1995). The terms have been related and conflated in different ways in folklore research (cf. Koski 2011: 322–324). On the one hand, the definition of genre has been subject to ongoing negotiation for some decades and is no more consistently employed than register. On the other hand, definitions of genre and register have been inclined to converge as a historical process. Genre definitions have become increasingly oriented to interest in cultural resources of expression and interpretation in the *parole* of folklore. At the same time, register has advanced from being viewed as a variety of language associated with particular situational circumstances to the cultural systems which provide models for expressive behaviours (verbal and otherwise) in contexts of social practice and interaction. The register as an entity can then be seen as reciprocally conferring role-relations on participants and as a cultural model for action (Agha 2007), in which case register and genre may seem to coincide. The purpose here is not to open the debate of how genre should be defined. However, a model for approaching genre will be outlined as a general framework for considering different approaches to register and for looking at what they include or exclude in relation to this particular model of genre. "Genre" will here be approached as an analytical category of a particular type which is modelled according to four aspects (as developed in Frog 2016):

1. *Form*. The form of a genre is characterized by the conventions of a mode or modes of expression, the signifying elements at multiple orders of representation, constructions and rules for the combination of elements as well as conventions of flexibility or conservatism in the production of generic expression.

2. *Content* or *enactment*. The content is what a genre is used to represent or communicate or the corresponding enactment is its effect on social, natural or imaginal realities (cf. Abrahams 1977; Austin's illocutionary act; Agha's performative act). The content or enactment is always genre-specific, and at an abstract level can simply be qualified by conventions of being appropriate rather than inappropriate. The combination of generic form with appropriate content/enactment produces a generic product in the same manner that a Saussurian signifier and its signified together form a sign (cf. Todorov 1977: esp. 248). According to this model, form without appropriate content (e.g. parody) does not qualify as a generic product *per se*, nor does appropriate content without conventional form (e.g. a summary of an epic or folktale).

3. *Practice*. The third aspect is practice, which covers conventions of the *who, where, when, why* and *how* of use (cf. Ben Amos 1976; Briggs & Bauman 1992). Practice can also be broadly qualified as appropriate versus inappropriate, emphasizing that it is always contextually situated, and appropriate practice may extend to co-occurrence with other performative behaviours or their absence (cf. Agha 2007: 58–59). Practice is fundamental to the construction and maintenance of the significance, relevance and indexical associations of the genre and its features (cf. Briggs & Bauman 1992; Agha's "enregisterment", this volume). The form–content/enactment–practice system of relations presents a description of the genre as a social, culture-specific phenomenon in relation to which expressions can be produced and interpreted.

4. *Functions*. Functions describe the social, societal and semiotic roles of a genre – what a genre does in broad social, cultural and semiotic senses and how it accomplishes this – not through individual occurrences, but through the general patterns of use in relation to other genres and within the broader semiotic system. Whereas specific aspects of form, content/enactment and practice are all culture-dependent, genres may be compared cross-culturally at the level of functions.

Two Sides of Register

Looked at against the above model, a convergence of register and genre becomes dependent on using the term register to refer to two different things. On the one hand, register refers to the signifying resources themselves and how these mean and refer, which is what Foley used the term for. These belong to the aspect of form according to the above model, and when used with the breadth of Foley, register correlates with form. On the other hand, register can also be used to refer to the abstract, identity-bearing entity of which the signifying resources are representative constituents. Thus, the appropriately concentrated co-occurrence of registral resources metonymically index the register as a metasemiotic entity – i.e. they allow a register as such to be recognized. This entity may in its turn index characteristics of practice. Foley distinguished this from his use of the term register, proposing the term *performance arena* for the experience-based frame of practice (according to the above model) indexed by a register (Foley 1995: 47–49). The metasemiotic entity may also index enactments, insofar as the relevant register may be associated with so-called speech-acts (on which see Austin 1962; Searle 1969) or performative expressions that affect social realities (Agha 2007: 55–64). Viewed in terms of structural relationships to other registers, the metasemiotic entity is also associable with areas of functions in the above model of genre. When all of these aspects of the metasemiotic entity are taken together, registers can also be approached not only as resources for expression, but also reciprocally as models for how to express – i.e. registers can be regarded as the models for social behaviours appropriate to particular situations. The resources of a register and the register as a metasemiotic entity can be considered clearly distinguishable objects of study. This difference is essentially the same as distinguishing the study of the lexicon and grammar of German from the study of people's inclinations to infer that a fluent speaker of German is "German" or that he is characterized by orderliness. This is not to deny the connection between registers and cultural models of behaviour. It is only intended to highlight that the convergence of register with the aspects of practice and function (and thereby with approaches to genre) occur at the level of this abstract, identity-bearing entity as a metasemiotic social reality.[6]

When register is placed in relation to the model of genre above, certain distinctions are also apparent. Approaches to registers outside of treatments of folklore tend to limit use of the term to the primary order of signification – i.e. linguistic verbalization or para-linguistic performative behaviours more broadly. Thus, for example, the range of conventional images, motifs, narrative sequences, structuring conventions and story-patterns associated with an epic tradition could easily fall outside of a register-based model. However, when the register is approached as broadly as by Foley, the models of register and genre may seem to more fully coincide. The most significant difference is that the register-based model accounts for verbal and non-verbal situated behaviours but does not give consideration to what the register is used to represent or communicate. This is unsurprising insofar as a major focus of research on registers has been situational variation in linguistic behaviours which – at least in principle – suggests that registers present "context-appropriate alternate ways of 'saying the same thing'" (Silverstein 2000: 430). However, *content* must be taken into consideration for certain genres of expression such as epic, through which the social valuation of what is represented confers authority on the register, and rendering even unfamiliar content through the register confers social value on that content with implications of shared social relevance as an "epic". In addition, rendering a narrative as epic simultaneously indexes it as a model and resource against which identities and behaviours are reflected while positioning it in an authoritative, hierarchical relationship to narrative characterized by representation through other genres. (Frog 2010a: 230–231; 2011b; cf. Honko 1998: 20–29; Foley 2004; Martin 2005.) It is therefore unsurprising that conversion processes to Christianity frequently produce renderings of Christian religious narratives in the vernacular oral authoritative form before this is gradually displaced by alternatives that became enregistered through Church authority and associated technologies of writing (Frog 2010a: 235–237). In many genres of folklore, the register may thus primarily index the identity or type of what is being communicated over the users and situations of use (cf. Lamb, this volume). The relationship between register and genre remains dependent on how each is defined, although use of the term register tends to place emphasis on expressive resources in relation to communicative situations while use of the term genre tends to place emphasis on the generation and reception of entextualized expressions. Although there has been a tendency for the use of these terms to converge, it is also worth observing that they may be applied in relation to one another as complementary tools.

Orders of Signification

As observed above, genres of folklore frequently exhibit conventional elements that are represented through language – i.e. signs mediated by linguistic signs. Images, motifs and themes are conventional elements that function as symbols that can be practically described here as a lexicon at the next order of representation or signification from language. Although these can be represented through different linguistic registers, they may also vary in semantics and conventions of use according to genre (cf. Honko 1989: 15). In other words, the lexicon of symbols exhibits contextual variation like a linguistic register and can appear in co-variation with the linguistic register.[7]

It can also be translated into other registers of discourse (e.g. a summary of an epic), repeated in parallelism while the lexical surface of expression varies, and so forth. These symbolic elements form conventional constellations such as a narrative or ritual sequence that also become socially recognizable and can become loaded with packages of significance – i.e. these complex entities can function as signs at a still higher order of signification. Foley defined the signifying integers of a register centrally in relation to the model of Oral-Formulaic Theory's *formulae*, *themes* and *story-patterns*. These can be considered conventional elements residing at three different orders of representation. Transposing the model of Oral-Formulaic Theory was consistent with Foley's central concern for the packages of word-power with which integers of the tradition became loaded through their regular patterns of use. Distinguishing relationships between orders of representation was not an analytical (or methodological) concern. The central adaptation of register to the study of oral poetries presented a precedent for addressing registers in terms of these multiple orders. Subsequent scholars have been inconsistent with regard to whether they include these higher order elements or use register more narrowly with reference only to the primary order of signification, or even only with reference to the linguistic register of a tradition.

Grouping multiple orders of representation together supports viewing their functioning as a systemic whole. However, it may also reduce sensitivity to the relationships between orders of signification and to cases where those relationships are not consistent. This can be illustrated by beginning with an extreme case and placing that in dialogue with more subtle phenomena. These issues become particularly complex when the methodological emphasis on resources used in *different* texts and contexts is acknowledged. Oral-Formulaic Theory research developed a parameter of qualifying elements as *formulae* in relation to statistical methods of identifying them in multiple contexts of use. This is inevitably dependent on the dataset (cf. also Wray 2002: 25–26). In larger corpora, it becomes apparent that expressions conventional only to a single context are social resources that may nevertheless be adapted and applied in exceptional ways (cf. Tarkka 2005: 65). The use of such elements may otherwise be so narrow and regular that they develop a distinct identity corresponding to a proper noun and thus index that conventional use referentially when applied or recognizably adapted in any other context. This is no less true of images, motifs and also of more complex symbols at still higher orders of representation, such as whole narratives and narrative cycles (Frog 2010b: 102–103). For example, the following reflects a highly conventionalized verbal system from kalevalaic epic that describes the outcome of a collision of the sleighs of two mythic heroes on the road:

(3) Puuttui vemmel vempelehe,   Touched shaft-bow to shaft-bow,
    Rahet rahkehe nenähän;   Traces to trace's end;
    Veri juoksi vempelestä,   Blood ran from the shaft-bow,
    Rasva rahkehen nenästä.   Fat from the trace's end.
    (SKVR I$_1$ 163a.4–7.)

This example reflects a distinctive verbal system characterized by an available set of formulae realized through a narrow set of metrically and semantically conditioned lexical choices to produce a tight textual unit.[8] The tight textual unit clearly belongs to the poetry's linguistic register. It specifically indexes this particular mythic image in almost all regions of the tradition. The parallel mythic images of the colliding sleighs can be seen as belonging to the next order of representation (see also Frog 2014c: 193). These images are associated with a single mythic event in a single mythological narrative that was maintained exclusively through the poetic genre rather than the story being told, for example, in prose, represented iconographically, enacted, etc. through different media and genres at the primary order of representation. The particular event of the colliding sleighs was invariably rendered with this verbal system. The narrative and its episodes were socially recognized identities, like the symbolic equivalent of proper nouns. When register is employed for resources across all of the orders of representation, the images, motifs and episodes of this narrative as well as the narrative itself can all be regarded as symbolic resources of the register at higher orders of representation. The multiple orders of representation are clearly interfaced, with higher orders informing the significance and meaning potential of their characteristic signifiers at lower orders of representation. However, when such elements are used in exceptional contexts, interpretation involves distinguishing the relevant order of signification for which it was employed – e.g. literal propositional description, as a mythic image or as a strategic reference to the epic narrative whole as a higher order sign (Frog 2010b: 102–103; 2011b: 57–58). The specific identity of this example highlights the interface of these orders of representation, whereas in other cases and in other traditions, the links between the verbalization and a particular motif or image may not be so comprehensive and the motif or image may be linked to a story-pattern realized in many different narratives. The emphasis in discussing this example is on the indexical interface of orders of representation, but it is also necessary to emphasize that integers of a register cannot be defined as excluding elements linked to their signifiers in the manner of proper nouns – i.e. that are *not* used as resources in *different* texts – any more than the personal name of the valkyrie Skǫgul (above), as a proper noun, should be omitted as an integer of the skaldic lexicon.

Old Norse eddic poetry on mythological subjects exhibits a degree of crystallization similar to kalevalaic epic. However, the verbalization of traditional images, motifs and themes may be conventional only to the narrative as a poem or textual entity while the element of narration develops broader indexical significance across all of its uses in different poems. For example, the gods at their divine (legal) assembly is a common mythic image linked to the motif of the gods making a judgement or decision. In the two examples of verbalization in (4) and (5), verbal correspondence is limited to the adjective *allr* ['all'] and the phrase *oc um þat* ['and about that'] whereas even the nouns for 'gods' are otherwise different:

(4) Þá gengo regin ǫll   Then went the gods (*regin*) all
    á rǫcstóla   to the judgment seats
    ginnheilog goð   magic-holy gods (*goð*)
    oc um þat gættuz   and about that considered
        (*Vǫluspá* 6.1–4, 9.1–4, 23.1–4, 25.1–4)

(5) Senn vóro æsir   Then were the gods (*æsir*)
    allir á þingi   all at their assembly
    oc ásynior   and the goddesses (*ásynjur*)
    allar á máli   all at a discussion
    oc um þat réðo   and about that discussed
    ríkir tívar   the mighty gods (*tívar*)
        (*Baldrs draumar* 1.1–6)

Each of these can be considered a distinct verbal system characteristic for rendering the same symbolic integer of content in different narrative poems. As in kalevalaic poetry, the crystallization of verbalization provides it with the potential to index the motif, but here the index becomes more specific to a particular text where use may be repeating as in (4) or context-specific as in (5)[9] among a variety of uses. This is more similar to Old Norse skaldic poetry, in which traditional links between verbalization and higher order integers *lack* general conventions in the register and are rather created as text-specific with each composition that advances into social circulation (and thereby a potential target of strategic reference). In traditions where verbalization is more flexible rather than crystallized into formalized texts, the expression of higher order elements may be much more variable. In South Slavic epic, the concentration of lexical material linked to a higher order integer like a theme is much lower than in the examples above. A poetic register oriented to situation-specific communication such as Karelian lament mandates variability, which in that case is augmented by parallelism at the level of motifs, requiring multiple situation-specific verbalizations for each element in performance (Stepanova E. 2014: 66–69). The crystallization of lexical material for signifying a higher-order element may also vary considerably even within a kalevalaic epic (Frog 2010b: 103–108). In South Slavic epic, this may only remain specific to idiolects of individuals rather than evolving socially recognizable indexicality with integers of narrative content (Foley 1990: 278–328). The use and evolution of particular elements at higher orders of representation may remain largely or wholly independent of conventionalized links to the mediating order of verbalization. The indexical relationship between integers at different orders of signification is always dependent on the poetic tradition and more narrowly on how the relevant elements of that tradition are conventionally used.

Systems of images and metaphors may also be quite flexible resources that are fundamental to expression in the poetry. This can be quite prominent in lyric genres, where symbolic representation can receive particular emphasis. In other cases, the framework of symbols and metaphors may be fundamental to understanding the linguistic register. For example, the kennings of skaldic poetry were generative, but their astounding lexical variation was enabled by building on conventional images and metaphors (e.g. *geira byrr* ['breeze of spears']), *Viðris dynr* ['din of Viðrir (a name of Odin)']), or even referring to socially recognized narratives.[10] The framework in the background was fundamental to interpreting verses. Its relevance extended from the rich lexicon of poetic synonyms and *kenning*s themselves to the clauses and sentences in which these were realized. Circumlocutions in kalevalaic wedding songs were built on corresponding (if quite different) systems of images and metaphors, such as referring to a maiden as a domestic bird like a 'chicken' (*kana*) or type of waterfowl, while referring to a suitor as some type of raptor like an eagle (*kokko*), suggestive of the relationship between them, whereas this symbolic structure of predator–prey was absent from wedding laments that equally had an established place in traditional weddings (Ahola et al. 2016; cf. Stepanova A. 2012). The relationship between the lexicon and image-systems of the poetic tradition are quite pronounced in each of these traditions (cf. Stepanova, this volume). They highlight the fact that image systems and metaphors are intimately bound up with human expression (cf. Lakoff 1986; Lakoff & Turner 1986), and more significantly that the frameworks which inform verbalization may co-vary with the linguistic register. This relationship is nevertheless easily taken for granted (especially in aesthetically unmarked discourse). Viewing these as belonging to a single register reduces or eliminates sensitivity to interactions between them, which may be unproblematic for many investigations but should still be recognized. For investigations in which such a relationship is brought into focus, the definition of register may require calibration for greater sensitivity to that relationship.

Perspectives

Register has proven a valuable analytical tool for the address of oral poetries. It can, however, be applied in a number of different ways with different degrees of inclusion and exclusion. At one extreme, it can be applied as a term more or less equivalent to genre. Attention was drawn to aspects of genre that have not been covered by such uses of register, but there is nothing to inhibit the adaptation of register to take these aspects into account as well. It is also possible to situate register in relation to genre as complementary tools for analysis and discussion. Similarly, a linguistic register or a performance register (inclusive of extra-linguistic features) can be distinguished with reference to a primary order of signification from systems of expressive elements and constructions at higher orders of signification. Such distinctions can facilitate keeping the different orders of signification and their interrelationships in focus, but in practice, this is relevant to only some investigations and not to others. No less relevant is the potential to discuss the register of a broad poetic system or that characteristic of a particular genre. Alternately, the term can also potentially be calibrated to exchange focus on the language mediating symbols to the symbols at higher orders of representation that may be mediated through multiple performance registers in order to discuss, for example, registers of mythology (Frog 2015b). In any of these cases, the usefulness of one or the other definitions of register is dependent on the investigation rather than dictated by the term itself. As a tool, register needs to be calibrated to the investigation. However, the range of potential variation in the use of register also mandates that the calibration of that tool for a particular investigation must be clearly stated, lest the author and the reader understand it as referring to different things.

Notes

1. See e.g. Hymes 1981; Silverstein 1984; Tedlock 1986; Blommeart 2006; Agha 2007: 98–103; Wilce 2008. It is interesting to observe that this was already acknowledged roughly two thousand years before the advent of ethnopoetics in Classical rhetoric by e.g. Cicero and Quintilian, for whom poetry was qualified by formalized meter whereas rhythm was fundamental to a much broader range of linguistic behaviour – *et contra nihil quod est prorsa scriptum non redigi possit in quaedam versiculorum genera uel in membra* ['and certainly there is nothing written in prose that cannot be reduced to some sort of verses or indeed parts of verses'] (*Institutio oratoria* IX.iv.lii, my translation).
2. E.g. Alembi 2002; Joubert 2004; Robbins 2006; Maroni 2010; Ramey 2012; Amodio 2014; see also articles published in the journal *Oral Tradition*; Foley's impact has been particularly pronounced in Finland, e.g. Harvilahti 2003; Tarkka 2005; Frog 2010a; Stepanova E. 2011; Koski 2011; Sykäri 2011; Kallio 2013; Stepanova E. 2014.
3. A significant factor in the difference in the scope of these formulae is associated with the lack of a colonic structure of the meter. In other words, South Slavic and Homeric epic poetries required word-breaks at certain points in a line. This caesura defined the *metrical capsules* in relation to which expressions conventionalized (cf. Foley 1999: 69–70). The lack of a colonic structure in Kalevala-meter situates the metrical line as the capsule for expression.
4. Following the survey in Meissner 1921; cf. also Clunies Ross et al. 2013. N.B. this includes exceptional kenning referents attested once and linked to a singular context (e.g. CAT, MOUSE, DUCK); it should also be stressed that the limited number of anticipated referents and crystalized semantic equations for referring to them made the interpretation of kennings predictable (Fidjestøl 1997: 45; cf. Frog 2014b: 106; 2015a).
5. This becomes more apparent as consideration shifts from local communities to variation in the traditions from the White Sea to the Gulf of Finland, in which local and regional traditions have historically developed interrelationships in somewhat different ways.
6. This can become important to distinguish, for example, because the historical construction of the resources of the register may lead to continuities not necessarily consistent with the image of the register as an entity. For example, Old Norse *dróttkvætt* poetry maintained its prestige status through the process of Christianization and was treated as a vernacular resource for treating Christian subjects. Nevertheless, the linguistic register remained interfaced with the vernacular (popularly "pagan") mythology and mytho-heroic traditions and the metaphors and image-systems of expression remained locked into the ideological environs of the pre-Christian royal courts.
7. Foley (e.g. 1999: 83–84) describes these higher order elements of tradition in terms of "units of utterance" and thus as *words* of the register.
8. Building on the approach of Lauri and Anneli Honko (1995; 1998; cf. Honko 1998: 100–116; 2003: 113–122), I have discussed these verbal systems in terms of *multiforms*.

Without elaborating on its potential variations, this example illustrates the pattern of two couplets each characterized by semantic parallelism while the second couplet presents syntactic parallelism to the first (although many variations can deviate from this structure). Within the system, the opening couplet is characterized by a two-syllable verb with a long initial (stressed) syllable (allowing alternation in word order between the first two words of the line). The verb is semantically conditioned with a meaning of becoming stuck. The couplet also employs two nouns able to refer metonymically to a sleigh. These are metrically conditioned as two-syllable nouns belonging to a class in which the inflected stem has a third syllable, and the inflected form has a long initial syllable (*vemmel / vempele-*; *rahis / rahkehe-*). Each word occurs twice in the line: once in nominative and once in genitive/accusative, with the postposition *nenä* concluding the second line. The second couplet (may) reuse the two metonyms for sleigh in parallel lines. The verb is metrically conditioned as in line 1 but semantically conditioned as a term for movement of liquid. The subject is a two-syllable noun with a short initial syllable (inhibiting alternation in word order for metrical reasons). Variation in the multiform is complex owing to the potential to repeat the syntactic structure of the first line of each couplet (rather than use of the prepositional phrase) as well as an additional available construction employing a three-syllable verb with a different class of noun. In practice, the verbal system would crystallize in the memory of the individual singer and significant variation in reproduction at the level of idiolect was exceptional. (Frog 2010b: 103–105.)

9   For discussion of the likely strategic reference to (5) in Þrymskviða 14.1–6, see Frog 2014a: 148–152, esp.n46.
10 For example, in the kenning *blað ilja Þrúðar þjófs* ['leaf of the soles of the thief of Þrúðr' = SHIELD], 'thief of Þrúðr' refers to an (otherwise unknown) myth of the abduction of the god Thor's daughter by a giant. The kenning 'leaf of the soles of a giant' is one of a system of shield-kennings that refer to the myth of Thor's battle with the giant Hrungnir, in which the giant is tricked into standing on his shield (Meissner 1921: 166).

References

Sources

Baldrs draumar. In Neckel & Kuhn 1963: 277–279.
Institutio oratoria. Fabius Quintilian. *The Institutio oratoria of Quintilian* I–IV. Ed. & trans. H. E. Butler. London: William Heinemann, 1920–1922.
SKVR = *Suomen Kansan Vanhat Runot* I–XV. Helsinki: Suomalaisen Kirjallisuuden Seura, 1908–1997.
Þrymskviða. In Neckel & Kuhn 1963: 111–115.
Þhorn Gldr = Þorbjǫrn *hornklofi*. *Glymdrápa*. Ed. Edith Marold et al. In *Poetry from the Kings' Sagas I: From Mythical Times to c. 1035* 1–2. Ed. Diana Whaley. Turnhout: Brepols, 2012. Part 1, pp. 73–90.
Vǫluspá. In Neckel & Kuhn 1963: 1–16.

Literature

Abrahams, Roger D. 1968. Introductory Remarks to a Rhetorical Theory of Folklore. *Journal of American Folklore* 81(320): 143–158.

Abrahams, Roger D. 1977. Toward an Enactment-Centered Theory of Folklore. In *The Frontiers of Folklore*. Ed. William Bascom. Washington, D.C.: American Anthropological Association. Pp. 79–120.

Abram, Christopher 2011. *Myths of the Pagan North: The Gods of the Norsemen*. London: Continuum.

Agha, Asif. 2007. *Language and Social Relations*. Cambridge: Cambridge University Press.

Joonas Ahola, Frog & Ville Laakso 2016 (forthcoming). Raptors in Iron Age and Medieval North Finnic Cultures up to c. AD 1500: Perceptions and Practices. *The Origin and Importance of Falconry until 1500 AD with an Emphasis on Northern Europe*. Ed. Oliver Grimm. Schriften des archæologischen Landesmuseums Ergänzungsreihe series. Wachholz: Neumünster.

Alembi, Ezekiel 2002. *The Construction of the Abanyole Perceptions on Death through Oral Funeral Poetry*. Helsinki: DataCom.

Amodio, Mark C. 2014. *The Anglo-Saxon Literature Handbook*. West Sussex: Wiley-Blackwell.

Austin, J. L. 1962. *How to Do Things with Words: The Williams James Lectures Delivered at Harvard University in 1955*. Oxford: Clarendon Press.

Bakhtin, M. M. 1981. *The Dialogic Imagination: Four Essays*. Ed. Michael Holquist. Trans. Caryl Emerson & Michael Holquist. Austin: University of Texas Press.

Bakhtin, M. M. 1986 [1952–1953]. The Problem of Speech Genres. In M. M. Bakhtin, *Speech Genres & Other Late Essays*. Ed. Caryl Emerson & Michael Holquist. Trans. Vern W. McGee. Austin: University of Texas Press.

Banti, G., & F. Giannattasio 2004. Poetry. In *A Companion to Linguistic Anthropology*. Ed. A. Duranti. Malden: Blackwell. Pp. 291–320.

Bauman, Richard 1984. *Verbal Art as Performance*. Prospect Heights: Waveland Press.

Bauman, Richard 1992. Genre. In *Folklore, Cultural Performances, and Popular Entertainments: A Communications-Centered Handbook*. Ed. Richard Bauman. Oxford: Oxford University Press. Pp. 53–59.

Bauman, Richard 1999. Genre. *Journal of Linguistic Anthropology* 9(1–2): 84–87.

Beck, Brenda E. F. 1982. *The Three Twins: The Telling of a South Indian Folk Epic*. Bloomington: Indiana University Press.

Ben Amos, Dan 1976. Analytical Categories and Ethnic Genres. In *Folklore Genres*. Ed. Dan Ben Amos. Austin: University of Texas Press. Pp. 215–242.

Bendix, Regina, & Galit Hasan-Rokem (ed.) 2012. *A Companion to Folklore*. Malden: Wiley-Blackwell.

Biber, Douglas 1995. *Dimensions of Register Variation: A Cross-Linguistic Comparison*. Cambridge: Cambridge University Press.

Bloch, Maurice 1989 [1974]. Symbols, Song, Dance and Features of Articulation: Is Religion an Extreme form of Traditional Authority? In Maurice Bloch, *Ritual, History and Power: Selected Papers in Anthropology*. London: Athlone Press. Pp. 19–45.

Blommaert, Jan 2006. Applied Ethnopoetics. *Narrative Inquiry* 16(1): 181–190.

Briggs, Charles L., & Richard Bauman 1992. Genre, Intertextuality, and Social Power. *Journal of Linguistic Anthropology* 2(2): 131–172.

Clunies Ross, Margaret 2005. *A History of Old Norse Poetry and Poetics*. Cambridge: D. S. Brewer.

Clunies Ross, Margaret, Kari Ellen Gade, Edith Marold, Guðrún Nordal, Diana Whaley & Tarrin Wills 2012. General Introduction. In. *Poetry from the Kings' Sagas I: From Mythical Times to c. 1035* I–II. Ed. Diana Whaley. Turnhout: Brepols. Vol. 1, pp. xiii–xciii.

Coleman, R. G. G. 1999. Poetic Diction, Poetic Discourse and the Poetic Register. In *Aspects of the Language of Latin Poetry*. Ed. J. N. Adams & R. G. Mayer. New York: Oxford University Press. Pp. 21–93.

Doane, A. N. 1994. The Ethnography of Scribal Writing and Anglo-Saxon Poetry: Scribe as Performer. *Oral Tradition* 9(2): 420–439.

Falk, Hjalmar 1924. *Odensheiti*. Videnskapsselskapets Skrifter II: Hist.-filos. Klasse 10. Kristiania: Brøggers.

Faulkes, Aanthony (ed.) 1998. *Snorri Sturluson, Edda: Skáldskaparmál*. London: Viking Society for Northern Research.

Fidjestøl, Bjarne 1997. The Kenning System: An Attempt at a Linguistic Analysis. In Bjarne Fidjestøl, *Selected Papers*. Ed. Odd Einar Haugen & Else Mundal. Trans. Peter Foote. Viking Collection 9. Odense: Odense University Press, 16–67.

Foley, John Miles 1988. *The Theory of Oral Composition: History and Methodology*. Bloomington: Indiana University Press.

Foley, John Miles 1991. *Immanent Art: From Structure to Meaning in Traditional Oral Epic*. Bloomington: Indiana University Press.

Foley, John Miles 1992. Word-Power, Performance, and Tradition. *The Journal of American Folklore* 105: 275–301.

Foley, John Miles 1993 [1990]. *Traditional Oral Epic: The Odyssey, Beowulf, and the Serbo-Croation Return Song*. Los Angeles: University of California Press.

Foley, John Miles 1995. *The Singer of Tales in Performance*. Bloomington: Indiana University Press.

Foley, John Miles 1999. *Homer's Traditional Art*. University Park: Pennsylvania University Press.

Foley, John Miles 2002. *How to Read an Oral Poem*. Urbana: University of Illinois Press.

Foley, John Miles 2004. Epic as Genre. In *The Cambridge Companion to Homer*. Ed. Robert Louis Fowler. Cambridge: Cambridge Univerity Press. Pp. 171–187.

Foley, John Miles, & Peter Ramey 2012. Oral Theory and Medieval Studies. In *Medieval Oral Literature*. Ed. Karl Reichl. Berlin: de Gruyter. Pp. 71–102.

Fox, James J. 2014. *Explorations in Semantic Parallelism*. Canberra: Australian University Press.

Frank, Roberta 1978. *Old Norse Court Poetry: The* Dróttkvætt *Stanza*. Islandica 42. London: Cornell University Press.

Frog 2009. Speech-Acts in Skaldic Verse: Genre, Formula and Improvisation. In *Versatility in Versification: Multidisciplinary Approaches to Metrics*. Ed. Tonya Kim Dewey & Frog. Berkeley Insights in Linguistics and Semiotics 74. New York: Peter Lang. Pp. 223–246.

Frog 2010a. *Baldr and Lemminkäinen: Approaching the Evolution of Mythological Narrative through the Activating Power of Expression*. UCL Eprints. London: University College London.

Frog 2010b. Multiformit kalevalamittaisessa epiikassa. In *Kalevalamittaisen runon tulkintoja*. Ed. Seppo Knuuttila, Ulla Piela & Lotte Tarkka. Kalevalaseuran vuosikirja 89. Helsinki: Suomen Kirjallisuuden Seura. Pp. 91–113.

Frog 2011a. Multiforms and Meaning: Playing with Referentiality in Kalevalaic Epic. In *Laulu kulttuurisena kommunikaationa: Proceedings from the Runosong Academy Jubilee Seminar, 8–10 October 2010*. Ed. Pekka Huttu-Hiltunen et al. Kuhmo: Juminkeko. Pp. 49–63.

Frog 2011b. Traditional Epic as Genre: Definition as a Foundation for Comparative Research. *RMN Newsletter* 3: 47–48.

Frog 2012. On the Case of *Vambarljóð* II: Register and Mode from Skaldic Verse to *sagnakvæði*. *RMN Newsletter* 5: 49–61.

Frog 2013a. The (De)Construction of Mythic Ethnography I: Is Every *þurs* in Verse a *þurs*? *RMN Newsletter* 6: 52–72.

Frog 2013b. Revisiting the Historical-Geographic Method(s). *RMN Newsletter* 7: 18–34.

Frog 2014a. Germanic Traditions of the Theft of the Thunder-Instrument (ATU 1148b): An Approach to *Þrymskviða* and Þórr's Adventure with Geirrøðr in Circum-Baltic Perspective. In *New Focus on Retrospective Methods*. Ed. Eldar Heide & Karen Bek-

Pedersen. FF Communications 307. Helsinki: Academia Scientiarum Fennica. Pp. 118–160.

Frog 2014b. Mythological Names in *dróttkvætt* Formulae I: When is a Valkyrie like a Spear? *Studia Metrica et Poetica* 1(1): 100–139.

Frog 2014c. Parallelism, Mode, Medium and Orders of Representation. In *Parallelism in Verbal Art and Performance: Pre-Print Papers of the Seminar-Workshop 26th–27th May 2014, Helsinki, Finland*. Ed. Frog. Helsinki: Folklore Studies, University of Helsinki. Pp. 185–207.

Frog 2015a (forthcoming). Metrical Entanglement and *dróttkvætt* Composition – A Pilot Study on Battle-Kennings. In *Approaches to Germanic Metre*. Ed. Kristján Árnason et al. Reykjavík: University of Iceland Press.

Frog 2015b. Mythology in Cultural Practice: A Methodological Framework for Historical Analysis. *RMN Newsletter* 10: 33–57.

Frog 2016 (forthcoming). 'Genres, Genres Everywhere, but Who Knows What to Think?': Toward a Semiotic Model for Typology. In Koski et al. 2016.

Frog & Eila Stepanova 2011. Alliteration in (Balto-) Finnic Languages. In *Alliteration and Culture*. Ed. Jonathan Roper. Houndmills: Palgrave MacMillan. Pp. 195–218.

Gade, Kari Ellen 1995. *The Structure of Old Norse dróttkvætt Poetry*. Ithaca: Cornell University Press.

Halliday, M. A. K. 1978. *Language as Social Semiotic*. London: Edward Arnold.

Harvilahti, Lauri 1992. The Production of Finnish Epic Poetry: Fixed Wholes or Creative Compositions? *Oral Tradition* 7: 87–101.

Harvilahti, Lauri 2003. *The Holy Mountain: Studies on Upper Altay Oral Poetry*. FF Communications 282. Helsinki: Academia Scientiarum Fennica.

Hasan, Ruqaiya 1989. *Linguistics, Language, and Verbal Art*. Oxford: Oxford University Press.

Honko, Lauri 1989. Folkloristic Theories of Genre. *Studia Fennica* 33: 13–28.

Honko, Lauri 1998. *Textualizing the Siri Epic*. Helsinki: Suomalainen Tiedeakatemia.

Honko, Lauri 2000. Thick Corpus and Organic Variation: An Introduction. In *Thick Corpus, Organic Variation and Textuality in Oral Tradition*. Ed. Lauri Honko. Studia Fennica Folkloristica 7. Helsinki: Finnish Literature Society. Pp. 3–28.

Honko, Lauri. 2003. *The Maiden's Death Song and The Great Wedding: Anne Vabarna's Oral Twin Epic Written down by A. O. Väisnen*. Helsinki: Suomalainen Tiedeakatemia.

Honko, Lauri, & Anneli Honko 1995. Multiforms in Epic Composition. In *XIth Congress of the International Society for Folk-Narrative Research (ISFNR), January 6–12, 1995, Mysore, India: Papers*. Mysore: Central Institute of Indian Languages. Vol. II, pp. 207–240.

Honko, Lauri, & Anneli Honko 1998. Multiforms in Epic Composition. In *The Epic. Oral and Written*. Ed. Lauri Honko, Jawaharlal Handoo & John Miles Foley. Mysore: Central Institute of Indian Languages. Pp. 31–79.

Hymes, Dell 1981. *"In Vain I Tried to Tell You": Essays in Native American Ethnopoetics*. Philadelphia: University of Pennsylvania Press.

Hymes, Dell 1989. Ways of Speaking. In *Explorations in the Ethnography of Speaking*. 2nd edn. Ed. Richard Bauman & Joel Sherzer. Cambridge: Cambridge University Press. Pp. 433–451.

Irvine, Judith T. 1989. When Talk Isn't Cheap: Language and Political Economy. *American Ethnologist* 16(2): 248–267.

Jakobson, Roman 1960. Closing Statement. Linguistics and Poetics. Thomas A. Sebeok (toim.), *Style in Language*. New York: Massachusetts Institute of Technology. Pp. 350–377.

Johnson, John William 2002. A Contribution to the Theory of Oral Poetic Composition. In *The Kalevala and the World's Traditional Epics*. Ed. Lauri Honko. Studia Fennica Folkloristica 12. Helsinki: Finnish Literature Society. Pp. 184–242.

Joubert, Annekie 2004. *The Power of Performance: Linking Past and Present in Hananwa and Lobedu Oral Literature*. Trends in Linguistics 160. Berlin: de Gruyter.
Kallio, Kati 2013. *Laulamisen tapoja: Esitysareena, rekisteri ja paikallinen laji länsi-inkeriläisessä kalevalamittaisessa runossa*. Tampere: Tammiprintti.
Kitts, Margo 2005. *Sanctified Violence in Homeric Society: Oath-Making Rituals and Narratives in the* Iliad. Cambridge: Cambridge University Press.
af Klintberg, Bengt 2010. *The Types of the Swedish Folk Legend*. FF Communications 300. Helsinki: Academia Scientiarum Fennica.
Koski, Kaarina 2011. *Kuoleman voimat: Kirkonväki suomalaisessa uskomusperinteessä*. Helsinki: Finnish Literature Society.
Koski, Kaarina 2016 (forthcoming). The Legend Genre and Narrative Registers. In Koski et al. 201t.
Koski, Kaarina & Frog with Ulla Savolainen (eds.) 2016 (forthcoming). *Genre – Text – Interpretation*. Studia Fennica Folkloristica. Helsinki: Finnish Literature Society.
Kristeva, Julia 1980 [1969] Word, Dialogue, and Novel. In *Desire in Language: A Semiotic Approach to Literature and Art*. Ed. Leon S. Roudiez. Oxford: Blackwell. Pp. 64–91.
Krohn, Kaarle 1926. *Die folkloristische Arbeitsmethode*. Oslo: Aschehoug.
Kuhn, Hans *Das Dróttkvætt*. Heidelberg: Carl Winter.
Kuusi, Matti 1953. Kalevalaisen runon alkusointuisuudesta. *Virittäjä* 57: 198–207.
Kuusi, Matti 1954. *Sananlaskut ja puheenparret*. Helsinki: SKS.
Kuusi, Matti 1994. Questions of Kalevala Meter: What exactly did Kalevala Language Signify to Its Users? In A.-L. Siikala & S. Vakimo (eds.). *Songs Beyond the Kalevala: Transformations of Oral Poetry*. Helsinki: Finnish Literature Society. Pp. 41–55.
Lakoff, George 1986. *Women, Fire, and Dangerous Things*. Chicago: University of Chicago Press.
Lakoff, George, & Mark Turner 1989. *More than Cool Reason: A Field Guide to Poetic Metaphor*. Chicago: Chicago University Press.
Lifton, Robert J. 1961. *Thought Reform and the Psychology of Totalism: A Study of 'Brainwashing' in China*. New York: Norton.
Lindow, John 1982. Narrative and the Nature of Skaldic Poetry. *Arkiv för Nordisk Filologi* 97: 94–121.
Lord, Albert Bates 1960. *The Singer of Tales*. Cambridge: Harvard University Press.
Lord, Albert Bates 1991. *Epic Singers and Oral Tradition*. Ithaca: Cornell University Press.
Moroni, Elisa 2010. Between Orality and Literacy: Parallelism and Repetition in Russian Folk Epics and Their Challenge to Translation. *Bergen Language and Linguistics Studies* 1: 1–28.
Martin, Richard P. 2005. Epic as Genre. In *A Companion to Ancient Epic*. Ed. John Miles Foley. Oxford: Blackwell. Pp. 9–19.
Meissner, Rudolf 1921. *Die Kenningar der Skalden*. Bonn: Schroeder
Missuno, Folip 2012. *'Shadow' and Paradoxes of Darkness in Old English and Old Norse Poetic Language*. Ph.D. thesis, University of York. White Rose eTheses Online. Available at: http://etheses.whiterose.ac.uk/3158/.
Neckel, Gustav, & Hans Kuhn (eds.) 1963. *Edda: Die Lieder des Codex Regius nebst vewandten Denkmälern* I. 4th edn. Heidelberg: Carl Winters Universitätsbuchhandlung.
Nikolaev, Ilya 2011. Izhorian Epic Songs as a Source of Linguistic Data: Synchronic and Diachronic Perspective. Unpublished paper presented at the Fifth International Symposium on Finno-Ugric Languages in Groningen (The Netherlands). Cf. the report: Database of Izhorian Epic Songs Morphology, *RMN Newsletter* 2 (2011): 69.
Niles, John D. 1999. *Homo narrans: The Poetics and Anthropology of Oral Literature*. Philadelphia: University of Pennsylvania Press.
Oral Tradition – available at: http://journal.oraltradition.org/
Parry, Milman 1928a. *L'Epithete traditionnelle dans Homere: Essai sur unprobleme de style homerique*. Paris: Société d'Éditions "Les Belles Lettres".

Parry, Milman 1928b. *Les Formules et la metrique d'Homere*. Paris: Société d'Éditions "Les Belles Lettres".

Peirce, Charles Santiago Sanders 1940. Logic as Semiotic: The Theory of Signs. In *The Philosophy of Pierce: Selected Writings*. Ed. Justus Buchler. New York: Routledge & Kegan Paul. Pp. 98–119.

Poole, Russell 1991. *Viking Poems on War and Peace: A Study in Skaldic Narrative*. Toronto Medieval Texts and Translations 8. Toronto: University of Toronto Press.

Price, Neil S. 2002. *The Viking Way: Religion and War in Late Iron Age Scandinavia*. Uppsala: Department of Archaeology and Ancient History.

Ramey, Peter 2012. Variation and the Poetics of Oral Performance in *Cædmon's Hymn*. *Neophilologus* 96: 441–456.

Reynolds, Dwight Fletcher 1995. *Heroic Poets, Poetic Heroes*. Ithaca: Cornell University Press.

Robbins, Vernon K. 2006. Interfaces of Orality and Literature in the Gospel of Mark. In *Performing the Gospel: Orality, Memory, and Mark*. Ed. Richard A. Horsley, Jonathan A. Draper & John Miles Foley. Minneapolis: Augsburg Fortress. Pp. 125–146.

Roper, Jonathan 2012. Synonymy and Rank in Alliterative Poetry. *Sign Systems Studies* 40(1/2): 82–93.

Saarinen, Jukka 2013. Behind the Text: Reconstructing the Voice of a Singer. *RMN Newsletter* 7: 34–43.

Salminen, Väinö 1934. *Suomalaisten muinaisrunojen historia*. Helsinki: Suomalaisen Kirjallisuuden Seura.

Sarv, Mari 1999. Regilaul: Clearing the Alliterative Haze. *Folklore* (Tartu) 10: 126–140.

Saussure, Ferdinand de 1967 [1916]. *Cours de linguistique générale*. Paris: Éditions Payot & Rivages.

Searle, John R. 1969. *Speech Acts: An Essay in the Philosophy of Language*. Cambridge: Cambridge University Press.

Sebeok, Thomas A. 1994. *An Introduction to Semiotics*. London: Pinter Publishers.

Seitel, Peter 2012. Three Aspects of Oral Textuality. In Bendix & Hasan-Rokem 2012: 75–93.

Sherzer, Joel 1999. Ceremonial Dialogic Greetings among the Kuna Indians of Panama. *Journal of Pragmatics* 31(4): 453–470.

Shuman, Amy, & Galit Hasan-Rokem 2012. The Poetics of Folklore. In Bendix & Hasan-Rokem 2012: 55–74.

Siikala, Anna-Leena 1991. Singing of Incantations in Nordic Tradition. In *Old Norse and Finnish Religions and Cultic Place-Names*. Ed. Tore Ahlbäck. Åbo: The Donner Institute for Research in Religious and Cultural History. Pp. 191–205.

Silverstein, Michael 1984. On the Pragmatic 'Poetry' of Prose. In *Meaning, Form and Use in Context*. Ed. Deborah Schiffrin. Washington, D.C.: Georgetown University Press. Pp. 181–199.

Silverstein, Michael 2010. "Direct" and "Indirect" Communicative Acts in Semiotic Perspective. *Journal of Pragmatics* 42: 337–353.

Stepanova, Aleksandra 2012. *Karjalaisen itkuvirsikielen sanakirja*. Helsinki: Suomalaisen Kirjallisuuden Seura.

Stepanova, Eila 2011. Reflections of Belief Systems in Karelian and Lithuanian Laments: Shared Systems of Traditional Referentiality? *Archaeologia Baltica* 15: 128–143.

Stepanova, Eila 2012. Mythic Elements of Karelian Laments: The Case of *syndyzet* and *spuassuzet*. In *Mythic Discourses*. Ed. Frog, Anna-Leena Siikala & Eila Stepanova. Studia Fennica Folkloristica 20. Helsinki: Finnish Literature Society. Pp. 257–287.

Stepanova, Eila 2014. *Seesjärveläisten itkijöiden rekisterit: Tutkimus äänellä itkemisen käytänteistä, teemoista ja käsitteistä*. Kultaneito 14. Tampere: Suomen Kansantietouden Tutkijain Seura.

Strömbäck, Dag 1954 Draken i Hjörungavåg. In *Scandinavica et Fenno-Ugrica: Studier tillägnade Björn Collinder, den 22 Juli 1954*. Stockholm: Almqvist & Wiksell. Pp. 383–389.

Sykäri, Venla 2011. *Words as Events: Cretan Mantinádes in Performance and Composition.* Studia Fennica Folkloristica 18. Helsinki: Finnish Literature Society.

Tarkka, Lotte 1993. Intertextuality, Rhetorics, and the Interpretation of Oral Poetry: The Case of Archived Orality. In *Nordic Frontiers*. Ed. Pertti J. Anttonen & Reimund Kvideland. NIF Publications 27. Turku: Nordic Institute of Folklore.

Tarkka, Lotte 2005. *Rajarahvaan laulu.* Helsinki: Suomalaisen Kirjallisuuden Seura.

Tarkka, Lotte 2013. *Songs of the Border People: Genre, Intertextuality and Tradition in Kalevala-Meter Poetry.* FF Communications 305. Helsinki: Academia Scientiarum Fennica.

Tedlock, Dennis 1983. *The Spoken Word and the Work of Interpretation.* Philadelphia: University of Pennsylvania Press.

Thorvaldsen, Bernt Øyvind 2006. Svá er sagt í fornum vísindum*: Tekstualiseringen av de Mytologiske Eddadikt.* Ph.D. Dissertation. Bergen: University of Bergen.

Todrov, Tzvetan 1977. *The Poetics of Prose.* Ithaca: Cornell University Press.

Tsur, Reuven 1992a. *Toward a Theory of Cognitive Poetics.* Amsterdam: North-Holland.

Tsur, Reuven 1992b. *What Makes Sound Patterns Expressive? – The Poetic Mode of Speech Perception.* Durham: Duke University Press.

Vargyas, Lajos 1983. *Hungarian Ballads and the European Ballad Tradition I.* Budapest: Akadémiai Kiadó.

Vleck, Van, & Amelia Eileen 1991. *Memory and Re-Creation in Troubadour Lyric.* Los Angeles: University of California Press.

Vološinov, V. N. 1930 [1929]. *Марксизм и философия языка.* Ленинград: Прибой.

Wilce, James M. 2008. Scientizing Bangladeshi Psychiatry: Parallelism, Enregisterment, and the Cure for a Magic Complex. *Language and Society* 37: 91–114.

Wray, Alison 2002. *Formulaic Language and the Lexicon.* Cambridge: Cambridge University Press.

Zumthor, Paul 1990 [1983]. *Oral Poetry: An Introduction.* Trans. Kathryn Murphy-Judy. Theory and History of Literature 70. Minneapolis: University of Minnesota Press.

Between Language and Register

II

Janus Spindler Møller

4. The Enregisterment of Minority Languages in a Danish Classroom

The human resource of language in the shape of linguistic features is primarily a resource for social action. *Languaging* (Jørgensen et. al. 2011) describes the processes involving the use of this resource in human interaction. *Registers* (Agha 2003; 2007) are ways these means of action are organized, and *enregisterment* (Agha 2003; 2007) describes the on-going discursive processes whereby any register comes into being, develops, and, potentially, disappears. Speakers may use, and even claim ownership of, certain registers in order to perform recognizable social roles in particular types of situations. Sometimes people may also refuse to use certain registers they are urged to use – not because they lack knowledge of the register but because the values attached to the register in a certain situation potentially result in ascriptions of identities that they do not want. In this article, I will analyze a case[1] where exactly such a refusal appears during a lesson in the 8th grade in a Danish school.

During a so-called "project week" in an 8th grade class in a school in Copenhagen, a group of girls consisting of the students Israh, Fartun and Mathilde carried out a project on terrorism. The school they attend is a standard Danish public school situated in an area of Copenhagen with a relatively large percentage of people with a linguistic minority background. The result of the project was to be a presentation held in front of teachers and classmates. At the end of their presentation, the girls wanted to play a recording made in advance of a poem made by themselves. The recording consisted of three versions of the same poem: a version in Arabic (Israh's home language), a version in Somali (Fartun's home language), and a version in Danish (Mathilde's home language). The girls recorded the three versions on a mobile phone in advance and placed the sound file on the school's intranet in order to play it for the class. But when they got to this part of their presentation, they could not find the file on the intranet and they did not have a back-up copy. From being a relatively streamlined presentation and, generally, a well-organized day in the class, the next 10 minutes appeared rather chaotic with the girls looking for the sound file, the two teachers making suggestions, the other students increasingly losing their patience, and so forth. After a while, the teachers suggested that, instead of playing the sound file, the three girls should read the poem in front of the class. Mathilde was to present the Danish version and Israh and Fartun should present the Arabic and Somali versions, respectively. That meant that Israh and Fartun would have to translate from Danish to Arabic and Somali once again on the spot as a written version of the poem only existed in Danish. Both Israh and Fartun refused to present the poem in Arabic and Somali. They did it in the end, but it took a considerable amount of persuasion from the teachers, accompanied by the other students present.

Personally, I experienced a "methodological rich moment" in the ethnography (Agar 1986) where the actions observed in the classroom did not meet my expectations at all. While experiencing the episode unfold in the class, I found it hard to understand what happened and what was at stake in the situation (cf. Jaffe-Walter 2013: 622). Why did the girls prefer to record the poem in advance? Why did the two girls with a minority background refuse to translate and perform the poem on the spot in Arabic and Somali? What made the teachers insist on the performance even though it seemed clear that the girls really did not want to carry out the task?

I will analyze the episode using the theory of registers and enregisterment (Agha 2003; 2007) combined with the theory of languaging (Jørgensen et. al. 2011) and discuss the possible patterns of identification (Brubaker 2004; Blommaert 2005) that could be behind the girls' reluctance to perform and the teachers' insistence that they do. Through micro-analyses of the interaction in central passages, I can obtain some answers to the questions above. At the same time, the episode reflects the valorization of minority languages at a level of societal discourse. In this chapter, I will combine observations of the enregisterment of "languages" as it unfolds in the classroom discourse with a discussion of the long-term enregisterment of minority languages in society at large.

Languaging and Enregisterment

The concept of languaging may be described as "the use of language by human beings, directed with an intention to other human beings" (Jørgensen & Møller 2014). This means that *languaging* practically covers all types of linguistic communication. Language is used in interaction to grasp, influence and shape the world (Jørgensen 2010) and the linguistic productions are always in some way designed to influence and make sense to the interlocutors just as interlocutors are occupied with the sense making of language use. Sometimes these processes of meaning making are carried out explicitly and, in the case sketched out above, the teachers not only ask the students to perform a specific type of languaging explicitly involving the use of different "languages", but also directly address how the linguistic production will affect the class. It is central in the theory of languaging that language use is *intentional* and that speakers are aware of this aspect of intentionality.

Another central element of languaging theory (cf. translanguaging, Garcia 2009) is that speakers use linguistic resources (and not "languages") as the fundamental elements in verbal communication. From a sociolinguistic perspective, there is no waterproof way to determine where one "language" begins and another "language" ends and there is no unambiguous way to determine when human beings "speak a language". From a linguistic perspective, it cannot be justified to claim that, for example, Danish and Norwegian are two different "languages" while e.g. West-Greenlandic and East-Greenlandic are two dialects of "the same language". When language users perceive categories such as Danish, Swedish, Serbian, French, English, Turkish, and so on, as fixed and delimitable language packages, this is not based in structural differences but rather on strong national ideologies. Ideas of languages as countable and separable from one another are *socio-cultural and socio-historical constructions* (Makoni &Pennycook 2006; Heller 2007). When I use terms for languages such as Arabic, Danish, etc. in this paper, it will be in this frame of understanding.

The problem of delimiting languages has obvious consequences for traditional ways of categorizing speakers as monolingual, bilingual, and so forth. In Copenhagen, a typical teenager will be familiar with expressions associated with a range of languages such as Danish, Norwegian, Swedish, English, French, German, Turkish and Arabic, and a range of adolescents will use the variability of available language in a range of different situations. Any threshold for when such adolescents can be said to "speak a language" must necessarily be arbitrary. But just as languages should be viewed as ideological constructions, so should language-based categorizations of speakers such as "native speaker of Danish", "bilingual", etc. Such labels must be treated as constructions rather than categories given in advance in sociolinguistic studies. The constructed relations between language, languages and groups of speakers become clearer when observed through the theoretical lens of registers and enregisterment (Agha 2007).

Viewing languages and their relations to speakers as socio-cultural and socio-historical constructions is in many ways similar to viewing them as registers in Agha' understanding of the term:

> A register formation is a reflexive model of behavior that evaluates a semiotic *repertoire* (or set of repertoires) as appropriate to specific types of conduct (such as the conduct of a given social practice), to classifications of persons whose conduct it is, and, hence, to performable roles (personae, identities) and relationships among them. (Agha 2007: 147, original emphasis.)

The theory of registers links the recognizable use of linguistic resources to interpersonal conduct, norms of situational use, and to metapragmatic classifications and evaluations of speech behavior. Situational language use is a social activity pointing to roles and personas. By using recognizable registers that index personas or stereotypes, speakers may construct identities. An important point for this paper is that speakers may also have an interest in not using linguistic resources associated with a particular register in order to avoid certain processes of identification.

Using registers in interaction necessarily involves the organization and evaluation of linguistic resources as well. The linguistic resources (in combination with other semiotic signs) associated with registers are by no means fixed just as their ascribed values are negotiable and situationally dependent and the formation of registers is an ongoing, never-ending process. Agha (2003; 2007) labels the process of registers becoming recognizable and meaningful among groups of speakers as enregisterment. These processes may involve societal discourses circulated over time in social space (cf. Agha 2003 on Received Pronunciation) and they may involve very local formations of shared ways of speaking associated with, for example, companies, youth groups, and so forth. What they have in common is that enregisterment always involves *socio-historically locatable practices* (Agha 2003: 232). The formation of registers and ascriptions of their value can take place simply through the frequency of use of certain linguistic resources in specific situations, and it may also take place in reflexive processes where attention is explicitly directed to the registers and their social implications.

The theories of enregisterment and languaging have in common that they view language use as fundamentally reflexive and language users as aware of the fact that language use involves processes of social positioning. On the basis of these theories, I can ask some more detailed questions for a microanalysis of the case introduced above:

1. How is the activity of performing the poem in minority languages described and evaluated by the different actors?
2. What values are ascribed to Arabic and Somali by the different actors in relation to the given social practice of presenting?
3. What possibilities for identification are situationally offered to Israh and Fartun?

However, before I turn to this analysis, I will introduce Israh's and Fartun's school and the class they attend, and I will first briefly discuss the connotations of the word "bilingual" in Danish society in recent years.

Being a "Bilingual" in the Danish School System

In a conference titled "More Languages = Valuable Resources" held at the University of Aarhus in 2012, the Danish translator and writer Thomas Harder captured the essence of how connotations of the term "bilingual" have changed in Denmark:

> In the last couple of years, Denmark has experienced the strange phenomenon [...] that the fine word 'bilingual' has changed to a more or less politically correct collective designation for a range of more or less serious problems with integration where only some of them are related to language. (Harder 2012, my translation.)

The essence of the "change" that Harder mentions is that bilingual (*tosproget* in Danish) was commonly used by researchers in the 1990s in public debate as a term replacing expressions like "immigrant children" in order to encourage a more positive view on children with a minority background in the public discourse with a particular focus on the children's linguistic resources. The researchers managed to establish the term but did not succeed concerning the more positive view. Politicians from both sides of the political spectrum have continuously treated bilingualism as a problem (see also e.g. Karrebæk 2013; Møller 2009; forthcoming), exemplified in the following quotes (my translations from Danish):

> Danish should be the mother tongue for everybody [in Denmark]. It is an illusion to think that one can integrate bilingual pupils if they don't learn Danish all the way through. (Brian Mikkelsen, Conservative People's Party, newspaper interview in *Berlingske Tidende*, 14th January 2000.)

> We cannot accept that Danish is only a second language. 80–90% of our bilingual pupils are born here [in Denmark] and that means that Danish is their mother tongue. (Svend Erik Hermansen, Social Democrats, newspaper interview in *Berligske Tidende*, 14th January 2000.)

> In Denmark, we speak Danish. One can learn all the languages one wants to, but that must be done in leisure time. It is not a public-sector assignment. (Inger Støjberg, Liberal Party (*Venstre*), newspaper interview in *Jyllandsposten* 18th August 2012.)

All three quotations are taken from debates on mother tongue tuition. All of them describe Danish language as what counts in Denmark and address bilingualism as problematic or unacceptable. A clear hierarchy of languages is established with Danish at the top and minority languages at the bottom. The first two quotes talk about "bilinguals" in connection to "integration" and to being "born here". This illustrates how the term "bilinguals" is commonly used as a cover term for descendants of immigrants from the Middle East, North Africa and more recently from Eastern Europe. Children with, for example, English, French, German or Scandinavian family background are generally not referred to as bilinguals. The quotes are chosen to illustrate the general tone in the political statements which tend to be rather harsh (see Taylor 2009 for discussion of the tone in statements from the Right Wing politicians in The Danish People's Party). Furthermore, they illustrate how the problematization of bilingualism in statements from politicians has not changed much over the last couple of decades. In 2002, for example, the political stance resulted in the abolition of state support for mother tongue tuition offered in the Danish public school system. Above, I described languages as socio-historical constructions. State regulations concerning access to learn particular "languages" and the continued description of "bilinguals" as a societal problem reminds us of the importance and very real impact on human's lives that these socio-historical constructions have (Holmen & Jørgensen 2010).

In the third example, the statement "In Denmark we speak Danish" is, of course, over-simplified. In the University of Copenhagen, Danish and English co-exist as officially accepted languages and the language is English in a range of workplaces in Denmark. Furthermore, with an immigrant population of around 20% in Copenhagen (Danmarks Statistik 2012), it is not possible to move around in the city without hearing other languages than Danish. It is not likely that Inger Støjberg (a high ranking member of parliament) who made the statement above does not know these things. In the light of this, the statement should rather be viewed as an ideological statement that metapragmatically typifies the use of Danish in a manner that departs from actual facts of language use in Denmark, thus formulating metapragmatic stereotypes of Danish usage that alter public frameworks of enregisterment. Inger Støjberg specifies a unique relation between a place ("Denmark"), a people ("we") and a speech register (Danish). Having a position at the absolute top of the Danish society, Inger Støjberg's statement potentially also adds an element of high status to the construction of the language-body-place connection (Quist 2010).

The central point here is that newspaper accounts like these ones tend to selectively reformulate public opinion on matters of language use. Being "bilingual" in Denmark is now formulated as a potential problem. The term "bilingual" further indicates that this problem is partly related to asymmetries of linguistic competence and differential practices of languaging. This is highly relevant for schools in the Copenhagen area and particularly for schools situated in ethnically heterogeneous areas such as the school where the girls involved in the situation described above are pupils. In a newspaper article titled "[School name] Has Started a Fight for a Better Reputation", the principal describes his vision for the school:

> the composition of students at the school should reflect the composition of people in the local community. And the first signs indicate that we are about to succeed. We get more children and they are more mixed ethnically and socially, and it looks like our share of bilinguals is going to be below 40 per cent. (Newspaper interview with the Principal, 25th February 2009, my translation.)

Behind the principal's vision is the concern that if some parents belonging to the Danish majority consider the percentage of "bilinguals" in a school to be too high and fear that this will lower its academic level, they may look for alternative schools for their children. In the Danish school system, it is possible for parents to choose a so-called "private" school instead of the public one located in their district. "Private" schools are still primarily publically funded, but the parents pay a monthly fee as well. There was a strong tendency of majority Danes to de-select the school where we worked in the mid-2000s, and the principal's statement should be viewed in this light.

The tendency of linguistic majority parents to de-select schools because of a high percentage of "bilinguals" illustrates the societal influence of mediatized discourse that formulate "bilingual" students as potentially causing problems for the majority. This being said, "bilinguals" are of course only one factor in the school's "reputation". In recent years, the school received a lot of positive media attention, for example, for being appointed a "health school", namely a school where a professional chef cooks healthy meals for the children's lunch with assistance from students from the upper grades.

In this section, I outlined some of the negative values ascribed to being "bilingual" in Denmark. This might explain partly why the girls do not want to use minority languages in class: because it involves identification with the "bilingual" stereotype. However, it does not explain why the girls wanted the performance of the poem to be carried out in three languages in the first place. I will return to this discussion after a sequentially based analysis of the particular episode.

Data and Analysis

In the so-called Amager-project (Madsen et. al. 2013; Madsen, this volume) a large group of researchers have carried out ethnographic fieldwork in and around the school since 2009. We have followed different groups of students over time in order to understand practices of everyday languaging as it takes place in an ethnically heterogeneous area of Copenhagen. The data that I use here are collected in a group that we followed from the 7th to the 9th grade. Data comes from a range of different settings such as school, leisure activities, family time and social media. The data consist of field diaries, video and sound-recordings, interviews, written school assignments, and so forth.

The particular class I focus on in this paper consisted of 20 students in the 8th grade, of whom 16 reported to have a mother tongue other than Danish. Eight students reported Arabic to be their mother tongue, four pupils said Urdu and/or Punjabi, and the languages Turkmen, Somali, Tagalog, and Farsi were represented by one student each. During our fieldwork in this class, the research group has not experienced general tendencies to conflicts between majority and minority Danes. This does not mean that linguistic and cultural diversity in the students' family backgrounds is not addressed. On a daily basis, students investigate and exploit diversities in a range of practices such as name calling, using "each other's" language, etc. (Møller 2010; Møller forthcoming). Minority languages are generally not used in regular classes in teacher controlled activities, but students may generally use all their linguistic resources in, for example, interaction with the person next to them without being stopped. The classroom can generally be described as a safe place with a supportive atmosphere among the students.

During the particular incident under discussion here, the 20 students, two teachers, and two researchers were present in the classroom. The teachers were Inger, the class teacher, and Janne, whom the students did not know as well. Both teachers were sitting in the back of the room. During the episode, Fartun and Israh were wearing radio-microphones and another recorder was placed on a table. This means that we were retrospectively able to capture the whispered conversation between the girls that we could not hear when the episode unfolded in class. After each presentation, the teachers left the classroom to discuss the presentation in solitude and returned to give their evaluation of the performance. There was an atmosphere of seriousness. In the situation, I was in charge of the recording equipment while my colleague Jens Normann Jørgensen was writing field notes. This is how he described the episode:

The girls have a poem (written by themselves?) in Arabic, Somali and Danish. Israh had the recording on her mobile, but can't find it. The teachers want her to read from the page. Some of the pupils join in. Israh says "I can't." Nobody buys it, but Inger has to put a lot of pressure on Israh to get her to read it aloud on the spot, which Israh does in the end. Thunderous applause. Fartun is not happy about reading aloud in Somali either. She says "I don't feel like doing it," but it does not sound like she is negative, only shy. Inger argues that nobody understands the Somali and that Fartun can say anything. Inger: "I just want to hear the tone in Somali". Therefore, according to Inger, it is risk-free to read aloud. Then she does it. Thunderous applause. At the end, Mathilde reads it in Danish. Hesitant applause. Inger asks her to read the whole poem again. Very hesitant applause from the class. (Excerpt of Jens Normann Jørgensen's field notes, 24 March 2010, author's translation.)

The field notes outline the chronology of the episode with a focus on the technical problems, the stretches of persuasion and the intensity of the applause from the girls' classmates. The applause illustrates the generally supportive atmosphere in the class and the louder applause after the performances in Arabic and Somali signals a positive reception which might be because their classmates acknowledge the good deal of self-conquest it took from Israh and Fartun to perform their poems.

The recording of the situation reveals that the main technical problem is that the girls cannot find the sound file on the school's intranet. The teachers then ask Israh if she still has it on her phone, which she does not. The use of technical equipment in the first place indicates that the girls want to include the polylingual poem performance in a way that they do not have to perform it directly in front of the class.

The field notes also pay particular attention to the way Inger convinces Fartun to read the poem in Somali. Inger argues that Fartun can safely do it because nobody understands it anyway. Inger actually succeeds in getting Fartun to perform. At the same time, Inger's line of argumentation explicitly addresses the value of Somali in the classroom and the reasons for making it a part of the performance. As we shall see from extracts of the recordings, this seemingly paradoxical observation is central in order to understand the situation: the teachers' main line of argumentation in order to convince the girls is that the girls should not take it too seriously and that others do not understand the languages anyway. I will return to this but first I will go through the episode as it unfolds in order to include some of the details revealed in the recordings.

The part of the presentation involving the poem is announced by Mathilde. Up to this point, the presentation has run relatively smoothly with the three girls taking turns reading aloud while presenting a visually creative PowerPoint show. From Mathilde telling the class that they are going to hear a poem until all three versions are read aloud lasts around ten minutes. I mention the time factor because the slow progression and the ensuing tension in the classroom indicates that the primary goal for the teachers, particularly when persuading Fartun, is to move the class out of the deadlock and back to the programme. This is a time-based chronological view of the episode divided into its central passages:

1. (0–1.21):	The three girls look for the sound file on the school computer while whispering together. There is muted talking in the rest of the class.
2. (1.21–2.50):	Mathilde informs the class that they cannot find the file and therefore only will read the poem in Danish. The teachers and then the rest of the class start giving advice on where to look on the computer. Mathilde and Israh keep looking. Inger asks questions for clarification in order to understand the technical aspects of the problem.
3. (2.50–3.40):	First Janne and then Inger ask Israh and Fartun if they can read the poem in front of the class as a plan B. Fartun says no and Israh says that it is difficult. Janne then says that Mathilde should just read the Danish version but Inger immediately dismisses this solution.
4. (3.40–5.36):	Inger insists that all the girls read the poem and appoints Israh to be the first. The teachers and an increasing number of students ask Israh to start. The pressure on Israh increases gradually (see excerpts 1–3 below).
5. (5.36–6.35):	Israh translates the poem from the Danish written version into Arabic.
6. (6.35–7.07):	Loud applause, followed by a student Isaam saying that he was moved by the poem. The class is silenced by Inger in order to pass the floor to Fartun, after which follows 6 seconds of silence.
7. (7.07–7.58):	Fartun says (giggling in a way I interpret as embarrassed) that she does not feel like doing it. Inger then tries to persuade her (excerpt 4 below).
8. (7.58–8.51):	Fartun translates the poem into Somali.
9. (8.51–9.04):	Loud applause, followed by a short introduction to the Danish version.
10. (9.04–10.02):	Mathilde reads the poem in Danish followed by more sporadic applause than the other readings. Mathilde is requested to read the poem a second time because Inger did not hear it all the first time around.

Viewing the episode in these passages makes it clear that a central turn happens between passage 3 and 4. In passage 1–3, Inger, the class teacher with the main authority, is struggling to find out what is happening in the presentation concerning the girls' general plans and their technical problems. It is evident from her questions in the situation that she did not know in advance that the girls would include the sound recording of the poem. From passage 4 onwards, Inger takes full control of the situation by insisting that the poem be read in Arabic and Somali and assigning Israh as the first presenter. Inger does this as a reaction to the other teacher's suggestion that only the Danish version should be read, and in spite of the girls' obvious aversion to translating the poem in front of the class. The negotiation of which path to take in the situation points to another central paradox: it is the girls themselves who wanted to include their multilingual capacity in the situation, but, as a result of changed conditions concerning the form of the presentation, they refrain from doing so. It is possible that, in this situation, Inger estimates that a small push will give the girls the satisfaction of sticking to their first plan and perhaps also wants to encourage Israh and Fartun to bring their home languages into play in the project. Inger has made her decision and sticks to it, no matter what; but, as it turns out, it is not easy to persuade the girls.

This leads to the question of why Israh and Fartun do not want to do it. In connection with her refusals, Israh says several times that it is difficult. Actually, the Danish version of the poem does contain several passages that could be potentially difficult to translate. So a possible explanation could be that the girls refuse because it is a technically difficult task. However, a look at the girls' actual performances shows that both of them are able to conduct high level translations of the poem. Israh's translation is precise and fluent without stops. Fartun leaves out a line from the Danish version and she stops one time, saying in Danish that she does not know the Somali word, but apart from that, she translates the poem fluently. The girls' performances indicate that it is not lack of linguistic competence that lies behind their rejection of the task.

To learn more about the girls' framing of the situation as it unfolds and about the enregisterment of Arabic and Somali usage, I will discuss passages 4 and 7, which are the passages where Israh and Fartun are (respectively) persuaded to carry out their tasks. The activity of persuading Israh consists of a range of short summons (actually more than 20) urging her to do it, with only one argument made by Janne in excerpt 3. The activity of persuading Fartun is done by Inger, and includes a rather detailed description of why Fartun should do it.

Excerpt 1 contains the whispered discussion between Fartun and Israh just after Inger insisted on them carrying out the translation:

Excerpt 1 (3.55-4.02) (transcription key in appendix)

1.	Fartun:	du begynder du begynder	you start you start *(whispering)*
2.	Israh:	[hold din kæft](>)	shut up *(whispering)*
3.	Fartun:	[du begynder Israh](<)	You start Israh *(whispering)*
4.	Inger:	prøv engang at gøre det	Just try to do it
5.	Israh:	jeg kan ikke det er svært	I can't do it it is difficult

In lines 1–3 Fartun and Israh started an argument over who should be first. Fartun "wins" when Inger appoints Israh to be the first in line 4. This short stretch of interaction illustrates how Israh verbally acts when interacting with classmates and the teachers respectively. When answering the teachers' request to carry on, Israh says that she cannot do it, and argues that it is difficult. When handling the classmates' demands, including when Fartun wants her to start, she is generally cursing and asking them to shut up in a whispered voice. In excerpt 2 we find an example of cursing:

Excerpt 2 (4.20-4.27)

| 1. | Inger: | så prøv lige at være stille I andre [i stedet for at komme] (>) med små kommentarer | would you mind being quiet the rest of you instead of giving small comments |

2.	Israh:	[inal abuuki] (<)	God curse your father *(low swearing in Arabic)*
3.	Israh:	jeg kan ikke (.)	I can't
4.	Israh:	jeg kan ikke finde ud af det	I can't figure it out

Israh expresses her frustration through a curse in Arabic in line 2 which is a linguistic practice we frequently observe (e.g. Ag 2010). The excerpt is another example of the pattern in which she refuses to translate the poem, and claims it is difficult when addressing the teachers, and simultaneously whispers a curse, which I interpret as whispered to herself because of her very low voice. The Arabic curse highlights that it is the activity of performing a school task in Arabic that she objects to – not the overall use of features associated with Arabic. Here it becomes clear that Israh views Arabic spoken as part of a presentation in front of teachers, classmates and researchers as a different register than curses in Arabic spoken to peers (for a similar description of how adolescents typify and revalorize other aspects of language use, see Madsen, this volume). At the same time, the curse reminds us that speakers use linguistic resources (and not languages understood as coherent systems) in their interaction. There are curses in Danish and curses in Arabic throughout the episode and these seem to reflect Israh's general stock of curses rather than being organized into "Arabic" curses and "Danish" curses. Again, Israh points to the task as being difficult by saying that she cannot figure it out (line 4). Seen in the light of her brilliant translation of the poem moments later, Israh's claim that it is difficult might be based in a social reluctance to do it, not on a lack of language proficiency. Anyway, the teachers cannot know that, and, in excerpt 3, Janne reacts to Israh's statement.

Excerpt 3 (4.30–4.45)

1.	Israh:	der er svære ord i jeg kan [ikke] (>)	there are difficult words in it I can't
2.	Janne:	[ja] (<)	yes
3.	Inger:	ja prøv at gøre [det så godt du kan] (>)	yes just try doing it as well as possible
4.	Janne:	[det har vi] (<) stor respekt for at der er jeg synes det kunne være rigtig flot hvis du prøver det er jo netop ikke en eksamen så alle mulige andre der måtte sidde der og synes de ved bedre de må jo (.) [bære over med situationen nu] (>) og have respekt for at du har mod til det	we have great respect for the fact that there is I think it would be really great if you try this is indeed not an exam so anybody who may think they know better they must (.) bear with the situation now and respect that you have the courage to do it
5.	Inger:	[de skal bare tie stille nu](<)	they should just be quiet now

In line 4, Janne points to two aspects of the situation: it is not an exam, and anyone wanting to comment negatively on the translation should refrain from doing so. Both remarks contribute to a specific framework of enregisterment for language use, though they do so indirectly. The first claim is probably intended to make Israh relax in the situation. At the same time, it is an example of the instances where teachers argue that the situation is not all that important, and so it is okay to use minority languages. This implies that in important situations in school, such as exams, minority languages are *not* relevant.

Janne also addresses the group of "anybody who may think they know better". This remark must necessarily be directed to the group of speakers of Arabic in the class. I do not hear anything specific on the recording that could trigger this remark. I interpret the remark as an attempt to secure Israh against intimidating remarks in advance and thereby making her feel more secure in the situation. Again, the remark indirectly corresponds to a framework of enregisterment: by assuming that the students who know Arabic will use this resource for negative purposes, Janne invokes a problem-oriented view of bilingualism, similar to the one described on a societal level above.

Janne's statement does not convince Israh right away. However, after a minute or more, when an increasing number of classmates (and not only Janne and Inger) have urged her to do it, Israh translates the poem, and her performance is followed by loud applause and the boy Isaam (of an Arabic speaking family background) says that he was moved by her performance. Right after this, Inger asks for silence in order to allow Fartun to present her poem. Notice that the excerpt begins with around 6 seconds of silence:

Excerpt 4: (7.01–7.58)

		(5.8)	
1.	Fartun:	jeg gider ikke	I don't feel like it
		(0.8)	
2.	Inger:	kom nu	come on *(decisive tone – several pupils laugh)*
		Fartun hop ud i det	Fartun jump into it
3.	Student:	xxx	xxx
4.	Inger:	kom så	come on *(talk in the background)*
5.	?:	ssh	shush
6.	Inger:	der skal være helt ro	there needs to be complete silence
		(13.2)	*(low whispering in the background)*
7.	Inger:	altså Fartun du kan bilde mig hvad som helst ind fordi jeg kan ikke somalisk så ved du hvad bare nogle lyde på somalisk	you know what Fartun you can make me believe anything because I don't know Somali so you know what just some sounds in Somali
8.	Boy:	bare sig [xxx](>)	just say xxx
9.	Inger:	[det ville være helt fint](<)	that would be just fine *(giggling in the background)*

10. Israh:	[Fartun](>)	Fartun
11. Inger:	[kom i gang] (.) så tag den derfra (.) og hvis du ikke ved et ord (.) så opfinder du det bare	get started (.) take it from there (.) and if you don't know a word (.) you just make it up
12. Student:	xxx	
13. Fartun:	okay	okay *(giggling)*
14. Student:	hun kan ikke forstå det	she can't understand it
15. Inger:	vi vil bare have den tone vi vil bare have sprogtonen (.) okay	we just want that tone we just want the language tone (.) okay
16. Fartun:	okay	okay
17. Inger:	du kan kalde det hvad det vil du kan sige det er en slikpind eller et eller andet altså på somalisk jeg ved det ikke (.) lad os så høre	you can call it anything you want you can say that it is a lollipop or something that is in Somali I don't know (.) let's hear it then
18. Israh:	hold din [kæft] (>)	good grief *(said low and giggling)*
19. Inger:	[ssh] (<)	shush
20. Israh:	det er [pinligt] (>)	this is embarrassing *(said low and giggling)*
21. Fartun:	[okay] (<)	okay
22. Inger:	ssh	shush

(Fartun performs the poem in Somali)

Whereas Israh denied the task verbally and claimed it was difficult, Fartun employs a strategy of complete silence. After the attempt to silence the class made by Inger in line 6 follows a pause of around 13 seconds. This pause triggers a longer persuasion attempt from Inger. This time, the persuasion attempt directly addresses the use of Somali. Fartun is the only speaker of Somali in the class. When Inger says in line 15, "we just want the language tone," the "we" most likely refers to the rest of the class including the teachers. She also highlights the fact that nobody else understands what Fartun is saying by stating that she can just "make up words" (line 11) or say "lollipop" (line 17). The strategy works in the sense that Inger manages to get Fartun to perform. From the probably toe-curling 13 seconds of silence (between line 6 and 7) she manages to create a joyful atmosphere in the class by addressing her own limited linguistic resources. At the same time she makes the purpose clear for Fartun which is to hear the sound of Somali and more specifically "the language tone". What consequences does this way of treating Somali have in terms of the enregisterment of Somali usage in class? Highlighting the fact that Fartun may as well say "lollipop" for all that matters in the class is another way of saying that Somali does not really serve any serious function in the classroom but rather should be viewed as exotic showcase material. In this sense the enregisterment of Somali as "sounds without meaning" locally leads to an exclusion of Fartun's linguistic competences at the same time as a friendly and jocular atmosphere is re-established in the class and the presentation is brought back on track.

A last point in relation to excerpt 4 is Israh's statements in line 18 ("good grief") and 20 ("this is embarrassing") which are put forward just before Fartun translates the poem into Somali. The statement is possibly a concrete reaction to Inger's statement including the "lollipop" advice and possibly an evaluation of the whole episode, in which Israh associates the use of Somali in front of the class with embarrassment.

Fartun's translation of the poem into Somali is received with loud applause by her classmates. After this, Mathilde reads out the Danish version. Inger asks Mathilde to repeat it because she missed the beginning and thereby underlines the obvious fact that Danish matters content-wise and the minority languages, including Arabic and Somali, do not.

Discussion

In the above episode, a group of girls wanted to include Arabic and Somali in their presentation, but when the conditions of presentation changed from playing a sound file to presenting poems individually, they strongly rejected the use of Arabic and Somali in the classroom. My analysis indicates that two of the girls were embarrassed to use their home languages in front of teachers and classmates. The teachers' treatment of minority languages in this situation, as well as common knowledge of mediatized political discourses that treat bilingualism as a societal problem, may account for this embarrassment. But this does not explain why the girls wanted to include minority languages in the first place. As was apparent from the recordings of this episode, the teachers were not prepared for this, and therefore the idea could not have come from them.

What should be remembered here is that the readings of the same poem in Arabic, Somali, and Danish was originally intended to be a creative element in the group's presentation of terrorism. The poem calls on peace and advocates for anti-terrorism (see appendix). Their PowerPoint presentation focuses particularly on terrorism conducted by Islamic groups and in this sense their peace poem conducted in Arabic, Somali, and Danish could be viewed as encouraging international and intercultural communication. When the sound file went missing, the girls were forced to perform not as a group but on an individual basis. The local values of "their languages" thus came to be in focus in their presentation rather than the role that the poem as a whole was intended to play in their collective presentation on terrorism. Arabic was treated by the teachers as potentially problematic because of the group of students who understands Arabic, Somali as an exotic showcase, and Danish as the language that mattered content-wise.

The poem's meaning or its potential significance for their group presentation on terrorism was not touched upon in the teachers' evaluation of the performance. This is perhaps not surprising. Several times during the episode, the teachers tried to tone down the seriousness of the situations involving Arabic and Somali. An explanation for this might be that the teachers were taken by surprise several times during the episode. At a certain point, their means of regaining control and getting the string of presentations back on track was to get the poem reading activity done as fast as possible. Probably in order to make the girls relax, the teachers downplayed the importance of the performance related to minority languages. However, the strategy also simultaneously reconstructed the minority languages as registers of low value and importance in the classroom and, by implication, in Danish society. In this sense, the teachers' response interfaced with societal discourses about "bilinguals", with which their remarks are consistent, thereby adding to an on-going enregisterment of these minority languages. This being said, Inger probably insisted on the girls' performance in Arabic and Somali with the intention of letting the students' diverse resources be brought into play in class. The teachers could not have predicted that the girls would refuse the way that they did, and that they would react with unconsidered or "instinctive" responses.

To sum up, the case has illustrated how the three girls exploited their different linguistic backgrounds to produce a shared creative poem in connection with a school assignment. In their handling of the situation the teachers treated the involved languages as distinct where they could have viewed them as a joined statement. The analysis has shown how the teachers pointed to Danish as academically important in the classroom and Arabic and Somali as non-academic and more of a resource for entertainment. I have illustrated how enregisterment can occur explicitly though probably unintentionally when teachers deal with situations involving minority languages in classrooms containing students with diverse linguistic backgrounds. Thus the case points to the need for a critical and reflective approach to concepts of languages when dealing with young students in order to prevent backbone reactions reflecting (and co-constructing) large-scale constructions of language hierarchies and monolingual ideologies.

The Girls' poem translated from Danish into English

> They talk about stuff they make up themselves
> Wear dark makeup – blow up bombs
> Some commit suicide but they take way too many with them
> To respect each other's faith and way of living is important if the world shall not become black
> One thing is for certain and that is that terror needs to be stopped
> Otherwise we will forget that happiness ever existed
> Our religion has the right to decide to decide but does it need to develop a nuclear war
> One day their strength will fail and terrorism will end

Note

1   When the episode unfolded I was present with my colleague Professor Jens Normann Jørgensen. Unfortunately Jens got sick before we got around to writing about the episode together, and in spring 2013 he passed away after a year-long battle with cancer. While he was still active, he used this case in several workshop discussions as a significant example of the influence that the enregisterment of minority languages in Denmark potentially has on people's lives. This article is written in honour of Normann – a great scholar, supervisor, colleague, and friend!

Appendix: Transcription Key

(1.0)	pauses in seconds
(.)	pauses shorter than 0.5 second
[hey you](>)	
[hey man](<)	brackets encloses overlapping speech, arrows indicate what is said simultaneously
( )	encloses my comments
xxx	inaudible

References

Ag, Astrid 2010. *Sprogbrug og identitetsarbejde hos senmoderne storbypiger*. Københavnerstudier i Tosprogethed 53. København; Københavns Universitet.
Agar, M. 1986. *Speaking of Ethnography*. London: Sage.
Agha, Asif 2003. The Social Life of Cultural Value. *Language and Communication* 23: 231–273.
Agha, Asif 2007. *Language and Social Relations*. Cambridge: Cambridge University Press.
Blommaert, Jan 2005. *Discourse: A Critical Introduction*. Cambridge: Cambridge University Press.
Brubaker, Rogers 2004. *Ethnicity without Groups*. Cambridge: Harvard University Press.
Danmarks Statistik 2012. Indvandrere i Danmark 2012, Danmarks Statistik. Available at: www.dst.dk/publ/indvandrereidk

García, Ofelia 2009. Education, Multilingualism and Translanguaging in the 21st Century. In *Multilingual Education for Social Justice: Globalising the Local*. Ed. Ajit Mohanty, Minati Panda, Robert Phillipson & Tove Skutnabb-Kangas. New Delhi: Orient Blackswan. Pp. 128–145

Harder, Thomas 2012. Sprogkundskaber er værdifulde ressourcer. Lecture delivered at the conference "Flere sprog = værdifulde ressourcer", Aarhus Universitet, Arhus, Denmaek, 25th October 2012, published on-line at: http://www.thomasharder.dk/da/node/122.

Heller, Monica 2007. Bilingualism as Ideology and Practice. In *Bilingualism: A Social Approach*. Ed. Monica Heller. London/Hampshire: Palgrave Macmillan. Pp. 1–24.

Holmen, Anne & J. Normann Jørgensen 2010. Sprogs status i Danmark 2010. In *Sprogs status i Danmark 2021*. Ed. Jørgensen, J. Normann & Anne Holmen. Københavnerstudier i Tosprogethed 58. Copenhagen: University of Copenhagen. Pp. 5–16.

Jaffe-Walter, Reva 2013. "Who Would They Talk about If We Weren't Here?": Muslim Youth, Liberal Schooling, and the Politics of Concern. *Harvard Educational Review* 83(4): 613–635.

Jørgensen, J. Normann 2010. *Languaging: Nine Years of Poly-Lingual Development of Young Turkish-Danish Grade School Students* I–II. Copenhagen Studies in Bilingualism, the Køge Series K15–16. Copenhagen: University of Copenhagen.

Jørgensen, J. Normann, Martha Karrebæk, Lian Malai Madsen & Janus Spindler Møller 2011. Polylanguaging in Superdiversity. *Diversities* 13(2): 23–38.

Jørgensen, J. Normann & Janus Spindler Møller 2014. Polylingualism and Languaging. In *The Routledge Companion to English Studies*. Ed. C. Leung & B. V. Street. New York: Routledge. Pp. 67–83.

Karrebæk, Martha Sif. 2013. "Don't Speak Like that to Her!": Linguistic Minority Children's Socialization into an Ideology of Monolingualism. *Journal of Sociolinguistics* 17(3): 355–375.

Madsen, Lian Malai, Martha Karrebæk & Janus Spindler Møller 2013. The Amager Project: A Study of Language and Social Life of Minority Children and Youth. Tilburg Papers in Cultural Studies 52. Available at: http://www.tilburguniversity.edu/research/institutes-and-research-groups/babylon/tpcs/

Makoni, Sinfree & Alastair Pennycook (eds.) 2006. *Disinventing and Reconsituting Languages*. Clevedon, Avon: Multilingual Matters.

Møller, Janus Spindler 2009. Poly-Lingual Interaction across Childhood, Youth and Adulthood. Ph.D. dissertation. University of Copenhagen.

Møller, Janus Spindler (forthcoming). "You Black Black": Polycentric Norms for the Use of Terms Associated with Ethnicity. In *Wasted Language: Super-Diversity and the Sociolinguistics of Interstices*. Ed. K. Arnaut, M. Spotti & M. S. Karrebæk. Clevedon, Avon: Multilingual Matters.

Quist, P. 2010. Untying the Language, Body and Place Connection: Linguistic Variation and Social Style in a Copenhagen Community of Practice. In *Language and Space: An International Handbook of Linguistic Variation* I. Ed. Peter Auer & Jürgen Erich Schmidt. Berlin: Mouton de Gruyter. pp. 632–648.

Taylor, Shelley K. 2009. Right Pedagogy/Wrong Language and Caring in Times of Fear? – Issues in the Schooling of Ethnic Kurdish Children in Denmark. *International Journal of Bilingual Education and Bilingualism* 12(3): 291–307.

Lian Malai Madsen

5. Investigating a Register Label
Integrated Speech in Copenhagen

Naming and labelling are key means of constructing linguistic codes. The understanding that certain speech practices and linguistic forms belong together requires taxonomic labels in the first place (Makoni 2012), and the metapragmatic labels we attach to such practices contribute significantly to their social enregisterment by hinting at indexical links between speech repertoires, typical speakers, social-interpersonal relationships and associated forms of conduct (Agha 2007: 145). Since giving names to speech practices is far from a trivial endeavor, recent sociolinguistic discussions have increasingly been concerned with research on the political and ideological aspects of professionals' metalinguistic labelling (e.g. Jaspers 2008; Jørgensen 2008; Heller 2007). But we can also learn a lot about speakers' sociolinguistic understandings by investigating register labels as participant practices.

The focus of this chapter is on such participant labelling. I aim to discuss the emergence (and change) of sociolinguistic structure and ideology by drawing on linguistic ethnographic data from a Copenhagen based collaborative research project (Madsen, Karrebæk & Møller 2015). In metalinguistic accounts given by the participants in our study, speech practices associated with respect, politeness, up-scale culture and academic skills are labelled "integrated" (Madsen 2013). In this chapter, I investigate the meaning contributed by the label "integrated" to the ongoing enregisterment of speech differences (Agha 2007) among urban Danish youth, and the meaning shift involved in the use of this term as a name for a conservative standard register. Before explaining how we came across this notion of integrated speech and the empirical context of its use, I briefly outline the theoretical approach to registers informing my work. After this, I discuss the history of use of the notion of "integrated" in Danish public discourse and how it relates to the particular usage we find in our field site. I illustrate this usage with examples from our data, and finally, I discuss the wider social and sociolinguistic implications of the reinterpretation of the term "integrated" and the corresponding reanalysis of standard linguistic practices that we witness in our data. The data that I present point to interconnections between cultural and ethnic diversity and dimensions of hierarchical stratification in the contemporary sociolinguistic order(ing) of speech behaviors among Copenhagen youth.

Enregisterment and Indexical Order

It is well documented in recent research on linguistic and cultural diversity that speakers in practice draw on their collective linguistic repertoires as resources to achieve communicative aims in a given situation, a fact also evident in the linguistic practices we observe among contemporary urban youth. Studies in such contexts have led to re-examinations of the traditional conceptions of a "language" or a "variety of language" as bounded sets of linguistic features. It has become clear that such concepts are representations of particular language ideologies (Jørgensen et al. 2011; Blackledge & Creese 2010) and sociolinguistics with inspiration from linguistic anthropology increasingly sees linguistic codes as socio-cultural and ideological constructions. Asif Agha's theory of enregisterment appeals to this kind of approach to language with its emphasis on "processes and practices whereby performable signs become recognized" as belonging to semiotic registers associated with particular values, users and types of situations (Agha 2003; 2007), and this approach has been widely employed and discussed in sociolinguistic research in recent years (e.g. Johnstone, Andrus & Danielson 2006; Newell 2009; Madsen et. al 2010). Enregisterment accounts for the processes through which linguistic registers are constructed, and takes into consideration metapragmatic activities on various levels ranging from widely circulating media stereotypes to local speaker practices.

The dialectics between situated metapragmatic activities and wider sociolinguistic processes is central to the discussion of "integrated" as a speech label. Michael Silverstein (2003) explains the dialectic relation between such micro-social and macro-social frames of analysis with the concept of indexical order. Distinct indexical orders can be seen as stages within a process of enregisterment. According to Silverstein, any sociolinguistic phenomenon can develop from a first order indexical stage, that is, from an identifiable and "presupposed" pattern of usage of particular linguistic forms, including a normative sense of their appropriate use and users (Silverstein 2003: 193). Since sociolinguistic change entails that new indexical links, when they are widely established, can become new first orders for subsequent change, Silverstein refers to this first order stage in a general sense as "n-th order indexicality". The sociolinguistic pattern of linguistic forms and usage makes linguistic forms available for more or less conscious social work and style shifting: "[...] within the n-th order ethno-metapragmatic perspective, this creative indexical effect is the motivated realization, or performable execution, of an already constituted framework of semiotic value" (Silverstein 2003: 194), and, finally, the noticing of such stylistic variation can result in the linguistic features becoming the topic of overt metapragmatic commentary. Thereby, speakers' contextual, ideology-invested, and sometimes creative, usage adds to and possibly transforms indexical links (Silverstein refers to this as $n + $1st indexical order) with the potential of becoming new sociolinguistic presuppositions. Hence, situated language use and metapragmatic activities are significant to studies of wider sociolinguistic change: the "dialectical effect of micro-realtime indexicality must therefore constitute a major vectorial force in formal linguistic change" (Silverstein 2003: 194). A concrete example that can illustrate first and second order indexicality is the "contemporary urban vernacular" (Rampton 2011) in Copenhagen, which is related to the integrated speech that I investigate here. At a first order indexical stage, linguistic signs such as vocabulary from Turkish, Kurdish and Arabic combined with non-standard grammar and non-standard prosody could index second-language speakers of Danish and thereby speakers with an immigrant background. More recently, however, these signs have become enregistered as a contemporary speech style associated with urban youth, cultural diversity and toughness more generally. I shall further suggest that the current enregisterment of the contemporary urban vernacular is closely related to the relabeling of standard linguistic practices as well. It involves a new ($n + 1$st) order of indexicality which implies a contrasting relation to a standard register and a distinct social status of speaker. To follow this argument, it is now necessary to turn to the data and the notion of integrated.

Discovering "Integrated"

From 2009 to 2011, we conducted a collaborative study of linguistic practices in the everyday life of 48 grade-school children and adolescents in a Copenhagen public school (Madsen et. al 2013). The overall focus of our research was to understand how language patterns and language norms are acquired, developed, and used in various everyday contexts. Most of the participants had a linguistic minority background and lived in a highly diverse area of the Danish capital. In the two grade-school classes that we studied, the percentage of students with a minority background was 75 and 82 percent. Over 3 years, we conducted team-ethnographic fieldwork, and collected data in a number of different settings: in school during classes and breaks, in youth clubs, at sports practice, in the local neighborhood, and in participants' homes. The data include field diaries, largely unstructured qualitative interviews with participants in groups and individually, as well as interviews with teachers, parents, and club workers. We have also recorded different kinds of conversations, both those initiated by researchers and participants' self-recordings. In addition, we have collected written data in the form of protocols, student essays and Facebook interactions.

The first round of interviews was carried out about 5 months into our first year of fieldwork. The adolescents were invited to come to the university in groups that they formed themselves, and we talked to them in one of our offices. These interviews were ethnographic and semi-structured. In all of these interviews, we went through certain topics such as groups of friends in the class, leisure activities and language, but we attempted to let participants lead the conversation in directions of their own choosing. The researcher usually initiated the topic of language by asking "in what way" or "how" the participants talked in various contexts (for instance with teachers, with friends, in the youth club, etc.). During some of the first interviews, the participants introduced labels for different ways of speaking, and one of these was the term *integreret* ['integrated']. This way of using the term was new to us when we began our fieldwork.

Integration in Public Discourse

The term *integrated* has a particular history of use in Danish public discourse that is related to the notion of integration into Danish society. It has overwhelmingly been employed in dominant macro-discourses on integration to describe minorities adapting themselves to a majority society (e.g. Rennison 2009; Olwig & Pærregaard 2007), and such integration discourses have predominantly been concerned with cultural minorities. During the 1980s and 1990s, attention to problems related to immigration increased in Danish public debate, where the notion of integration has been very prominent since the mid-1990s (Olwig & Pærregaard 2007: 18). In 2002, the government even established a distinct Ministry of Integration. The government of 2011–2014 closed down this ministry and instead immigration and integration are dealt with in other ministries, such as the Ministry of Law and the Ministry of Social Affairs. Although the Ministry of Integration has been reestablished (2015), it certainly changed the official political texts about integration, and it is rather unclear what precisely the concept of integration refers to in the general debate as well as in much research on integration (Ejrnæs 2002). In fact, Bettina Wolfgang Rennison (2009) identifies eight different discourses on diversity related to the integration debate in Denmark (with a complete assimilationist understanding as one extreme, and a human rights understanding as the other). Still, by far the most dominant such discourse of the past decade in Danish media and political debates is an ethnocentric discourse on diversity (Yilmaz 1999: 180–181; Rennison 2009: 120–158). The ethnocentric discourse emphasizes values related to culture. Cultural differences are understood within the frames of stereotypical ideas of "us" and "them", and the "us" is imagined as a coherent cultural and national community (Rennison 2009: 128–131; Yilmaz 1999). The ethnocentric discourse on integration is not an exclusively Danish phenomenon, but characteristic of public debate and policy-making in a range of Western European countries (e.g. Blommaert & Verschueren 1998; Yilmaz 1999; Jaspers 2005; Extra et. al 2009). Because of its history of use in the Danish context, the term *integrated* carries traces of an association with minorities adapting themselves to mainstream Danish cultural practices.

Excerpt 1 below makes clear that this understanding of integration is also relevant to the everyday interactional conduct of the participants in our study. The excerpt is from a self-recording by Bashaar in the youth club. Bashaar calls for the other participants' attention to tell them about a new rap song he is working on with Mahmoud in their rap group Mini G's.

Excerpt 1. Self-recording in the youth club by Bashaar (Bas); Mahmoud (Mah); Israh (Isr); Selma (Sel)

1.	Bas:	ew har I hørt vores nye	ew have you heard our new
2.		omkvæd mig og	chorus me and
3.		Mahmoud (det har han ikke)	Mahmoud (he hasn't)
4.		vi skal	we are
5.		lave en sang i Mini G's	making a new song in Mini G's
6.		den handler	it's about
7.		om integration	integration
8.		(vi siger sådan der)	(we go like)
9.	Isr:	hvis det er jer der har lavet	if it's you who made it
10.		den [så er den dårlig]	[then it's bad]
11.	Sel:	[lad være med at]	[don't]
12.		spille integreret	play integrated
13.	Bas:	(vi siger sådan der)	(we go like)
14.		endnu en fremmed (.)	another stranger (.)
15.		hun er bare en fremmed (.)	she's just a stranger (.)
16.		hun er en dansker	she's a Dane
17.		på Nørrebro ((synger)) (.)	in Nørrebro ((sings)) (.)
18.		gi'r det ikke	doesn't that
19.		mening?	make sense?
20.	Mah:	næ:	no:

Bashaar calls for the others to listen to the chorus of their new song and includes the information that the song is about integration. The concept of integration as a process of adaptation involving minority and majority relations is clearly relevant to the lyrics of the rap song. Towards the end of the excerpt, Bashaar performs the chorus and, by referring to a "dansker" ['Dane'] in "Nørrebro" (an area of Copenhagen known for its highly ethnically diverse population) as a "fremmed" ['stranger'], the boys turn the stereotypical societal discourse upside down. A different meaning of integrated is at play in Selma's teasing comment before this. In the expression "play integrated", integrated is employed as a derogative term and in this combination it invokes elements of fakeness. This is also a regular usage of the notion of integrated among the participants in our study. They use the term to point out behavior of peers that is regarded as uncool, fake or overly adapted to adult, mainstream or school-related models (see Madsen 2011; 2013). Excerpt 1 is an example of how the terms *integration* and *integrated* are used in senses corresponding to the widespread understanding of integration as the process whereby minorities adapt themselves to cultural practices of the majority. This meaning is actively employed, brought about and co-exists with the use of *integrated* as a term for a way of speaking which expands and transforms its minority-majority related meaning, as we shall see.

Integrated Speech

In the interviews and essays we collected, integrated speech was mainly presented as the way of speaking to adults, especially to (and by) teachers. In excerpt 2 Lamis emphasizes relatively complex and abstract vocabulary as an important feature of the integrated register and Selma's stylized performance of such speech (marked in Italics) also reveals other associated values:

Excerpt 2. Lamis (Lam) in group interview with Selma (Sel);
Yasmin (Yas); Tinna (Tin); Interviewer (Lia)

1.	Lia:	hvad taler I så med	then what do you speak with
2.		lærerne i skolen	the teachers at school
3.	Lam:	integreret	integrated
4.	Sel:	integreret	integrated
5.	Lia:	[integreret]	[integrated]
6.	Sel:	[*vil du*] *gerne bede om*	[*would you*] *like to have*
7.		*en kop te* hhh	*a cup of tea* hhh
		((forvrænget lys stemme))	((shrieky high pitched voice))
8.	Lam:	hhh nej der bruger man de	hhh no there you use all those
9.		der integrerede ord	integrated words
10.	Sel:	der [prøver xxx]	there [tries xxx]
11.	Lam:	[nogle gange] nogle gange	[sometimes] sometimes
12.		når jeg har trip	when I trip out
13.		over lærerne så taler jeg	about the teachers then I speak
14.		det der	that
15.		gadesprog	street language
16.	Lia:	hvad øh kan du give	what eh can you give
17.		eksempler på integreret	examples of integrated
18.	Yas:	[integration]	[integration]
19.	Sel:	[sådan der] [*hvad*] *laver du*	[like] [*what*] *are you doing*
20.	Lam:	[int]	[int]
21.	Yas:	hhh	hhh
22.	Sel:	*har du haft en god dag*	*have you had a nice day*
		((forvrænget lys stemme))	((shrieky high pitched voice))
23.	Lam:	nej nej nej ikke sådan noget	no no no nothing like that
24.		ikke sådan noget	nothing like that
25.		sådan noget hvor	more like where
26.		de kommer med	they come out with
27.		[rigtig rigtig]	[really really]
28.	Sel:	[*god weekend*]	[*have a nice weekend*]
		((forvrænget lys stemme))	((shrieky high pitched))
29.	Lam:	rigtig svære ord	really difficult words
30.	Yas:	mm	mm
31.	Sel:	sådan der rigtig	like this really
32.	Lam:	(.) nej nej [nej]	(.) no no [no]
33.	Sel:	'[ube]høvlet' hhh	'[im]pertinent' hhh
		((dyb stemme))	((deep voice))
34.	Lam:	ja hhh [og sådan der]	yes hhh [and like that]
35.	Lia:	[det lyder rigtigt]	[it sound really]
36.	Lam:	'det så uaccep[tabelt Lam]'	'it's so unaccep[table Lam]'
37.	Yas:	[ja men også]	[yes but also]

When the girls are asked how they speak to their teachers, they claim to speak integratedly. An exception to this may occur when they are angry with the teachers or "trips out" about something, as Lamis puts it. In such situations "street language" may be used (a contemporary urban vernacular in the sense of Rampton 2011; see also Madsen 2013). Selma demonstrates throughout the sequence, integrated speech with a stylized performance marked by a shrieky, high-pitched voice. In her performance, she emphasizes politeness with ritual phrases such as *have a nice day, have a nice weekend*, and *would you like to have some tea?* The politeness, the tea offer, and the high-pitched shrieky voice bring about stereotypical associations of upper-class cultural practices. Lamis underlines so-called "difficult words" as the significant trait of integrated speech, and Selma supports with the example of "impertinent". Because it is exemplified with words like "impertinent" and "unacceptable", integrated speech is related to reprimands or corrections of behavior typically performed by authority figures. So, integrated speech appears associated with authority, control and aversion to rudeness, and also to be combined with ritual politeness and upper-class cultural practices. More generally, when examples of vocabulary are presented in the interview accounts and in the written essays, academic activities, complex and abstract adjectives and ritual politeness are emphasized in addition to vocabulary related to corrections of behavior (Madsen 2013). With respect to the stylizations in excerpt 2, it is worth noting that the performance of integrated speech is accompanied by quite a bit of ridicule in the girls' representations. This is detectable, for instance, in the change of voice and in the laughter following the examples of difficult words. In this manner, the girls present a certain distance from this register.

When the participants had mentioned integrated as a way of speaking, we elaborated by asking the adolescents about who spoke this way. Most of them mentioned teachers, and initially, also the ethnic Danes among them as typical users. After further discussion, it turned out that in most cases their Danish classmates did not actually use many "difficult words". However, it seemed that, to the minority students participating in our study, the integrated register was also partly associated with Danish ethnicity: "But one usually uses the integrated language with teachers or other adults. It's to talk very beautifully and try to sound as Danish as possible" (Mark, 15, minority background, written essay 2).

However, not all of the participants regarded integrated as predominantly a Danish register. In her essay, Lamis presents an understanding of integrated as disassociated from the idea of a specific national language. Instead, speaking integrated seems related to stylistic adjustments:

> But slang and integrated are also important, because there are some people who cannot tolerate listening to slang, then you have to be able to talk to them so that they are comfortable. But slang and integrated are not just in one language, but they are in English, Danish, Arabic, and all languages there exist. :D (Lamis, written essay 1.)

In a few of the essays, we also find accounts of the use of "integrated Arabic": "but with my parents [I] speak integrated Arabic, like polite" (Fadwa, 15, minority background, written essay 2), or:

> With my family I speak completely integrated/normal Arabic but when I speak to my cousins it is street language Arabic. When I speak to my family: I speak normal Arabic to my family, I also speak integrated Arabic to show respect. (Jamil, 15, minority background, written essay 2.)

In addition, some of the participants referred to Urdu as "the integrated Punjabi". Finally, it is worth noting that several of the students of majority background also describe in their essays "integrated Danish" as a register relevant to their everyday encounters particularly with elderly adults and teachers. This listing of rules of language by a girl of Danish heritage is an example:

> Speak integrated to people you need to show respect to
> Speak normal to your relatives
> Speak normal/street language to your school friends
> Speak integrated to elderly people to show respect
> (Marie, 15, majority background, written essay 2.)

These observations suggest that "integrated" practices seem to be undergoing reinterpretation. The term *integrated* carries traces of an association with minorities adapting to mainstream Danish cultural practices (as sketched above). Here, however, we see *integrated* reinterpreted as describing conservative standard practices (respectful, polite, up-scale) in a more general sense. In its use among these adolescents, the term is not tied exclusively to the "foreigner" and "Dane" categorizations typical of dominant integration discourses, even though it may include an ironic reference to these discourses. In fact, there is an account in the written essays which explicitly links successful integration ("well integrated") to high socio-economic status ("rich"):

> Integrated can be used by everyone, by and large, but if one speaks integrated language one is considered polite, rich, well-integrated person because people who speak integrated are like that. (Isaam, 15, minority background, written essay 2.)

From the overt metalinguistic reflections presented in the interviews and essays, we can see that there is an awareness among these Copenhagen adolescents of a register labelled "integrated". The enregisterment of this way of speaking involves accounts or demonstrations of:

> Performable signs:
> distinct pronunciation, abstract and academic vocabulary (long, posh words), high pitch, quiet and calm attitude, ritual politeness phrases
>
> Stereotypic indexical values:
> higher class culture (wealth), sophistication, authority, emotional control and aversion to rudeness, academic skills, politeness and respect, (Danishness)
> (See further Madsen 2013; Madsen et al. 2010; Møller & Jørgensen 2013.)

In addition, the ethnographic study suggests that presenting the integrated register as an available linguistic resource is part of a social school-positive practice, and emphasizing distance from this register is part of a practice more resistant to the school institution (Madsen 2013). A range of varied cultural practices have been drawn into these overt evaluations of integrated speech: ways of orienting to academic skills, ways of engaging with emotions, and with typical interlocutors. In fact, the associations of the integrated register seem to map onto value ascriptions that allow us to link integrated practices to the value-system that previous Danish sociolinguistic studies associate with "conservative Copenhagen" and school-related standard ideology, where excellence is perceived in relation to "superiority" (Kristiansen 2009: 189) and associated with values of intelligence, articulation, ambition, independence, rationality and conscientiousness. And the participants in our study label the speech that indexes these values "integrated".

The Wider Currency of Integrated as Speech Practices

We have seen that in this empirical context a traditionally recognizable way of speaking (standard Danish) has been given a new name. But how wide is the currency of this meaning of *integrated*? A google search (January 2014), in fact, predominantly results in a couple of linguists' recent descriptions of integrated speech (inspired by our own research), and when we first encountered this metalinguistic label in 2009 it certainly seemed a new notion. However, a recent comedy sketch show, *Det slører stadig* ['It Still Veils'] from 2013, broadcast on the national television channel DR2, suggests that integrated speech is by now a more widespread concept. DR2 is targeted at adults, but the sketches from the show have been circulated widely through social media among children and youth (Hyttel-Sørensen 2015). Contrasting speech styles play a central part in several of the sketches on this show. In particular, the Copenhagen version of a contemporary urban vernacular (also referred to by the participants in our study as "slang" or "street language") is a key feature in the construction of the character of Latifah, a young woman who dresses in tracksuit bottoms and large hooded sweatshirts, and wears heavy make-up, a gold chain and large earrings. In several ways she represents an image of a tough streetwise urban female gang member, and consistently speaks in a style which is referred to as "gangster language" within the frame of the show. This style is characterised by several of the features described by linguists as characteristic of the contemporary urban vernacular (Madsen 2013). In her search for achieving more power, Latifah interviews different societal gatekeepers, for instance, professors, politicians and a police officer. The speech of the Latifah character contrasts with the standard speech of the people she interviews, and in two of the sketches, standard and academic speech is specifically referred to as "integrated". One example is an interview with a professor of management philosophy. She stops him after he delivers a sequence of heavy academic and theoretical explanations and asks him to speak "ik så integeret men bare lidt almindeligt dansk" ['not so integrated but just a little ordinary Danish']. Another example is a special Latifah episode of the show where she is on a quest to become more integrated and, as part of this quest, visits a professor of Danish language to learn to "tale integreret" ['speak integrated'].

The show invokes a relatively sophisticated metapragmatic discourse in comparison to earlier media examples of linguistic parodies of contemporary youth speech, which tended to typify such speech as simply "the language" of young minority gangster types. In one of the program's sketches, the actor who plays the role of Latifah is portrayed as a student (wearing jeans, cardigan, subtle make-up and large glasses) who talks to a fellow student (a young blond female) about particle physics in a standard and highly academic register. However, when her mobile phone suddenly rings, she switches into the "gangster" register associated with the Latifah persona, thus bringing the "gangster" way of speaking into sharp contrast with the academic register. The humor of this sketch builds on a dramatic shift in registers by a single speaker, as well as on the clash in stereotypical associations between the street speech used and the academic look of the character. In this way, the comedy show invokes a view of the contemporary urban vernacular as a stylistic resource that can be used flexibly, and by speakers who also command standard and sophisticated academic registers. It parodies and exaggerates both the youth register and the standard register, and it plays on the contrast between them. Moreover, it refers to the standard speech as "integrated", and specifically links "speaking integrated" to the more traditional meaning of integration as social adaptation. Thus integrated as a register label has made the move "from the streets to the screen" (Androutsopoulos 2001) and the indexical meanings associated with the register formulated as "integrated" in the comedy show correspond to those described by adolescents in the oral metapragmatic data we collected in 2009–2011. Likewise, the contrast between the integrated speech and the contemporary youth register that is exploited for humorous effects on the television show corresponds to contrastive metapragmatic descriptions given by adolescents (Madsen 2013). This contrast is illustrated in several excerpts from interviews and essays above, where "slang" or "street language" is described as suitable in some situations and "integrated" in others.

It is worth noting that the television show is framed overall as concerned with minority–majority relations. It is an explicit aim of the program to make fun of cultural stereotypes about both minority people (and stereotypical Moslem personae in particular) and majority people (stereotypical Danish personae). This framing contributes to an understanding of the gap between everyday vernacular speech and standard integrated speech as particularly relevant for cultural and ethnic minorities. In this way, the notion of integrated speech in the parodies of the television show involves a stronger association with Danish (in contrast to an ethnic minority speech style) than the understanding of *integrated* as a stylistic dimension across different national languages that we see when the participants refer to "integrated Arabic".

Meaning Potentials and Sociolinguistic Ideologies

Registers are created, maintained and sometimes transformed through communicative practice (Agha 2003; 2007; Silverstein 2003). I have addressed different types of metapragmatic commentary among the participants in our study such as characterizations of speech in interviews, descriptions in essays, performed stylizations, and, especially, practices of labeling. I have shown how *integrated* as a speech label has recently been mediatized and taken up in television comedy. I argue that these metapragmatic activities suggest a development of the register. It is clear from the data that I have discussed that the term *integrated* has several meaning potentials. It is used to refer to processes of minorities adapting to mainstream society in a sense that is equivalent to its typical use in public discourse, but it is also used to refer to forms of adaptation in a more general sense, often with derogatory connotations of fakeness among young peers. Finally, it is used to refer to speech practices whose form and value associations correspond to traditional standard Danish.

My main concern in this chapter has not been to show that certain linguistic signs are used in a new way, but rather to show that giving a new name to a register formulates new indexical values for existing practices. Further, I argue that the label "integrated" not only adds meaning to the register it describes, but also to those with which this register is contrasted. In contemporary Copenhagen, it makes sense to refer to academic standard speech as integrated because it is opposed to the youth register variously referred to as "street language", *perkersprog* ['Paki language'] or "slang", a youth register that has traditional indexical connections to social groups that are targets of integration (in the stereotypical political and public discourses discussed earlier). As Agha (2015) notes, slang as a register type can only be identified at a value boundary, and negative evaluations of slang are institutionalized in standard oriented-practices such as schooling, which formulate slang as sub-standard language or vulgar. Agha (2015) also notes that the term "slang" is not itself a slang term but a term in the standard language, so that to label a speech variety "slang" is to inhabit an out-group perspective on the speech variety named. When speakers in our data employ terms like "slang" or "street language" for their own speech they are voicing their metalinguistic commentary from the out-group perspective of Standard Danish. However, when they apply the term "integrated" (in its expanded sense) to standard Danish or to other standard languages (as when they speak of "integrated Arabic", or describe Urdu as "integrated Punjabi"), they are engaged in an ironic metapragmatic commentary on the very idea of a standard, formulating such out-group adult speech in oppositional contrast to their own in-group youth practices.

I have shown that the label "integrated", which is traditionally linked to a discourse of ethnic and cultural differences in majority discourses, is now used to typify contrasts of social status (and class) more than contrasts of ethnicity in youth discourses. There is of course nothing new about associating standard linguistic practices with higher social status and academic skills.

What is new is the use of the term "integrated" for a high-cultural register and the contrasting values this implies for contemporary youth registers (see further Madsen 2013). This is, I argue, an example of a recent $n + 1$st order of indexicality in Copenhagen, a new stage in the sociolinguistic enregisterment of speech differences. This labeling and the sociolinguistic position of the youth register it implies, reflects, perhaps, an awareness among youth of the social inequalities embedded in dominant understandings of cultural differences and of minority cultural (speech) practices as worthless in relation to schooling and societal power. It certainly suggest that linguistic signs that used to be seen as related to immigration, or identified as emblems of ethnic minority positions within the nation state (rather than of the majority) or of the outsider (rather than the insider) are now clearly linked to low (rather than high) socioeconomic status as well, and that contrasts of social status are profoundly interwoven with aspects of ethnicity in metapragmatic narratives and labels. According to Silverstein (2003: 194) different indexical orders tend to be "in dialectic competition one with another". The recent media uptake of the notion of integrated speech seems to reflect this, as the minority–majority relationship has a stronger prevalence in this type of metapragmatic commentary than among the adolescents in our project. It remains to be seen whether these mediatized sociolinguistic images influence future enregisterment or how exactly they do so when they move back to the streets from the screen.

Appendix: Transcription Key

[overlap]	overlapping speech
xxx	uintelligible speech
(questionable)	parts I am uncertain about
((comment))	my comments
:	prolongation of preceding sound
under<u>l</u>ined	stress
(.)	short pause
(0.6)	timed pause
hhh	laughter breathe

References

Agha, Asif 2003. The Social Life of Cultural Value. *Language and Communication* 23: 231–273.

Agha, Asif 2007. *Language and Social Relations*. Cambridge: Cambridge University Press.

Agha, Asif 2015 (in press). Tropes of Slang. *Signs and Society* 3(2).

Androutsopoulos, Jannis 2001. *"From the Streets to the Streets and back Again": On the Mediated Diffusion of Ethnolectal Patterns in Contemporary German*. Duisburg: L.A.U.D.

Blackledge, Adrian, & Angela Creese 2010. *Multilingualism: A Critical Perspective.* London: Continuum.

Blommaert, Jan, & Jef Verschueren 1998. *Debating Diversity: Analysing the Discourse of Tolerance.* London: Routledge.

Ejrnæs, Morten 2002. Etniske minoriteters tilpasning til livet i Danmark: Forholdet mellem majoritetssamfund og etniske minoriteter. *AMID Working Paper Series* 18/2002. Aalborg: The Academy for Migration Studies in Denmark.

Extra, Guus, Max Spotti & Piet Van Avermaet (eds.) 2009. *Language Testing, Migration and Citizenship: Cross-National Perspectives on Integration Regimes.* London: Continuum.

Heller, Monica 2007. Bilingualism as Ideology and Practice. In *Bilingualism: A Social Approach.* Ed. Monica Heller. London/Hampshire: Palgrave-Macmillan. Pp. 1–24.

Hyttel-Sørensen, Liva 2015. Gangster Talk on the Phone. In *Everyday Languaging.* Ed. Lian Malai Madsen, Martha Karrebæk & Janus Spindler Møller. Trends in Applied Linguistics. Berlin: Mouton De Gruyter. Pp. 49–70.

Jaspers, Jürgen 2005. Linguistic Sabotage in a Context of Monolingualism and Standardization. *Language and Communication* 25: 279–297.

Jaspers, Jürgen 2008. Problematizing Ethnolects: Naming Linguistic Practices in an Antwerp Secondary School. *International Journal of Bilingualism* 12: 85–103.

Johnstone, Barbara, Jennifer Andrus & Andrew E. Danielsen 2006. Mobility, Indexicality and the Enregisterment of "Pittsburghese". *Journal of English Linguistics* 34: 77–104.

Jørgensen, J. Normann 2008: Poly-Lingual Languaging around and among Children and Adolescents. In *International Journal of Multilingualism* 5(3): 161–176.

Jørgensen, J. Normann, Martha Karrebæk, Lian Malai Madsen & Janus Spindler Møller 2011. Polylanguaging in Superdiversity. *Diversities* 13: 23–38.

Kristiansen, Tore 2009. The Macro-Level Social Meanings of Late Modern Danish Accents. *Acta Linguistica Hafniensia* 41: 167–192.

Madsen, Lian Malai 2011. Interactional Renegotiations of Educational Discourses in Recreational Learning Contexts. *Linguistics and Education* 22: 53–67.

Madsen, Lian Malai 2013. 'High' and 'Low' in Urban Danish Speech Styles. *Language in Society* 42(2): 115–138.

Madsen, Lian Malai, Janus Spindler Møller & J. Normann Jørgensen 2010. 'Street Language' and 'Integrated': Language Use and Enregisterment among Late Modern Urban Girls. In *Ideological Constructions and Enregisterment of Linguistic Youth Styles.* Ed. Lian Malai Madsen, Janus Spindler Møller & J. Normann Jørgensen. Copenhagen Studies in Bilingualism 55. Copenhagen: University of Copenhagen. Pp. 81–113.

Madsen, Lian Malai, Martha Karrebæk & Janus Spindler Møller 2015. *Everyday Languaging.* Trends in Applied Linguistics 15. Berlin: De Gruyter.

Makoni, Sinfree B. 2012. A Critiqiue of Language, Languaging and Supervernacular. *Muitas Vozes* 1(2): 189–199.

Møller, Janus Spindler, & Jens Normann Jørgensen 2013. Organizations of Language among Adolescents in Superdiverse Copenhagen. *International Electronic Journal of Elementary Education* 6(1): 23–42.

Newell, Sasha 2009. Enregistering Modernity, Bluffing Criminality: How Nouchi Speech Reinvented (and Fractured) the Nation. *Journal of Linguistic Anthropology* 19: 157–184.

Olwig, Karen, Frog & Karsten Pærregaard (eds.) 2007. *Integration: Antropologiske perspektiver.* Copenhagen: Museum Tusculanum.

Rampton, Ben 2011. From 'Multiethnic Adolescent Heteroglossia' to 'Contemporary Urban Vernaculars'. *Language and Communication* 31(4): 276–294.

Rennison, Bettina Wolfgang 2009. *Kampen om integrationen.* Copenhagen: Hans Reitzel.

Silverstein, Michael 2003. Indexical Order and the Dialectics of Sociolinguistic Life. *Language and Communication* 23: 193–229.

Yilmaz, Feruh 1999. Konstruktion af de etniske minoriteter: Eliten, medierne og "etnificeringen" af den danske debat. *Politica* 31(2): 177–191.

Kapitolina Fedorova

6. Foreigner Talk
A Register or Registers?

More than thirty years ago, Charles Ferguson (Ferguson 1981) started discussion on the foreigner talk register and defined it as a conventional variety of simplified speech which is regarded by the speakers as appropriate for use with non-native speakers of a certain language. In this sense, we can speak about English or German or Russian foreigner talk as a linguistic subsystem with specific lexical and grammatical features differentiating this type of communication from the "normal", i.e. native-to-native, variety. Ferguson's approach and his own studies on English foreigner talk were important at that time since he provided researchers with a useful instrument to investigate a phenomenon which before that had been generally neglected by linguists – transformations made by people to their speech when addressing someone whose native language is not the same as their own. But later empirical studies revealed that the situation with native-to-non-native communication is much more complicated and very different strategies could be employed by speakers which sometimes make combining them under the common label "foreigner talk", if not totally impossible, then at least problematic. Should we consider discrepancy in data found in different research to be just different stages of the same simplification process, is there one "true" foreigner talk, or should we speak about separate strategies? And, consequently, does the term "register" make our understanding of interethnic communication more profound, should we keep it or put it on the shelf? In this article, I will try to address these questions by analysing verbal behaviour of Russian native speakers in different situations, both real and imagined, where their communication partner lacks full knowledge of Russian. However, first I need to give a brief overview of studies on foreigner talk in different languages.

Foreigner Talk Studies: An Overview

Numerous empirical studies conducted in the past decades (see e.g. Ferguson 1975; Meisel 1975; Arthur et al. 1980; Hinnenkamp 1982; Jakovidou 1993) demonstrated that there are some almost universal means employed by native speakers in their conversations with foreigners. These include slower and louder speech, frequent repetitions, and grammar simplification. At the same time, the level of this simplification can vary significantly from using shorter sentences to fully "ungrammatical" speech, i.e. breaking grammar rules. The most typical "ungrammatical" feature of foreigner talk is morphological oversimplification, with just one noun, pronoun or verb form used for any role in the sentence. As a result, such grammar categories as case, gender or tense dissolve. Articles, copulas, and other grammar elements tend to be omitted as well. Simplifications of this kind resemble pidgins, making foreigner talk research often useful in pidgin studies. Naturally, structurally different languages can vary rather significantly in respect of their morphological complexity. And this means that the same linguistic strategy – morphological oversimplification – will result in more serious structural changes in languages with "rich" morphology, like German or Finnish, in comparison with languages using less morphological categories and markers, such as the English language. Therefore "ungrammatical" speech can be perceived as more "incorrect" by speakers of the former languages; at the same time, these languages present more options for linguistic transformation.

What is more, it was discovered that research results in foreigner talk studies have been heavily influenced by the methods used for obtaining data and the settings in which communication takes place. In the beginning of foreigner talk studies, Ferguson suggested three possible methods of approaching the phenomenon of foreigner talk. The first of these is asking informants about how they and others speak to foreigners. Ferguson himself used this method in his study of English foreigner talk (Ferguson 1975). He asked his students to transform some sentences (like "I have not seen the man you are talking about") to make them more understandable for a foreigner and then to answer some questions on their attitudes towards this type of talk. The second method is setting experimental conditions – a researcher pretending to be a foreigner, for example. Experiments of this kind were usually set in a university classroom, and not in real-life situations (e.g. Henzl 1973). The final method is the observation of real-life situations. The Heidelberg Project of 1975, for example, studied German foreigner talk used by German employers to address expatriate employees, mostly Turks (Heidelberger Forschungsprojekt 1975). Ferguson believed that all these methods were applicable to investigate the same phenomenon; he did not differentiate among various aspects of foreigner talk. However, as was demonstrated through comparison between the results of many different studies (Long 1981), when asked to transform some sentences to make them more understandable for non-native speakers, informants produce a lot of ungrammatical utterances whereas in actual communication this type of speech may be used or not used depending on social conditions of a given interethnic contact. Formal settings and high social status of both communicating parties demand maintaining more strict communication rules and avoiding "grammar mistakes" acceptable in other circumstances. Therefore, on the one hand, the linguistic stereotype of foreigner talk register (what people think about such communication) differs from actual communication in real-life situations; on the other hand, the register itself is susceptible to situational variation. The problem is that most studies have employed only one method of obtaining data and did not try to compare several cases of using foreigner talk by native speakers of a particular language. It makes sense, then, to fill in this gap and investigate thoroughly different foreigner talk situations.

In this paper, I will try to address all these questions on basis of my research on Russian native speakers' verbal behaviour in communication with non-native speakers. Three sets of data will be used for comparison: (1) stereotypical representations obtained through interviews and questionnaires; (2) actual speech records made in St. Petersburg of native Russian speakers with foreign visitors and students; and (3) actual speech records made in the Russian–Chinese border area of Zabaikalie in the rather different social situation of native Russian speakers with Chinese labour migrants.

Russian Foreigner Talk as a Stereotype

It was already mentioned above that there is rather a strong stereotype among speakers of different languages according to which communication with non-native speakers should involve breaking grammar rules. It seems that in folk metalinguistics, "speaking broken language" means imitating the way foreigners speak the language. Russian speakers are not exceptional in this respect, but at the same time, there are interesting differences in their attitudes. Ferguson created the term "foreigner talk" on the analogy of baby talk, speech directed to small babies; and indeed, in the English speaking world, communication with foreigners sometimes is described in lay language as "baby talk" as well: people tend to simplify their speech the same way that they would if they were addressing small children. Thus, in one of Jake Allsop's short stories, an Englishwoman in Italy tries to be understood using what is called by the author "baby talk": "Me no understand Italian! This car no good" (Allsop 1991: 14). In contrast, Russian lacks terms for referring both to baby talk or foreigner talk; one can only use descriptive phrases for these such as "communication with babies / foreigners". There is one rather expressive word for baby talk, referring mostly to its phonetic features, *siusiukanie*, but it definitely cannot be used for naming the speech addressed to non-native speakers. This lack of terms matches Russian native speakers' generally negative attitude towards both phenomena as well as towards any other non-normative speech variety (Fedorova & Gavrilova 2004).

In my study, conducted in 2000–2001 in St. Petersburg, the informants were asked to transform some sentences for foreigners (in written form). In most cases, schoolchildren had no problems with the task but many adult informants felt uncomfortable and sometimes even refused to take part in the research, explaining that they do not want to use this "stupid broken language". Naturally the very fact of their negative attitude confirms the existence of the stereotype and its non-normative, "anti-grammar" nature evident in the data obtained from other informants. Altogether 90 questionnaires were completed; no significant differences between informants from different age groups and social groups were discovered.

My study revealed that, for Russian speakers, the most obvious way to simplify Russian grammar is to avoid declination and conjugation using nouns, adjectives and pronouns in the nominative case, and verbs in their infinitive form. Thus, the phrase *Khochesh' poiti zavtra so mnoi na kontsert?* ['Would you like to go to the concert with me tomorrow?'] is transformed into e.g.: *Ty i ia idti den' posle segodnia slushat' muzyka* ['You and I to go day after today to listen music' in word for word translation]. Furthermore, in stereotypic Russian foreigner talk, simpler syntactic structures are employed. When transforming sentences with subordinating conjunctions, informants tend to omit them by asyndetic connection: *Ia ne videl cheloveka, o kotorom Vy govorite.* ['I haven't seen the man you are talking about'] turns into *Ia ne videt' chelovek – ty govorit'* ['I not to see man – you to talk']. Or another example: *Esli zavtra ia budu svoboden, pokazhu Vam samuiu krasivuiu tserkov'* ['If I have spare time tomorrow, I'll show you the most beautiful church'] gives *Den' potom ia net delat', ty pokazat' khorosho dom* ['Day later I not to do, you to show well house'].

A rather striking feature of stereotypic Russian foreigner talk, which differentiates it from foreigner talk in other languages, is the function of the copula *est'*, the only surviving present tense form of the verb *byt'* ['to be']. Its use in the language is rather restricted in contrast to most European languages (cf. Eng. *he is good*; Germ. *er ist gut* vs. Rus. *on Ø khoroshii*). It is important to observe that Ferguson regarded the absence of copulas as an almost universal strategy of grammar simplification, found both in simplified registers (such as foreigner talk, baby talk or telegraphic style) and pidgins: "In pairs of clauses differing by presence and absence of a copula in a given language, speakers will generally rate the one without the copula as simpler and easier to understand" (Ferguson 1996: 119). It is sentences with the copula, however, that are perceived as much more appropriate in communication with foreigners by Russian native speakers: *Ty – khoroshii chelovek* ['You are a good person'; literally 'you good person'] transforms into *Ty est' khoroshii chelovek* ['You are a good person']. What is more, the copula *est'* can be used in combination with a verb when communicating with foreigners, which is absolutely impossible in Standard Russian grammar: e.g. the phrase *Skol'ko ty uzhe zhivesh' zdes'?* ['How long have you lived here?'] was transformed as *Ty skol'ko est' zhit' zdes'?* ['You how long are to live here'] or *Esli by ty vchera ne opozdal, my by posmotreli etot fil'm* ['If you weren't late yesterday we would have watched this film'] was turned into *Ty vdrug idi vovremia, my est' videt' kartinki* ['You suddenly go in time, we are to see pictures']. In fact, such incorrect use of the copula *est'* serves as a stereotypic linguistic marker of communication with foreigners in modern Russian culture. The same feature is used for imitating the way foreigners speak Russian.

Summing up, the study of Russian speakers' reflexive perception of foreigner talk reveals a strong stereotype of "broken language" to be used in communication with foreigners. This language lacks grammatical inflections which is typical for foreigner talks in general but, unlike foreigner talks in other languages, makes excessive use of the copula *est'*. It is possible to say that stereotypic Russian foreigner talk has some features determined by the linguistic structure of the Russian language. At the same time, cultural conventions are important as well, and should be taken into account as well as the attitudes toward foreigner talk: the existence of this stereotype does not mean it is regularly used in real communication.

"Talking Up": St. Petersburg Data

When we turn from stereotypical representations obtained in interviews and questionnaires to data from real life, the situation proves to be very different. When faced with "real" foreigners, Russian native speakers demonstrate several sets of linguistic strategies, which vary mainly by the social roles of interlocutors. In my research conducted in St. Petersburg in 1999–2002, dialogues between foreign (mostly Western) guests and students and their Russian hosts and friends were recorded in real-life situations. In most cases, Russian speakers were not previously informed about the aims of recording and behaved naturally. In total, 75 Russian speakers took part in the study, consisting of 37 males and 38 females and representing different age groups and different educational groups. Generally speaking, social parameters influenced informants' speech in the following way: middle-aged people displayed the highest proportion of foreigner talk features in their speech, while elderly people demonstrated them least of all, largely retaining the speech patterns common to native-to-native communication. In terms of gender, women tended to communicate with foreigners more easily than men. But of all characteristics, educational background was the most influential: people with higher education tended to adapt their speech more to a foreigner's needs in order to make themselves more easily understood.

The most striking characteristics of personal everyday communication between Russians and Russian-speaking foreigners can be described as the Russian speakers' hyperactive speech behaviour. When communicating with foreigners, Russians tend, over the course of the conversation, to take responsibility for (and to dominate) the dialogue. As a result of their behavior, conversations between Russians and foreigners look asymmetrical; the amount of input by non-native speakers (NNS) is less than half of the input by native speakers (NS). Indeed, to minimise the foreigner's role in conversation, the NS often begins to speak as if guessing the NNS' hitherto unarticulated thoughts:

(1) NNS: *My mnogo...* We were... a lot...
  NS: *Guliali?* Walking?
  NNS: *Po gorodu /** Around the city, yes, yes.
    da da / We saw
    My videli kakaia.../ which...
    My smotreli s... Is... Is... We look... from... Iss... Iss...
  NS: *Isaakievskogo sobora.* St. Isaac's Cathedral.

* The sign "/" is used to show short (less than 2 seconds) pauses in informants' speech

Sometimes native speakers practically exclude foreigner speakers from the conversation. Consider the following interaction, which involves several NSs and a single NNS:

(2) NS1 (to NNS): *Vy byli / v blinnoi /* Have you been in the pancake café
na Gagarinskoi? on Gagarinskaya street?
NS2: *Ne / ne uspeli esche.* No, they haven't had time yet.
NS3: *Net / ne uspeli.* No, they haven't had time.
NS1: *A / oni priekhali tol'ko…* Aha, they've just arrived.

The domineering behavior of Russian native speakers can manifest itself in other traits as well: question types, the use of phatic elements and repetitions of different kinds (see examples in Fedorova 2006).

In modern Russian colloquial speech, ellipsis is widespread (see e.g. Zemskaya et al. 1981). But when communicating with foreigners, speakers prefer to use fuller structures. Such sentences look neutral out of context, but they cause redundancy when they are prevalent. It seems that this "hypercorrectness", along with a slower tempo of speech, is the main diagnostic feature that allows native speakers to detect the foreigner talk situation, e.g. while listening to someone else's conversation with a foreigner on the phone. That this minimisation of ellipsis is a conscious strategy can be confirmed by the fact that even when some elliptic form is used, it is often immediately followed by a "self-correction" on the part of the native speaker – a reconstruction in fuller grammatical form: *Potomu chto u vas lodka zhens… korabl' zhenskogo roda. A u nas muzhskogo. Vo vsiakom sluchae voennyi korabl' u nas muzhskogo roda.* ['It's because in your language the boat… ship belongs to the feminine gender. And in ours – to the masculine. A military ship, in any case, belongs to the masculine gender.'] Native speakers also tend to avoid asyndetic connections, rather common in colloquial speech.

Finally, most foreigner talk researchers (see e.g. Freed 1981; Hatch 1983) list shorter sentences and the use of simpler syntactic structures as typical of the register. In this type of communication with foreigners, however, the situation is reversed: the average number of words in a sentence (9.58) is twice as large as that found in sentences exchanged by native speakers (4.56). Utterances addressed to a non-native speaker are not only longer, they are more complex due to the use of a greater number of subordinate clauses, on average 1.55 per sentence vs. 1.3 in colloquial speech. (For purposes of comparison, samples of speech by the same informants were recorded during their communication with other native speakers.)

Thus, although it is commonly believed that foreigner talk is a simplified register characterised by such traits as short sentences, a limited lexicon, and, less frequently, ungrammatical constructions, Russians conversing with foreigners in real-life situations in St. Petersburg tend to use more formal, grammatically correct forms of speech despite their artificiality and unnaturalness. At the same time they aim at discourse dominance making their communicative partners play subordinate roles in conversations which can be, and often are, perceived as impolite or rude by foreigners accustomed to different rules of communication. Interestingly, this situation resembles cultural differences in hospitality between Russians and Westerners as described by Laurent Thévenot and Nina Kareva: "He [the foreigner] is not able to take part in creating a community on equal terms with locals. Instead, Russians believe they should always help him to overcome his disability i.e. treat him as a small child. A foreigner is accepted most favourably when he does not interfere with anything that does not concern him directly, or, in other words, with anything not intended for his eyes." (Thévenot & Kareva 2009: 691.) It looks like Russian speakers acting as "hosts" towards foreigners tend to treat them as unequal partners in conversation and demonstrate it with both verbal and non-verbal means. But at the same time, this should be seen as a positive discrimination rather than a negative one.

"Talking Down": Zabaikalie Data

The situation in the Russian–Chinese border area differs in many ways from the situation described above. The present case is based on research that I conducted in 2008–2010, obtaining data through observation and interviews in the Zabaikalsii territory of Russia and in the Chinese border town Manzhouli. On the Russian side of the border, most foreigners are Chinese. Most of them have some (often extremely limited) knowledge of Russian, and very few Chinese immigrants, especially those employed in manual labour, get any formal language instruction. The overwhelming majority learn Russian during their communication with Russians in everyday situations or pick up some words from their linguistically more competent fellow countrymen. The resulting "Chinese-Russian language", or Chinese ethnolect of Russian, is perceived by native Russian speakers as "broken language", either ugly or amusing. Imitating "Chinese Russian" is a popular form of language play, especially among younger people. At the same time, Russian speakers almost never try to learn Chinese in everyday communication; if necessary, they turn to formal language instruction, but the number of people able to speak some Chinese is small. It is therefore Russian that serves as a main means of communication, and at least two language variants used by Russian native speakers can be observed.

The most common linguistic behavior in interethnic contacts in Zabaikalie is the full or partial ignoring of the situation. In spontaneous communication with Chinese speakers in the market place, native speakers of Russian do not generally accommodate linguistically less competent partners: they use colloquial forms and speak rather fast. At the same time, some markers in their speech allow the observer to guess that the addressee is a speaker of Chinese and not of some other language. First, all Chinese, regardless of age, are addressed with the informal pronoun *ty* [sg. 'you'] and corresponding verb forms even though the polite *Vy* [pl. 'you'] is normatively used in communication between strangers in Russian society. Russian rules of politeness do not apparently apply to Chinese people. Second, there are lexical clues as well: some words used by the Chinese trying to speak Russian have become popular with Russian native speakers and are used now in communication with Chinese (as well as for referring to the contact situation – e.g. when speaking about shopping at Chinese markets or border crossing practices). This lexicon thus turns into a local jargon, a restricted set of lexemes used in interethnic communication or used (metaphorically) to refer to contact situations. Typical and frequently used examples of this jargon are such words as *kapitana* (Russian *kapitan* ['captain'] as pronounced by Chinese speakers) with the rather broad meaning of chief, master or anyone in a higher position than the speaker, or *kunia* (Chinese *gūniang* ['girl'] in adapted pronunciation) used as a form of address to any female (in Chinese this word is not normally used for address – see Tsze 2007). (For more examples, see Fedorova 2011a; Fedorova 2011b.) Chinese speakers are treated as non-equals to their Russian speaking interlocutors both linguistically and socially: one cannot expect full understanding from them but, at the same time, they are not "important" enough for the Russian speakers to make serious efforts to be understood.

Another type of communication can be found in everyday conversations between Chinese and Russians who are involved in some form of ongoing business or personal relations, whether as spouses, business partners, or in employer–employee relations, etc. Since they are not just strangers to each other, they communicate with each other on a regular basis. Linguistic strategies used by Russian native speakers in such "closed" communication (and extremely difficult to witness, I should add) differ dramatically from those I discovered in St. Petersburg data, in which "hypercorrectness" as well as a slower tempo of speech were the main diagnostic features of a foreigner talk situation. Instead of artificially correct grammar, here we can find a lot of ungrammatical utterances. Some typical examples are presented in items (3–5):

(3)   *Ty chto khochu?*   What do you want?
                                   (lit. 'you what want?')

In (3), the verb *khotet'* ['to want'] is inflected in the first person instead of in the second person. In (4), the noun *Chita* ('the name of the city') is used as an adjective, which is not normative in Russian grammar.

(4)   *Zavtra esche odin gost'*   Tomorrow another guest will come.
        budet. Chita-gost'.   Chita guest.

In (5), the verbs *kupit'* ['to buy'] and *rabotat'* ['to work'] are used in the imperative form instead of in the past or present tense form:

(5)   *Takoi muzhchina kupi.*   The man bought this one.
        Ne rabotai.   It doesn't work.

In some of its forms of morphological oversimplification, this version of "broken Russian" resembles the stereotypical foreigner talk described above.

On the other hand, there are some differences too. The most important difference is the use of the imperative rather than the infinitive as a basic verb form. Imperatives are apparently considered to be the "proper way" to speak to the Chinese. Interestingly, the same feature was typical in the so-called Russian-Chinese pidgin, which had been used in the Russian–Chinese border area in the eighteenth and nineteenth centuries (Fedorova 2012). What is more, the extended use of imperatives seems to be perceived as natural for foreigner talk by local people of this border area but is not perceived as natural by outsiders from Western parts of Russia. This linguistic feature is thus culturally specific. One may infer that it is related to the long tradition of interethnic communication and social inequality of the contacting groups in the region. In a sense it is possible to speak about "the sociology of grammar": prevailing imperatives (as well as avoiding polite forms) are matched by very strong ethnic stereotypes that Russian speakers have about Chinese (Fedorova 2013).

It is also important to mention that all informants who use the second, "ungrammatical", strategy express rather negative feelings towards this "broken language" and are reluctant to admit the fact that they themselves speak this way. Their usual justification is: "They won't understand otherwise." But even though they view it as unavoidable, this type of speech is shameful and disgusting in their own eyes. Linguistic attitudes both towards the way Chinese speak Russian and towards the way that they make Russians speak Russian are strongly negative in the border region.

As we can see, in communicating with Chinese speakers who are probably felt to be "inferior" in some ways, Russian speakers use different language strategies: they either ignore their communicative partners' needs, and avoid making any modifications to their own speech, expecting instead that the Chinese will make all necessary adjustments; or they imitate their partners' imperfect speech on a lexical and / or grammatical level. Chinese speakers have no choice but to make some efforts to learn Russian. Speakers of Russian, on the other hand, are free to choose their linguistic means. Linguistic ways of domineering (grammatically informal address; extended use of imperatives) are used as well. Of course, this can be explained by the fact that it is the Chinese who are more "interested" in negotiations because they depend economically on Russian customers. But this is not always the case. In many instances, the relations are reversed, and Russians are subordinate to a Chinese boss. However the linguistic strategies used by Russian speakers remain the same in such cases.

Most probably in Russian–Chinese cross-border communication, Russians dominate over Chinese not economically but symbolically – everyone knows "who is the boss". And being the boss, Russian speakers can choose (if they like) to use strategies of "talking down" by speaking language that they themselves perceive as "inferior", and by breaking grammar rules in interactions with Chinese interlocutors.

Conclusions

I have tried to demonstrate that very different linguistic phenomena can be studied under the name "foreigner talk". In both the cases of foreigner talk in live use discussed above, informal conversations between native and non-native speakers of Russian were recorded in similar ways. However, the social roles performed by Russian speakers in relation to foreign interlocutors were quite different in the two cases. In the St. Petersburg case, communication occurred between foreign (mainly Western) visitors and students and their Russian friends and hosts. In the Zabaikalie case, we observe communication between Chinese migrants (of different social statuses) and their Russian partners, employers and friends. Very different linguistic strategies were revealed in these records. Playing the role of a "host" for a foreigner speaking Russian tends to "overprotect" foreigners. The NS tends to linguistically limit the verbal space of the NNS by using hypercorrect and extremely formal speech. On the other hand, when communicating with Chinese speakers in the border regions, native speakers of Russian can avoid any modifications in their speech, thus making interethnic communication a one-way process; or use ungrammatical utterances and "jargon" words, justifying themselves by invoking the linguistic incompetence of their interlocutors. This latter type of speech is much closer to what has been called "foreigner talk" by Ferguson and others. However, the hypercorrect variety observed in the St. Petersburg data cannot be described in the same terms, or be understood as a simplified register akin to "baby talk". This discrepancy in data brings up an important question: is Russian foreigner talk a unified phenomenon?

Ferguson's notion of "foreigner talk" as a simplified sub-code seems inadequate: simplification is not the only means by which native speakers of Russian deal with non-native speakers. Producing longer and more syntactically complex sentences, on the one hand, and destroying standard grammar, on the other hand, are by no means the same strategy, nor are they employed in the same situations. Other situational parameters, such as social roles or settings can influence communicative patterns in significant ways. We should bear in mind, therefore, that definitions of "foreigner talk" that refer to just one parameter of the situation – namely, the linguistic proficiency of the addressee –cannot fully define the phenomenon in question. We need to consider the social milieu in which native speakers and non-native speakers interact, and the types of footings and alignments they achieve with each other in specific social settings. Another important aspect of analysis is what one could call the "cultural construction" of foreigner talk, which turns out to be strongly ideologically marked for Russian speakers. Linguistic means employed in communication with non-native speakers correspond with historically rooted cultural models for treating "others" either as guests or subordinates. Thus the notion of register should be considered as not only a linguistic category but also as a socio-cultural category as well, which means that anthropological research methods can add more depth to register studies.

References

Allsop, Jake 1991. *Ladybirds and Other Stories.* London.

Arthur, B. et al. 1980. The Register of Impersonal Discourse to Foreigners: Verbal Adjustments to Foreign Accent. In *Discourse Analysis in Second Language Research.* Ed. Diane Larsen-Freeman. Rowley: Newbury House Publishers. Pp. 111–124.

Fedorova, Kapitolina 2006. Russian Foreigner Talk: Stereotype and Reality. In *Marginal Linguistic Identities. Studies in Slavic Contact and Borderland Varieties.* Ed. Dieter Stern & Christian Voss. Wiesbaden: Harrassowitz Publ. Pp. 177–190.

Fedorova, Kapitolina 2011a. Language Contacts on the Russian–Chinese Border: The 'Second Birth' of Russian-Chinese Trade Pidgin. In *Perpetual Motion? Transformation and Transition in Central, Eastern Europe and Russia.* Ed. T. Bhambry, C. Griffin, T. Hjelm & O. Voronina. London: School of Slavonic and East European Studies, University College London. Pp. 72–84.

Fedorova, Kapitolina 2011b. Transborder Trade on the Russian–Chinese Border: Problems of Interethnic Communication. In *Subverting Borders. Doing Research on Smuggling and Small-Scale Trade.* Ed. Bettina Bruns & J. P. Miggelbrink. Wiesbaden: Verlag für Sozialwissenschaften, Springer. Pp. 107–128.

Fedorova, Kapitolina 2012. Interethnic Communication and Cultural Memory in the Russian–Chinese Border Area. In *Bridging Cultures: Intercultural Mediation in Literature, Linguistics and the Arts.* Eds. Ciara Hogan, Nancy Rentel & Stephanie Schwerter. Stuttgart: Ibidem Verlag. Pp. 197–214.

Fedorova, Kapitolina 2013. Speaking with and about Chinese: Language Attitudes, Ethnic Stereotypes and Discourse Strategies in Interethnic Communication on the Russian-Chinese Border. *Civilisations* 62(1&2): 71–89.

Fedorova, Kapitolina & Tatiana Gavrilova 2004. Мнимое сходство и сходная мнимость: регистр общения с иностранцами vs. регистр общения с детьми в русском языке. In *Труды факультета этнологии.* Вып. 2. Санкт-Петербург: Издательство Европейского университета. Pp. 203–220.

Ferguson, Charles A. 1975. Toward a Characterization of English Foreigner Talk. *Anthropological Linguistics* 17(1): 1–14.

Ferguson, Charles A. 1981. "Foreigner Talk" as the Name of a Simplified Register. *International Journal of the Sociology of Language* 28: 9–18.

Ferguson, Charles A. 1996. *Sociolinguistic Perspectives: Papers on Language in Society, 1959–1994.* New York / Oxford: Oxford University Press.

Freed, Barbara 1981. Foreigner Talk, Baby Talk, Native Talk. *International Journal of the Sociology of Language* 28: 19–39.

Hatch, Eveline 1983. Simplified Input and Second Language Acquisition. In *Pidginization and Creolization as Language Acquisition.* Ed. William Andersen. Rowley: Newbury House Publishers. Pp. 64–86.

Heidelberger Forschungsprojekt Pidgin-Deutsch: Sprache und Kommunikation auslandischer Arbeiter 1975. Kronberg: Scriptor.

Henzl, Vera 1973. Linguistic Register of Foreign Language Instruction. *Language Learning* 23(2): 207–222.

Hinnenkamp, Volker 1982. *Foreigner Talk und Tarzanisch.* Hamburg; Buske Verlag.

Jakovidou, Athanasia 1993. *Funktion und Variation im "Foreigner Talk".* Tübingen: Gunter Narr Verlag.

Long, Michel H. 1981. Input, Interaction and Second Language Acquisition. In *Native Language and Foreign Language Acquisition.* Ed. Harris Winitz. New York: The New York Academy of Sciences. Pp. 259–278.

Meisel, Jürgen M. 1975. Ausländerdeutsch und Deutsch Ausländischer Arbeiter: Zur Möglichen Entstehung eines Pidgins in der BRD. *Zeitschrift für Literaturwissenschaft und Linguistik* 5 (18): 9–53.

Thévenot & Kareva 2009 = Тевено, Лоран & Нина Карева 2009. "Чудесный хлеб" гостеприимства (недоразумения, проясняющие открытость и закрытость сообществ). *Новое Литературное Обозрение* 100: 678–701.

Tsze 2007 = Цзе, Ян 2007. Забайкальско-маньчжурский препиджин: Опыт социолингвистического исследования. *Вопросы языкознания* 2: 67–74.

Zemskaya et al. 1981 = Земская, Е. А, Китайгородская, М. В., Ширяев, Е. Н. 1981. Русская *разговорная речь: Общие вопросы: Словообразование: Синтаксис*. Москва: Наука.

Alejandro I. Paz

7. Stranger Sociality in the Home
Israeli Hebrew as Register in Latino Domestic Interaction

From the perspective of linguistic anthropology, the study of register has been revolutionized in the last twenty-five years through a careful re-reading of Mikhail Bakhtin's framework for conceptualizing textuality as a contextualized social achievement that arises in relation to "heteroglossia" (as Bakhtin's term has come to be translated; 1981). That is, the linguistic anthropological concept of register helps us understand better how interactional cohesion is achieved (see Silverstein 1997), even in large-scale social formations where it is usual to find constant and complex processes of socio-linguistic variation and distinction. This volume itself shows a lot of this re-thinking, which is in general a re-thinking of twentieth century notions of language or semiotics more generally, including Ferdinand de Saussure's foundational relation of *langue* and *parole* (Saussure 1955). In particular, Asif Agha's seminal work (1998; 2005; 2007) gives us a guiding framework for thinking about register as part of how sociolinguistic stability forms from heteroglossic conditions. To move beyond concepts of registers as stock forms, Agha speaks of enregisterment, a social process whereby:

> diverse behavioral signs (whether linguistic, non-linguistic, or both) are functionally reanalyzed as cultural models of action, as behaviors capable of indexing stereotypic characteristics of incumbents of particular interactional roles and of relations among them. (Agha 2007: 55.)

In this process, forms are enregistered just as (metapragmatic) stereotypes about corresponding speakers crystallize. That is, registers emerge as do concomitant social identities – whether national, ethnic, gendered, professional, or other – and thus shape the trajectories of heteroglossia. Instead of a relatively stable linguistic form (*langue*) being displayed in utterances (*parole*), we can speak of enregisterment and trajectories of change across landscapes of sociolinguistic variation. Registers are not simply special linguistic forms in this framework, but rather they are aspects of social history – a history driven by complex, cross-cutting and diverse social projects.

Agha's approach to enregisterment is useful to the study of bilingualism as a form of heteroglossic trajectory, especially in contexts of immigration.

To focus on bilingual contexts as a question of register means a shift away from speaking about "codeswitching", "codemixing", or "borrowing", as Agha (2009) himself has noted. Instead, it becomes possible to consider the relation of social groups to the emergence of stereotypes, and how this stereotyping occurs as languages are linked through practice to institutional sites, roles or domains of use. Albeit not utilizing the current formulation of register, this social understanding of languages in bilingual context became common to linguistic anthropological studies since John Gumperz's early work, as part of the ethnography of speaking tradition (e.g. Gumperz & Wilson 1971; Blom & Gumperz 1972). In many studies of bilingualism since then, linguistic anthropologists place as much emphasis on describing the social processes that shape the ideologies and practices that help connect a given "language" to a group of speakers – or, often, a stereotypic speaker – as they do on describing the lexical, phonological, semantic or morphosyntactic phenomena.[1] Indeed, the linguistic anthropology of bilingualism shows how the lexical, phonological, semantic and morphosyntactic phenomena are part of social histories that propel heteroglossia.

Here, I would like to add to this research by considering how, for a highly marginalized migrant group, the dominant national language is also a register of stranger sociality within intimate, domestic contexts. Non-Jewish Latin America migrant workers – who collectively refer to themselves as Latinos – began arriving to live and work in Israel in the early nineties and stayed without legal residence status. They increasingly lived under the fear of deportation in the early 2000s, even as their children were growing up and receiving their schooling in Hebrew and participating in multiple Hebrew-based youth programs. Marginalized in multiple ways, Latino families accept the nationalist ideology that (standard) Hebrew is the language of the Jewish people, while Spanish – in several national and regional varieties – is "our" language, a language of diaspora. These social conditions produce a deep, if shifting, sociolinguistic contradiction from the perspective of Latinos: while Hebrew is considered the language of a nation to which they do not belong, Latino children tend to be Hebrew-dominant.[2] To complicate these matters, as in many other cases of immigration, the boundary between Hebrew and Spanish is not well-demarcated in most daily contexts of Latino interaction, leading to what Latinos themselves think about as "mixing" of the two languages.

Moreover, for Latinos, Hebrew is not only a language of official national public discourse, like that emanating from government, schools, and journalism. Hebrew is also understood to be the language of the street, of the marketplace, of their employers, and more generally of everyday stranger sociality. This everyday stranger sociality is conducted in a more informal register of Hebrew than that used in the official public sphere.

Linguistic anthropologists have written extensively on how linguistic categories and standard national registers help to produce frameworks of mass public participation (for example, Errington 1998; Silverstein 2000; Gal & Woolard 2001; Agha 2003; Inoue 2005; Bate 2009). More generally, literature on public sphere discourse has emphasized how literary and news genres can produce interactional pragmatics of stranger sociality at a mass scale, where a sense of imagined community is projected on the basis of anonymous participation.[3]

These literary and official contexts of national stranger sociality are related to but not identical with the more general sense of stranger sociality that I focus on here. The nationalist projects to establish and attempt to unify the official public sphere through the use of a standard register certainly affect unofficial, everyday contexts, but they never fully determine the transient or even long-term indexical meanings associated with the forms used. These everyday contexts occur outside of spatial and temporal zones construed as Latino sites of interaction, what Bonnie Urciuoli (1996) calls the "outer sphere". It is in outer sphere contexts that most Latinos gain their sense of Israeli interactional behavior as strangers, to which they attribute the characterological attributes of roughness and aggression.[4]

In what follows, I will consider Latino perceptions and practices of everyday, outer sphere Israeli stranger sociality. First, I will briefly contextualize the presence of Latinos in Israel, including their perception of Israelis as rough and aggressive. Second, I will go through a story told by a Latino that exemplifies the common idea that, in sites of stranger sociality in Israel, Latinos need to act more aggressively to match Israeli behavior. Here also it is possible to see how Hebrew becomes a term for a register associated with this footing of stranger sociality. Third, I will examine an interaction between a mother and her twelve-year-old son which shows how the son takes up this stranger footing within a domestic context of intimacy. In part, he draws on Hebrew to index his shift in footing. Together, the examples suggest how domestic, inner sphere contexts of migrant groups are buffeted by the enregisterment processes of centralizing national language.

Latinos in Israel

My description and examples are from my study of noncitizen Latino labor migrant families in Israel, with whom I did more than three years of ethnographic and linguistic fieldwork, including a sustained period between 2004 and 2006. The Latino families that I worked with are not Jewish, and comprised Spanish-dominant parents who largely migrated to Israel as adults in search of better economic opportunities, while the Hebrew-dominant children largely grew up in Israel, attending Israeli schools. Latinos work mostly in domestic cleaning, child care, or light industries. Known by state officials and in most public discourses as "foreign workers", both parents and children arrived as part of a large wave of non-citizen migrant workers that began in the early nineties, and continues in different form today. Although by some estimates, Latinos had numbered some 15,000–20,000 prior to the advent of the Immigration Police in 2002, at the time of my fieldwork, they probably comprised 5,000–8000 people.[5]

Latinos see their domestic spaces as a site for socializing their children into Latin American pragmatics of *educación*, the refinement and delicacy of polite behavior. To fully and appropriately inculcate *educación* in their own children would mean to reproduce the sites of interaction as remembered from their Latin American upbringing and social settings. This is something most Latino parents concede is impossible to do in Israel, especially because children spend a lot of time in an outer sphere space Latinos call "the street". Yet, at the same time, Latinos believe that their children show greater *educación* than Israeli children, and that this distinguishes Latinos ethnically. Indeed stories about the rudeness of Israeli children, and how they speak to their Israeli parents, are ubiquitous, and often include the highly salient figure of the Israeli child played out in Hebrew. In the domestic worlds of Latino diaspora, these frequent representations have led to the emergence of a metapragmatic stereotype about the Israeli, and the Hebrew language itself, which some argue is incapable of any softness or other qualities of *educación*.

For Latinos, then, Israelis lack *educación*. In reaching this conclusion, they are ironically participating in a more general "moral panic" about Israeli interactional behavior (Katriel 2004: 211–219). Certainly, in the past, Israelis have been conscious of themselves and have been perceived more broadly as speaking with directness, and avoiding elaborate rhetoric (Katriel 2004: 21–23, 139–164). The highly ideological perception of Israeli directness is then cast by Latinos, in a Herderian mold of equating interactional pragmatics with the named language, as a feature of Hebrew (see Paz 2015). Indeed, in Latino domestic contexts, the forms classified as Hebrew work as a register associated with the stereotyped Israeli stranger.

In these domestic spaces, Spanish and Hebrew can be used like register alternants, capitalizing on these stereotypes. Like in other migrant contexts, families generally use a more syncretic code that neutralizes the apparent distinction of Spanish and Hebrew in much interaction. Yet the contrast is available, and one that is felt to be important, especially to parents who worry about their ability to maintain authority over children given the palpable marginality in which they live.

Stereotyping Israelis as Strangers

In contrast to the domestic spaces and other Latino contexts where *educación* can be found, there were the multiple outer sphere sites where Latinos encounter Israelis. Especially among adults, these encounters were the subject of continuous story-telling about Israelis' interactional behavior, and Latino responses. In these stories, that is, Israelis are stereotyped as aggressive, rough, short-tempered, and overly inquisitive – in short, liable to interactional acts that threaten their interlocutors' face.[6]

As an example, here is a story about interacting with an Israeli stranger, told by a Chilean, Rodrigo. The story came up in the context of a group conversation, which I recorded, about the differences in *educación* between Latinos and Israelis. Included in the conversation were two flatmates, Fred from Ecuador and Enrique from Venezuela, as well as Rodrigo's wife, Ester, who had arrived to Israel from Chile at the age of fourteen and finished high school there, and thus was fluent in Hebrew. All had been in Israel between three and ten years, and belonged to the same Evangelical church. Rodrigo's story is about how he had used a Hebrew phrase MA IXPAT LI ['WHAT DO I CARE'] as part of defending his seat on the bus from an Israeli stranger. (To the extent it is possible to distinguish, I use *italics* for (etymological) Spanish and SMALL CAPS for (etymological) Hebrew; where the language boundary has been clearly neutralized, I use both.) The story begins before the portion excerpted here, with Rodrigo explaining that a young man approached him on a crowded bus, and first tried to address a sleepy Rodrigo in English. When Rodrigo asked him if he knew Hebrew, the Israeli asked Rodrigo for the seat. In Rodrigo's rendition, the story develops as a series of well-played lines that reject the Israeli strangers attempt to gain the seat. These toppers win Rodrigo laughs from the rest of us (lines 3, 8, 14, 23). Rodrigo gives this story as an example of how of stranger sociality in Israel requires aggressive interactional pragmatics, and, at the same time, he uses Hebrew to directly quote his own speech to the Israeli stranger. Such a poetic juxtaposition serves to reinforce the stereotype of Israeli stranger sociality as aggressive, and thus requiring an aggressive response, which is the conclusion he reaches (line 25). Further, in lines 5-7, Rodrigo singles out the intonation contours and voice quality of his own represented speech for comment, using dummy syllables to produce a caricatured contrast of (roughly) phlegmatic and aggressive intonations. All of this is meant to show how, by speaking like Israeli strangers do, he managed to keep his bus seat:

Excerpt 1. Rodrigo's story about defending his seat on the bus. Some false starts have been removed as well as orthogonal segments to save space. In lines 18 and 28, Rodrigo uses the Chilean dialect colloquial verb forms for second person

1. R: *eh yo le dije* "ANI LO ROTSE" R: *eh* I told him "I DON'T WANT TO"
2. *y después- y dije* "ZEHU" *and after-* and I said "THAT'S IT"
3. [everyone laughs] [everyone laughs]
4. R: "ANI LO ROTSE, ZEHU" R: "I DON'T WANT TO, THAT'S IT"
5. *no así como* <e:h> [phlegmatic tone] *not like* <e:h> [phlegmatic tone]
6. *eh,* **fuerte** *eh,* **strong**
7. <e:h> [aggressive tone] <e:h> [aggressive tone]
8. [some laughs] [some laughs]
9. R: *cuando (al rato)* R: *when (after a while)*
10. *y se quedó ahí* *and he stayed there*
    [...]* [...]
11. *y me dice eh* "ATA SHILAMTI"** *and he says to me eh* "DID YOU PAY"
12. *acaso yo había pagado en lugar de el* *whether I had paid instead of him*
13. *y yo le dije* "MA IXPAT LEXA" *and I said to him* "WHAT'S IT TO YOU"
14. [several laugh] [several laugh]
    [...]*** [...]
15. R: *(es)* "MA IXPAT LEXA" R: *(it's)* "WHAT'S IT TO YOU"
16. *y me dice* "*ay*" *and he says to me* "*ay*"
17. *y se coloca a hablar* *and he starts to talk*
18. *y que* "*tu teni que pagar*" *and that* "*you need to pay*"
19. *y le dije* "ATA NAHAG SHEL OTOBUS?" *and I said to him* "YOU ARE DRIVER OF BUS?"

20. "MA? MA ATA?"	"WHAT? WHAT ARE YOU?"
21. y no sé, me dijo (...)	and I don't know, he said (...)
22. y también le dije "MA IXPAT LI"	and I also said to him "WHAT DO I CARE"
23. [several laugh]	[several laugh]
24. R: pero **fuerte**	R: but **strong**
25. como les gusta a ellos que les diga	like they like being spoken to
26. "entonces ahora que te quedai callado"	"so now you keep quiet"

* The omitted lines are where Rodrigo attempts to calculate how much time elapsed before the Israeli fellow re-initiated his interrogation.
** Rodrigo uses the first person form of the verb, rather than the second person *shilamta*.
*** In the omitted lines, Rodrigo explains again the nature of the second question, and then notes that he had been sleeping until interrupted by the Israeli fellow.

The story plays out as a series of challenges by the Israeli stranger (the first is not represented, but then lines 11, 18, and 21) which Rodrigo answers. Rodrigo represents his winning lines – which draw laughter – as using Hebrew (lines 1-2, 4, 13, 15, 19-20, 22).[7] He not only describes his winning lines, but also characterizes his own tone and general interactional orientation as *fuerte* ['*strong*'] in lines 6 and 24. In lines 25, Rodrigo adds explicit commentary: he was speaking firmly just "like they [Israelis] like to being spoken to." Finally, in line 26, Rodrigo re-iterates the upshot of his answers to the Israeli stranger in transposed speech, using a highly colloquial Chilean dialect form: he was telling the Israeli to just keep quiet. That is, line 26 is a version of how he might have spoken in a similar situation in Chile, complete with the informal register of everyday stranger sociality.

Stories about such encounters with Israelis in everyday contexts were legion among adult Latinos. Just as common was the conclusion that one had to respond in kind. However, crucial here is that in such stories, Hebrew as a set of forms is associated for Latinos with the stereotype of the aggressive Israeli. Further, these outer sphere contexts are where most adult Latinos actually speak Hebrew with Israelis, and, thus where many pick up a jargon variety of Hebrew.[8] In other words, within Latino inner sphere contexts, Hebrew is *incipiently* enregistered as the speech used among strangers – indeed strangers who lack *educación*. This is not to argue that this small group of marginalized labor migrants has achieved a long-term degree of sociolinguistic stability, or imposed their understandings on a larger society. Rather, this enregisterment process is a localized response to the aforementioned Israeli ideas and practices of interactional directness.

Hebrew forms, as they are perceived by Latinos in inner sphere contexts, do not stay within the boundaries of stories of encounters with strangers, like Rodrigo's in Excerpt 1. More importantly, the interactional directness that is associated with speaking in Hebrew does not stay within the boundaries of such stories. Both Hebrew and the aggressive characteristics associated with Israeli interactional directness continually seep into the bounds of what Latinos consider contexts for Latino *educación*. This seepage is especially evident in interactions between adults who were socialized in Latin America and their children growing up in Israel. The next example illustrates how, from the perspective of Latino parents, their own children may behave in ways that seem uncannily Israeli.

The Stranger at Home

The example features a Colombian mother, Luna, and her twelve-year-old son, Juan, who had lived some nine years in Israel. Also present was their flatmate, another Colombian mother, Marla. During the course of a casual conversation, which they recorded for me, Juan takes offense when Luna and Marla laugh at his error speaking in Spanish. When this happens, Juan first shifts his interactional footing, leaving the friendly conversational alignment with Luna and Marla for a more adversarial one, and this precedes his eventual change in denotational footing (cf. Agha 2007: 134–142) to Hebrew. After transcribing this recording, I used this excerpt in an interview with 52 Latinos to ask for commentary. Those who know him consider Juan to be a very well-behaved young man, always polite to elders; he also shares his mother's quick sense of humor. However, in this interaction, many found that Juan begins to act in an "Israeli" fashion.

The excerpt begins after a long conversation between Luna and Marla about an event that occurred the day previous to when they made the recording. The context is as follows: I had been contacted by two Spanish-language television reporters who were interested in doing a two-minute segment on Latinos in Israel. During the session, the reporters continually asked the interviewees to repeat their answers in an effort to make them shorter. In the recording from the following day, Luna and Marla had a lengthy and animated discussion about this experience, and Juan's error (line 2) comes just as he attempts to be included in this intimate recollection. Juan's lines 1–2 have a great deal of tone contrast in the contour, which sound *alegre* or jovial to Latinos. He even uses strong sentential stress exactly on the word he mispronounces. Juan wants to comment on the constant repetition the reporters requested, and mispronounces the word *repetirse* ['to repeat']. There are three other points to note in these two lines: he uses IMA for 'mom', an acceptable hebraicism in this context; he simplifies a denotational distinction in adult Spanish by using *grabación* ['recording'] instead of *entrevista* ['interview']; and also he uses *referirse* ['to refer'] at the end of line 2 instead of *decir* ['to say'], probably due to hypercorrection. When Luna and Marla snicker at his error, he is clearly offended (line 7), where he then shifts footing completely from the *alegre* son sharing in a good story to an angry young teenager that ends up speaking over her in Hebrew (lines 36–39).

Excerpt 2. Juan's Error. Luna is Juan's mother and Marla is Lola's mother. A false start has been removed in the interest of saving space. Square brackets signal overlapping turns. [T] is used in the translation to indicate singular (informal) second person address and [V] to indicate plural (formal) second person address.

1. J: *IMA, cuando uno habla
   en esa grabación*
2. *hay que **re-(vergarse)**
   lo que uno se refiere*
3. L: *re-qué?*
4. J: *referiarse*
5. L: *repetiarse?*
6. M: *repe-repe* [laugh]
7. J: *qué?* [offended]
8. L: *referirse?*
9. M: *repetirse?*
10. J: *no, bueno, no hablo en español*
11. L: *no, Juan, no*
12. *al contrario*
13. *tiene que hablar más Español*
14. *para que suelte esa lengua*
15. J: *y tú tienes que hablar más hebreo*
16. L: *bueno, enséñame tú*
17. *porque es que tú vas a un colegio*
18. *mientras que [tú no me educas*
19. J: [*y tú no me enseñas a mi
    hebreo- eh español*
20. L: *no, aquí en la casa?*
21. [*(... español)*
22. M: [*(... español)*
23. L: *Marla habla hebreo?*
24. *yo hablo hebreo?*
25. *Lola habla hebreo?*
26. *nosotros aquí hablamos todo el día-*
27. J: [BESEDER, BESEDER
28. L: [*(todo el día, no)*
29. [*cuando llegamos a la casa*
30. [*hablamos en español*
31. J: [BESEDER, BESEDER, BESEDER
32. L: [*pero usted . a (refirear)*
33. [*cómo es que dijo?*
34. J: [BESEDER, BESEDER, BESED-
35. L: *a repitearse*
36. J: MA ANI AMARTI
37. ANI LO AMARTI KLUM
38. [ANI LO YODEA SFARADIT
39. [MI AMAR
40. L: [REGA, *hablando (de ...)*
41. [ANI LO MEVINA IVRIT
    [pause]
42. ALO

J: MOM, *when one talks in that
   recording*
*you have to **re-(unclear)**
   to what you refer*
L: *re-what?*
J: *referpeat*
L: *reperpeat?*
M: *repe-repe* [laugh]
J: *what?* [offended]
L: *refer?*
M: *repeat?*
J: *no, okay, I'm not speaking in Spanish*
L: *no, Juan, no*
quite the opposite
you[V] have to speak more Spanish
so you[V] loosen that tongue
J: *and you[T] have to speak more
   Hebrew*
L: *okay, you[T] teach me*
because it's that you go to a school
while you [don't educate me
J: [*and you[T] don't teach me any
    Hebrew- eh Spanish*
L: *no, here in the house?*
[*(...Spanish)*
M: [*(...Spanish)*
L: *Marla speaks Hebrew?*
I speak Hebrew?
Lola speaks Hebrew?
we here speak the whole day-
J: [OKAY, OKAY
L: [*(not the whole day)*
[*when we get home*
[*we speak in Spanish*
J: [OKAY, OKAY, OKAY
L: [*but you . (referpeat)*
[*how was it that you[V] said?*
J: [OKAY, OKAY, OKAY
L: *to referpeat*
J: WHAT DID I SAY
I DIDN'T SAY ANYTHING
[I DON'T KNOW SPANISH
[WHO SAID
L: [WAIT, *speaking (of ...)*
[I DON'T UNDERSTAND HEBREW
[pause]
HEY

As Juan stated in his interview after hearing himself in the excerpt, he spoke with "chutspah" (Heb. XUTSPA), because he knows that his mother does not speak that much Hebrew and he spoke rudely. Furthermore, he acknowledged that when his mother starts to ask him questions, he ignores her (repeating BESEDER at lines 27, 31, and 34). As many of my Latino interviewees commented, Juan is treating her "like another person" – that is, *like an outsider or stranger*. From their perspective, starting at least at line 27, Juan no longer treats Luna with the respect one should show one's mother.

This interactional fact is matched by Luna's response. Luna picks up on this stranger sociality, and also shifts denotational footing by the end of the interactional segment shown here. Luna attempts across several turns to encourage Juan to speak more Spanish, as well as to answer his accusation that she does not help him learn. That is, Luna attempts to maintain the role of a mother educating her son. When Juan repeatedly treats her using devices to signal distance, Luna tellingly uses her jargon Hebrew (line 41) to state that she does not understand him when he speaks Hebrew. Then there is a pause, and she follows up his silence with a vocative call, ALO ['hey'] (line 42). This use of ALO is found within non-stranger contexts (often as a kind of pragmatic metaphor), but – especially with the intonation contour Luna used – is more resonant of calling to a stranger in the street, like in the open-air markets (SHUKIM) of Tel Aviv. That is, Luna has interactionally shifted to match Juan's stranger footing.

Given this, it is possible to see from line 7 onward how Juan becomes progressively more distant (and therefore insolent), leading up to Luna's own shift. Juan first loses the *alegre* intonation of lines 1–2 in favor of more angry intonation starting at line 10. Then, when Luna, in educating mother mode, uses a second person V-form honorific (not unusual in this context), Juan returns a T-form in his accusation that Luna does not speak Hebrew any more than he speaks Spanish (line 15). Such a response also suggests a footing of equals, rather than a respectful son speaking to his mother. Then Juan becomes a cold, disinterested outsider, using only a Hebrew-derived form (BESEDER) at line 27 to talk over Luna. Juan takes on the persona of the aggressive stranger, speaking only Hebrew and raising his voice (lines 36–39). Finally, Juan does not even respond to Luna's Hebrew-language complaint that she cannot understand him. That is when Luna shows her awareness that they are speaking to each other as strangers, using the aforementioned ALO-vocative (line 42).

Excerpt 2 shows how Hebrew can function as a register of stranger sociality within Latino inner sphere contexts.[9] Moreover, it exemplifies the complexity of the enregisterment process among marginalized and marked populations like these non-citizen Latinos. Not only is Hebrew used in stories like Rodrigo's (Excerpt 1) to represent speech during encounters with Israelis in outer sphere contexts. Hebrew also seeps into and becomes cross-indexed with hostile and distant footings in inner sphere contexts. This patterning helps to strengthen the association of Hebrew with the aggressive stranger sociality Latinos perceive in outer sphere contexts.

Conclusion

Heteroglossia was Mikhail Bakhtin's term for the open-ended, constantly unfolding process of sociolinguistic variation. The question that Bakhtin's insights helps to answer is how relative stability is achieved in the face of constant historical change. This question is especially important to consider in complex, mass social formations. In many modern nation-states, migration generates constant vectors for heteroglossic change, many of which are considered to be structured by bilingualism. In linguistic anthropology, register – and in particular conceiving of a process of enregisterment – has helped to explain relative sociolinguistic stability. Furthermore, as opposed to many studies of bilingualism that assume the genetic distinction between languages continues to hold in all contexts, the framework of enregisterment allows us to examine the practices and institutions through which forms are functionalized as belonging to distinct named languages.

Here, I have considered the bilingual situation of a small, marginalized group of noncitizen Latino labor migrants in Israel. The noncitizen Latinos associate Hebrew with what is perceived as the aggressive behavior of Israelis in contexts of everyday stranger sociality. No doubt their stereotype of an Israeli is an expression of their social marginalization. During my fieldwork, most Latinos in Israel lived in highly precarious circumstances, and had few openings for social mobility. The enregisterment process in which they were part saw Spanish and Hebrew come to mean different registers in inner sphere contexts: Spanish was especially useful for showing *educación*, while Hebrew was especially useful for both portraying and enacting the stereotype of the aggressive Israeli in outer sphere contexts.

Such an enregisterment process is very different than those supported by extensive state or private capital resources, as in language standardization campaigns. Instead, as part of the process of integrating into Israeli social spaces, Latinos perceptions of and reactions to what they consider to be typical Israeli interactional behavior helps to stabilize the indexical meanings of Hebrew and Spanish as registers. This enregisterment is supported by the metapragmatic stereotyping of speakers from a treasure of stories, told again and again by the noncitizen Latinos as they attempt to explain the transformations that migration has brought upon them.

Notes

1. Some classic studies in this tradition are Gal 1979; Hill 1985; Irvine 1989; Heller 1988; Woolard 1989; Mannheim 1991; Kulick 1992; Urciuoli 1996; Errington 1998; Eisenlohr 2006.
2. Space does not allow for a full elaboration of these issues here; please see further Paz 2010; 2015.
3. Foundational works here are Habermas 1989 and Anderson 1991. For commentary and literature, see further Cody 2011.
4. Potentially, Latinos are picking up on some of what Tamar Katriel (2004: 208–211) has described as a style of *kasax*, a term used for a competitive verbal or physical blow to an opponent. Katriel suggests that this style is perhaps converging with direct speaking style of *dugri*.

5 On these noncitizen Latinos, see further Schammah Gesser et al. 2000; Raijman et al. 2003; Kalir 2010; on noncitizen labor migration to Israel, see further Willen 2007; Kemp & Raijman 2008.
6 On facework and politeness, two classic works are Goffman 1967 and Brown & Levinson 1987.
7 Besides this, it could be noted, he represents his adversary's words embedded in narrative nonpast tense in lines 11 and 16, and then his topper responses come framed in the relatively more presupposing past tense forms in lines 13 and 19, which no doubt ratchets up the sense of having outdone the usurper.
8 The sociolinguistic skill and grammatical competence among adult migrants varied in ways that cannot be described here due to space limitations.
9 This is not true of all Hebrew-derived form. Although space does not allow for an expanded discussion, the use of IMA (line 1) by Juan and of REGA (line 40) by Luna shows something of an incipient syncretic register, that neutralizes the distinction between Spanish and Hebrew.

References

Agha, Asif 1998. Stereotypes and Registers of Honorific Language. *Language in Society* 27: 151–193.
Agha, Asif 2003. The Social Life of Cultural Value. *Language and Communication* 23(3–4): 231–273.
Agha, Asif 2005. Voice, Footing, Enregisterment. *Journal of Linguistic Anthropology* 15(1): 38–59.
Agha, Asif 2007. *Language and Social Relations.* Cambridge: Cambridge University Press.
Agha, Asif 2009. What Do Bilinguals Do? A Commentary. In *Beyond Yellow English: Toward a Linguistic Anthropology of Asian Pacific America.* Ed. Angela Reyes & Adrienne Lo. Oxford Studies in Sociolinguistics. New York: Oxford University Press. Pp. 253–258.
Anderson, Benedict R. O'G. 1991. *Imagined Communities: Reflections on the Origin and Spread of Nationalism.* London: Verso.
Bakhtin, Mikhail M. 1981. Discourse in the Novel. In *The Dialogic Imagination: Four Essays.* Austin: University of Texas Press. Pp. 259–422.
Bate, Bernard. 2009. *Tamil Oratory and the Dravidian Aesthetic: Democratic Practice in Southern India.* New York: Columbia University Press.
Blom, Jan-Petter, & John J. Gumperz 1972. Social Meaning in Linguistic Structure: Code-Switching in Norway. In *Directions in Sociolinguistics: The Ethnography of Communication.* Ed. John Joseph Gumperz & Dell H. Hymes. New York: Holt, Rinehart & Winston. Pp. 407–434.
Brown, Penelope, & Stephen C. Levinson 1987. *Politeness: Some Universals in Language Usage.* Cambridge: Cambridge University Press.
Cody, Francis 2011. Publics and Politics. *Annual Review of Anthropology* 40: 37–52.
Eisenlohr, Patrick 2006. *Little India: Diaspora, Time, and Ethnolinguistic Belonging in Hindu Mauritius.* Berkeley: University of California Press.
Errington, James Joseph 1998. *Shifting Languages: Interaction and Identity in Javanese Indonesia.* Cambridge: Cambridge University Press.
Gal, Susan 1979. *Language Shift: Social Determinants of Linguistic Change in Bilingual Austria.* New York: Academic Press.
Gal, Susan, & Kathryn Ann Woolard. 2001. Constructing Languages and Publics: Authority and Representation. In *Languages and Publics: The Making of Authority.*

Ed. Susan Gal & Kathryn Ann Woolard. Manchester: St. Jerome Publishing. Pp. 1–12.

Goffman, Erving 1967. *Interaction Ritual: Essays on Face-to-Face Behavior*. Garden City, NY: Anchor Books.

Gumperz, John Joseph, & Robert Wilson 1971. Convergence and Creolization: A Case from the Indo-Aryan/Dravidian Border in India. In *Language in Social Groups*. Ed. Anwar S. Dil. Stanford: Stanford University Press. Pp. 251–273.

Habermas, Jürgen 1989. *The Structural Transformation of the Public Sphere: An Inquiry into a Category of Bourgeois Society*. Ed. Burger Thomas & Lawrence Frederick. Cambridge, MA: MIT Press.

Heller, Monica 1988. *Codeswitching: Anthropological and Sociolinguistic Perspectives*. Berlin: Mouton de Gruyter.

Hill, Jane H. 1985. The Grammar of Consciousness and the Consciousness of Grammar. *American Ethnologist* 12(4): 725–737.

Inoue, Miyako 2005. *Vicarious Language: Gender and Linguistic Modernity in Japan*. Berkeley: University of California Press.

Irvine, Judith T. 1989. When Talk Isn't Cheap: Language and Political Economy. *American Ethnologist* 16: 248–267.

Kalir, Barak 2010. *Latino Migrants in the Jewish State: Undocumented Lives in Israel*. Bloomington: Indiana University Press.

Katriel, Tamar 2004. *Dialogic Moments: From Soul Talks to Talk Radio in Israeli Culture*. Detroit: Wayne State University Press.

Kemp, Adriana, & Rebeca Raijman 2008. *Migrants and Workers: The Political Economy of Labor Migration in Israel [Hebrew]*. Jerusalem: Van Leer Jerusalem Institute.

Kulick, Don 1992. *Language Shift and Cultural Reproduction: Socialization, Self, and Syncretism in a Papua New Guinean Village*. Cambridge: Cambridge University Press.

Mannheim, Bruce 1991. *The Language of the Inka since the European Invasion*. Austin: University of Texas Press.

Paz, Alejandro I. 2010. Discursive Transformations: The Emergence of Ethnolinguistic Identity among Latin American Migrant Workers and Their Children in Israel. Unpublished Ph.D. dissertation, University of Chicago.

Paz, Alejandro I. 2015. The Deterritorialization of Latino Educación: Noncitizen Latinos in Israel and the Everyday Diasporic Subject. In *A Sociolinguistics of Diaspora: Latino Practices, Identities and Ideologies*. Ed. Rosina Márquez Reiter & Luisa Martín Rojo. New York: Routledge. Pp. 151–165.

Raijman, Rebeca, Silvina Schammah-Gesser, & Adriana Kemp 2003. International Migration, Domestic Work, and Care Work: Undocumented Latina Migrants. *Gender & Society* 17(5): 727–749.

de Saussure, Ferdinand 1955. *Cours de linguistique générale*. Ed. Bally Charles, Sechehaye Albert & Riedlinger Albert. Paris: Payot.

Schammah Gesser, Silvina, Rebeca Raijman, Adriana Kemp & Julia Reznik 2000. 'Making It' in Israel? – Latino Undocumented Migrant Workers in the Holy Land. *Estudios Interdisciplinarios de América Latina y el Caribe* 11(2): 113–136.

Silverstein, Michael 1985. The Functional Stratification of Language and Ontogenesis. In *Culture Communication, and Cognition: Vygotskian Perspectives*. Ed. James V. Wertsch. Cambridge: Cambridge University Press. Pp. 205–235.

Silverstein, Michael 1997. The Improvisational Performance of 'Culture' in Realtime Discursive Practice. In *Creativity in Performance*. Ed. R. Keith Sawyer. Greenwich, CT: Ablex. Pp. 265–312.

Silverstein, Michael 2000. Whorfianism and the Linguistic Imagination of Nationality. In *Regimes of Language: Ideologies, Polities, and Identities*. Ed. Paul V. Kroskrity. Santa Fe, NM: School of American Research Press. Pp. 85–138.

Urciuoli, Bonnie 1996. *Exposing Prejudice: Puerto Rican Experiences of Language, Race, and Class*. Boulder, CO: Westview Press.

Willen, Sarah S. 2007. *Transnational Migration to Israel in Global Comparative Context.* Lanham, MD: Lexington Books.

Woolard, Kathryn Ann 1989. *Double Talk: Bilingualism and the Politics of Ethnicity in Catalonia.* Stanford: Stanford University Press.

Registers in Transition

III

Timo Kaartinen

8. The Registers and Persuasive Powers of an Indonesian Village Chronicle

Register and genre often seem to point to the same thing: language which stands out as a particular kind of discourse. The use of these terms reflects two, related insights of language use. Genre, in the Bakhtinian understanding, is an "organizing principle that guides us in the process of our speaking" (Bauman 2004: 3). Genre thus highlights the speaker's wish to be understood, quoted, and responded to – an awareness of the continuity of discourse before and after the current speech event. Register has more to do with the social conventions of speaking. As a "predictable configuration of codal resources that members of a culture typically associate with a particular reoccurring communicative situation" (Malcolm 2005: 60), register indexes various features of the speech context and the cultural understandings and models which organize it (Agha 2004: 23).

This article discusses register as an element of a metapragmatic model of language and communication. It explores the models of speech and writing which orient the rhetoric of an Eastern Indonesian literary chronicle which uses several different types of formal language to signify traditional authority and truth. As a literary text, this chronicle constructs the reader as a participant in a world of public communication centered on the author and raises questions of its social poetics and genre. As a collection of documents and stories about contested past events, the chronicle invites the question of how people frame its rhetorical effects. These depend on the audience's metapragmatic models about powerful language. Such classifications are not concerned with particular utterances or texts, but with registers of speech. This article explores what makes this text significant as a statement about the collective past. Register is an essential complement to an analysis focused on the chronicle's genre and style as it reveals how the chronicle's meaning depends on the author's special position in his society's communicative field.

Registers index the position of speakers in a speech context. The articulation between different registers is therefore crucial for satisfying the aesthetics of particular types of social engagement (Brenneis 1990). In the church assemblies of some Pacific societies, for instance, formal and entextualized language is the source of truth and conviction, but the conviction manifests itself in subjective statements and questions which draw from everyday speech. Preachers who direct this performative process cite the Bible as a confirmation of the proper, introspective attitude which their sermons instil in the audience (Miyazaki 2004: 93). Even if formal language signifies absolute truth and the conformity of belief, the autonomous, introspective qualities of the person are equally important for the rhetoric of pursuing them (Besnier 1995: 158).

The chronicle I will discuss here was written by an Eastern Indonesian village elder towards the end of his long life. He was 94 years old when I witnessed his efforts to record the oral history of his family and village in the Malay language in Arabic script. His text resembles several other examples of Malay literacy which has been present in Eastern Indonesia since the 16th century (van der Chijs 1886: 87; Collins 1996: 32; Manusama 1977; Riedel 1888: 158; van Ronkel 1945). Instead of locating himself within one, established genre, however, this author used stylistic, thematic and constructive features from several discursive frameworks. The result was a "boundary genre" (Hanks 1987: 677; Kaartinen 2013: 401), an emerging literary form which incorporates and echoes multiple registers of speech and writing which have been socially shaped to anticipate reception by different audiences within different ideological frameworks.

It is fitting to think of these styles as genres if the goal is to understand the author's communicative intent: his wish to be recognized and understood by the actual and imagined audiences of the chronicle. Register points to a different set of questions which have more to do with the chronicle's reception among the author's own people. How did these people frame and construct the writer's traditional authority? How would they construct the linguistic forms of the chronicle as a connected speech repertoire?

I ask these questions because the author was in fact recognized as a traditional leader, even if many members of the community could not read or make sense of his texts. Just like Biblical truth, the chronicle's totalizing interpretations of the past were not simply meant to be accepted as truth. They were designed to interrogate the audience about different, fiercely contested historical perceptions. Village politics revolved around conflicting interpretations of the past precisely because these conflicts could not be resolved by public debate in the village: people only expected to find certainty about their personal value among strangers and outsiders. For this reason, any speech that revealed some crucial aspect about the collective past or the self would always veil something else. Linguistic registers in this view are entangled with different registers of self-knowledge and truth, raising further questions about the politics of memory and representation.

Universal and Local History

The ethnographic material of this article is based on fieldwork among the Bandanese, a small ethno-linguistic group that originates in the Eastern Indonesian islands of Banda.[1] Banda is a group of small volcanic islands in central Maluku, known as the only source of nutmeg and mace in the 16th century.

The islands were colonized by the Dutch East India Company in 1621, and the original Bandanese were exiled to the Kei Islands, a remote part of the Eastern Indonesian archipelago. One of their new settlements was Banda Eli, a village which has preserved the ancestral Bandanese language, oral tradition, and Islamic faith until the present day.

One impulse behind my fieldwork in Banda Eli was to uncover the Bandanese people's own account of their role in colonial history. Old men who understood that I wanted to write a book about their past referred me to an old man, Kadim Nurdin Serwowan, better known as Kende, whom everybody recognized as the authority on this subject. In the following weeks and months, I spent numerous sessions at his house, typing stories which he read aloud from his *jawi*[2] manuscripts, and eventually photographing his original texts.

Kende's chronicle is based on written documents and oral narratives from different sources. Instead of presenting his stories as a connected narrative he underlined that they were "excerpts", "citations", or "documents", which were part of a larger textual work, dialogue, or oral performance.

After presenting all of this material to me, Kende declared that his story was "complete" and insisted that I should inquire from other people about its veracity. At the same time, I was told not to show my copies of his writing to other villagers. The paradoxical need to keep the texts confidential reflected an awareness of the written documents as an interface between oral discourse and textual production. The texts were intended as an authoritative account of the past, and within the community such authority was located in specific persons.

The chronicle brings together diverse accounts about the localized origins of the different groups in the village. Through his own heroic ancestors, the past of the village is connected to the ruling dynasty of Tidore and the history of Islam. Alliances with Keiese groups and their subordination to the immigrants are the subject of another body of narratives which seek to establish the land claims of the immigrant founders of the contemporary village. This is a list of the narratives by topic in the order I collected them:

1. Genealogical relations and intermarriages between Kende's family and the Sultan of Tidore during the ancestral period in the Banda Islands.
2. An ancestral war between an indigenous Keiese ruler and his brother which took place after Kende's ancestors arrived in Kei in 1602. This story explains how the Bandanese immigrants acquired land rights in the southern part of the village.
3. The arrival of first Dutchmen in Banda and a victory over them through magic in 1599.
4. Jan Pieterszoon Coen is defeated by the Bandanese in battle but manages to defile the islands and cause the flight of their inhabitants.
5. An ancient visit to Banda by an Islamic saint (identified as Abubakar, the Prophet's Companion) which resulted in the conversion of the Bandanese.
6. The succession of imams in ancestral Banda.
7. Land tenure in the contemporary Banda Eli village, with reference to the ancient war described in story (2).

8. The founding of a separate mosque congregation in the southern part of contemporary Banda Eli in 1911.
9. The ancient war in which the community of Efruan, south of Banda Eli proper, was incorporated in the village.
10. The creation of the Banda Islands.
11. The ancestral migration from Banda to Kei.
12. The genealogy of the indigenous ruler who used to rule over Banda Eli land and the boundaries of his domain.
13. An exegesis of the tree symbol of the Golkar party of Indonesia.

The sessions during which Kende offered these stories to my transcription took place over a period of three months. The fact that he often initiated them suggests he was working with a comprehensive plan in mind. As a glance over the list makes clear, however, Kende did not frame the stories as a continuing narrative, nor did he try to place them on a coherent timeline. It makes more sense to look at the chronicle as a work of translation in which each story provides a charter for certain significant relationships. Stories (3) and (4) can be read as native commentary on Dutch historical accounts about the colonial conquest of Banda. During my research, people of Banda Eli had recently become aware of Dutch colonial documents and monographs published in the 1880s (e.g. van der Chijs 1886), perhaps through the Indonesian translation of Willard Hanna's popular account of how the Dutch East India Company displaced the original population of Banda and turned the islands into a part of its colonial empire (Hanna 1978). Another historical discourse in the background of the chronicle concerns the relations between Keiese villages and chieftainships. The current political order on the Kei islands is said to derive from an ancient, naval war which involved most chiefly domains on the islands, and in which the Bandanese played a decisive role. Kende's chronicle does not address this war directly, but he is careful to mention the allies and opponents in more local warfare which established the territorial rights of his ancestors in the southern part of the village in stories (2), (7), (9) and (11) and (12). The narrative motifs and names in stories (1), (5), (6) and (10) reverberate with traditions of dynastic succession and mythical geography known throughout Maluku. Story (8) is written as a commentary on a misplaced policy by the local government of limiting the number of mosques in the village, and text (13) is a commentary on the political symbolism of current state power.

Viewed in this way, the chronicle as a whole appears as a narrative of encounters between Kende's community and diverse kinds of foreign powers: colonizing Europeans, the indigenous chiefs of the Kei Islands, other Muslims in Maluku, the broader Islamic world, and agents of the modern state. The result is a necessarily fragmented view of history, as if the author did not worry about the match between his version of events and the broader discourse about them. In each narrative, the chiefly office held by Kende and his ancestors is presented as the counterpart of these political and religious powers, as if to encompass them under a single, locally recognized category of authority. One by one, specific historical others appear to yield power and recognition to the main Bandanese protagonist of the chronicle. The narrative never questions or re-interprets mainstream historical accounts, but it centers their relevance on Kende's own position within the Bandanese community.

While Kende's chronicle shows little interest in constructing a continuous historical narrative, the stories do indicate precise dates and years for specific events. Invariably they are dated immediately prior to some external, political changes which show in the historical record. The founding of the new mosque congregation in story (8) takes place in 1911, the year which preceded the colonial appointment of new village chiefs. By this device, Kende's stories emphasize that the Bandanese were active agents of their own history, rather than victims of external circumstances.

This view of the historical agency of the Bandanese should be understood in terms of local, cultural categories which are also key to the internal coherence of Kende's writings. In his discussion about historical narrative, Hayden White makes a difference between annals, chronicles, and genuinely historical discourse. His point is that genuinely historical discourse relies on a notion of a legal or moral subject who can serve as the agent or subject of narrated events (White 1987: 10). When the impulse to moralize events and rank them according to their significance is absent, we are dealing with annals; a chronicle, on the other hand, is organized around specific characters and relations rather than universalizing notions about order and authority. By this definition, "chronicle" appears to be the best description of Kende's efforts to write down the past. The idea of the Bandanese as a community does not consist of a universalizing self-definition; instead, it is constructed on several, alternative views of the larger social world surrounding it.

Models of Speaking

Kende held the chiefly office of *kapitan*, which was officially recognized by the Dutch colonial government in 1912. It is one of several chiefly offices in his community, and it refers to the task of interacting with state power and outsiders. Another chief who holds the title of *ratu* is responsible for agricultural rituals, land rights, and taboos. A similar division exists between the chiefs in charge of the other part of the village. The Banda Eli classification of chiefly positions implies that traditional leaders exercise authority in two distinct domains: the kinship-based hierarchies between persons and entire groups, on the one hand, and the larger political and economic relations outside the village.

The people of Banda Eli describe the nature of traditional leadership in explicitly linguistic terms. *Ratu* is the kind of chief who "speaks inside the house" and settles disputes within the community. *Kapitan* "speaks outside the house" and represents the unity of his community to outsiders. This is not a distinction between public and private language: instead, it points to an ideological view in which powerful speech that reveals or makes transparent some aspect of social reality always has to veil something else.

In practice, "speaking inside the house" refers to an attempt to settle a dispute between relatives. It begins with a heated, bitter protest about personal grievances and insults and the embarrassment they have caused among other people. This protest is usually made in Bandanese, the language of intimacy which is largely unknown outside the community. The talk about embarrassment appeals in a powerful way to people's sense of shared origin and collective honor. The usual reasons for it are love affairs, distant friendships, or the alienation related to long-distance travel. These personal engagements are always considered as risks to relatives, because if something goes wrong, the whole family will be subject to public evaluation and gossip. As people "inside the house" are reconciled with each other, they are supposed to forget the gossip and focus on their feelings towards each other (Kaartinen 2010: 133).

There is a cost to this reconciliation. Marriages, travels and distant friendships are also a source for personal differentiation and value. By engaging in them, people achieve some respite from personal relations with kinsmen which are always to some extent hierarchical. Younger siblings defer to elder ones, and children to parents. Submitting to "inside speech" deprives people of some of the esteem and sense of being their own person that they have earned among outsiders. Indeed, a measure of "outside speech" is always present in tense, emotional discussions. The senior figures who have been called upon to testify and mediate such an event frequently switch codes from Bandanese to Malay/Indonesian, as a gesture to their autonomous, "reasonable" perspective on the issue at hand (Collins & Kaartinen 1998: 550).

Kende's chiefly position entitled him to a full display of the kind of authority which manifests itself in a fleeting, veiled manner "inside the house". His chronicles present his ancestors (also *kapitans*) as the equals of foreign conquerors, colonial officers, and other leaders of the Kei Islands society. Facing such outsiders, the "outside" chief stands for the collective agency of all his people. Kende affirmed this construct with a frequent use of what Marshall Sahlins (1985: 47) calls the "heroic I". His oral explanations of narrative events from a few centuries ago culminated in such statements as "I made a miracle that sunk the enemy's ships," or "I punished him with death for his crime."

In most cases, Kende aligned his narrative voice with the identity of his ancestors when he turned to me and clarified the meaning of a particular narrative event. A similar voicing structure appears when the narrative refers to the author in the third person by mentioning his chiefly title. In this example, drawn from Kende's narrative about the Islamic conversion of the ancestors, the author underlines the collapse between ancestral time and his own time with an added comment: "this is me."

Maka dengan segera pergi memanggil kepada yang terhormat saudara Kapitan Sairun (<u>ini saya</u>) dengan segala bersama-sama datang di sini

Therefore go right away to call my venerable brother Kapitan Sairun (<u>this is me</u>) to summon everybody and come here

Sahlins argues that in certain hierarchical societies, such first-person accounts about the acts of an ancestral hero are not just a bizarre extension of the narrator's biography into the distant past. They are evidence that hierarchical relationships can be embodied personally and projected historically at the same time. The relevance of this perspective in Banda Eli society is shown by the fact that Kende's stories were taken seriously by his rivals and opponents, even if these persons might disagree with his claims or tell entirely different stories about similar events.

Whereas the "royal We" is often used to address the subjects, Kende's use of the "heroic I" was directed at outsiders. The colonial state used to interpret it as a claim to actual power within the community, and it appointed leaders like Kende to collect taxes from their subjects with mixed results. Kende's own case shows that it was not easy to translate external recognition into power to one's own people. Kende's own attempt to declare his end of Banda Eli as a sovereign village relied on support from the subordinate class – people who speak Bandanese but originate from the Kei Islands society – but it foundered against opposition from his own high-status relatives. Within society, the title of *kapitan* does not come with much personal power: the entire family of its holder claims it as part of their collective estate.

The Banda Eli model of communication uses the boundaries of the house (both as a social group and an assembly space) as an index for mapping the connections between register and context. Inside the house, the emotional exchanges between relatives are witnessed and evaluated by a relatively silent outsider. Outside the house, the relatives and familiars of the leader are witnesses for the politically assertive speech between their leader and outsiders. Kende was used to being evaluated by the effect of his discourse on distant social others. This explains why he constantly aligned his discourse with foreign genres, as if he was still mediating the intervention of various outsiders in his community. One example of this is the use of precise times and dates in anecdotal and mythological narratives. A "modern" reader, such as an Indonesian civil servant or outside scholar, would presumably appreciate such precise reporting, even if the meaning of the reported event would only be intelligible to the local audience. Such an attempt to coordinate and join the response of foreign and local audiences is evident in the entire corpus of Kende's writings, and offers an explanation for his use of widely circulating writing conventions and literary models in his chronicle.

Models of Literacy

The practice of Quranic education has for centuries maintained a certain degree of general literacy in any Muslim community in Maluku. Modern schools and the relatively cosmopolitan outlook of Banda Eli leave no doubt about most villagers' ability to read and write letters and other short pieces of written discourse. While the availability of books and newspapers is very limited, people speak of "books" with reference to any larger-scale literary works. Clearly, however, the production of such works is a specialized activity.

To someone familiar with Malay states, Kende's role as the village scribe might seem reminiscent of the officers charged with producing messages and letters in the Sultan's court of a Malay state.[3]

One must note that the activity of writing in Maluku was not monopolized by courts. More often than not, it provided a medium for the symbolic appropriation and diffusion of power, and the authority it signified could only be claimed by reference to local, cosmological schemes. During the centuries of inter-island trade which preceded effective colonization, trading communities envisioned themselves as linked to a plurality of shifting, regional trade centers (Ellen 2003: 8). Their loose political unity was not based on subjection to any particular, centralized polity but rested on "legitimizing myths which established the physical and social parameters of their world" (Andaya 1993: 49). Since the Indonesian word *mitos* has the connotation of untruth it may be safer to say that any local claims to authority relied on cosmological models in which the signs of its external derivation (such as writing) had to be connected to signs that stood for the local origins of society.

One literary model in terms of which people of Kei organize knowledge about society is the list. Each local society transcends its nature as a kin-based group by representing itself as a whole composed of numbered elements which stand in relations of subordination and contrast to each other. By one account, Banda Eli is part of a chiefly domain called Maur Ohoi-Vut, the "kingdom of ten villages", which extends over the northern tip of the island and has a supreme chief in Watlaar, a coastal village south of Banda Eli. In another view, Banda Eli is an autonomous historical entity with two "tribes" connected by a ritual center. Each tribe consists of smaller, numbered elements called "houses". Particularly on ceremonial occasions the names of these groups, as well as the ritual titles they claim, are cited as part of a finite list. Succession to chiefly office is another topic in which ritually significant information is memorized as lists. The recitation of ancestral names, place names and titles occurs generally in the performance of magic spells and ritual speech, and James Baker (1993) has suggested that this model of ritual speech may have given additional, local significance to Quranic recitation in the North Maluku society of Tidore.

In Kende's chronicle, the list is used particularly to identify elements of the Keiese society in interaction with the Bandanese ancestors, for instance in stories (2), (7) and (12). In an example from story (2), a list of names refers to *all* subjects of a princely family preparing for war.[4]

> Maka raja minta bantuan kepada orang-orang Fanfaf Futlim dengan beralat senjata lengkap, yakni berupa busur, anapana, lembing, tombak, dan pedang, taji dan keris. Cari aksi untuk melawan dengan Harfarat dengan keluarganya seisi rumah hanya sembilan orang dengan pembantuan lima orang saja tetapi dengan mempunyai kekuatan batin, yakni:
>
> 1. Kadru
> 2. Riyat
> 3. Silkoit
> 4. Sef

5. Silyam
Cuma lima orang ini sebagai panglima perang untuk membantu Harfarat dengan mempunyai kekuatan batin.

Thus the raja applied for help on behalf of the people of Fanfaf Futlim who were fully armed with bows, arrows, javelins, spears, knives, spurs, and daggers. They made ready to resist Harfarat whose family and children numbered only nine people, and who only had five people to help him, but these five possessed the Inner Power. They were:
1. Kadru
2. Riyat
3. Silkoit
4. Sef
5. Silyam

A mere five people led the troops who helped Harfarat and possessed the Inner Power.

The notion of completeness here is similar to the idea of siblings as an indivisible unity – an idea which often finds expression in the series of homophonous personal names, as Janet Carsten (1997: 85) observes about the Langkawi society. A parallel to such naming practices in Keiese rituals is the recitation of homophonous names which are actually said to be chiefly titles. By repeating a sound shape with minimal variation such lists of names suggest an underlying, cosmological whole. While the recitation of such lists may create an impression of them as texts in their own right, Kende's chronicle also uses them as one of its sources of schematic coherence.

Ancestral Voices

In addition to the narrative voice of the writer, the chronicle frequently quotes what ancestral characters said at a crucial turn of events. Their reported words take the form of songs and verbal formulas. Some songs represent the "weeping" of powerful people defeated in a war. Songs of another type represent dialogue between ancestral figures. Both weeping and dialogue can be recognized as registers of contemporary storytelling and verbal art. As Kende projects such language into the distant past, he underlines that his ancestors communicated with strangers from a stance of sympathy, equality, and mercy, and never deferred to their superior status. In each case, the song stands not for the voice of Kende's own ancestors, but rather for the voice of ancestors of linguistic and ethnic others.

Kende presented the songs as the "proof" of his narrative, with the implication that the song would immediately prompt the song's "owners" to recognize the truth of what is being told about them. In this sense, reported speech appears as an "objective document" of the social reception of speech (Hanks 1987: 679). Kei Islands people have often deployed oral historical narratives as evidence in dispute settlement, which is the ultimate test for their performative effects. It is easy to imagine that if some people hear a quotation of their ancestors begging for mercy in such a context, they will present an equally vicious response. Dialogue, on the other hand, suggests an alliance between two groups. Citing ancestral dialogue would therefore be a way to get another group to defend one's own position in a dispute.

Songs and formulas are recognized as typical registers of oral historical discourse in the Kei Islands society. Most people of Banda Eli are fluent in the Keiese language (Evav), and they are also familiar with oral traditions performed at public festivals. In this context, formulas which condense the role of a particular village or community in ancient wars are woven together into long songs called *ngel-ngel* and interpreted as parts of a shared tradition. I have also been present at a dispute settlement which ended in solemn silence when one of the participants performed the kind of song quoted in Kende's chronicle. The singers are typically common people and do not assume the kind of interpretive authority manifested by Kende's chronicle. At the same time, it is difficult to see their performances as a submissive gesture either. A performer who understands well the ongoing social engagement will time the song in such a way that singing, together with the somewhat emotional silence that follows it, obviates the social hierarchy between participants.

One of Kende's stories was used as an argument in a dispute over marine resource rights in 1990. The people considered as the descendants of the defeated, ancestral ruler were invited to witness in favor of one party in the conflict, but they anticipated the insult to their honor and never showed up. Consequently Kende did not include the song in the draft (Ind. *konsep*) of the decision which he wrote at that time, but only performed it when we discussed my transcription of the text four years later.

Formulas are incorporated in the narratives in a similar way as the songs. They paraphrase the meaning of a particular past event in a condensed way that is easily repeated and memorized:

> Watlaar felled the big trees, Banda Eli cut off the small grass.

In this parallelistic expression, the practices of shifting agriculture are a metaphor of ancient warfare in which the whole population of a village was exterminated to punish the rape of a noblewoman. Ironically, much of Kende's own knowledge about oral traditions came from this village where he served as an imam, the Islamic leader of prayers, during the 1930s. The people of this village have since then affirmed their social and political autonomy relative to the conquering villages mentioned in the formula, and it would be an insult to cite it in their face. Some other people in Banda Eli would also contest the story because it recognizes that their village belongs to a political domain ruled from Watlaar, a village located four kilometers south along the coast.

The effect of pronouncing a formula or singing a song engages a socially recognized register to form a complete, distinct utterance. This corresponds to the aesthetic effect of "finalization" in the reading of a literary work, in the sense that the writer, for that moment, has said everything there is to be said (Bakhtin 1986: 76). A related effect of discourse is officialization, a process through which the speakers signal the authentic, authoritative grounds on which they speak (Hanks 1996: 244). In literary discourse, there is no question of timing the change of registers with actual social engagements. These effects are achieved by other means. In Kende's chronicle, reporting the speech of ancestors is an important device for officializing discourse, and accordingly the chronicle refers to songs as the "proof" of narrated events.

> Insya Allah dengan membuktikan dengan satu nyanyian:
> > Waliyo Tadore sia waliyo Tidore
> > Destar naik naku sombak warotop si ya wali yo Tadore
>
> Artinya: membuktikan sehelai kain sutera dilipat menjadi serban atau destar sebagai seutas tali yang dapat memperikatkan atau memperhubungkan silatu rahim kakak dan adik dari Banda Neira ke Tadore. Dari kedua kampung itu semua hidup dengan selamat.

> God willing there is a song to prove it:
> > Guardians of Tadore, guardians of Tidore
> > Raise the headdress and fold it into a rope for the guardians of Tadore
>
> The meaning: it proves that a sheet of silk cloth folded into a turban or headdress is a binding rope to bind or connect sisters and brothers from Banda Neira in love and compassion with Tadore. Everyone from these two villages will live in peace and prosperity.

The songs and formulas stand for narrative truth claims which are extremely contested by most parties. For this reason, Kende never showed his writings to other villagers. At the same time, most people knew well what they contained. Old people had seen him debating the same issues in public; young people heard him recite the day's writings in the evening when Kende sat at the window where he had enough light to read. Much of his authority hung on the perceived effect that his writings might have on other people. In this sense, Kende's authority depended on the metapragmatic ideas about what would happen if he made his knowledge public, and less on the direct effects of his rhetoric.

Literary Discourse

Kende's chronicle clearly presents us with several, different examples of what, in the eyes of Maluku villagers, constitutes literary text. A significant device to accomplish this is the engagement of the register and strategies for written texts, such as the Arabic title words which appear in the opening of several narratives. Instead of referring to his writings as *hikayat* ['story'], Kende indicates that they are excerpts from a larger work by using words like *muqaddimah* ['introduction'], *bab* ['part'], or *pasal* ['chapter'] as the title of specific passages. Words like *konsep* ['draft'] and *salinan* ['excerpt'], derived from other languages, carry the same implication. Text (1) is called 'genealogy' (*Keturunan silsila*) but consists of a larger narrative account. In a manner similar to the Malay Annals, the story does not merely offer genealogical information but makes a performative statement about the claim of the "owner" of the story to ancestral characters mentioned in it. Such ownership is implied by the statement, at the end of the text, according to which the text was originally written on behalf of the Tidore Sultan's daughter who was Kende's ancestress in Banda. This can be seen as a strategy from written discourses comparable to the use of the "heroic I" as an orally based device mentioned above.

The cues and strategies associated with written registers are not exclusive to a single genre. Instead, Kende appears to draw on these communicative resources intuitively, according to an (at least somewhat) idiolectal understanding of these registers and associated genres including how and when they should be used. Through the deployment of these devices, he positions himself and his reader and the communicative relationship between them. At the end of several texts the reader is greeted with *wassalam*, the formal, Arabic ending of a letter. This phrase, as well as words like *tamat* ['end'] or *sekian* ['thus'], marks the text as a letter or document rather than a part of a larger literary work. The fact that most texts bear a date has a similar implication. In this case, the chronicle invites one to recall the circumstances of an important social context that involved written communication. Such contexts may have involved powerful outsiders: religious and government officials, visiting chiefs, or marriage partners, who represent the direct authors or addressees of the documents. However, oral historical genres in Banda Eli hardly make any reference to dates, whereas Kende's manuscripts coordinate narrative and calendric time with more precision than any practical or evidential purposes would seem to call for. One underlying impulse for this is the current availability of historical documents about the colonization of Banda in which dates are the most accessible information to people who do not read Dutch. In the chronicle, events located in the ancestral homeland are clustered around the time of the first Dutch visits to the islands. According to texts (1), (2), and (3), the intermarriages with the Sultan of Tidore are completed in 1597; the history of Dutch–Bandanese interactions during 1599 and 1621 is condensed in a few months at the turn of the 17th century, and the exodus to the Kei Islands takes place at 1602.

The use of Christian rather than Islamic dates in these texts suggests that they are written explicitly to challenge the European account of the same events. Whenever the text mentions the month of the event, however, it refers to Islamic months by their Arabic names. This is how Kende dates the text about his ancestor who opposed the Dutch in Banda (3):

Pada hari peringatan Kapitan Sairun yang berpulang ke Rahmat Ullah pada malam Rabu yang tepat pada waktu terbit fajar sidik bertanggal 1 Muharram pada tahun 1601 Masehi.

On the day of commemorating *Kapitan* Sairun who returned to God's Mercy on the night against Wednesday exactly at the breaking of day on 1 Muharram of the year A.D. 1601.

In another text, (8), Islamic prayer times are determined by cannon shots, ordered by the imam, as well as by precise clock times:

> Bapak Datuk Imam tua kembali di Kubtel disuruh lagi ditembak meriam itu berbunyi menandahkan pada hari Jumat itu penghulu segala hari serta berbunyi meriam itu dipanggil pada umat Islam yang berakal balik di kampong Efruan itu semuanya turun bersama kita pergi bersembahyang Jumat. Maka kita semua datang sampai di muka pintu masjid Jumat tiba-tiba sudah selesaikan sembahyang Fardhu Jumat pada jam 11:00 kemudian sembahyang Johor 4 (empat arkat) pada jam 12:00...

> The senior Lord Imam back in Kubtel ordered again to fire the cannon whose sound on Fridays was a signal to all chiefs to summon reasonable Muslims back to the village of Efruan and to come and join us for the Friday prayers. Thus when we all came at the door of the Friday mosque the obligatory Friday prayers had just finished at 11:00 followed by the Noon 4 prayers (four prostrations) at 12:00 ...

In either case, the reader has no independent way of coordinating the different calendars and temporalities conjoined in Kende's account. On the one hand, the dates indicate that the writing itself took place at a specific moment. On the other hand, the stories describe external events with a moment's precision. Social time, calendric time, and the time of writing are presented as a single regime of events. By constructing such models of time, Kende situates his account in a discourse of historical documents and the authority of such documents as accounts of history. The strategy of employing registers associated with literature extends from linguistic resources and structuring devices associated with different genres to engagements with ideologies, alternative ways of thinking about time, that belong to discourses "outside the house".

In spite of engaging the register of written literature, the classification of Kende's chronicle as a total, literary work remains ambiguous. To be able to classify the chronicle in such terms, we would need to single out the conventions and expectations which enable a particular community or audience to identify a text as belonging to a certain type of literature. Instead, this work emerges as a "boundary genre": Kende's mediating position between his own community and outsiders means that his writings are addressed to several audiences and respond to multiple horizons of expectation at once. As a consequence, the chronicle incorporates a number of distinguishable genres and the metapragmatically interpretable registers of distinct discourses are juxtaposed and interpenetrated within the chronicle as a coherent work. There are several different ways in which they can be finalized, or constructed as complete messages, to the puzzlement of people who expect to "make sense" of them as a coherent account of history.

Recent anthropological discussions of textuality offer some keys for approaching this puzzle. Once it was assumed that the finalized, complete nature of a literary work is based on the formal coherence and consistency of the linguistic expressions contained in it. More recent views expand the notion of texts from literary works to a more general idea of text as a metadiscursive notion that emerges from the communicative events mediated by writing or other forms of objectified discourse (Silverstein & Urban 1996: 2). The discourse that goes on in such events is sometimes interpreted as dialogue, at other times as text; in either case the "event" consists of utterances – efforts by speakers or authors to project a final or complete meaning to what they have said. What scholars in this tradition call entextualization means that the "original" author and the "final" recipient of the message are projected somewhere beyond ongoing interaction, often by formal devices which indicate that the discourse contains meanings or logic evident to others than those immediately present (Kuipers 1990: 4). From this point of view, the textuality of Kende's writings is enhanced rather than undermined by their overlapping indication towards multiple communicative contexts.

These views of textuality have been helpful in accounting for the authority and cultural significance of oral mythology and ritual speech. One measure of the authority of traditional texts is the degree to which they resist commentary and re-interpretation (Hymes 1981; Urban 1996). The source of such resistance is the poetic patterning of discourse which is easiest to recognize in songs, speeches, and stories that conform to a particular genre. Discourse that moves between genres is also structured by its component features – form, plot, register, temporal horizon, appropriate subject matter – and their reception by the audience (Bowen 1991: 141). The poetic structure of Kende's chronicle is not obvious to someone who simply reads it because it was based on his life-historical relationship to different audiences outside his own community. Songs, dates, literary formulas, and mundane-sounding dialogue are examples of his use of register as an index of his standing among such outsiders. This use of register was perfectly in line with the cultural model of Kende's leadership role. Many of the songs he performed while dictating a narrative to me were not actually written down in his manuscript: singing them added a twist to the story's intended effect when Kende read it aloud from his notebook. His performance, like his text, did not respond to any stable expectations on genre. It is suggestive of a pragmatic deployment of register to modify the audience's response, or what Elizabeth Tonkin (1992: 53) has called different "modes" (rather than "genres") of discourse.

Kende's writings do not evoke an interpretive horizon by using a consistent linguistic or poetic style. Hence their classification as a total, literary work remains ambiguous. We are thus left with the question of how Kende's readers are able to recognize the authority of his writings; what, in the stories themselves, indicates that they are concerned with truth about the past.

The answer suggested by literary theory is that something intervenes between the meaningful units of language and the objectivity of the things they represent. Words and phrases do not simply add up to a complete story with a logical, narrative scheme. Instead, literary works and stories engage their readers with interpretive logics that operate on a lower level and encourage them to "fill in the blanks", or supply the work with meanings which arise from their own, previous knowledge and experience. Following Roman Ingarden's (1973) aesthetics of reception, William Hanks (1989: 104) has suggested that the boundaries of texts (what the text "says", what it is "about", whom it "concerns") are constituted by the interplay between schematic and concretized moments in the text's progression. Instead of providing all concrete information about the objective things it represents, the text gives the reader "schematic aspects" – indications and vantage points – from which s/he can imagine them in concrete terms and incorporate them in the description or narrative of the text.

In Kende's chronicle, these schematic aspects are exemplified by place names and characteristics of the landscape. Text (7) is organized around the landmarks which the ancestral founders of their contemporary village passed on entering the settlement; what might be told as a temporally advancing narrative is thus condensed into a list of place-names which outline territorial boundaries:

> Mulai dari Sirwang, Maslairfofan turun di Gurmas sampai di hender suku 30 bagian selatan sampai di Siwar (Howarfit) sebelah utara di pantai sampai di Taub Matbelngutdo diserahkan kepada Kapitan Sairfofan yang berdasarkan ke perangan dengan Fufaifuk.

> Starting from Sirwang, Maslairfofan and descending to Gurmas up to the brook at Tribe 30 the southern part up to Siwar (Howarfit), the northern half of the beach up to Taub Matbelngutdo was handed to *Kapitan* Sairfofan on the basis of the war against Fufaifuk.

Text (7) is clearly composed as a land rights document, and its underlying narrative is that of text (2) – an extensive narrative in which Kende's ancestor arrives in the Kei Islands and rescues the indigenous ruler who gave him the land. Here the focus is not on territories and places but on the names, persons, and social entities that define the indigenous land owners. The same is true for text (9) which describes an ancient conflict between several, carefully named ancestral groups. The familiar environment of mundane life thus provides the concrete reference for mythological warfare, underlining the implications of this war for current society, even if its parties and their connections to presently living people are vague and disputed.

In spite of their common subject matter – land rights – these stories fall in different genres. Whereas text (7) maps its events on place, texts (2 and 9) refer to place only as the general scene of a narrative that focuses on human characters. Text (10), on the other hand, extends subjective knowledge beyond the domain of concrete experience: imagined flights above the landscape or dives in the depths of the sea. Some of this diversity of chronotopes is understandable in the light of the specific claims of each text. Text (7) was written in the context of a territorial dispute, as a document of an agreement between community leaders. Texts (2) and (9), on the other hand, are concerned with excluding the territorial claims of groups which still exist as recognized social entities. Even as the narratives recognize certain people as the original inhabitants and owners of village land, the stories affirm that they have either become extinct or moved away.

Even text (10) can be seen as an origin myth concerned with justifying some aspect of the present society. It contains a number of magic spells which allow one to approach the protective spirits of the volcano and the sea. On closer look, however, this text is more than a statement about the autochthonous status of the Bandanese in their ancestral home. It is written around a large, drawn image of the volcanic cone in the Banda Islands, as if to help the reader to recognize it during his sea travels. The writing is mixed with other images as well: a passport photo of Kende's son is glued to the original. The text also invites the reader to imagine the map of the Banda Islands. Their most conspicuous feature is the volcanic cone enclosed inside another, curved island formed by the volcano's caldera. Kende's text claims that this feature, or the cartographic image of it, carries a hidden insight: from a bird's eye view, Banda resembles the Arabic letter nun (ن). For someone who knows the Arabic letters, "seeing" is "reading."

This example suggests that Kende was not merely concerned with producing an authoritative account of past events. His use of different registers – ranging from the objective, "documentary" reference to clock times and calendars to the subjectively immersive reading of the Arabic Quran – demonstrates a concern with the aesthetics of truth and conviction. The chronicle quotes passages from the Quran particularly in texts (3–4) where they emphasize the religious motivation for the resistance against Dutch power. These narratives, as well as text (8), are not modeled after local origin narratives but respond to global discourses about colonial and Islamic history. While these texts contain polemical statements, they also invite the reader to disagree about a wide range of details. Even as they present a close, concrete account of certain key events, the use of calendric dates allows the reader to schematize the events as part of several alternative master-narratives or temporal frameworks. For instance, the meticulous account about the summons to the Friday prayer in text (8) gives the reader full freedom to imagine what has just been going on in secular life before the cannon sounds. In this way, precise, documentary description creates what Hanks (1989: 105) calls schematic aspects: interpretive possibilities that depend on the reader's ability to "fill the gaps" in the story.

Register is relevant for understanding the reader's subjective involvement with discourse because it determines what kind of language would be appropriate for talking about the gap. Kende's simultaneous use of several registers confronted his audience with interpretive gaps in a powerful way. Although he liked to be in the position to explain what his story meant, I believe that his first concern was to throw the ball to the audience and create an awareness that they were in the presence of powerful discourse. This, of course, was a gesture towards Kende's own mediating role between different aesthetics of truth and conviction.

At the same time, Kende was clearly interested in aligning his discourse with different sources of power. It is noteworthy that the religious schism in text (8) falls in 1911–1912, the years in which the chiefly domains of Great Kei were reorganized by the colonial state. The ancient dispute narrated in text (8) was revived in the early 1970s when Kende wanted to remove the mosque presided over by his relatives away from the village center in order to affirm it as the center of an independent congregation. The narrative backs up this agenda by presenting an earlier dispute from 1912 as a founding event that split the village in two different mosque congregations. The narrative obscures the fact that the colonial government produced a similar split in the secular domain by appointing a different chief in each side of the village around the same time (Kaartinen 2010: 174).

The precise hours and minutes mentioned in the story finalize it in a particular way and turn it into evidence about a state intervention in the distant past. It is likely that the model for officializing comes from the Kei Islands experience of various customary and formal courts and other administrative proceedings during the past century (Adatrechtbundels 1922: 26). In the 1970s dispute Kende faced the intervention of officials from the official religious court. No one in that court had access to documents about the government intervention that fell two generations earlier. Ironically Kende, who had succeeded the first, Dutch-appointed *kapitan* as the secular leader of his side of the village, was the only one who could create a precedent for its decision which allowed Kende's family to build a new mosque further away from the village center.

Kende's precise reporting about the 1912 dispute was not merely a device for convincing state officials. In addition to precise hours of the clock, the events of his narrative are also timed with reference to the Islamic daily prayers (Kaartinen 2010: 171). The double use of secular and sacred registers points to Kende's unique position as community leader. He served as imam in a subordinate hamlet of Banda Eli during his youth before he was appointed as *kapitan*. In this narrative, Kende uses register to coordinate the religious and secular sources of his authority – a combination of powers which must have been decisive in his encounters with other powerful people in the village.

Kende's chronicle says almost nothing about his career as a community leader and state-appointed chief before and after decolonization. Making more of his personal access to state power would, of course, reveal the negative, incomplete aspect of his power. A chief who speaks outside the house draws some of his authority from the recognition of outside powers. He can only convince his own people by placing himself on a level with outsiders and talking to them in their language. By animating the speech of such outsiders, Kende's chronicle obscures their agency.

Audiences and Authorship

The literary text that I have discussed presents a paradox. It revolves around various public registers of language which are easy to identify with such contexts as dispute settlements, traditional performances, religious observances, pleas, oaths, confessions, and reports to the authorities. In spite of his constant reference to these public contexts, Kende declined to make his chronicle public in his own village. I have already pointed to some obvious reasons for this: debating his representations of past events would have revived forgotten conflicts over land, status, and authority. There was nothing to gain from that.

But Kende was ready to respond to any outsider – including myself – who showed interest in his writings. When he passed away in 1997, his writings were divided among relatives who lived in faraway towns. In this way, the chronicle turned into a monument of Kende's history of communicating with various powerful outsiders – the substance of his position as the "chief who speaks outside the house".

As I have already noted, speaking outside the house represents the community as an undivided group to outsiders. Using a foreign register of authoritative language is not a gesture of submission to a larger sociopolitical order because it veils the dimension of self which is revealed in the emotional engagements "inside the house". On the contrary, it puts the speaker, and his whole group, on a level with other speakers in the foreign arenas of political assertiveness. In short, the Banda Eli language ideology avoids placing all speech under a single regime of discourse. Instead of recognizing one, uniform public space it is a model for affirming nobility.

It would be easy to dismiss Kende's chronicle as an obsolete, nostalgic glance at the high points of his life. I believe, however, that in his nineties he had not entirely abandoned his political projects. Above all, he attempted to make sure that people would not forget his ancestry and status, and that his descendants could still make claims on them. Submitting such memory to interpersonal evaluation among his fellow villagers would have been a certain way to dilute and destroy it. A scholarly outsider like myself offered little more guarantee of preserving the chronicle's emphasis on Kende's personal eminence, his rhetoric of "heroic I". Therefore he cultivated the interest of urban, literate relatives in his manuscript and ordered it to be sent to them at his death. These people are now in position to reveal their personal connection to well-known historical events, and to carry on the same aesthetic of social and political involvement which characterized Kende's role as a chief.

The classification of chiefly offices in Banda Eli points to two genres of powerful speech. On a closer look, these genres are ideal types that describe the relationship between the speaker and audience. Particularly the chief who "speaks outside the house" has to engage different kinds of audiences. His use of different registers of speech is an index of his relationship to different forms and sources of power. In Kende's case, the situation is further complicated by the fact that many relevant engagements with powerful outsiders have taken place in the past. Kende's manuscript is an effort to reconstruct personal authority from the registers of language that commemorate these historical interactions with foreign cultural, religious, and state authority.

The registers of powerful speech discussed in this article are suggestive of Johannes Fabian's distinction between two different politics of memory. Public memory, as Johannes Fabian (2007: 95) puts it, "documents itself." Its substance and truth claims are evaluated in public performances and social engagements. Its opposite is collective memory, one that is declared as a closed territory or possession. Fabian's figure allows me to suggest that Kende not only wrote down oral traditions in order to claim ownership of them: essentially he was concerned with "collecting" knowledge that could be lost and discredited as soon as it became public.

Where exactly is the politics of such memory? Preserving an aristocratic family tradition is merely the surface of it. During his late years, Kende's keenest wish was to be recognized by educated younger relatives who lived an entirely different life in rapidly changing Indonesian cities. All who have stayed in the Banda Eli village struggle in their own way to maintain a temporally continuing social engagement with distant relatives, who often live in very different socioeconomic conditions. As long as distant kinsmen keep visiting, writing and helping them, most people do not mind that they also have a quite different, "modern" outlook and priorities.

For a literate, cultural authority such as Kende, modern thinking presents a more fundamental difficulty. Traditional knowledge about the past is habitually classified as inferior to academic, national, and Islamic historical discourse. The people at its source are therefore not included in its public evaluation. In spite of the respect Kende enjoyed as a person, he suffered from what Fabian (1983) has called denial of coevality. His response to urban relatives who dismissed his knowledge as "myth" (Ind. *mitos*), or remarked that it did not make sense to them, was to produce a slight mismatch between the dates of his account and the publicly accepted master narrative. Kende's politics of memory was geared to create alterity as a condition of communication (Fabian 2007: 27).

Fabian's discussion focuses on the failure of anthropologists to recognize that they live in the same time and participate in the same politics as the people they study. Kende's chronicle presents a challenge for recognizing the author's coevality with his audience. In order to do so, we cannot simply approach the chronicle as an item of cultural knowledge: we have to recognize it as an argument which offers itself to response and contestation.

What kind of argument did Kende want to make? To me, an academic outsider, he insisted that his chronicle was a "complete" account about the past. He told me to find out whether other people in the community agreed with it. I understood this as a didactic strategy: the teacher engages the student in a debate and forces him or her to disagree about the details in order to reveal the full story and convince the student of is truth.

This strategy relies on some kind of public debate. In order to participate in the revealing and aesthetic powers of Kende's songs and stories, I needed access to other people who knew them. I found, however, that other villagers had little knowledge about the discourse which Kende presented as the proof of his accounts. The people of Banda Eli enjoy public debate about their culture and history, but this debate is not aimed at placing past events in a comprehensive master narrative. In the absence of a stable, historical genre, their debate revolves around each speaker's knowledge about a particular register of cultural discourse.

I doubt that Kende's aim was to create a master narrative or to teach his knowledge about the past. Instead of placing it in the center of a field of generalizable knowledge, his chronicle reflects a position which Emiko Ohnuki-Tierney (1990: 18) has called "symbolic marginality." One of its features is the modification of the speaking "I" in each discourse situation (Ohnuki-Tierney 1994: 63). Kende's use of religious, official, and traditional registers – not to mention his "heroic I" – appealed to a model of the self in which the core of one's ancestry and origin can only be known outside the context of familiar, interpersonal relations. The desire for such self-knowledge is the source of the Bandanese interest in long-distance travel which promises to bring one into encounters with distant, forgotten relatives. Ohnuki-Tierney's (1994: 64) notion of the "absent subject" points to another possibility. With reference to the Japanese use of pronouns, she argues that discourse which deliberately violates the normal registers of interpersonal communication has powerful self-revealing effects. I argue that Kende was using registers with a related purpose: to encourage his listeners and readers to assume an introspective, questioning attitude about their own selves and origin, and to pursue for insights about them by talking to him.

The positive powers of symbolic marginality are evident in the possibility of mobilizing intercultural relations for new social and political ends. Traditional verbal arts were disappearing quickly from the Kei Island villages which I studied in the 1990s, but they continue to signify alliance and kinship between different communities. This means that genres are lost but registers remain. The interest in obsolete items of language is not limited to people who look for family heritage among old relatives. Kende made an effective appeal to it when he ordered his writings to be sent to a number of distant relatives. In this way, his long-lost political influence was reproduced in another form, as an ethnic-cultural network which continues to have relevance in urban Indonesia.

Notes

1. My field research in the village of Banda Eli took place over 15 months in 1994–1996, with funding from the Academy of Finland and the Väinö Tanner Foundation and under the sponsorship of the University of Gajah Mada, Yogyakarta. In 2009 I did fieldwork in Ambon and the Kei Islands with funding from the Academy of Finland, sponsored by the Indonesian Institute of Sciences (LIPI) at Jakarta and Ambon. I would like to express thanks to these agencies and the Banda Eli community for their generous support to my research.
2. *Jawi* refers to the use of the Arabic alphabet for writing in the Malay language. It has been used in Islamic Southeast Asia since the 12th century, and became widespread in the Eastern Indonesian islands of Maluku in the 15th century. In my field area, the Latin alphabet has replaced *jawi* as the medium for reading and writing Indonesian and other Malay dialects, even if religious education continues to emphasize the ability to recite the Quran in Arabic.
3. The closest examples of Malay trading states are Ternate, Tidore, Jailolo and Bacan – the four historical sultanates of North Maluku (Andaya 1993).
4. In social and cosmic classifications known throughout Maluku, the number five (the number of war leaders on the enemy side) signifies the completeness of the male body, whereas the number nine (the number of people in the enemy's domestic unit) signifies the union of husband and wife (Valeri 1989).

References

Adatrechtbundels 1922 = *Adatrechtbundels bezorgd door de Commissie voor het Adatrecht.* Vol. 21. Gravenhage: Martinus Nijhoff.

Agha, Asif 2004. Registers of Language. In *A Companion to Linguistic Anthropology.* Ed. A. Duranti. Malden, MA: Blackwell. Pp. 23–45.

Andaya, Leonard 1993. *The World of Maluku: Eastern Indonesia in the Modern Period.* Honolulu: University of Hawaii Press.

Baker, James 1993. The Presence of the Name: Reading Scripture in an Indonesian Village. In *The Ethnography of Reading.* Ed. J. Boyarin. Berkeley: University of California Press. Pp. 98–138.

Bakhtin, Mikhail 1986. *Speech Genres and Other Late Essays.* Austin: University of Texas Press.

Bauman, Richard 2004. *A World of Other's Worlds: Cross-Cultural Perspectives on Intertextuality.* London: Blackwell.

Besnier, Niko 1995. *Literacy, Emotion, and Authority: Reading and Writing on a Polynesian atoll.* Cambridge: Cambridge University Press.

Bowen, John R. 1991. *Sumatran Politics and Poetics: Gayo History, 1900–1989.* New Haven: Yale University Press.

Brenneis, Donald 1990. Shared and Solitary Sentiments: The Discourse of Friendship, Play, and Anger in Bhatgaon. In *Language and the Politics of Emotion.* Ed. Catherine Lutz & Lila Abu-Lughod. Cambridge: Cambridge University Press. Pp. 113–125.

Carsten, Janet 1997. *The Heat of the Hearth: The Process of Kinship in a Malay Fishing Community.* Oxford: Clarendon Press.

van der Chijs, Mr. J. A. 1886. *De vestiging van het Nederlandsche gezag over de Banda-Eilanden (1599–1621).* Hague: M. Nijhoff.

Collins, James T. 1996. *Malay, World Language of the Ages.* Kuala Lumpur: Dewan Bahasa dan Pustaka.

Collins, James, & Timo Kaartinen 1998. Preliminary Notes on Bandanese: Language Development and Change in Kei. *Bijdragen tot de Taal-, Land- en Volkenkunde* 154(4): 521–570.

Ellen, Roy 2003. *On the Edge of the Banda Zone: Past and Present in the Social Organization of a Moluccan Trading Network.* Honolulu: University of Hawaii Press.

Fabian, Johannes 1983. *Time and the Other.* New York: Columbia University Press.

Fabian, Johannes 2007. *Memory against Culture: Arguments and Reminders.* Durham, NC: Duke University Press.

Goody, Jack 1977. *The Domestication of the Savage Mind.* Cambridge: Cambridge University Press.

Hanks, William 1987. Discourse Genres in a Theory of Practice. *American Ethnologist* 14: 668–692.

Hanks, William 1989. Text and Textuality. *Annual Review of Anthropology* 18: 95–127.

Hanks, William 1996. *Language and Communicative Practices.* Boulder: Westview Press.

Hymes, Dell 1981. *"In Vain I Tried to Tell You": Essays in Native American Ethnopoetics.* Philadelphia: University of Pennsylvania Press.

Ingarden, Roman 1973. *The Literary Work of Art.* Evanston: Northwestern University Press.

Kaartinen, Timo, 2010. *Songs of Travel and Stories of Place: Poetics of Absence in an Eastern Indonesian Society.* Folklore Fellows Communications 299. Helsinki: Academia Scientarium Fennica.

Kaartinen, Timo 2013. Handing Down and Writing Down: Metadiscourses of Tradition among the Bandanese of Eastern Indonesia. *Journal of American Folklore* 126(502): 385–406.

Keane, Webb 1997. *Signs of Recognition: Powers and Hazards of Representation in an Indonesian Society*. Berkeley: University of California Press.

Kuipers, Joel 1990. *Power in Performance: The Creation of Textual Authority in Weyeba Ritual Speech*. Philadelphia: The University of Pennsylvania Press.

Malcolm, Karen 2005. What Communication Linguistics Has to Offer Genre and Register Research. *Folia Linguistica* 39(1–2): 57–74.

Manusama, Z. J. 1977. *Hikayat Tanah Hitu: Historie en Sociale Structuur in Ambon*. Doctoral dissertation, University of Leiden.

Miyazaki, Hirokazu 2004. *The Method of Hope: Anthropology, Philosophy, and Fijian Knowledge*. Stanford: Stanford University Press.

Ohnuki-Tierney, Emiko 1990. Introduction: The Historicization of Anthropology. In *Culture Through Time: Anthropological Approaches*. Ed. E. Ohnuki-Tierney. Stanford: Stanford University Press. Pp. 1–25.

Ohnuki-Tierney, Emiko 1994. The Power of Absence. Zero Signifiers and their Transgressions. *L'Homme* 130(2): 59–76.

Riedel, J. G. F. 1888. *De Sluik- en Kroesharige Rassen tusschen Selebes en Papua*. Gravenhage: Martinus Nijhoff.

Ronkel, Ph. S. van 1945. Een maleisch geschrift met nautische illustraties, over de geschiedenis van Banda. *Cultureel Indie* 7: 123–130.

Sahlins, Marshall 1985. *Islands of History*. Chicago: University of Chicago Press.

Schrieke, B. 1955. *Indonesian Sociological Studies: Vol. I*. The Hague: van Hoeve.

Silverstein, Michael & Greg Urban 1996. The Natural History of Discourse. In *Natural Histories of Discourse*. Ed. Michael Silverstein & Greg Urban. Chicago: The University of Chicago Press. Pp. 1–20.

Tonkin, Elizabeth 1992. *Narrating our Pasts: The Social Construction of Oral History*. Cambridge: Cambridge University Press.

Valeri, Valerio 1989. Reciprocal Centers: The Siwa-Lima System in the Central Moluccas. D. Maybury-Lewis & Uri Almagor (eds.) *The Attraction of Opposites: Thought and Society in the Dualistic Mode*. Ann Arbor: University of Michigan Press. Pp. 117–142.

White, Hayden 1987. *The Content of the Form: Narrative Discourse and Historical Representation*. Baltimore: Johns Hopkins University Press.

James M. Wilce and Janina Fenigsen

9. Mourning and Honor
Register in Karelian Lament

This chapter considers the language used in traditional Karelian lament and its counterpart in the Finnish "lament revival" as particularly interesting examples of honorific register where honorific forms routinely combine respect and intimacy. This special language, which revivalists call the *itkukieli* ['lament language'], will be referred to here as the "lament register". This register is realized through the use of a range of devices, of which we will focus on nominal circumlocutions, diminutivization, and frequentativization of the verbs, from which key words in the circumlocutory noun phrases derive. Although expressions of respect and intimacy are by no means unique to lament register, their implications for our thinking about power and solidarity and distance and intimacy have remained undertheorized. We suggest that the lament register provides an excellent case for re-examining these issues. Furthermore, we suggest that in its (discursive and functional) use of the honorific register to address and influence the world of spirits in ways that are tangible to the lamenters, the Karelian (and, in some respects, the neo-Karelian) lament in particular invites a re-thinking of conventional scholarly perspectives on funerary lament such as to realign the socio-psychologically functional perspectives with the metapragmatic realities of the lamenters. This metapragmatic functionality (Silverstein 1993) straddles and connects two phenomena – the linguistic forms and the understood honoring that they enact, which together constitute Karelian *itkuvirži* ['crying song, lament'] or *iänellä itkie* ['with-voice to cry', i.e. 'to cry aloud, lament'][1] and the lament register *per se*. Moreover, that honoring is realized, as Finnish lament revivalists say, through *pehmennys* ['softness/softening'], a metapragmatic term that captures deference and intimacy.

We set forth the case for regarding the lament register as closely related to "honorific registers", particularly those associated with ritual discourse. In doing so, we rely on local commentary and cross-linguistic/cross-cultural comparison. We underscore what some have noted previously (Irvine 2009) – that the common association between honorifics and power and the dichotomizing of respect and intimacy are oversimplifications. Wilce's study of the so-called[2] "lament revival" in Finland, which draws on Karelian tradition, indicates that the "tenderness" or linguistic "softening", mentioned by those revivalists as a desideratum of laments and clearly manifested in such registral features as diminutivization, is paradoxically congruent with "respect".

Human beings are constantly doing things with words. That is to say that speaking *is* a kind of doing or action. Yet it is also true that speech *becomes* action – social action – insofar as culture gives it significance. The view that language merely expresses things that already exist, including inner states such as emotions and thoughts that are in need of therapeutic venting, is a modern language ideology, one that crops up in the literature on lament (Gamliel 2007). This chapter works from the opposite assumption – that speech as action creates as much as it expresses. Registers will be regarded here as metapragmatically conventionalized tools for such action. The particular speech genres of interest here are what have been treated as subgenres of Karelian lament, especially funerary, wedding, and "occasional" laments, the latter being performed apart from stereotyped ritual contexts though nonetheless using the lament register that lamenters understand to target spirits as their ratified audience.

Work on register has moved toward centre stage in the fields of linguistic anthropology (e.g. Irvine 1990; 1998; Philips 2007; Agha 2007; Silverstein 2010) and folkloristics (e.g. Stepanova 2014 and various contributors to this volume) as an important lens through which to view the use of language and related sign systems (Agha 2007).

While building on that work, we suggest that register phenomena are best analysed together with the sociocultural function of discursive acts, the participant structure and permutations of "voice" in particular events of discourse, and the nature of semiotic acts construed in terms of performance genres. This chapter seeks to demonstrate the utility of such a multifaceted analytic approach *vis-à-vis* mourning rituals and their use of registers of deference or honorification, and particularly *vis-à-vis* the nature of the traditional Karelian lament register. What we find particularly compelling is the apparent paradox that this register makes an offering, as befits its ritual nature, yet a very complex offering combining respect, endearment, pity, and emotional pain. We not only propose this case as an exception to the typically taken-for-granted assertion of the mutual exclusivity of honorifics and diminutives or other marks of endearment, but bring together evidence that there are many such "exceptions" – with important implications for our models of honorific registers.

Considerations of space limit us to merely touching on the relationship between register, genre, and the participant structure and voicing of communicative events such as acts of lamentation and do not allow us to address phenomena that include parallelism at the level of text and word (such as alliteration); prosodic requirements (such as the crying voice, pharyngeal constriction and cry breaks), melodic features (Tolbert 1988); or embodied acts with props (cocking the head to one side and holding a handkerchief to the cheek in order to collect tears), considering them features of performance, textuality, or genre.

A "register" is, for our purposes, *a set of linguistic resources that are used to carry out particular routinized (genred) sociosemiotic activities and are denotatively equivalent to, but indexically contrasting with, another set.*[3] Our focus is on "discursive registers" (Agha 2007: 79–81) rather than the more inclusive category of "semiotic registers", which are repertoires "of performable signs linked to stereotypic pragmatic effects by a sociohistorical process of enregisterment" (Agha 2007: 80). Our focus is thus close to that of Douglas Biber and Susan Conrad, for whom "register features" are "words or grammatical characteristics that are pervasive – distributed throughout a text from the register – and frequent – occurring more commonly in the target register than in most comparison registers" (Biber & Conrad 2009: 53). In addition to nominal circumlocutions typically marked with diminutive suffixation and co-occurring in the lament register with frequentative verbs, Karelian laments are also marked by alliteration – a feature that lies outside of our purview. These lexico-grammatical features occur in all Finnic languages. However, echoing Biber & Conrad, such elements are both more pervasive and frequent in Karelian laments than in other genres and thus part of what makes those laments stand out.

While Agha notes that "[d]iscursive registers typically involve non-linguistic signs as well" (Agha 2007: 80), the question of whether to ascribe to genre instead of register features of textuality like alliteration and text-level parallelism, let alone performance features such as particular melodic patterns, stylized weeping, or cry-breaks is complex. Limitations of space do not allow for more than acknowledgement of this issue. Certainly, the "density" of alliteration and the unique melodic structure and voice quality in Finnic lament registers enable us to clearly distinguish them from other regional performance genres and their registers (Frog & Stepanova 2011; Eila Stepanova and Frog, p.c.). The present discussion, however, will not venture into these aspects of the tradition and, while recognizing their centrality for the lament tradition, we do not engage with the question of whether these are features of the lament register *per se*.

Earlier definitions of registers treated them as relatively fixed sets of linguistic features, related objectively to a relatively fixed notion of context, and later, of social persona. By contrast, recent accounts hold that the very existence of "a register" is the sort of "total social fact" that includes language ideologies.[4] Agha defines register as a model of action which (a) "links speech repertoires to stereotypic indexical values, (b) is performable through utterances (yields enactable personae/relationships), and (c) is recognized by a sociohistorical population" (Agha 2007: 81).

What the literature has not dealt with, says Susan Philips, is the fact that "multiple possibilities for making indexical connections between speech and its meaning are constantly available [...]" and that "by virtue of the nature of indexicality [...] a given situation or social context in itself will not ultimately constrain the meaning assigned to speech" (Philips 2011: 249). Philips proposes an approach to register that recognizes that the ideologies that help constitute the register's "facts" – and by implication, those facts themselves – vary, and that a "phenomenological" approach to the (ideological, i.e. metapragmatic) reflections on register use is needed.

Honorific Registers

We adopt here Judith Irvine's definition of an honorific register as the "linguistic means of expressing" as well as entailing "conventionalized differences of rank" (Irvine 2009: 251). Defined broadly, "honorific registers" are used in encounters involving *a*) kin who reciprocally observe taboo relations; *b*) situations governed by other sorts of taboo, e.g. on naming the recent dead (*a* and *b* often designated "avoidance registers"); *c*) differences of rank or status, but also situations in which one might trope on such norms (status);[5] and finally, *d*) in encounters with the sacred.

Like other registers or types of register, the literature on honorific registers has defined them as consisting of lexical (or lexicalized) and grammatical (or grammaticalized) features inextricably linked to cultural models of person, status, honor – and to models of language and its relation to genres of performance / communicative action, social and ritual function, etc. Models of honorific registers include the representation of honorific speech as "beautiful". This is how lament register is ideologized by Finnish revivalist (or "neo-Karelian") lamenters. The Tongan honorific register (Philips 2010) and its Japanese counterpart are linked with locally perceived "beautification". Japanese words with certain honorific prefixes are regarded as "more elegant or beautiful than their non-prefixed counterparts" (McClure 2000: 80).

Honorific registers "are euphemistic, disengaging the respected person from unpleasantness and from the concrete, mundane, messy details of everyday life," writes Irvine (2009: 161–162). In some accounts, being addressed directly is intrusive by its very nature.[6] The idea that the semantic meaning and pragmatic effect of the expressions that constitute honorific language are mitigated (or mitigating) echoes in Michael Silverstein's account of honorific registers: "All maximally respectful language" is softened (a metapragmatic term we have borrowed from the Finnish lament revivalists) "in effect constituting denotation by 'hint' and by allusion" (Silverstein 2010: 349–350).

As Philips suggested, a phenomenological approach to register – one that regards registers-qua-models (Agha 2007) as emergent in social interaction, and as peculiarly reflective of the emotional experience shared and constituted in interaction – has something to add to these older approaches. It fits honorific registers particularly well. In an article on honorific usage on the Micronesian island of Pohnpei, Elizabeth Keating asks, "what feeling categories (or perhaps embodied sensory experiences) are linked to honor in discourse" (Keating 1998: 404) and discovers that Pohnpeian "orators frequently relate honor to the feeling of love" (1998: 405). Perhaps a bit closer to a Husserlian phenomenology is Irvine's description of what Senegalese griots (praise singers, descended from slaves) may well experience as they perform emotion on behalf of their patrons (or "nobles", descended from local slave owners). Irvine writes, "To speak like a griot... [involves taking] on the mantle of the griot's supposed emotionality, [in contrast] with some more restrained interlocutor" who pays for your performance while interlocking with you in a dance that entails your ongoing subalternity. "Your subjective experience presumably includes *knowing that you sound like a griot. If you are* a griot" your awareness of your status and that of your audience, which includes the principal behind your words as animator (Goffman, 1981) – colors "your attitude toward the griot status you are for the moment typifying as well as toward those for whom you perform" (Irvine 1990: 156). To paraphrase words omitted from the foregoing quotation, whether or not expert Karelian lamenters "really felt" the grief they displayed – and much evidence indicates that they did – their subjective experience presumably included a sense of the power and precariousness of their embodiment-in-performance-with-spirit-addressees, and as Keating (1998) reminds us, of the entwinement of honorification and affectivity. We return to this theme below.

Lexical and Morphosyntactic Features of Honorific Registers

A special *lexicon*, or set of pronouns, is the most salient, and in some cases the only, marker of honorification in some languages. Deference registers consisting primarily of honorific *words* often entail "praise-epithets", as in the Wolof griot-praise register (Irvine 1998: 56). From the perspective of lexical semantics, the shift from the everyday to the honorific lexicon is a shift toward obscurity or opacity. Contrasting sets of pronouns can be as simple as Roger Brown and A. Gilman's famous (1960) contrast between V- and T-pronouns ("V vs. T" standing for *vous* and *tu*), but deictic systems in non-Indo-European languages are often more complex. They may have referent as well as addressee honorific pronominal forms, as in Nepali (Ahearn 2012: Table 4.2), and Pohnpeian, in which honorification is performed through, among other features, (addressee-)status-raising nouns and (speaker-)status-lowering pronouns (Keating 1997). Finally, what may be most salient about some respect or avoidance registers, like those in Dyirbal (Dixon 1972), is the breathtaking reduction of the total lexicon *vis-à-vis* everyday speech.

Morphosyntactic features of many honorific registers include nominal and/or verbal suffixation with indexical significance regardless of its referential meaning, or lack thereof. Among the less intuitive findings regarding grammatical tendencies of honorific registers is not nominal but rather verbal morphosyntax and semantics. In Pohnpeian, status-raising and status-lowering possessive classifiers have different properties of control and temporality. In combination with verb morphology, honorific speech can signal a particular aspectual form interpreted as both the completion of an action and the self-depletion of the speaker (Keating 1998: 403). Such facts may shed light on the grammatical features of the Karelian lament register.

Can an Honorific Register also Index Intimacy, Endearment, or Warmth?

For Brown and Gilman (1960: 258), intimacy implied a lack of either power differential or honorification, hence exchanging reciprocal T; giving asymmetrical T meant at best a condescending type of intimacy. The possibility of honorification via the use of an intimate register is not considered. Likewise, grammaticalized honorifics or high "speech levels" are typically linked with distance / distancing and the suppression of emotion, while ordinary speech or low "speech levels" (sometimes indexed by the use of diminutive marking) are linked with intimacy and/or the expression of warmth or positive affect.

Indeed, respect and intimacy appear to be incompatible in Javanese (Keeler 1984) and indigenous Australian languages such as Dyirbal (Dixon 1972) and Guugu-Yimidhirr (Haviland 1979). However, the apparently opposed functions can coincide as the performative meaning of honorific morphology. This less common phenomenon is found in Koya, Japanese, and Xavante, an Amazonian language. In Xavante, "in addition to the use of endearment terms, certain respect/intimacy relationships are reflected in the morphology" (Harrison 2001: 1). Another example is Nahuatl (also known as Mexicano: Hill & Hill 1978; Sullivan 1988). Nahuatl has a morpheme class that Sullivan calls "reverential-diminutive" or simply "reverential", a suffix denoting "respect, endearment, or compassion" (Sullivan 1988: 19). Sullivan also describes "the postposition [...] *tzinco*", as indicating "respect or affection" (1988: 136).

The use of honorifics has long been documented in situations as apparently disparate as paying deference to mere humans and divine beings. The very distinction, however, is problematic and, as we shall see, this is true of traditional Karelian lament. Evidence from unrelated languages is useful to consider here. As at least recent forms of insular Pacific languages (including Japanese) demonstrate, honorific registers were not somehow lifted from their normal context of use (in addressing people) and applied to religious forms of address.[7] Rather, a single principle of rank seems to have applied. It seems, for instance, that the idea of distinguishing honorification based on human and divine addressees was never culturally meaningful on Tonga:

> Traditionally the person of the Tu'i Tonga, the sacred ruler of Tonga, was to be avoided, and he was the primary target of the higher level of honorification. Lexically everyday words were avoided in use to and about the Tu'i Tonga by replacing them with other words." (Philips 2010: 318, 325.)

Today the Tongan honorific register is used in church to address God and Jesus. Registers, their features and uses are flexible, adaptable, and open, allowing even for the borrowing of some features across registers. This is particularly relevant to Finnish-Karelian lament whose recent history and revival demonstrate such flexibility by adopting many formal features of the register and using them in the ways that are similar to, yet distinct from, the tradition.

Lament as an Object of Research

Studies of lament genres around the world have, with a few exceptions, focused on the living expressing grief on behalf of lamenters themselves or the community. There are compelling accounts of lamenting as one of the few outlets for women's protest that are relatively safe – particularly where lamenting is choral so to speak, rather than soloistic (Briggs 1993). Far fewer studies have revealed laments as "ritual" *sensu stricto*– as part of the community's activities for enacting their connection with and collectively managing (and subjecting themselves to) the sacred. In almost every society that practices lament, women take the lead, and thus in ritual lament women invoke the sacred. Although this sacrality may be either hidden or absent in many societies, from ancient Egyptian laments to revivalist neo-Karelian laments performed by Finnish women, lamenting *is* a sacred act (Wilce 2011).

Although the language and poetics of lament traditions have received attention in different contexts and with different emphases – e.g. as traditional psychotherapy (Gamliel 2007), a rhetoric of grievance (McLaren 2000), or magico-religious intervention affecting the dead (Wickett 2010) – it has received little attention within the framework of registers. Karelian lament language has previously been approached as a "register" in the work of Eila Stepanova (e.g. 2009; 2011; 2012; this volume) as well as of Frog & Stepanova (2011). This work has provided a stimulus and very valuable basis for the present discussion, as has Aleksandra Stepanova's *Karjalaisen itkuvirsikielen sanakirja* ['Dictionary of the Karelian Lament Language'] (2012), listing over 1,400 different circumlocutions. In addition to this work, we know of only one previous study of a local "lament language" that has treated it as a register, and that is William Robert Hodges' dissertation on the rapidly disappearing Toba Batak *hata andung* ['lament register']: "This specialized linguistic register is comprised of some 500 metaphoric terms for individuals, kin and sib relations, parts of the body, food, animals, and other elements in the Toba Batak material and relational world" (Hodges 2009: 227). Throughout his work, Hodges stresses the honoring function of Toba Batak lament and its register in general, and makes passing reference to the use of honorific titles in addressing the dead (2009: 36). Elsewhere, he mentions the synthesis of respect and endearment indexed by the use of clan titles in interaction, but not in the context of lament (2009: 85). Hodges' description is of particular interest owing to some analogies to the Karelian tradition discussed below.

Karelian itkuvirži

The Karelian genre label *itkuvirži* derives from *itku* ['a cry, a lament'] and *virži* ['a song, poem, lament']. Until roughly 1900, *itkuvirži* ['crying song, lament'] was commonly performed by women at funerals and weddings throughout the transnational region of Karelia (Stepanova, this volume; see further e.g. Tolbert 1988; Laaksonen 1999; E. Stepanova 2011; 2012). Regional genres of lamenting, defined as "tuneful weeping with words", are generally considered to belong to the shared Finnic linguistic-cultural heritage, with roots that may be much older (e.g. Honko 1963; 1974; Frog & Stepanova 2011; Stepanova 2012; on cross-cultural areal features of lament traditions in this part of the world, see Stepanova 2011). In Karelia, these traditions continued until roughly 1900, when wedding laments stopped being performed, funeral lamenting waned, and Finnish folklorists busied themselves collecting samples to archive. In fact, Finnish and Russian folklorists have been describing Karelian lament and lamenters for almost 170 years (see Lönnrot's account [1836]), and the folklorist Eila Stepanova is still interviewing the remaining handful of aged rural women in Karelia and its neighboring regions who now and then lament by the body of the deceased. (E. Stepanova 2011; 2012.)

In this regional tradition, a primary cultural function of ritual laments was to honor the living and the dead and to communicate with various beings in the unseen world. Fundamental to the tradition was an understanding that effective lamenting at funerals was necessary in order for the deceased to successfully complete the journey to the otherworld and be integrated into the community of the dead. If the journey of the newly deceased were unsuccessful, he or she could remain in the world of the living and cause harm to the family. (Stepanova 2011: 137–138; cf. Stepanova 2012: 266.) In undergoing the transformation from individual member of the living community to integrated member of the community of dead ancestors, deceased members of the family advanced toward the status of supernatural beings (E. Stepanova, p.c., February 2014). This potential fluidity between ancestral dead and gods reflects the fact that the vernacular category 'god' (*jumala*) could be used more flexibly than in Christian and Classical traditions and could refer to a range of positive beings with great supernatural power (Frog 2013: 62). Karelian laments thus warded off danger from inhabitants of the unseen world, paid honor to them, expressed tender feelings toward them, enabled the last journey of the recently deceased, comforted the bereaved, and helped the community navigate the complexities of the sacred (or sacred realms).

The primary addressees of at least ritual laments were the ancestors and divine powers.[8] The tradition and its vocabulary were historically rooted in vernacular mythology and with these addressees, but the lament register also adapted to address the Christian God (see E. Stepanova 2012; 2014) much as the Tongan honorific register mentioned above became used in church to address God and Jesus. If the primary addressees of Karelian ritual laments were supernatural beings in the unseen world, then in some sense the bereaved human audience were overhearers, albeit "ratified overhearers" rather than "eavesdroppers" (Goffman 1981: 132). Yet they were also "principals", those whose emotions were being performed.[9] This makes the lead lamenters – ideally, women who had earned a reputation for the *magico-ritual efficacy* of their lament performances – "animators" of the emotions experienced by the bereaved families (Goffman 1981).[10] Karelian lamenters offered themselves as bridges between this world and the other world – an act so powerful and yet stressful that it entailed risk of heart attack and death (Tolbert 1988: 80).

Centuries of European thought sharply divided mind from body and thought from feeling, relegating women, peasants, and non-Europeans to a passion-dominated realm of the primitive (Bauman & Briggs 2003). Yet the old Karelian lamenters were honored: the perceived sacredness of the Karelian lament register enabled those who pay honor to sacred beings (lamenters) also to receive the community's respect. In this, their very emotionality was regarded as a sign of their powerful state, not unlike the power of the Finnic male ritual specialist called a *tietäjä* ['knower'], or of Siberian shamans (E. Stepanova 2012: 276–277; cf. Honko 1974: 58n). It is the quality of that emotionality, however, that is at the centre of our argument. If humility and fear are the affective qualities most commonly associated with honorification, this chapter argues that, along with humility, the Karelian lament register indexes warm, tender affect.[11] The union of "emotional expression," honorification, and power is certainly seen in the Finnish "lament revival", and affectivity and power are intertwined in Karelian laments old and new.[12]

The power of lament was or is fundamental to it, yet it had/has to be harnessed for specific aims. Finnic laments could include requests for aid or support from the inhabitants of the otherworld (E. Stepanova 2012: 176–177).[13] Such requests directed to inhabitants of the otherworld constitute more than a quarter of some old Karelian laments. The Karelian lamenters' power to facilitate communication with the supernatural has been highlighted by Eila Stepanova (2012: 263; cf. 2009: 14), who points out that its ritual use "remained bound to beliefs that the dead ancestors could not understand normal spoken language, and could only understand the special language of laments," and dream visitations by the deceased provided a potential channel for reciprocal communication (E. Stepanova 2012: 271; see also Honko 1974: 40, 43). Although all Karelian women were traditionally expected to know something about lamenting, and the community joined in weeping over the dead in funerary observances, women known to possess particular skill were generally preferred to lead lamenting at funerals and weddings. Skill was evaluated in relation to outcome, since a lamenter's performance was something like that of the *tietäjä* ['knower'] mentioned above – a ritual healer filled with supernatural power.[14]

The deferential function of registers like the Karelian and neo-Karelian *lament registers* does not, of course, lie primarily in denotatively explicit expressions of respect, although these may have been fairly common in Karelian laments (see forms of address such as *n-armahat kallehet syndyzet* ['dear precious divine powers'].)[15] Rather, respect was conveyed in large part as an indexical effect, i.e. reflecting the creative indexicality of register choice. The solemnity of lament and its association with respect can be illustrated by an early 1980s interview with an old lamenter in Russian Karelia conducted by several Finnish scholars representing the Finnish Literature Society (Järvinen, p.c. 2010).[16] The lamenter told a particular story about an invitation she had received to lament over someone who had recently died. The story illustrates her insistence on the solemnity of the event. After observing the family of the deceased laughing and otherwise *ei kunnioiteta* ['not respectful'] to the dead, she decided she could not lament there. She concluded by reiterating that she only laments if the family cries and *žiälöiččöy* ['shows pity'] to the dead.[17] This close conjoining of terms indicates that the lamenter understood pity in some close relationship to respect. In assessing what might be meant by calling at least some lament registers (and especially Karelian) honorific – and particularly assessing local ideologies that constitute lament as honorific, for particular reasons – we must take into account the mix of feelings that should surround and infuse the lament.

The combination of the following features can be considered to make the Karelian lament "language" unique as a register, keeping in mind that they only do so as objects or products of a language ideology:

1. Nominal circumlocutions: a system at the perceived core of the *register*, with 1,400[18] distinct lexical substitutions identified (A. Stepanova 2012)
2. Heavy use of three particular grammatical features:
   a. Diminutivization of nouns
   b. Frequentativization of verbs (i.e. adding *-ele-* to mark a category of verb aspect often called "iterative")
   c. Plural forms where singular forms would be expected

In what follows below limitations of space force us to focus on features (2a) and (2b).

The Karelian Lament Register

Like all registers, the Karelian "lament language" was (or is) ideologically conceived. Those whom we might call "elders of bygone days"[19] considered it able to affect the unseen world and communicate with the dead and other supernatural powers, although traditional laments also respectfully addressed the living (cf. e.g. Asplund et al. 2000). Moreover, old lamenters and their communities understood that "language" primarily *as a lexicon* (feature 1 above). Finnish and Karelian scholars have said that the circumlocutory practices characterizing this lexicon reflect old naming taboos, and particularly a concern that the deceased can hear what is said in his or her old neighborhood, especially when it is articulated in laments (Honko 1963: 128). "In an earlier period, people believed in the magic power of the name, and therefore in order to avoid harming relatives, either living or deceased, they did not mention names directly" (E. Stepanova 2012: 263). The circumlocutions of the Karelian lament register involved substitutions for all manner of everyday things and certainly not just proper names or common nouns related to the deceased and familial relations (A. Stepanova 2012; cf. E. Stepanova 2011: 135; 2012: esp. 263). "The language of laments diverges so significantly from colloquial speech that it poses a considerable barrier to understanding the content" (Frog & Stepanova 2011: 204; cf. E. Stepanova 2012: 257). The relative opacity of these expressions did little to limit their effectiveness, since lamenters believed that their supernatural addressees *did* understand the lament register and not everyday language.

It should be noted that many of the circumlocutions constituting the core of the lament register are phrases and not (just) isolated words (see further A. Stepanova 2012). In the terminology of generative grammar, they are noun phrases realized either as isolated nouns or as longer strings whose heads are nouns. As noun phrases, they almost all reflect the process of diminutivization (feature 2a, above). Moreover, the nouns are often deverbal, derived from verbs – "frequentative" verbs (feature 2b above).[20] While the circumlocutions may most closely reflect the range of honorific register features discussed in the cross-cultural survey above, diminutivization reflects the subset of registers that index both honor and intimacy or warm affect.

In his article "Itkuvirsirunous" ['Lament Poetry'], Honko mentions features identified as 2a and 2b above:

> The most striking common feature is the abundant use of diminutives, which is also found in the Baltic and Mordovin lament poetry. One can say that most of the diminutive nouns – and in the Karelian region also *frequentative verbs* – have become stylistic indexes of a particular folklore genre, which no longer have grammatical meaning. (Honko 1963: 125, emphasis added.)[21]

This can be compared with an analysis of aspectual morphology offered by William Labov two decades later in his essay "Intensity" (1984). Labov (1984: 45–46) observes that, "Certain aspect categories tend to acquire the feature of intensity, and eventually the aspect marker is used to signal intensity even when its other associations do not apply." Labov himself linked intensity of the sort he said is signalled by aspectual forms with "emotional expression", "emotional meaning", and "emotional content" (1984: 1, 45, 68). This appears consistent with the Karelian frequentatives.

Example 1. From a Tver Karelian funerary lament, recorded 1977, from Anna Andrejevna Šutajeva, o.s. Smirnov, and recorded by Helmi and Pertti Virtaranta (Asplund et al. 2000: 10-12, 41)

1. O kum mie koorottelin nämä   Oh how I reared these
   n-ihalat ijättyzeyt yksistä   gentle children alone
2. puoluluziin armahiitago n-abuziitta. without a husband's dear help.
3. O šie miun armahane n-ihalane   Oh my dear gentle mother…
   n-imettäjäzeni

In example 1, we see both frequentativization and diminutivization. In line 1, *korottelin*[22] is a frequentative verb whose root Aleksandra Stepanova (2012: 136) glosses as "kasvattaa" ['to rear'] thus the frequentative *korotella* means 'to keep rearing'. The denotatively explicit *armahane ihalane* ['dear gentle'] underscores the positive affect that is "merely" indexed by the diminutive suffix *-ne/-ni* (varying by dialect and inflected *-ze-*, noting that in some dialects the diminutive suffix is a homophone of the first person singular possessive suffix *-ni* also seen in *imettäjä-ze-ni*, ['my breast-feeder, one who suckled me' = 'mother'], one of the lament register's "metaphors" or circumlocutions).

Diminutivized nouns are primarily forms of (second-person) address, as in Example 1. First-person forms are often possessive, as for example in the expressions *vaimelon vartuvo-ni* ['my wilting body' (trans. E. Stepanova 2011: 133)] (see also A. Stepanova 2012: 197, 201) and *vaivažien rukkažen* ['[me] the miserable pitiful one' (E. Stepanova 2011: 135)]. According to Eila Stepanova (2012: 264), the "lamenter's representation of her own ego […] is qualified by negative epithets" (e.g. *mie maltomatoin* ['I, the one lacking in understand-

197

ing']; Asplund et al. 2000: 15; trans. A. Stepanova 2012: 157) in marked contrast to the use of positive epithets for all other people objects and phenomena. One possible interpretation of these practices is that it entails self-lowering of the sort found in most honorific registers.[23]

The Practices and Ideologies of "Lament Revivalists"

Tenhunen (2006) describes Karelian lament as having three "lives". The first – "traditional" lament – was as an integrated part of the living verbal culture of Karelia described above. The second was the brief efflorescence of lament, especially in Finland between the 1940s and 1970s, following Finland's loss of most of Karelia to the Soviet Union, which led hundreds of thousands to leave all behind and restart their lives in Finland. These second-life laments were often performed on stage in large gatherings of Karelian refugees. Lament's "third life" began in the 1980s – also in Finland. Our account of this third life reflects Wilce's participation in six revivalist lament workshops in which he made video and audio recordings of all of the pedagogical discourse and some of the students' end-of-class lament performances. In addition, he has interviewed dozens of people and, at greatest length, six people who have taught such workshops and "alumni" known to him from one such event.

The so-called "lament revival" that started the 1980s is largely the product of two women with different but overlapping notions of the Karelian lament register – Pirkko Fihlman and Liisa Matveinen. Fihlman and her co-teacher Tuomas Rounakari represent the only real revivalist organization – *Äänellä itkijät ry*. ['Those Who Cry with Voice/Words, registered association']. Matveinen, a professional musician with a Masters in Folk Music, and an important contributor to Finnish New Wave folk music, leads the other group. Neither collectively named nor formally organized, Matveinen and her students are, in comparison with *Äänellä Itkijät*, "lament purists". The key to the so-called revival is the lament workshop, typically spanning a weekend. Both revivalist groups hold courses that train women (the vast majority of students) to perform their own laments. We return to Fihlman, Matveinen, and their work below. First, however, we address the relationship between the revivalists and the genre they seek to revive.

The dialectical relationship between performance and local reflections on performance, and between local and non-local reflections, is well-trodden scholarly ground. Of course, scholarship that reflects on both dialectics mentioned here represents a third kind, and there is no necessary end to such layering, as Silverstein has pointed out (2003). Lament performances that we have been calling traditional (i.e. Tenhunen's "first life" of Karelian laments) were never innocent of metadiscursive reflection. In our view, revivalistic versions of lament have a claim on authenticity, particularly insofar as neo-lamenters in fact attempt to achieve "authenticity." Actually, they might well achieve *four different authenticities* via four semiotic interventions (Fenigsen & Wilce 2012):

1. They claim a direct link with the old lamenters.
2. They self-consciously shape their performances after the traditional model.
3. Paradoxically, some modern lamenters then anchor their authenticity in a match between inner experience and outward expression – a modern preoccupation.
4. They testify to the spiritual efficacy of their admittedly contemporary lamenting.

The revival of the tradition by neo-lamenters has not been limited to the language and practice of lament. It also extends to its connections with belief traditions drawn not only from literature on the subject but from the famous transition-generation lamenter Martta Kuikka (Fenigsen & Wilce 2015). This includes the idea that the inhabitants of the unseen world only understand the lament register (E. Stepanova 2009: 14; 2012: 263) – or that lamenting in the proper register reaches the unseen world, with or without an expectation or intention of doing so. Pirkko Fihlman lamented at her brother's funeral. The following night, her brother appeared in a dream to her husband, who said he expressed his thanks for the "soft pillows she had lamented to him,"[24] which parallel's Karelian traditions about the deceased visiting lamenters in dreams (Honko 1974: 40) coupled with the neo-lamenters' ideology of "softness" and laments providing comfort for the deceased (here reflected symbolically as pillows). Liisa Matveinen tells of having dream visitations that she thought indicated she had disturbed her ancestors, until Martta Kuikka explained that she had opened the door, and that the ancestors' intentions were positive.

Matveinen and Fihlman have Finnish-Karelian ancestry. Both have also studied the literature on Finnic lament and listened often to archival recordings. They endeavour to teach people how to create new laments that are respectful, authentic, and efficacious, and this means they concur that new laments should mimic old Karelian examples and be realized in what they call the *itkukieli* ['lament language']. Revivalist lamenters capture the honorific spirit of old laments, and demonstrate their laments' prayer-like function, in passages like this from a lament by revivalist Sirpa Heikkinen: "We greet the beloved ones in the other world, those who have walked in front of us, those who have waited at the door. Lead her to the bright road."

Neo-laments include some traditional register features such as frequentative verbs. A publicly performed lament by Karoliina Kantinen included the phrase *vielä istuksentelen* ['I am still sitting'], a frequentative form. Neo-laments also may use diminutive forms (Finn. *-inen*, infl. *-ise-*). For example, one of Pirkko Fihlman's laments uses the phrase *miun maalle synnyttäjä-ise-ni* ['you who have given birth to me on this earth'].

Thus, despite some internal diversity in the "lament revival", and specifically some previous disagreements between Pirkko Fihlman and Liisa Matveinen, they both present old Karelian laments as their model and thus embrace the old Karelian lament register. They agree that the lament register is deferential, and that in at least in some cases even today, spirits are its intended honorees. Both women testify to having dreams in which their ancestors appear to them. Both groups also draw middle-class women, objections by some participants that modern Finland has no class distinctions notwithstanding.[25] Even objectors would likely admit that many of those who take ÄI-Lamenters' "Healing Lament" courses are artistically oriented or practice some form of therapy – and they clearly have at least a minimum of leisure and money to devote to things like lament courses.

Although they differ over just what a modern lament register should entail, Matveinen and Fihlman have great respect for elderly Karelian tradition-bearers. They both learned much from one such woman – Martta Kuikka, the speaker of the words below, in Example 2.[26]

Example 2. Martta Kuikka on "softened" lament words

[Itkun] sanoja on etsittävä ja kerättävä	[Lament] words have to be sought and collected
ja jopa kirjoitettava ylös niitä	and even written down –
jotka on kelvollisia siihen itkuvirteen	those that are acceptable in that lament
että siis niitä sanoja *pehmennetään*[27]	that is, those words are *softened*
ja tehdään *suloisemmaksi*.	and made *sweeter*.
ja ne ei saa olla *kovia*.	and they can't be *hard*.

Kuikka's description of what lament "words" should be like resonates with academic descriptions of "honorific-intimate" registers discussed earlier in this chapter.[28]

Example 3 below shows that Matveinen analyses the function of the lament register as honorific, and justifies its use – even today – on the basis of its target audience, namely "spirits" (3.15).

Example 3. Excerpt from English interview with Liisa Matveinen

3.1 With this language [we] can reach something about the other world
(one minute gap)
3.15 Spirits only understand the lament register
(one minute gap)
3.30 Somehow you have *to talk very beautiful language* to them
3.31 I think it's very clear that we have to speak to them with a *very beautiful language*
3.32 *because we respect them.**

* Limitations of space do not allow us to discuss revivalists' statements that lamenting is a sacred act that must receive respect.

The mention of respect in Example 3 is not the only example in Wilce's corpus of transcribed recordings from revivalist lament courses and interviews, but makes clear that at least one highly regarded contemporary lamenter considers the lament register honorific. Here Matveinen goes beyond the more commonly invoked reason for using lament register – because the spirits *understand* it (and only it). Noteworthy as well is her description of the (honorific) register as *beautiful* – a quality that Tongan and Japanese speakers attribute to their honorific registers.

Example 4 shows Pirkko Fihlman stressing to a group of ten lament students (including Wilce) the importance of the lament register, albeit a modern adaptation of it in which the traditional circumlocutions taken from traditional laments stored in the archives of the Finnish Literature Society serve only as a model for improvisation by Fihlman (in this example) and her students. Prior to where Example 4 picks up, Pirkko Fihlman has been speaking about "modern laments".

Example 4. Pirkko Fihlman teaching about "Normal" and Poetic Speech in the "Modern Lament" Register, Lament Course October 2008) (with metapragmatic labels italicized).

4.1	mutta se että niissä käytetään sitte	But then they use
4.2	näitä tämmösiä *hellyyttäviä* ja	these kinds of *tender*, and
4.3	*hyväilevämpiä* ja	more *endearing*, and,
4.4	tämmösiä *kuvauksellisia sanoja*:	those kinds of *imagistic words*:
4.5	Ne ei oo ihan sitä *arkikieltä*	They aren't exactly *everyday speech*,
4.6	koska se *arkikieli* on aika töksähtävää	because *everyday speech* is really abrupt.
4.7	mut- jos me lähetään esimerkiks	But if we start for example
4.8	puhumaan niinkun	to talk [in the lament register] about
4.9	armaasta äidistä niin se voi olla	"dear mother", it might be thus –
4.10	kantajaiseni ja tuutijaiseni ja	"the one who carried me" and "one who rocked me"
4.11	joku maallensynnyttäjäiseni	"the one who brought me to earth."
4.12	pitäs koitaa käyttää	One should try to use
4.13	niinku niis itkuissa *sellasii sanoja*	in these laments *those kinds of words*
4.14	jotka koskettaa	that touch

Fihlman declares *arkikieli* ['everyday speech'] (4.5-6) – exemplified in emails, which she says are full of "abbreviations" or "half words" – inappropriate for lamenting. She invokes the metapragmatic labels *hellyyttävä* ['tender'] (4.2) and *hyväilempi* ['endearing'] (5.3). Fihlman is arguing that modern Finnish laments – like their traditional Karelian counterparts – must consist of forms that are tender. Although this is hardly a cross-culturally typical description of the entailment of using honorific register, Fihlman's practice and ideology fit with the scattering of registers discussed above that are ideologically construed as honorific and endearing and fills the notion of honorification with affect.

Examples 5a and 5b represent a discussion of the features that, according to Liisa Matveinen (L), every new lament must have, because every such lament must reflect the tradition, the genre. The discussion took place in a workshop for those whose interest has been so piqued by learning to lament that they were in training to become teachers of their own lament courses. Women participants are labeled W1, W2, etc.

Example 5a. Excerpt from a course for lament teachers taught by L. Matveinen (Helsinki 2010)

5.1	L: mitkä ovat itkuvirret tyylikeino	L: What are the stylistic methods of laments?
5.2	niinku runoullisesti, kielellisesti	poetically, linguistically?
5.3	W1: alkusointu	W1: Alliteration
5.4	W2: nii, ja metaforat	W2: Yes, and metaphors
5.5	L: Metaforakieli	L: Metaphorical language
5.6	L: elikkä just-a kiertoilmaisut	L: that is, circumlocutions

Matveinen's metadiscourse takes an interesting turn after line 5.6; we have thus labelled the last example, below, 5b. Note in lines 5.5 and 5.6 the reference to 'metaphorical language' (*metaforakieli*) and 'circumlocutions' (*kiertoilmaisut*), referring to the set of canonical circumlocutions that, we have argued, were the most characteristic feature of Karelian lament and particularly associated with this as an honorific register. Matveinen's commitment to tradition is such that she brings a list of many of the canonical circumlocutions to her lament classes. In Example 5b, she indicates her interpretation of circumlocutions as a matter of lengthening (5.7). (We have repeated line 5.6 in Example 5b below to make its relationship with 5.7 obvious.) Matveinen then illustrates how such lengthening works at the word level, starting with the unmarked verb stem (i.e. lacking explicit aspectual marking, line 5.8), then adding -*eskel*- to change "walked" (*kulj-i-n*) to "repeatedly walked" or "wandered" (*kulje-skel-i-n*) (5.10), then repeating the morphological change (*kulje-skele-ntel-i-n*), producing what we are calling a "hyper-frequentative" form.

Example 5b. Second excerpt from L. Matveineen's Helsinki 2010 course

5.6	L: elikkä just-a kiertoilmaisut	L: that is, circumlocutions
5.7	pidenellä sanoja	lengthening words
5.8	sanota esimerkiksi että minä kuljin*	For example, it could be said "I walked"
5.9	se voi sanoa että kuljeskelin**	[or] one could say "I wandered"
5.10	tai sitten kuljeskelentelin	or then "I wandered about randomly"
5.11	((L laughs loudly, others join))	

* From *kulkea*.
** From *kuljeskella* (frequentative).

The features of the Karelian lament register represented by Fihlman and Matveinen shine a light on the connection between honor and affect. Their metadiscourse bears a strong affinity to that of the Karelian lamenter who refused to lament because the family had not shown pity to the deceased, even if, when viewed from outside their respective cultural ideologies, there may have been a pronounced difference between the potential emphasis and emotive concern for comforting the deceased in modern Finnish culture and perhaps more formal concerns with presentation of grief and behaviour conforming with commiseration for the deceased in a traditional Karelian community. The link between diminutivization-as-honorific, and affect in the form of misery, is common in old Karelian laments as in Example 6:

Example 6. Illustrative example of the link between diminutivization-as-honorific, and affect (text and translation according to Stepanova 2011: 139)

Kuin mageih da menestyrskoib	When [I] go to the sweet
oi magavosijazih vieriin	and monasterial sleeping place.DIM.PL
i eino, kylnui, kyzyn	and always, cold [lamenter], [I] ask [you]
hotti ozuttuagua udralla unisse	to appear to the miserable's [lamenter] in dreams.

Semiotic ideologies, such as local understandings of the social context and function of the lament register, are the glue that holds its various features together. Not only can *analysts* identify features that the lament register shares with contemporary "indirect speech" varieties – such as diminutivization and the metaphoricity and indirectness of phrasal substitutes for everyday terms – but *lamenters* invoke their own metapragmatic tropes, representing those very features as achieving the desired quality of 'softness' or 'softening' (*pehmennys*) or correlating it with 'showing pity' (*žiälöiččöy*). Thus both scholars and lamenters characterize the lament register as blunting communicative directness on both the referential and indexical levels.

The Karelian lament register achieves the denotational blurring Silverstein described (2010) through the circumlocutions or metaphoricity of, and the phrasal substitutes for, everyday terms that define the register. That which blunts referential directness indexes respect. Now, if we substitute any of the tropes of mitigation that neo-Karelian lamenters use – "softening" or "beautifying" – we see that, not only for them but perhaps for many other social groups who have honorific registers, honor and intimacy (or tenderness, or endearment) are potentially quite compatible.

Conclusion

The Karelian lament register, we have argued, is an enactment of deference and endearment. The complexity of the register, consisting of a set of lexified and grammaticalized alternants, contributes to the complexity (i.e. multifunctionality) of Karelian lament. Circumlocution exemplifies the avoidance of direct reference, a feature of all honorific registers according to Silverstein (2010);[29] yet lament register circumlocutions are diminutivized, indexing endearment. As for the frequentativization of verbs in laments, Labov's (1984) work would indicate that such aspectual changes may creatively index affective "intensity". According to Liisa Matveinen, it contributes to linguistic indirection and thereby to honor. We might even venture to say that the use of the frequentative builds a temporality that, while not mythical, is still out of the ordinary.

It may seem odd that an account of an honorific register, particularly one like the lament register, would need to assert the centrality of affect, which is so salient in lament that at times the question of lament's ritual function, *sensu stricto*, is overlooked (as in Tenhunen's short [2007] account of neo-lament). The issue is that scholarly accounts rarely treat "honor" as affect, and for good reasons, such as the fact that the performance of high affectivity counts as deference in some situations, and low affectivity in others (Irvine 1998). Even this fact, however, points to affect as an important dimension of honorification. The lament register shares with at least a few other honorific registers a healthy dose of positive affect – which lament revivalists call tenderness, warmth, or softness (and which scholars call "intimacy"). Where they are found to play an important role in local performances of honor, those affective stances help to define or inflect "honor". The contemporary understanding that "words" must undergo "softening" to suit neo-Karelian lamenting may have had its analog in traditional understandings, but in any case is interesting for its relationship to descriptions by Silverstein, Irvine, and others of honorification involve softening (as a "softening of the lines" around a semantic core and as ameliorating the impact of a speech act).

Our exploration of the lament register raises intriguing questions: given the global trend toward the rejection of conventionalized linguistic indirection (*Is not communicative directness rational and efficient?*), is the development by Finnish lament revivalists of new circumlocutions a model of resistance to modernity through the genre and its register, at the very time when modernity has been dealing death blows to lament (Wilce 2009)? What do traditional Karelian lament (which apparently empowered rural lamenters) and neo-Karelian revivalist lament (which has received a remarkable amount of public/media attention) have to tell us about gender, performance, power, and public(ity)?

Does the honorific nature of the lament register really involve self-lowering of the kind enacted via other honorific registers? If self-lowering is evident in the Karelian practice, is there a difference in how this aspect of the tradition has been adapted (or neglected) by neo-lamenters in the modern culture of Finland? If the honorific nature of the lament register really does involve self-lowering, while also being a highly honorable act and thus taking its place alongside other registers that are conceived as both respectful and respectable,[30] what light does the discovery of its duplex nature as *honoring and endearing* (and, even more strikingly, *honoring and pitying*) shed on "orders of indexicality" (Silverstein 2003)? Some answers to these questions and more may come as a result of investigating honorifics *as used in ritual and specifically to address the sacred*, synthesizing insights from the Karelian and other cases of honorific-religious registers. We hope that our study might serve as a model in a world where, increasingly, affectivity is no stranger to power.

Acknowledgements

For their comments on earlier drafts, we would like to thank Eila Stepanova, Susan Philips, and particularly Frog.

Notes

1. Our source for the idiomatic Karelian expression is E. Stepanova (p.c.). See the Finnish expression *äänellä itkijät* ['those who cry with voice/words'], taken by the chief lament revivalist organization as its name.
2. "So-called", because Finns' borrowing and transforming Karelian tradition is controversial.
3. Our definition resonates with Silverstein's: Registers are "context-appropriate alternate ways of 'saying the same thing' such as are seen in so-called 'speech levels', i.e. stratified lexico-grammatical principles of denotational coherence)" (2010: 430).
4. "There is no such thing as a social fact without its ideological aspect or component" (Silverstein 1998: 126).
5. As an example of "honorific" speech used for purposes other than honoring, see Tolstoy's anecdote (cited by Friedrich 1972: 280) about a Russian "grandmother's" use of the respectful pronoun *vy* to a young prince – with a look of contempt.
6. In his classic treatment of the semiotics of Javanese linguistic etiquette, J. Joseph Errington (1988: 248) writes, "An experience of 'intrusion upon the mind' may be intrinsic to the proper significative effect of indexical signs." A linguistic example of this might be "a pronoun demonstrative or relative, [which] forces attention to the particular object intended without describing it" (Peirce 1931–1958: 195) – or "Hey you!"
7. Thanks to Susan Philips for suggesting this pattern (p.c., September 2013).
8. "The cult of ancestors was not only significant at funerals: for example, ancestors were given a central place in weddings when the bride performed farewell laments not only to the living members of her family, but also to the dead." (Honko et al. 1993: 570; Imjarekov 1979: 8.)
9. Compare the case of nobles and griots described above (Irvine 1990).
10. On the importance of the bereaved family's sincere "pity" and "respect" to the animators, the lamenters, see the discussion of "pity" in this text.
11. It is worth noting that power has accrued to the addressee *and the giver* of honor in at least some cultural settings involving honorific registers around the world (Silverstein 2003).
12. A contemporary lamenter from rural Finland describes her lamenting in terms of power and alterity: "I am a mediator/connector. The power comes from somewhere else." The union of power and emotion is visible, also, wherever leaders of business, schoolchildren, church members, and New Age followers receive training in emotional intelligence, and "emotion pedagogies" (Wilce and Fenigsen forthcoming) or "pedagogies of feeling" (Hayashi et al. 2009) touch millions of people.
13. For example, a wedding lament by Viena Karelian Olga Pavlova included pleas to the *spuassuzet* to "bless this young woman as she prepares for marriage," followed by similar pleas to the lamenter's sister, brother, and parents. (Asplund et al. [2000: 17–18, 44] recorded in 1938 by Jouko Hautala and Lauri Simonsuuri). *Spuassuzet* is an interesting term in the lament register: as Eila Stepanova (2012) has discussed, this term reflects a loan from Russian *Spas, Spasitel'* ['Saviour'] borrowed under influence from Christianity, but inflected in diminutive and plural forms according to the rules of the register and used as a parallel to the vernacular *syndyzet* (diminutive plural of *syndy* ['origin, creation, birth'] and used with reference variously to 'divine powers' and to the 'land of the dead'. (See Stepanova 2012; 2014.)
14. An example comes from Karelian lament scholar Unelma Konkka, who quotes a woman talking about the efficacy of her mother's wedding laments: "She was a real master. She gave 44 women to husbands in marriage. Not one was divorced." (Konkka 1985: 107; translation by Wilce.)
15. The phrase is from the same source as Example 1 below – a dirge performed in 1977 by Anna Andreijevna Sutjajeva, o.s. Smirnov and recorded by Helmi and Pertti

Virtaranta (Asplund et al. 2000: 9). Asplund et al. 2000: 11, 41; on the form "armahat," see A. Stepanova 2012: 102).

16 Among the several folklorists who conducted the original interviews, special thanks to Irma-Riitta Järvinen of the Finnish Literature Society (Suomalainen Kirjallisuuden Seura), who produced the recording notes, and who gave generously of her time, playing and interpreting the recordings, despite some technical difficulties.

17 We are indebted to Irma-Riita Järvinen for discussing this episode with JMW in Finnish and English. We would also like to thank Eila Stepanova for providing the third-person singular form of the Karelian verb *žiälöiččöy* (p.c., August 2010).

18 Although the number 1,400 leads us to think otherwise, the number of circumlocutions was not fixed, and in fact new ones were always being generated. Still, the Karelian lament register stands apart from similar registers used in other genres of Karelian folk performance for the sheer number of different circumlocutions used and the intensity of their use. Karelian laments also stood out for their melody, rhythm, crying voice, etc.

19 We borrow this phrase from northern New Mexico, and specifically from Charles Briggs (1988), who – during fieldwork there – learned the phrase, and what it meant to talk like such an elder.

20 "The agent-expressing suffix, the diminutive suffix and the possessive suffix can in turn be connected to the frequentative suffix of the basic verb *(synnytellä, kyluetella): synnyttelijiini, synnyttelijaiseni, kyluettelijani, kyfuettelijaiseni*" (Leino 1974: 116).

21 The translation is Wilce's, as corrected by Heidi Haapoja.

22 Apparently the spelling *koorott...* (with two initial /o/ vowels) in the transcript is an error.

23 Wilce has recorded the same tendency in revivalist lament courses.

24 The expression *Pirkko itki hänelle ne niin pehmeät pielukset* ['Pirkko lamented to him soft pillows'] – i.e. the use of the verb *itkeä* ['to cry'] as ditransitive – is as remarkable in Finnish as it is in English.

25 For a Finnish sociological exploration of the widespread denial that Finland has a class system, see Järvinen & Kolbe 2007.

26 Wilce recorded Kuikka's words while a documentary featuring Kuikka and other tradition bearers was played during a 2009 lament course in which he participated.

27 This derives from *pehmentää* ['to soften'], which is used rarely, and never in regard to *sanoja* ['words'].

28 We find a close ideological parallel to Kuikka's words (Example 2) in Pirkko Fihlman's musings on the lament register's required softness, warmth, and obscurity as somehow connected to the need to protect the soul's journey. Fihlman's invocation of "obscurity" (3.4) may reflect precisely the sort of semantic process Silverstein (2010) attributes to all "maximally respectful" registers. Yet just what sort of connection she had in mind between the linguistic and cosmic is not clear.

29 The orthodox Jewish practice of avoiding the pronunciation of any of the most important Hebrew names for divinity – and in English, writing G—d – would be another example of avoidance in a religious register of honorification.

30 Examples include Javanese "speech levels" as discussed by Silverstein 2003, and other honorific registers discussed by Irvine 2009: 165. On the honorability of lamenting among the Toba Batak, see Hodges 2009: 245.

References

Agha, Asif 2007. *Language and Social Relations*. Studies in the Social and Cultural Foundations of Language. Cambridge: Cambridge University Press.

Ahearn, Laura M. 2012. *Living Language: An Introduction to Linguistic Anthropology*. Malden MA: Blackwell Publishers.

Asplund, Anneli, et al. 2000. *Itkuja: Karjalasta, Inkeristä, Suomesta* ['Laments from Karelia, Ingria, Finland']. SKS CD 3. Helsinki: Finnish Literature Society.

Bauman, Richard, & Charles Briggs 2003. *Voices of Modernity: Language Ideologies and the Politics of Inequality*. Social and Cultural Foundations of Language. Cambridge: Cambridge University Press.

Biber, Douglas, & Susan Conrad 2009. *Register, Genre, and Style*. Cambridge: Cambridge University Press.

Briggs, Charles 1988. *Competence in Performance: The Creativity of Tradition in Mexicano Verbal Art*. Philadelphia: University of Pennsylvania Press.

Briggs, Charles 1993. Personal Sentiments and Polyphonic Voices in Warao Women's Ritual Wailing: Music and Poetics in a Critical and Collective Discourse. *American Anthropologist* 95(4): 929–957.

Brown, Roger, & A. Gilman 1960. The Pronouns of Power and Solidarity. In *Style in Language*. Ed. Thomas A. Sebeok. Cambridge, MA. MIT Press. Pp. 253–276.

Dixon, Robert M. W. 1972. *The Dyirbal Language of North Queensland*. Cambridge: Cambridge University Press.

Errington, J. Joseph 1988. *Structure and Style in Javanese: A Semiotic View of Linguistic Etiquette*. Conduct and Communication. Philadelphia: University of Pennsylvania.

Fenigsen, Janina, & James Wilce (in press). Authenticities: A Semiotic Exploration. *Semiotic Inquiry* 32(1–3; "Semiotics in Anthropology Today", guest ed. Sally Ann Ness): 103–122.

Friedrich, Paul 1972. Social Context and Semantic Feature: The Russian Pronominal Usage. In *Directions in Sociolinguistics: The Ethnography of Communication*. Ed. John J. Gumperz & Dell Hymes. New York: Holt, Rinehart & Winston. Pp. 270–300.

Frog 2013. Shamans, Christians, and Things in between: From Finnic–Germanic Contacts to the Conversion of Karelia. In *Conversions: Looking for Ideological Change in the Early Middle Ages*. Ed. Leszek Słupecki & Rudolf Simek. Studia Mediaevalia Septentrionalia 23. Vienna: Fassbaender. Pp. 53–98.

Frog & Eila Stepanova 2011. Alliteration in (Balto-) Finnic Languages. In *Alliteration in Culture*. Ed. Jonathan Roper. Houndmills: Palgrave MacMillan. Pp. 195–218.

Gamliel, Tova 2007. "Wailing Lore" in a Yemenite-Israeli Community: Bereavement, Expertise, and Therapy. *Social Science & Medicine* 65: 1501–1511.

Goffman, Erving 1981. *Forms of Talk*. Philadelphia: University of Pennsylvania Press.

Harrison, Alec J. 2001. Xavante Morphology and Respect/Intimacy Relationships. *SIL Brazil Technical Publications*. Summer Institute of Linguistics. Available at: http://www.sil.org/americas/BRASIL/publcns/anthro/XavHonor.pdf.

Haviland, John B 1979. Guugu Yimidhirr Brother-in-Law Language. *Language in Society* 8: 365–393.

Hayashi, Akiko, et al. 2009. The Japanese Preschool's Pedagogy of Feeling: Cultural Strategies for Supporting Young Children's Emotional Development. *Ethos* 37: 32–49.

Hill, Jane H., & Kenneth C. Hill 1978. Honorific Usage in Modern Nahuatl: The Expression of Social Distance and Respect in the Nahuatl of the Malinche Volcano Area. *Language* 54: 123–155.

Hodges, William Robert 2009. *Ganti Andung, Gabe Ende (Replacing Laments, Becoming Hymns): The Changing Voice of Grief in the Pre-Funeral Wakes of Protestant Toba Batak (North Sumatra, Indonesia)*. Santa Barbara: Music University of California.

Honko, Lauri 1963 Itkuvirsirunous ['Lament Poetry']. In *Suomen Kirjallisuus* I: *Kirjoittamaton kirjallisuus*. Ed. Matti Kuusi. Helsinki: Suomalaisen Kirjallisuuden Seura. Pp. 82–96.
Honko, Lauri 1974. Balto-Finnic Lament Poetry. *Studia Fennica* 17: 9–61.
Irvine, Judith 1990 Registering Affect: Heteroglossia in the Linguistic Expression of Emotion *Language and the Politics of Emotion*. Ed. Lutz, Catherine & Lila Abu-Lughod. Cambridge: Cambridge University Press. Pp. 126–161.
Irvine, Judith 1998. Ideologies of Honorific Language. In *Language Ideologies: Practice and Theory*. Ed. Bambi Schieffelin et al. New York: Oxford University Press. Pp. 51–67.
Irvine, Judith 2009. Honorifics. In *Culture and Language Use*. Ed. G. Senft et al. Handbook of Pragmatics Highlights 2. Amsterdam: John Benjamins. Pp. 156–172.
Järvinen, Katriina, & Laura Kolbe 2007. *Luokkaretkellä hyvinvointiyhteiskunnassa: Nykysukupolven kokemuksia tasa-arvosta* ['Class in the Welfare Society: Equality in the Experience of the Modern Generation']. Helsinki: Kirjapaja.
Keating, Elizabeth 1997. Honorific Possession: Power and Language in Pohnpei, Micronesia. *Language in Society* 26: 247–268.
Keating, Elizabeth 1998. Honor and Stratification in Pohnpei, Micronesia. *American Ethnologist* 25: 399–411.
Keeler, Ward 1984. *Javanese: A Cultural Approach*. Monographs in International Studies, Southeast Asia Series 69. Athens OH: Ohio University Center for International Studies.
Laaksonen, Pekka 1999. Sellin Kylässä, Pohjois-Aunuksessa ['In Selli Village, Northern Olonets Karelia']. In *Kotimailla*. Ed. Pekka Laaksonen. Helsinki: Suomalaisen Kirjallisuuden Seura. Pp. 44–107.
Labov, William 1984. Intensity. In *Georgetown University Round Table on Languages and Linguistics*. Ed. Deborah Schiffrin. Washington, DC: Georgetown University Press. Pp. 43–70.
Lönnrot, Elias 1836. Itkuvirsistä Venäjä Karjalassa ['On Lament in Russian Karelia']. *Mehiläinen* (Sept.–Oct. 1836).
McLaren, Anne 2000. The Grievance Rhetoric of Chinese Women: From Lamentation to Revolution. *Intersections* 4 ("Displacements, Transitions and Diasporas"). Available at: http://intersections.anu.edu.au/issue4/mclaren.html.
McClure, William 2000. *Using Japanese: A Guide to Contemporary Usage*. Cambridge: Cambridge University Press.
Peirce, Charles S. 1931–1958. *Collected Papers of Charles Sanders Peirce*. Cambridge, MA: Belknap (Harvard University).
Philips, Susan 2010. Semantic and Interactional Indirectness in Tongan Lexical Honorification. *Journal of Pragmatics* 42: 317–336
Philips, Susan U. 2011. How Tongans Make Sense of the (Non-) Use of Lexical Honorifics. *Journal of Linguistic Anthropology* 21: 247–260.
Silverstein, Michael 1993. Metapragmatic Discourse and Metapragmatic Function. In *Reflexive Language: Reported Speech and Metapragmatics*. Ed. J. A. Lucy. Cambridge: Cambridge University Press. Pp. 33–58.
Silverstein, Michael 2003. Indexical Order and the Dialectics of Sociolinguistic Life. *Language & Communication* 23: 193–229.
Silverstein, Michael 2010. 'Direct' and 'Indirect' Communicative Acts in Semiotic Perspective. *Journal of Pragmatics* 42: 337–353.
Stepanova. Aleksandra 2012. *Karjalaisen itkuvirsikielen sanakirja* ['Dictionary of the Karelian Lament Language']. Trans. E. Stepanova. Helsinki: Suomalainen Kirjallisuuden Seura.
Stepanova, Eila. 2009. Itkukielen metaforat ja itkujen dramaturgia ['Metaphors of the Lament Language and the Dramaturgy of Laments']. In *Kantele, runolaulu ja itku-*

virsi: Runolaulu-Akatemian seminaarijulkaisu. Ed. Pekka Huttu-Hiltunen, Frog, Janne Seppänen & Eila Stepanova. Kuhmo: Juminkeko. Pp. 13–25, 113.

Stepanova, Eila 2011. Reflections of Belief Systems in Karelian and Lithuanian Laments: Shared Systems of Traditional Referentiality? *Archaeologia Baltica* 15: 120–143.

Stepanova Eila 2012. Mythic Elements of Karelian Laments: The Case of *syndyzet* and *spuassuzet*. In *Mythic Discourses: Studies in Uralic Traditions*. Ed. Frog, Anna-Leena Siikala & Eila Stepanova. Helsinki: Finnish Literature Society. Pp. 257–287.

Stepanova, Eila 2013. 2014. *Seesjäveläisten itkijöiden rekisterit: Tutkimus äänellä itkemisen käytänteistä, teemoista ja käsitteistä.* Kultaneiro 14. Joensuu: Suomen Kansantietouden Tutkijain Seura.

Sullivan, Thelma D. 1988. *Thelma D. Sullivan's Compendium of Nahuatl Grammar.* Salt Lake City: University of Utah Press.

Tenhunen, Anna-Liisa 2006. Itkuvirren kolme elämää: Itkuvirsien käytön muuttuminen ['The Three Lives of Lament: Transformations in Lament Usage']. Helsinki: Suomalaisen Kirjallisuuden Seura.

Tenhunen, Anna-Liisa 2007. Times Change, Laments Revive. *Finnish Music Quarterly* 2007: 30–36.

Tolbert, Elizabeth 1988. *The Musical Means of Sorrow: The Karelian Lament Tradition.* Los Angeles: Department of Ethnomusicology University of California.

Wickett, Elizabeth 2010. *For the Living and the Dead: The Funerary Laments of Upper Egypt, Ancient and Modern.* London: IB Tauris & Company Limited.

Wilce, James M. 2009. *Crying Shame: Metaculture, Modernity, and the Exaggerated Death of Lament.* Malden, MA: Blackwell Publishers.

Wilce, James M. 2011. Sacred Psychotherapy in the Age of Authenticity: Healing and Cultural Revivalisms in Contemporary Finland. *Religions* 2: 566–589.

Wilce, James, and Janina Fenigsen (eds.) Forthcoming. *Advancing the Study of Globally Circulating "Emotion Pedagogies".* (Special Issue of *Ethos.*)

Dorothy Noyes

10. Inimitable Examples
School Texts and the Classical Register in Contemporary French Politics

After the first round of the French presidential election in April 2012, incumbent Nicolas Sarkozy announced that on the first of May he would hold "a celebration of *real* work". Quickly realizing his slip, he corrected himself and said that May Day would be "a *real* celebration of work".[1] Labor unions and public employees were not impressed. Socialist candidate François Hollande responded with a celebration of his own. While the unions marched and the other parties held meetings in Paris, Hollande went to the Loire valley town of Nevers to lay a wreath at the grave of Pierre Bérégovoy, the last Socialist prime minister of François Mitterrand's presidency, who committed suicide on May Day, 1993.

Why Hollande should rebuke Sarkozy by invoking the memory of this obscure figure will, I hope, become clear in due course. What Labor Day celebrations have to do with my topic, the classical register in French politics, also requires elucidation. But I want to reflect precisely on the question of how trade unionists, public employees, and the left have come to claim rights in that classical register; what kind of investment they have in a performative repertoire that is not their own vernacular and indeed has never been anybody's vernacular.

Registers in political communication are easily recognized, exciting both visceral responses and suspicious scrutiny. Common Western registers include the Habermasian, the technocratic, and the populist, with their variants according to ideology, regime type, and national tradition (for example, the evangelical inflection of much US political oratory). Each is complexly rooted in political memory, indexing resonant political ideals. In manipulating registers, therefore, political actors do not simply legitimate or position themselves but strive to frame the debate, defining a scene of meaning on which the desired dramaturgy can be played out (Burke 1969). As with all registers, the semiotic range extends beyond linguistic signs to gesture, voice, bearing, dress, even lifestyle and conduct (Agha 2007: 147). Given the importance of the human body to most ideologies of political representation, these extralinguistic repertoires merit special attention.

The French political register that I am calling classical is proper to ceremonial occasions and to particular offices, notably the presidency as it was established by Charles de Gaulle after the Second World War. Drawing on a repertoire elaborated from the early seventeenth century through the Napoleonic period and looking back to antique models, the classical register makes heavy demands on performers, who must not only master its linguistic, kinesic, and visual forms, but have access to the material signs and stages that sustain it. One might place the classical among the codes of distinction that Bourdieu claimed were essentially beyond the reach of those not born to them (1984). Certainly the classical bodily habitus of "dignity" is maintained among the upper bourgeoisie. At the same time, the more fully encoded forms and artifacts of the classical register are no longer the property of an elite. Appropriated as public symbolic goods during the French Revolution, they are reproduced today in the universal formal socialization of public schooling.

In the late nineteenth century, after a hundred years of recurrent revolutions, external wars, and regime changes in France, the architects of the Third Republic sought to create institutions that would reconcile monarchists and republicans and stabilize the social violence of a modernizing France. Key among these institutions was the free, secular, and compulsory public schooling instituted in the early 1880s by education minister Jules Ferry. Designed to integrate French regions, train modern citizens, and recruit a bureaucratic elite, the new system fostered a fervent "secular faith" among teachers, for they were not only the agents of the transformation but the immediate beneficiaries of its meritocratic promise (Ozouf & Ozouf 1992). But although these new state functionaries overwhelmingly voted on the left, the literary and historical culture they disseminated was in no way revolutionary. For the Greek and Latin texts of humanist education, the new centralized curriculum substituted French "classics": the authors of the *ancien régime*, the absolutist monarchy that preceded the Revolution. Even today the secondary school curriculum that prepares students for the *baccalauréat* examination is strongly weighted toward works of the seventeenth century. Among these, preference was long given to those that hailed back most fully in turn to Greek and Roman precedents. School texts were selected for their moral as well as their aesthetic qualities: a school text had to be "a model to imitate... above reproach" (Jey 1998: 31). In short, Republican education maintained "an old cultural model destined for social elites" as it sought to form a new middle class (*ibid.*: 9). Classical exemplars were intended to anchor the democratic progress of a society that had undergone the Terror and the Commune.

Thus the "school classics" were kept at a remove from contemporary high cultural production, a point not always understood by petit-bourgeois aspirants (Bourdieu & Passeron 1979; Milo 1984). New exclusive idioms of distinction were cultivated by elites, particularly in commerce and industry, where advancement did not depend on higher education and state examinations. The classics became, in effect, *déclassés*. But just as schoolteachers had done earlier, much of the larger population that entered secondary education after 1945 embraced the "secular faith" of Republican culture. The school texts were hardly exciting and rarely taken up once the exams were passed, but school culture offered a clear path by which lives could both be measured in principle and advance in practice. To be sure, the promise was not always kept; schooling in practice might be exclusionary and oppressive, and what Bourdieu called the "cultural goodwill" of the lower middle classes was often its own reward (1984). Nonetheless, the school classics instilled a common vocabulary and a framework of ideal expectations through which ordinary citizens might criticize the failures of the actual.

The economic and political shocks of the 1970s began to shake this security. Those who had gained most from the state in the postwar era, those unionized workers and public functionaries who had trusted most in the Republican promise, became critical actors in the episodes I will now recount. I examine the awakening of the dormant classical register in the public reactions to Pierre Bérégovoy's 1993 suicide and to a series of confrontational gestures made by Nicolas Sarkozy at the beginning of his presidency in 2007 and 2008. Both political outsiders by birth and education, both avowed reformers within their respective parties, the two men positioned themselves differently in relation to the classical register. Bérégovoy's suicide was celebrated by both the political elite and ordinary citizens as restoring a dead rhetoric to life: it was a supreme act of cultural and political goodwill. Sarkozy's explicit criticisms and performative rejections of French tradition, understood as all of a piece with his unpopular institutional reforms, provoked a public reclamation of that tradition's most inflexibly classical exemplars.

Bérégovoy: From Honest Man to Man of Honor

"People of quality know everything without ever having learned anything," says one of Molière's disguised valets. Bourdieu showed us, however, that supposedly natural distinction is really learned so early that its acquisition is forgotten. The complexity of high bourgeois style is such that it can never be fully acquired through formal schooling: the nonnative speaker always betrays herself in the details, typically by trying too hard and hypercorrecting. Conscious efforts to attain distinction are by definition doomed to failure.

The social barriers to meritocracy trump political ideology. In the 1980s during the presidency of François Mitterrand, Socialist party membership drew its demographic base from the provincial petty bourgeoisie – particularly from schoolteachers. But the party elite was overwhelmingly bourgeois and Parisian in origins, graduates of the select École Nationale d'Administration: they were there from the start.

Pierre Bérégovoy was the emblematic exception.[2] The child of small shopkeepers in Normandy, one a Ukrainian immigrant, he was forced to abandon his education when his father became ill, beginning his career as a metalworker in a textile factory. Through union activism and party militancy, he rose slowly to the secretariat of the Socialist party. Valued for his discipline and loyalty, he was named Minister of Finance in 1984 to implement the unpopular new doctrine of "rigor". Praised by international bankers, he was denounced by many voters as a traitor to the increasingly hard-hit working class. The thoroughness of his conversion to free-market economics could, indeed, be understood as ideological hypercorrection. But Bérégovoy defended himself by his origins: "The socialists understand me: I belong to them profoundly." Despite continual social snubs – he and his team were known to the civil servants as "the Zaïrians" – and despite the long delay of the political rewards he felt he had earned, Bérégovoy responded to his rise with glee, boasting to those around him, "Me, the son of a worker, among all these *énarques*,[3] and I can govern! Socialism has given this to me." (Youri Roubinski, personal communication, March 1994; Virard 1993:100, 103; Rimbaud 1994: 8).

Other members of the government pointed to Bérégovoy's participation in every phase of postwar Socialism to argue for the legitimacy of the current policy turn to the right. Among themselves they confessed they found him tedious, but as Mitterrand said: "Never forget where he comes from. It is socialism that has made him" (*Paris Match*, 13 May 1993). The press never let go of Bérégovoy's humble origins: he was continually qualified as "the former metalworker" and the "autodidact". He was depicted in cartoons as bursting out of too confined a space: his buttons popping, his socks falling down, his untrimmed eyebrows projecting, grinning from ear to ear, never attaining the calm self-containment of the born bourgeois at ease in his position. Even his nickname, Béré, recalled the classic working-man's headgear.

With the eruption of multiple financial scandals in the late 1980s, minister Pierre Joxe proffered Bérégovoy as the icon of the party's innocence. "This government is composed of honest people... None of us have earned money on the stock market... Pierre Bérégovoy used to be a mechanic. Has he gotten rich? Go look at his apartment, his furniture, look at his suits, his shoes, his socks! Why should you seek to dishonor him?" But the television audience understood the sort of honor that Joxe himself denied the former mechanic: soon afterwards Bérégovoy received socks in the mail from all over France.

Bérégovoy's lack of elegance could not save the Socialists en masse. Mitterrand finally named him prime minister in 1992 in a last-ditch attempt to redeem the party for a voter base alienated by scandal and beset by recession. But a month before the March 1993 legislative elections, Bérégovoy himself became entangled in one of the government's insider trading scandals. The revelations proved more humiliating than incriminating: the consensus was that "Béré"'s desire for social acceptance among Mitterrand's cronies had led him to naive involvement. When the Socialists lost the election, he is widely agreed to have assumed more responsibility than he actually bore. Increasingly marginalized in Party affairs, he was still the MP for the Nièvre and mayor of its capital Nevers, returning to his constituency every Friday to perform his mayoral duties.

On Friday, April 30th, he spent the day on municipal business, surprising his staff by his determination to clear his desk. Saturday was May Day: he hosted a reception for union leaders and opened the annual bicycle and kayak races along the Loire. In the late afternoon, he left his bodyguard at the kayak race and had his chauffeur drive him to the side of a canal off the river, a tree-lined avenue where he liked to walk and which he had used in the photographs for his last election campaign. He sent the chauffeur back to pick up the bodyguard, a few minutes away. Then he went into the trees and shot himself in the head. By the time the car returned, he was in a coma; he died in the helicopter on the way to the hospital in Paris in time for the evening news.

In the consternation that followed, two principal interpretations of the suicide emerged. For the press on the left, the meaning of the act was clear. "A trade unionist does not kill himself on May 1st by chance," declared one journalist (Clément 1993: 16). "Pierre Bérégovoy was the symbol of the French left," began *Le Monde*'s biography (4 May 1993). His act was a confession that in the Mitterrand years Socialism itself had committed suicide. The mourners who brought Socialist red roses to the Paris hospital felt a less abstract connection. "I came because my father was a Socialist and an autodidact," said one young man. "Bérégovoy was his model." For many, the allegorical and the autobiographical came together. One self-declared "nobody... since I have lost my job at fifty-three years old" described Bérégovoy as "a simple, honest man who did not need to attend an elite school to become the Prime minister of the Republic. He is for me the exact symbol of the great Republic of 1789" (Labi & Rimbaud 1995: 100–101).

Individuals claimed diverse particular identifications with him in more than two hundred thousand letters sent to his widow. "He was one of ours, and they killed him," said a railwayman. Rural people called him the voice of *la France profonde* ['deep France']; a Jewish writer spoke of him as a *tsaddik* ['a righteous man'], and residents of the working-class suburbs defined him as *un exclu* ['excluded'], representative of all the immigrants and unemployed whose place in the nation-state was rapidly becoming the central question in French politics (*ibid*: 38–39, 55, 89). The press spoke of the "little dinners" to which Bérégovoy was not invited, the unreturned phone calls, Bérégovoy sitting alone (*Paris Match* 13 May 1993). Cast off to the margins when his utility was gone, Bérégovoy was a working man put back in his place.

The politicians, who of course had a different story to tell, had also a different idiom, bridged only by the ambiguous phrase "honnête home". Members of all parties declared themselves intimate friends of a man driven to destroy himself by the persecution of the media – from which they too suffered. Bérégovoy "preferred to die rather than endure the affront of doubt," said Mitterrand in his eulogy, adding that "no explanation can justify casting the honor of a man to the dogs" (*Le Monde* 6 May 1993). Said Bernhard Kouchner "A suicide... expresses in an honorable fashion, in a *geste* ['deed'] of honor, his disgust and his impotence" (*Le Monde* 4 May 1993). François Léotard declared, "Pierre Bérégovoy has exited on his own authority from a story that was not his own. A story that, with a single *geste* ['gesture'] – becoming thus superior to all of us – he abandons to us in his last disdain" (*ibid*.). Since that time, successive homages, memorials, monuments, academic studies, documentaries, and place names have inscribed Bérégovoy securely into the national memory. Certainly both a sense of guilt and an eye to public opinion contributed largely to the politicians' efforts; certainly public resentment fed the acceptance of them; but what explains so extraordinary a rhetorical elevation?

The suicide was no less rhetorical: a *geste*, at once symbolic gesture and material action. It can be seen, indeed, as the ultimate hypercorrection, an apology wholly disproportionate to the offense: overkill. Many politicians had recovered from worse setbacks and were not taking their own scandals so seriously. This raised Bérégovoy to truly classical stature. Former minister Léo Hamon wrote of Bérégovoy's "civic virtue in the strong, Roman sense of the term" and his consistency, "exemplary in this struggle as in his entire career" (Labi & Rimbaud 1995: 106–107). Like Lucretia or Cato of Utica, Bérégovoy was understood as taking his life in protest of general corruption under tyranny, to shame and inspire more accomodating members of the elite. And indeed, while never mastering the minutiae of bourgeois style, he clearly internalized the grand narratives of bourgeois legitimation. Along with his evening reading, he is said never to have missed an opening night at the Comédie Française (*ibid*: 105–106). Unlike the more careless inheritors, Bérégovoy took seriously both Corneille's enactments of honor and Molière's strictures about the high price of honor for the upwardly mobile.

He was an *honnête homme*, said everyone: a man of honor/an honest man. The ambiguous phrase goes straight back to that slippery moment of the seventeenth century when an upwardly mobile class of state officials, the absolutist ancestors of Ferry's Republican bureaucrats, sought to redefine *honnêteté* from aristocratic style to bourgeois substance – while simultaneously working to acquire the style. La Rochefoucauld defined the almost impossible ideal that resulted: "It is truly to be a man of honor to wish to be always exposed to the gaze of honest people."

The unity of appearances and reality, honor and honesty, was temporarily restored by Bérégovoy's act. "Sometimes they believe in it, then!" wrote Daniel Schneidermann of *Le Monde*.

> Sometimes…politicians believe in their promises, in their ideals, … in all that… one supposed had become purely utilitarian and mechanical. … Those words, by now hollow from so many repetitions – my honor, my conscience, socialism – resonated secretly in him, so distant, so deep, that the thousand suspicious eyes of the crowd never guessed it. From this bloody recalling on Saturday evening, the political word, all political words found themselves instantly as if revalorised, recharged with authenticity and truth. What if, despite appearances, political life were not a … vain spectacle? …And what if [politicians] were really men after all, men of flesh and blood? (*Le Monde*, 4 May 1993.)

Bérégovoy's *geste* went beyond hypercorrection to sacrifice. Its excess paid, at least for a moment, the debts of the entire political class. Like several of Molière's plebeian heroes, Bérégovoy attempted all his life to purchase symbolic capital with more material kinds, to exchange his substance for style. This time, he spent enough. His gesture shifted not just register but the genre of his own narrative, from the reversible struggles of comedy to the decisive action of tragedy. To be sure, the shift to a register so far removed from the everyday also removed Bérégovoy from everyday rewards: though it bought him a place in memory, it was an act that put him out of action. But in sacrificing himself, he redeemed the classical tradition of political representation.

Sarkozy: From Gesture to Gesticulation

The election of Nicolas Sarkozy in 2007 brought another outsider to the very forefront of French political life. As president, Sarkozy took on a complex responsibility. In the words of the inaugural ceremony, he incarnated France, symbolized the Republic, and represented the French people. He raised some anxieties from the beginning as the child of divorced parents and mixed ethnic ancestry, a new man in his cultural style behaving more like an American tabloid celebrity than the successor of Charles De Gaulle. His political style was equally new, not polished, but aggressive and "hyperactive", passing "from gesture to gesticulation" (Courtois 2008). Sarkozy embraced this characterization, boasting of a politics of "rupture" that would shake up a stagnant France. He defined himself explicitly in opposition to classical norms: "I myself have created my character by transgressing certain rules" (Reza 2007: 139–140). Indifferent to dignity insofar as it constrained his own conduct, Sarkozy was likewise contemptuous of solidarity. In the eyes of many, his liberal politics and individualist, even narcissistic, conduct undermined his capacity to incarnate, symbolize, *or* represent. Satirists highlighted "Sarko"'s physical restlessness, mimeticism, intrusiveness into the space of others, imperfect self-control. These were evident in a series of confrontational incidents in which he was said by all parties to have "debased the dignity" of the presidency, above all in the celebrated slanging match at the Paris Agricultural Show of 2008, when he told a farmer, "*Casse-toi, pauvre con*" ['Screw you then, dumbass']. Above all, said psychologist Joseph Messinger, "He absolutely does not disguise himself" (En trois mots 2008). If classical French politics are based in hypocrisy, a maintenance of group norms that allows differences and deviations their private space, Sarkozy broke through the screen: he incarnated rupture.

While refusing the Republican political repertoire, Sarkozy also denounced its archive and the exemplary logic connecting literary and historical forebears to present conduct. This dual refusal excited a surprising consensual reaction across the French public, which became clear in a strange confrontation between Sarkozy and a fictional aristocrat from the seventeenth century.

A relatively recent arrival to the *lycée* curriculum, *La Princesse de Clèves* is by now an established "classic" in every sense. The 1678 novel by Mme. de Lafayette is a powerful psychological exploration of how individual fears and desires interact with the honor code. The protagonist is a beautiful woman at the French court, raised by her mother to strict virtue and mistrust of the seductions of men. Married off very young to a nobleman she respects, she soon meets the glamorous Duc de Nemours, who wins her heart, but woos her without success. Made aware of her passion, her husband dies of a broken heart. The Duc presents himself after a decent interval, expecting to gain his happiness now that it can be lawfully granted, but the Princess refuses him once more, ruled not by the social forms but by her own deeper sense of honor. She retires to a convent and "her life," concludes the novelist, "which was rather short, left inimitable examples of virtue."

Possibly weary of uncooperative women given his impending divorce, Sarkozy was observed during the period of the presidential campaign to have it in for the Princess, who became his proxy for everything recalcitrant in French life. Talking in February 2006 of the need for administrative reform, Sarkozy declared, "The other day, I was entertaining myself..looking at .... the entry exams for public sector jobs. A sadist or an imbecile, you choose, had put in the program to interrogate the examinees on *La Princesse de Clèves*. I don't know whether you've often happened to ask the receptionist what she thinks of the Princesse de Clèves. Imagine the spectacle!" As president he returned to the theme several times, suggesting in July 2007 that volunteer work ought to be recognized as a qualification for the public sector competition, for this after all, he said "is worth as much as knowing *La Princesse de Clèves* by heart." Seeing raised eyebrows around the room he gave a little twisted smile and said "Well, I have nothing against it, but, well...I suffered a lot for her." (*Le Monde* 7 September 2008).

This peculiar obsession, deriving presumably from youthful boredom in the classroom, was justified to the press by the allegation that Sarkozy's own secretary had failed to receive a promotion because she had not been able to name the book's author on a state exam. But by making the Princess a multivalent symbol of all that he sought to change, Sarkozy provided his opponents with a unified figure of resistance to his reforms. In addition to the bureaucracy and the exam system, Sarkozy also had his eye on higher education: in 2007 he declared, "The taxpayer is not necessarily obliged to pay for your studies in old literature.....The pleasure of knowledge is fantastic, but the State should concern itself first of all with the professional success of young people." (*L'Express* 26 February 2009)

When the government's proposals to cut research funding and increase the teaching loads of university lecturers came forward in the early months of 2009, the Princess became the poster child for the ensuing strike and for broader anti-government protest in the face of the economic crisis. Perhaps for the first time in history, Clèves was made to rhyme with *grève* – the strike, a by now equally classic French institution. In addition to the traditional street marches, students and professors organized public marathon readings of the novel in front of universities across France (Pires 2009). A film updating the novel to a French *lycée*, the setting in which the French people encounter it, was shown to acclaim on the Arte channel (Honoré 2008). Facebook groups formed; the novel sold out in bookstores; the most popular item at that year's *Salon du Livre* was a button saying "Me, I'm reading La Princesse de Clèves."[4] In dissing the princess, according to his critics, Sarkozy showed his contempt for general culture, his contempt for the receptionist who should not be expected to need or want it, and his contempt for schooling as the medium of national and class integration (Cassin 2009; Cixous 2011). Teachers showed their contempt for him in turn in a host of unlovely caricatures and parodies.

Endless commentaries contrasted Sarkozy's rough discourse to the classical style celebrated in the novel. One of the more surprising evaluations came from *L'Humanité*, the newspaper tied to the French Communist Party. Columnist François Taillandier exhorted the French to stop lowering themselves to Sarko's level by quoting or parodying the vulgar "Screw you then, dumbass," with which he had insulted the farmer. He went on:

> This perhaps is what the wearers of the button, "Me, I'm reading La Princesse de Clèves"…wanted to say in their fashion. If we could be sure that all of those who wore the button have read or reread the novel of Mme. de Lafayette, that would be a beautiful thing. In any case, these two little events, placing face to face one of the most beautiful musics of the French language and the triviality of an obscene reply, are in my opinion joined by an invisible, but solid thread. A certain idea of language and literature has since time immemorial constituted one of the pillars of French identity. Our schools and our universities knew it, and up to François Mitterrand, our presidents knew it also. You could even deplore a rather conventional veneration of this heritage: but in short it was respected. One did not always still understand why it is necessary to read the "classics" and to make the effort to speak well, but at least no one was advising against it. (*L'Humanité* 26 May 2009.)

Bérégovoy's action revitalized the classical register by placing the body behind it, "recharging it with authenticity and truth," as Schneidermann had said. Conversely, Sarkozy restored it by his failure of hypocrisy: his refusal even to pay lip service to the classical. Against this rupture of registers, the order of French political life reasserted itself. Even the Communist Party newspaper aligned itself, as we see, not behind Liberty leading the people, but behind an aristocrat standing fast against change. The hard surface of classicism, resisting both inner impulse and external pressure, now informed not just the literature of the court of Louis XIVth but the prerogatives of bureaucrats, the examination as rite of passage, the power of labor unions, the right to strike, the *Salon du Livre*, the *Salon de l'Agriculture*, the farmer's *terroir* and the Communist party. All of these rather disparate entities were now integrated with the personal integrity of the chaste Princess, united against the blandishments of the hyperactive president. No one was going to bed with Sarkozy.

Jules Ferry, Vindicated?

Sarkozy's verbal explosions point to a realm felt as foreign: American and cinematic, focused on the pursuit of individual appetites. Perhaps an inevitable future, it is not one owned by the French in the present. Bérégovoy's suicide caught him up into a tradition at once intimate and half-forgotten to the French, a world deeply inscribed in literature which he restored to the body. Bérégovoy showed that the dead bones of school texts could live, that outsiders could both value them and come to inhabit them. Vaulting into that virtual world, Bérégovoy justified all those who routinely gesture towards it. His extremism was in fact that of the Princess of Clèves, whose life, you recall, "was rather short and left behind it inimitable examples of virtue." The paradox of the classical action in French culture is that it is both exemplary and inimitable. The authentic exception validates the hypocritical rule.

To be sure, Bérégovoy is dead and Sarkozy is still kicking – but he did lose that second election, and while it was surely a challenging moment for political incumbents, both polls and analysts emphasized his personal unpopularity as a key factor in his defeat. Sarkozy's endeavor to wake up "a mummified France" succeeded all too well. By violating register expectations he provoked a reaction of unusual solidarity: not with him but against him. As the press observed, it is rare that students and professors, literati and service workers, speak with one voice. It is perhaps unfortunate that the voice belongs to the Princesse de Clèves, for the novel makes clear that her astonishing fidelity to an ideal of duty stems in fact from the fear of change and pain. Just saying no, as the public did to Sarkozy, would not allow the French to meet the challenges of the present.

Oddly for a president who wanted to create a Ministry of National Identity, Sarkozy set himself apart from the public he represented by thumbing his nose at common French experience. On the contrary, the reception of Bérégovoy's death pointed up not only the power of that national experience but something interesting about its source. The suicide produced a temporary solidarity between "deep" France and "excluded" France, a common mourning to which even the political class was forced to pay lip service. What all these constituencies had in common was *not* inherited communal tradition: it was the classical civic culture that informs French state institutions from the public schools to the bureaucrat's office to the Elysée palace.

The inclusive promise of French republicanism, French schooling and French *civilisation* have been much debunked, not least by Bourdieu in his demonstration that these are not the real avenues to status and power in French society. In 2012, nonetheless, the new president François Hollande risked a storm of criticism by laying another wreath on the very day of his inauguration. It was before the statue of Jules Ferry, that creator of the Republican educational system. Hollande was careful to insist that Ferry must be condemned for his other major contribution, the energizing of French colonialism with the formulation of the explicitly racist "civilizing mission". Nonetheless, said Hollande, who based his promise of national recovery on the hiring of sixty thousand new teachers, Ferry is "the builder of this great communal house that is the school of the Republic."

Unhappily for the tidiness of my narrative, at the time of this writing Hollande's mastery of the Republican classical register and his approach to reform by consensus have made little headway against the economic crisis, while his promised "return to dignity" has been undermined by the irruption of his private life into the ceremonial realm of the Presidency. Still, despite this and despite all that we know about schooling as a vehicle of class discipline, I too feel an inclination to revisit Ferry's statue.

The classical register has always been restricted both by performance context and by access: it has always been public, ceremonial, and high in status. With the severe reduction of that public ceremonial sphere in a neoliberal consumer society, it is detached from the habitus even of the traditional political elite. Indeed, considering François Mitterrand, Jacques Chirac, Dominique Strauss-Kahn, and the rest, there is hardly a figure in recent French politics who lives up fully to the ideal of the *honnête homme*, especially with La Rochefoucauld's stringent demand that he wish to live *always* under the gaze of honest people. The classical is a residual register indexing an impossible social persona – an "inimitable example".

But this very abandonment leaves the register open to appropriation by anyone. It is what folklorists used to call a *gesunkenes Kulturgut*: a fallen cultural good (Naumann 1935). Because it is a register that costs the actor something to inhabit, demanding self-control and even self-sacrifice, it allows dignity to be earned. It offers symbolic social mobility and a performative meritocracy on paradoxically more objective terms than the actual recruitment practices of French elites. The performances are validated or rejected not by those few but by the public as a whole.

In support of Bérégovoy and against Sarkozy, unexpected social consensus emerged in response to the activation of a register that was dormant or even moribund, at best the object of lip service. Schooling and public institutions have converted a prestige repertoire into a common property, largely maintained by citation and allusion but available as a resource for occasional full performance. The French case suggests a need for comparative research into the nature of ceremonial registers as well as a reframing of current polemics over school curricula. Right-wing calls for defense of national culture mistake the social location of what is held in common. Left-wing critiques of the canon underestimate the potential of imposed texts for appropriation. Vernaculars have their own force, identitarian or revolutionary or both. But the register that holds together a plural society must be deliberately constituted and sustained by institutions. Its performance is necessarily effortful.

Notes

1 All translations are mine unless otherwise noted.
2 For a fuller account, see Noyes 2000.
3 Graduates of the elite École Nationale d'Administration.
4 Long afterward intellectuals continued to defend the novel's contemporaneity, notably in a documentary exploring its relevance to the lives of girls in the immigrant suburbs of Marseille (Sauder 2011).

References

Sources

En Trois Mots 2008, Entretien avec Joseph Messinger, psychologue, auteur de "La Sarko attitude". France 3, 27 mai. http://www.lesmotsontunsens.com/video-joseph-messinger-psychologue-analyse-la-gestuelle-de-sarkozy-la-sarko-attitude . Retrieved 15 February 2014.
L'Express.
L'Humanité.
Le Monde.
Paris Match.

Literature

Agha, Asif 2007. *Language and Social Relations*. Cambridge: Cambridge University Press.

Bourdieu, Pierre, & Jean-Claude Passeron 1979 [1964]. *The Inheritors: French Students and Their Relation to Culture*. Trans. Richard Nice. Chicago: University of Chicago Press.

Bourdieu, Pierre 1984 [1979]. *Distinction: A Social Critique of the Judgment of Taste*. Cambridge MA: Harvard University Press.

Burke, Kenneth 1969 [1945]. *A Grammar of Motives*. Berkeley & Los Angeles: University of California Press.

Cassin, Barbara 2009. Sarkozy "m'à tuer". *Le Monde* 1 March.

Cixous, Hélène 2011. Nicolas Sarkozy, the Murderer of the Princess of Cleves. *The Guardian* 22 March.

Clément, Jérome 1993. *Lettres à Pierre Bérégovoy: Chronique du mois de mai 1993*, Paris: Calmann-Lévy.

Courtois, Gérard 2008. Entretien avec Denis Muzet: "Sa présence a valeur de solution". *Le Monde* 6 May.

Honoré, Christophe 2008. *La belle personne*. Paris: Arte France Cinema.

Jey, Martine 1998. *La littérature au lycée: Invention d'une discipline (1880–1925)*. Recherches textuelles 3. Metz: Université de Metz.

Labi, Philippe, & Christiane Rimbaud 1995. *Lettres à Béré: Une nation sous le choc*. Paris: J. C. Lattès.

Milo, Daniel 1984. Les classiques scolaires. In *Les lieux de mémoire*, t. II, *La Nation*. Ed. Pierre Nora. Paris, Gallimard. Pp. 517–562.

Naumann, Hans 1935. *Deutsche Volkskunde in Grundzügen*. Leipzig: Quelle & Meyer.

Noyes, Dorothy 2000. Authoring the Social Drama: Suicide, Self, and Narration in a French Political Scandal. *Narrative* 8: 210–231.

Ozouf, Jacques, and Mona Ozouf 1992. *La République des instituteurs*. Paris, Seuil.

Pires, Mat 2009. Diary: La Princesse de Clèves at the Barricades. *London Review of Books* 9 April.

Reza, Yasmina 2007. *L'aube le soir ou la nuit*. Paris: Albin Michel.

Rimbaud, Christiane 1994. *Bérégovoy*. Paris: Perrin.

Sauder, Régis 2011. *Nous, princesses de Clèves*. Paris: Nord/Ouest Documentaires.

Virard, Marie-Paule 1993. *Comment Mitterrand a découvert l'économie*. Paris: Albin Michel.

Corpus and Performance

IV

William Lamb

11. Verbal Formulas in Gaelic Traditional Narrative
Some Aspects of Their Form and Function

> One story grows out of another, and the tree is almost hidden by a foliage of the speaker's invention. Here and there comes a passage repeated by rote, and common to many stories, and to every good narrator. – John Francis Campbell (1994 [1860]: 34)

Research in fields as diverse as language acquisition, speech pathology and corpus linguistics has demonstrated the central role that formulaic language plays in human communication and cognition (Wray 2013). Once sidelined in theoretical linguistics as a peripheral concern (Wray 2002: 13),[1] formulas are now recognised as pervasive and natural, and key to our understanding of human language (Bybee 2006: 712-713). Some registers, especially those that are repetitive and constrained in some way, seem to exhibit distinct types and a greater proportion of formulas than others. Scottish Gaelic traditional narrative is one such variety.[2]

The book-length treatment of Gaelic storytelling formulas mooted by Ó Duilearga (1945: 35)[3] remains unwritten, and few articles have examined the topic, *per se*. In fact, relatively little work has been published on the formulaicity of traditional prose in any language, in contrast to that on metrical verse.[4] To an extent, this dearth can be attributed to the hegemonic legacy of Oral-Formulaic Theory, and the difficulty that scholars have had thinking past its margins at times (Frog 2011: 21; 2014a: 111–113).

The theory's originators, Milman Parry and Albert Lord, transformed our understanding of Homeric verse and the composition-*cum*-performance of epic poetry, but they effectively ignored prose (Gray 1971: 293; cf. Clover 1986: 12n). This is understandable, given their main objective (O' Nolan 1971: 234), which was to explain how the complex hexameter lines of the *Odyssey* and *Iliad* could have been composed at a time when literacy was scarce. Examining a living, oral tradition of epic verse in former Yugoslavia, Parry realised that modern poets could extemporise thousands of lines at a time by using prefabricated, metered phrases; that is, formulas (Lord 2000: 43). He concluded that, regardless of who had composed the *Odyssey* and *Iliad*, the presence of similar constructions in those works indicated that they had emanated from oral tradition (*ibid.*: 144).

As insightful as Parry and Lord's work was for the Homeric question, it restricted a universal human tendency – to recycle language, where possible – to a narrow communicative domain. Although it would be inaccurate to construe poetry and prose as dichotomous categories,[5] even a cursory glimpse at the literature indicates that work on verbal formulas in oral tradition has tended to emphasise metred over non-metred narrative.[6] In the present article, I hope to redress this deficiency somewhat by providing a preliminary account of the formula in Gaelic traditional narrative, focussing on form and function. Before commencing, let us expand the term "formula" further, and discuss how it is to be used here.

Although formulaic language has been much discussed in the literature, scholars still disagree on its fundamental characteristics (Zeyrek 1993: 162). So far, most definitions have been influenced by authors' specific agendas and assumptions (Wray 2013: 317; cf. Rosenberg 1981: 443). Certainly, this is evident in Parry's own influential definition, which states that a formula is "a group of words ... regularly employed under the same metrical conditions to express a given essential idea" (1930: 80; cf. Lord 2000: 4).[7] This definition proved too limiting even for the traditions for which it was originally intended,[8] but subsequent alterations did not readily accommodate non-metrical registers (O' Nolan 1971: 234n). The breadth of research on the subject belies the notion that formulas are restricted to metred poetry. As O' Nolan (*ibid.*: 235) remarks, "the formula is a device which arises from the nature of oral narrative" – whether metred or not.

It would be beneficial to have a definition of formulaicity applicable to a wide set of linguistic contexts. Towards this aim, consider the following, from Wray:

> [A formulaic sequence is] a sequence, continuous or discontinuous, of words or other elements, which is, or appears to be, prefabricated: that is sorted and retrieved whole from memory at the time of use, rather than being subject to generation or analysis by the language grammar (2002: 9).

As Wray states (2008: 96), this definition is not theory neutral, because it makes a claim about how formulas are encoded and decoded in human memory. At the same time, it is procedural and inclusive – allowing for lexical sequences that *appear* to be prefabricated – and imposes no further stipulations, such as the requirement for metricality. The main difference between Wray's definition of "formulaic sequence" and a subsequent term proposed by her, the "morpheme equivalent unit" (MEU), is that the latter takes a stronger position on the cognitive status of formulas:

> [it is] a word or word string, whether incomplete or including gaps for inserted variable items, that is processed like a morpheme [...] without recourse to any form-meaning matching of any sub-parts it may have (Wray 2008: 94).

Although formulaic language may well be processed in a similar way to morphemes, without direct observation of our neurolinguistic functioning, we have no decisive way of identifying MEUs (cf. Wray 2008: 97). Furthermore, one wonders what additional nuances may be required for this theory in order to accommodate a language such as Gaelic, in which morphemes are remarkably protean. Due in part to the complex morphophonemics of Celtic languages, Ternes (1982: 72) averred, "There is hardly a language [family] in the world for which the traditional concept of 'word' is so doubtful."[9] So, until we better understand the interaction between "meaningful units" and grammar in human language, it seems best to accept a certain amount of fuzziness when dealing with formulaic language (see Wray 2008: 116-121), whilst striving for clear operational definitions.

In this article, I follow Wray's definition of "formulaic sequence" (2002: 9), that a formula is an expression that seems to be prefabricated. An indicator of prefabrication is its presence across more than one narrator's texts. Such consistency suggest that it has been conventionalised within a language community (cf. Wray 2008: 8n), and not generated *ex novo* by a speaker's grammatical apparatus. I do not consider phrases that appear to be idiolectic here, although formulaic conventions, of course, probably originate in well-chosen idiolecticisms. I also make few stipulations about rigidness of form; both "fossilised" strings and lexico-grammatical templates[10] are included. As discussed below, some of the formulas characteristic of Gaelic storytelling show open, semi-open and closed elements. In all, this conceptualisation of the formula is general, but empirically derived: any sequence of "meaningful units" – continuous or discontinuous – that is common for more than one language user in the dataset (see below) is included. It seems cogent to work with broad strokes at the risk of tentativeness in places, given the preliminary nature of the present study and the fact that theoretical models continue to be evaluated (cf. Wray 2008: 96).

The material surveyed here comes from the first three volumes of Campbell's *Popular Tales of the West Highlands* (hereafter, *PTWH*), republished by Birlinn as two volumes in 1994. Unlike many collections of nineteenth-century folklore, it was transcribed closely from contributors across the Highlands and Islands and presents a faithful representation of oral narrative.[11] Altogether, the sample consists of roughly 90,000 words of text across 33 tales and 17 narrators, from the Argyllshire mainland, Barra, Colonsay, Islay, and mainland Ross-shire (see Figure 1). My method involved noting candidate formulas as I read through the texts and placing them in a database. Those that recurred between narrators were highlighted and analysed, whilst those only used by single narrators were discarded.

We will begin by considering the consistency and geographical distribution of formulas in the Gaelic narrative tradition, and touch upon the semantic "substance" of formulaic recurrence along the way. After this, we will consider functions, in two sections. The first of these is devoted to macro-functions of formulas in traditional narrative, especially memory facilitation and semiotic reference. The second concerns the micro-functions of Gaelic storytelling formulas (e.g. register marking and the realisation of motifs), which provide insight into the core communicative features of the register.

Stability of Form and Geographical Distribution

Storytellers across the Gaelic-speaking region drew upon a common stock of formulas and produced them with impressive consistency. In essence, these sayings comprised an extended lexicon of narrative language, which would have been acquired[12] by any good storyteller during his or her enculturation in the tradition (cf. Davies 1992: 243). As mentioned above, some are fossilised structures, particularly the shorter formulas, which resist variation. Others are lexico-grammatical templates, also known as frames (see Wray 2008: 10). Some of the longer formulas (e.g. Example 8) are composites, which occasionally resemble poetry, evincing features such as rhythm, alliteration and rhyme. These are sometimes referred to as "runs"[13] in the literature (e.g. Bruford 1966: 36; cf. Lord 2000: 58-60), and seem to be built from smaller elements or chunks (cf. Bruford 1966: 37; Lord 2000: 58; Wray 2008: 5).[14] Let us consider three common, conventionalised formulas, with a focus on their variability and geographical distribution. I have tried to distinguish between three levels of formulaicity here, with "closed" elements underlined, semantically constrained "semi-open" ones in bold type, and "open" elements left unmarked.

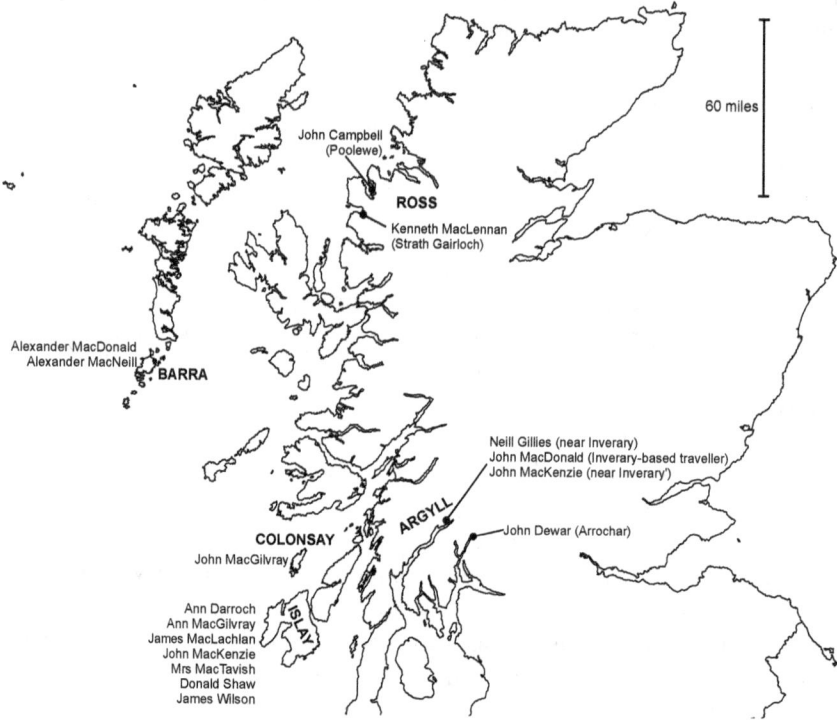

Figure 1. Narrators' places of origin

Beginning with a simple, mostly fixed formula, the expression *thogadh cèol is leagadh bròn* ['music was raised and sadness vanquished'] typically occurs at the end of a tale, once a hero has routed his enemy and returned from battle. It is geographically well-dispersed (see Figure 2a), common in Gaelic narrative and consistent across the sample. Here are four instances of it in four different tales, collected from narrators in Islay, Colonsay and Barra (N.B.: the orthography has been silently modernised by the present author, but no changes have been made to lexis or grammar):

(1) (a) *thogadh ceòl is leagadh bròn* 'music was raised and sadness vanquished'
(Alexander MacNeill, Barra: *PTWH* II, 175)

(b) *thogadh an ceòl is leagadh am bròn* 'the music was raised and sadness vanquished'
(Donald Shaw, Islay: *PTWH* I, 549)

(c) *thog iad ceòl is leag iad bròn* 'they raised music and vanquished sadness'
(James Wilson, Islay: *PTWH* I, 100)

(d) *Thog iad ceòl is leag iad bròn* 'they raised music and vanquished sadness'
(John MacGilvray, Colonsay: *PTWH* II, 196)

These phrases are nearly identical, so no underlining or bold type have been used. The only differences are in the morphology of the verb, which is impersonal[15] in (1a) and (1b), and two words – *ceòl* ['music'] and *bròn* ['sadness'] – which are definite in (1b) and indefinite in the rest. As we will see in the examples below, open and semi-open formulaic elements tend to be deixis-sensitive.[16] Deixis involves the way in which a language anchors an utterance to person, place and time. Typical deictic categories are voice, tense, person, definiteness and number.

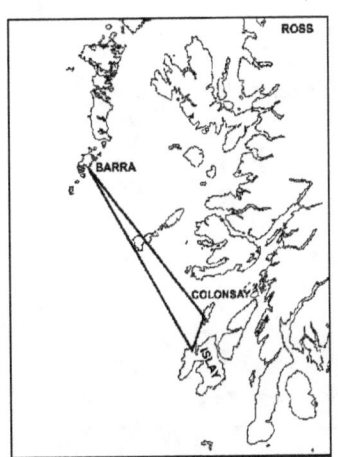 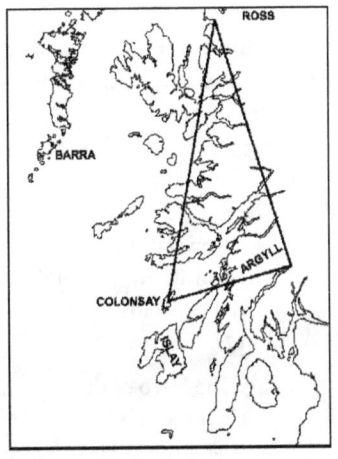 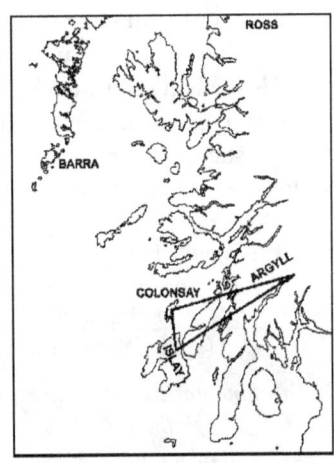

a. 'Lifting of music'   b. 'The three narrows'   c. 'Near to enemies'

Figure 2. Maps of formula occurrences

Our next example, the imprisoning formula "the binding of the three[17] narrows", appears in the tales of three different narrators, from Colonsay, Argyll and Ross (see Figure 2b):

(2)(a) <u>Chuir</u> e_i <u>ceangail nan trì chaoil</u> air$_j$ 'He$_i$ put the binding of the three
                                                                   narrows on him$_j$
      <u>gu daor</u> agus <u>gu</u> **docair**   <u>firmly and</u> **painfully**'
      (John MacGilvray, Colonsay: *PTWH* II, 201)

  (b) <u>Chuir</u> e_i <u>ceangal nan trì chaoil</u> orra$_j$ 'He$_i$ put the binding of the three
                                                                narrows on them$_j$
      <u>gu daor</u> 's <u>gu</u> **docair**   <u>firmly and</u> **painfully**'
      (Neill Gillies, Argyll: *PTWH* I, 199)

  (c) Chaidh <u>ceangail nan trì chaoil</u> a <u>chuir</u> 'The binding of the three narrows
                                                          was put on
      orra$_j$ <u>gu daor</u> 's <u>gu</u> **daingeann**   them$_j$ <u>firmly and</u> **tightly**'
      (Kenneth MacLennan, Ross: *PTWH* I, 212)

Given the mix of fixed and facultative elements in this formula, it is clearly a template. This is a two-protagonist expression with the semantic roles AGENT and PATIENT. We see variation in the deictic categories of person, number and voice, and a valence decrease in (2c), leaving us with PATIENT only. Like Example 1, the formula is well-distributed and consistent. As will be evident even to non-Gaelic-speakers, there is a degree of parallelism here, or "language marked by extra regularities" (Bauman 1984: 16). The primary element is alliteration: ch_ + c_l + ch_l and gu d_r + gu d_r/n. Such regularity helps to constrain the formula and facilitate its continuity (cf. Rubin 1995: 88). On this note, (2c) ends with *daingeann*, which is semantically related to *docair* (both have the connotation of "unmovable"), and which also alliterates with *daor*. This formula will be discussed again in detail in the following section, when we deal with semantic function.

Our third example, and the most complicated from a semantic point of view, is the battle formula "far from friends and near to foes". This tends to appear when a protagonist rallies himself before a last, great effort. Here are three instances from three different tales, collected from narrators in Islay, Colonsay and Argyll (see Figure 2c):

(3)(a) *smaointich* mi$_i$ *fhèin* <u>gu robh</u> mi$_i$ 'I$_i$ myself **thought** <u>that</u> I$_i$ <u>was</u>
     fagus <u>d</u>om nàimhdean 's   near <u>to</u> my$_i$ <u>foes</u> and
     <u>fad o</u> m'$_i$ <u>chàirdean</u>   <u>far from</u> my$_i$ <u>friends</u>'
     (James Wilson, Islay: *PTWH* I, 187)

  (b) *Smaointich Gaisgeach na*   'The Hero of the Red Shield$_i$
       Sgiatha Deirge$_i$ **thought**
     <u>gun robh</u> e_i <u>fad' o</u> a$_i$ <u>chàirdean</u> 's   <u>that</u> he$_i$ <u>was far from</u> his$_i$ <u>friends and</u>
     fagus <u>d</u>a$_i$ *nàimhdean*   near <u>to</u> his$_i$ <u>foes</u>'
     (John MacGilvray, Colonsay: *PTWH* II, 195)

  (c) *chunnaic* e_i <u>gu robh</u> e_i 'he$_i$ **saw** <u>that</u> he$_i$ <u>was</u>
     <u>fada bho</u> a$_i$ <u>charaid</u> 's   <u>far from</u> his$_i$ <u>friend and</u>

> dlùth $\underline{da}_i$ nàmhaid   **near** $\underline{to}$ his$_i$ foe'
> (John MacKenzie, Argyll: *PTWH* I, 158)

The wording of (3a) and (3b) is identical, apart from the referents used and the order in which the two main elements are presented (i.e. NEAR to POSS FOE(S) | FAR from POSS FRIEND(S)). Like Example 2, this formula is a template, as it shows a combination of fixed and facultative elements. For example, *smaointich* ['thought'] can be substituted by *chunnaic* ['saw'] and vice versa. Indeed, any apposite *verbum sentiendi* will do in this "semi-open" slot; lexical freedom is constrained by semantic parameters (cf. Bybee 2006: 718). In (3c), the word for "near" differs: it is *dlùth* as opposed to *fagus*. Again, although several words are plausible here,[18] they are all close synonyms and, thus, constrained to a class of semantic equivalence. The only "open" element in Example (3) is the subject NP (e.g. "The Hero of the Red Shield"). "Friends" and "foes" show deixis-sensitive morphological variation between the singular and plural, although this is difficult to indicate using the present annotations.

Turning to the obligatory elements, we can include the phrasal prepositions "near to" and "far from" – with their friend(s) and foe(s) complements – as well as its propositional structure and the semantic roles that obtain. The "near to enemies" formula is a one-protagonist template with a particular, stable pattern of co-reference ($\underline{V}^{cog}$ NP$_i$ | NP$_i$ $\underline{\text{near to}}$ NP$_i^{POSS}$ FOE^{NUMBER} $\underline{\text{and far}}$ $\underline{\text{from}}$ NP$_i^{POSS}$ FRIEND^{NUMBER}). Propositional structure and semantic roles tend to be deixis-independent, and remain consistent between different narratives and renditions. In a nutshell, it is the interplay between the open and obligatory in formulaic templates – being moderately constrained, mnemonically primed routines – that promotes creativity[19] (cf. Rubin 1995: 90) and ensures their durability. As Lord said, "formulas are not the ossified clichés which they have the reputation of being [...] they are capable of change and are indeed highly productive" (2000: 4).

Before leaving this example, we can use it to illustrate the importance of diachronic considerations when studying traditional Gaelic formulas. We find an analogue for this orally collected formula in a romantic tale[20] from a 17th-century manuscript (see Bruford 1966: 187), which is similar in semantics and form:

(4) Is $\underline{fada}$ ó gach aon$_i$ agaibh$_i$ 'Every one$_i$ of you$_i$ is $\underline{far}$ from
    a$_i$ dhuthchas dílis 7 a$_i$ bhaile bunaidh 7   his$_i$ native culture and his$_i$ town of
                                                                     origin and
    is líonmhor bhur$_i$ $\underline{námhaid}$ 7   your$_i$ $\underline{\text{enemies}}$ are many and
    is tearc bhúr$_i$ $\underline{gcarad}$ annso   your$_i$ $\underline{\text{friends}}$ few here.'

Although this excerpt is temporally removed from the others by at least two hundred years, it is clearly related. It also occurs during a battle scene and features the same juxtaposition between nearby foes and distant friends, although the latter is implied. We see the same propositional pattern and can infer the same relationship between variability and deixis (e.g. voice, tense, number and person). Importantly, we should not assume that the formula originated in literate composition (cf. Davies 1992: 243), although it illustrates the dynamic confluence of orality and literacy in Gaelic tradition (see Ó Duillearga 1945). Given the prolixity of the medieval and early modern romances (Bruford 1966: 37), it seems likely that the author of the tale in question took liberty with the original phrase. Then again, as dubious as it may seem, perhaps he cited the formula verbatim as a mark of authentic orality (cf. Wray 2008: 45).[21] Further research, with a larger and diachronic corpus, could elucidate these and related issues.

As many other formulas in the sample had a similar degree of consistency and geographical distribution as the three we have discussed so far, it seems that an established, consistent and geographically distributed phrasal lexicon was associated with the Gaelic storytelling register. The indications are that traditional narrative was of central importance to Gaelic society in generations past, and that certain individuals, at least, were expert "acquirers" of these enregistered expressions. In the next section, we will consider the way in which the formulas were used by narrators, and especially the referential meanings that they had for participants in the tradition.

Macro-Functions of Formulas in Traditional Narrative

A myriad of functions have been ascribed to traditional formulas in the literature, but it is useful to differentiate between their primary *raison d'être* – dealing economically with a recurrent communicative need – and secondary functions that become available once they have been conventionalised. Undoubtedly, some formulas function as register markers (see the discussion of "boundary markers" below). Yet, when we identify a formula as a register marker, we often reveal more about our etic perspective than how it functions within a speech community. Before examining functions in more depth, let us briefly discuss conventionalisation.

Linguistic conventionalisation is the normative adoption of a word or phrase by a community of language users. This seems most likely to happen when a word or phrase: 1) is prompted with regularity (Coulmas 1979: 252);[22] 2) expresses something important to the community, within a context that is similarly valorised; 3) is encoded memorably, by incorporating features such as strong imagery,[23] rhythm, alliteration and assonance (Ong 2005: 34); and 4) has specificity, such that it does not compete with other forms.[24] When considering the link between frequency and linguistic conventionalisation, it is important to remember that a lexeme or phrase may be rare across a language, generally, but common in particular domains or, indeed, particular narratives. Additionally, those specific domains or narratives may be highly valorised. Gaelic narrators had such reverence for the Fenian hero tales, for example, that they would remove their bonnets during recitation (MacNeil 1987: xxiii; cf. Campbell 1872: 218).

Once a formulaic expression has been conventionalised in traditional narrative, a number of functions become available to its users. Let us now examine two that have been frequently discussed in the literature: mnemonic and semiotic functions.

Several authors have suggested that one of the primary functions of formulas in narrative, particularly the longer composites, is to rest a narrator's memory (Ó Duilearga 1945: 35; cf. Campbell 1994 [1860]: 34; Bruford 1966: 33). This parallels assertions from Oral-Formulaic Theory (Lord 2000: 43) and linguistics (Kuiper 2000: 280) that formulaic language alleviates the demands of rapid, on-line composition and communication on working memory by automating lexical output into chunks. Ó Duilearga proposes that "they serve as resting-places [...] from which [the narrator] can view swiftly the ground he has to cover" (1945: 35). The argument is that once a long passage has been memorised, a narrator is able to invoke it as a prefabricated block and focus on the upcoming sequence. This seems plausible given the length of some passages (e.g. *PTWH* I, 193 and 200). However, complex tales exist in Gaelic without these long, semi-poetic passages, such as versions of ATU[25] 313, The Girl as Helper in the Hero's Flight, and other elaborate *Märchen*. It is also curious to suppose that narrators would have required such a break; I am not aware of any narrators breaking down mid-course without them. Finally, it is difficult to see how memory would have needed to be conserved in the literate Romantic tales (see Bruford 1966), in which formulas frequently occur. Therefore, conservation of working memory does not seem to be the primary function of formulas, although it may be a concomitant of their use in oral registers. We shall now turn to semiotic functions.

Any linguistic behaviour that co-varies with another behaviour, communicative function, situational context, or any other observable phenomenon, can serve to index it. It follows that the greater its specificity – that is, its absence from general behavioural or situational contexts – the greater its indexical potential. As an example, linguistic forms associated with particular persons or types of people can serve as semiotic markers of them (Agha 2005: 39). When not all members of a community are able to convey a particular register fluently (*ibid.*: 39–40), its unusual forms may be highly indexical of those who are able to do so.

The language of Gaelic traditional storytelling - like traditional and ritualistic registers in other cultures - diverges from common discourse to the extent that many fluent speakers have difficulties understanding it (Shaw 1999: 316–317; cf. Ó Duilearga 1945: 32 and Akinnaso 1985: 340). Much of the difficulty seems to involve the formulas themselves, which are produced rapidly and sometimes incorporate language that is antiquated, obsolete or otherwise opaque.[26] Even storytellers themselves have struggled to explain the meaning behind common formulas (Zall 2013: 132–133).

Ó Duilearga (1945: 35; cf. Jackson 1952: 135; Bruford 1966: 37) says that obscure phrases in formulas were meant "to impress the listener":

> [O]bscurity of language held an attraction for the pedantically minded though unlettered listener. One old story-teller friend of mine, speaking of old men who he had known in his youth, was full of admiration for their 'hard Irish'[27] (*crua-Ghaoluinn*), remarking that "they had such fine hard Irish you would not understand a word from them" (Ó Duilearga 1945: 33).

At least in part, this seems to be an instance of formulas being used by individuals to increase their status in a group (Wray 2002: 96). What is curious is that it conflicts with the prevailing use of formulas for decreasing processing efforts in the listener, through a shared reservoir of expressions (*ibid.*: 97). Perhaps, in this case, the prestige-raising and referential functions (see below) eclipse this tendency, with "hard Gaelic" being emblematic of the richness of oral tradition and its diachronic aspect. Presumably, by keying a prestigious variety of narrative, a narrator could confer a degree of prestige upon himself. Nonetheless, conservative language is commonly found in Gaelic heroic narratives known to have historical literary associations, or in those that emulate these types of tales (Bruford 1966: 182 *et passim*; Zall 2010: 217; cf. Bruford 1979; Lamb 2013: 179). As a parallel, in kalevalaic poetry, the language of mythological epic was more conservative than other poetic genres – even other narrative ones – although they shared the same form (Frog p.c., 16 March 2014). To summarise, certain formulas might have served to increase the prestige of the narrator, but this is a secondary development: they are integral to the register itself.

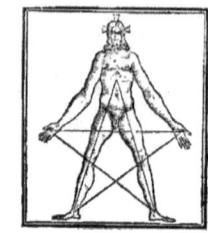

A second semiotic function frequently discussed in the literature is the activation of framed, associative knowledge. Formulas are said to invoke tradition (Hymes 1994: 330–331n), summoning "a larger context via a specialised code" (Foley 2002: 113; cf. 1991: 60). MacInnes (2006: 275) remarks that "even the shortest utterance [can set] off a train of memories". Due to the repetitive and restricted nature of Gaelic traditional narrative, participants have copious opportunities to form associative bonds between formulas and their surrounding contexts. A resonant example of this is the imprisoning formula mentioned already, *chuir e ceangal nan trì chaoil air gu daor agus gu docair* ['he put the tying of the three narrows on him firmly and painfully']. Formulas like this are used intentionally by narrators to invoke sets of associations in their audience (Zeyrek 1993: 165), including similar episodes in other tales. Powerfully, this particular formula also references the binds suffered by Christ. It relates to the Christian symbol of the Five Sacred Wounds (Figure 3), as we see in a prayer known as *Ùrnaigh ri Naomh Colum Cille* ['Prayer to St. Columba']:

Figure 3. The Binding of the Five Narrows and the Sacred Wounds of Christ (from Valeriano Balzani, Hieroglyphica (1556)).

(5) *Tha mi 'coisrigeadh nan trì Chaoil* 'I consecrate the three Narrows
(Caol nan dùirn [recte: *dòrn*], (Narrow of the hands,
Caol na cuim, Narrow of the torso,
agus Caol nan cas) mar chuimhneachan and Narrow of the legs) in memory
air Naomh Colum Cille. of St Columba.
Tha mi 'coisrigeadh nan trì chaoil, I consecrate the three narrows,
's gach nì a th' agam and every thing that I have
an làthair Nh. Choluim Chille, in the presence of St Columba,
's nan Naomh Gàidhealach uile. and every Gaelic Saint.'
    (*Lòchran an Anma*: 10)

This type of associative network – called "traditional resonance" by Foley (2002: 134) and the "tension of essences" by Lord (2000: 97–98) – is known to cognitive scientists as a *schema*.[28] Assuming a Catholic listener enculturated in oral tradition, the phrase *ceangal nan trì chaoil* would have triggered powerful associations beyond hero tales. As Foley argues (2002: 121), in order to understand the referential quality of an expression – which he calls "immanence"[29] – in a traditional register, one must be cognisant of how it operates *across* the tradition, not simply how it functions within a particular textual "cenotaph" (Foley 1992: 290). Given that we cannot now collect Gaelic traditional narrative in a way that was possible even forty years ago, this mandate is of key importance when we interpret the bounded snapshots available to us in archives such as the School of Scottish Studies, and other primary sources.

To summarise this section, formulas are a type of linguistic conventionalisation that propagate through a language community via repetition, valorisation, memorable encoding and specificity. Like formulaic language at large, the formulas of oral tradition may help to conserve working memory for the narrator, but this cannot be their primary function. Similarly, they may increase the perceived status of the speaker, in line with formulas more generally, but this is also a secondary development; they are a constituent part of the register. A formula's referential qualities, augmented through repetition across a range of linguistic and thematic contexts, make it a fecund symbol of the tradition as a whole, and "a commonplace that reverberates with the associative meaning derived *pars pro toto* from other uses in the continuing tradition" (Foley 1988: 111). In all, formulaic phrases in traditional storytelling are a history of past solutions to frequent communicative requirements (Rubin 1995: 209), which gain powerful associations through their employment across the tradition. Having discussed some of the macro-functions of formulaic language in traditional narrative, we shall now examine some of the more specific themes and micro-functions involved.

Micro-Functions of Gaelic Storytelling Formulas

If formulas lexicalise the habitual communicative needs of a register, then it follows that they reflect its basic characteristics and functions. Certainly, many formulas in Gaelic narrative express recurrent motifs,[30] such as those catalogued in *The Types of the Irish Folktale* (Ó Súilleabháin & Christiansen 1963). As will be clear, however, this is not always the case. Lord grouped the formulas that he found according to the elements that recurred most often in Yugoslavian sung epic: actors, actions, and settings (2000: 34; cf. Zeyrek 1993: 163 and Davies 1992: 243–252). This is a neat, three-way division but it does not suffice here. I found that formulas relating to actors were rare, and generally idiosyncratic, when they appeared. It seems imprudent to have an empty category, when only three are available. Although I have maintained "actors" under the broader label "nominal reference", I found a need for five categories altogether, arranged in a slightly different manner (see Table 1).[331]

Table 1. A Brief Taxonomy of Gaelic Storytelling Formulas
- I. BOUNDARY MARKERS
  - a. Openings
  - b. Closings
- II. CHARACTER EXPRESSION & INTERACTION
  - a. Greetings and partings
  - b. Emotive-expressive language
- III. POWER TRANSACTIONS
  - a. Cursing
  - b. Be-spelling
  - c. Battle
- IV. DESCRIPTIONS AND TRANSITIONS
  - a. Temporal transitions
  - b. Geospatial transitions
  - c. Descriptions (e.g. arming)
- V. NOMINAL REFERENCE
  - a. Names
  - b. Epithets

I will take each in turn, providing illustrative examples.

Certain formulas index BOUNDARY MARKERS, rather than motifs. This seems to pertain mainly to the beginnings and ends of tales. As Belcher found for African narratives, beginnings in Gaelic tales are "frequently introduced by formulas that define the subsequent content as something set apart from ordinary discourse, and [...] invite the audience's attention and participation" (2008: 17; cf. Bauman 2004: 4). Almost one half of the tales in the sample begin with a variation on *bha* NP *ann roimhe seo* ['there was before this a NP'] (e.g. *bha bànrigh ann roimhe seo a bha tinn* ['there was before this a queen who was ill']). Most of the rest use a similar phrase: *bha* NP *aon uair* ['there was one time a NP'] (e.g. *bha rìgh air Lochlainn aon uair* ['there was one time a king of [lit. 'on'] Scandinavia']). Still, some tales – in particular the hero tales – begin with richer language:

(6) (a) *Dh'fhalbh an Gruagach bàn, Mac Rìgh Èireann, le mhòr-chuideachd a chumail cùirt agus cuideachd ris fhèin*   'The fair-haired chief, son of the king of Ireland, went with his nobles to keep **court** and **company** with him'

(*PTWH* II, 166)

(b) *An latha an tàinig O Domhnaill a-mach a chumail còir agus ceartais, chunnaic e òglach a' tighinn*   'The day that O' Donnell came out to keep **righteousness** and **justice**, he saw a youth approaching'

(*PTWH* I, 345)

While the first two examples use the matrix verb *bha* ['was'], examples (6a) and (6b) use the more informational *dh'fhalbh* ['went'] and *chunnaic* ['saw']. Additionally, both of the latter examples use a similar non-finite verbal phrase (underlined). Although the two phrases have separate meanings – noted in the gloss – both contain the verb *cumail* ['keep, maintain'], followed by an alliterative, two-noun NP. In light of their similarity, it is worth posing the question: what is the minimum requirement of formulaicity? Can this particular formula be specified simply as a particular head verb followed by two alliterative nouns pertaining to the domain of what a king might 'keep'? This example illustrates one of the difficulties involved in cataloguing individual formulas.

Turning to the endings, many are consistent with Propp's (1968: 63–64) observations about *Märchen* and conclude with a wedding and ascension of the hero. It is common to find composite formulas here, for instance: *rinn iad banais mhòr ghreadhnach a mhair seachd latha 's seachd bliadhna* ['they made a large, magnificent wedding that lasted for seven years and seven days']. Weddings are usually stated as lasting a year and a day (*latha is bliadhna*), but sometimes, even more hyperbolically, seven years and seven days, as above. It is also typical for narrators to say that they were at the wedding themselves, where they had been given useless gifts that later expired (see Bruford 1966, 198; Shaw 2007: 98):

(7) *'s dhealaich mi riutha,* 'and I parted from them,
     's thug iad dhomh ìm air èibhleig, and they gave me butter on a cinder,
     's brochan-càil an crèileig, 's bròga pàipear, kale broth in a creel, and shoes of paper,

     's chuir iad air falbh mi le peileir gunna-mhòir and they sent me away with a bullet from a large gun
     air rathad-mòr gloine gus an on a road of glass until
     d'fhàg iad am shuidhe staigh an seo mi they left me standing here'
     (*PTWH* I, 340)

This trope of "useless gifts" is found across Europe (Bruford 1966: 52) and is attested in the Irish tradition as well (see Ó Ceannabháin 2000: 136). Whether or not the narrator deploys an outlandish *dénouement*, it is common for them to finish with a definitive boundary marker in the first person, such as *agus dhealaich mi riutha* ['and I departed from them'] or *dh'fhàg mise an sin iad* ['I left them there'].[32]

Human or anthropomorphic characters are the central focus of any story. Numerous formulas in the current sample involve CHARACTER EXPRESSION AND INTERACTION, both dialogic and monologic. Many of the greetings, in particular, are formulaic.[33] The hero tales are especially interesting; greetings often take the form of courtly exchanges, contrasting with the mayhem and violence that characterise the genre more generally (cf. Shaw 1999: 309–311). Strangers bless one another with words that are wise, soft, peaceful and so on: e.g. *bheannaich Brian Bòrr e ann am briathran fisniche, foisniche, file, mile, ciùin* ['Brian Boru blessed him in words [that were] wise, peaceful, poetic, sweet, mild'] (*PTWH* I, 545). Partings are similarly polite, if shorter: *dh'fhàg iad beannachd aig a' chèile is dh'fhalbh e* ['they left a blessing at one other and he left'] (*PTWH* I, 102).

EMOTIVE-EXPRESSIVE formulas are also prominent. Expressions of joy and sadness are particularly compelling in that they commonly exploit a systematic opposition in Gaelic between positive 's' words and negative 'd' words (e.g. *soilleir* ['bright, clear] and *doilleir* ['dark, obscure']) and the alliterative possibilities that obtain: *chaidh e dhachaidh <u>dubhach</u>, deurach, dall-bhrònach* ['the man went home mournful, tearful, blind-sad'] (*PTWH* I, 288); *dh'fhalbh an gobhainn gu <u>subhach</u>, sunndach leis a' chrùn* ['the blacksmith departed joyfully, happily with the crown'] (*PTWH* I, 291). Heroes who have returned home to find their loved ones abducted, may take an oath of self-deprivation, such as *chan ith mi greim, 's chan òl mi deoch, 's cha dèan mi stad ach a-nochd, gus an ruig mi far a bheil an duine sin*[34] ['I won't eat a bite, I won't drink a drink, and I won't stop but tonight, until I reach that man'] (*PTWH* I, 511). The "far from friends" formula above is also in this category.

A POWER TRANSACTION involves one character acting upon another for the purpose of gain or control, or as a consequence of a prior action. Power transactions are a central aspect of most folktales, and the tales surveyed show a variety of formulas involving control, threats, curses, subjugation, manipulation and one-upmanship. The "binding of the three narrows" formula, discussed in depth above, is an example of a power transaction. When a hero or heroine manages to escape magical bondage after obtaining inside help, he or she may hear: *mo bheannachd dhutsa 's mollachd do d' oid-ionnsachaidh* ['my blessing for you and a curse for your tutor'] (*PTWH* I, 98). An extremely prevalent blessing-cursing formula, typically occuring as a form of initial complication,[35] involves a mother or grandmother offering either a small or a large piece of cake to each of her progeny in succession[36] before they set off on a journey. The small portion is given with her blessing, while the large is given with her curse: *cò aca as fheàrr leat, a' bhlaigh bheag 's mo bheannachd, no a' bhlaigh mhòr is mo mhollachd?* ['which do you prefer, the small portion with my blessing, or the big portion with my curse?'] (*PTWH* I, 288). In the hero tales, be-spelling formulas are common. In these, one character places an injunction (*geas*, pl *geasan*) upon another, and specifies certain conditions to be fulfilled under mortal threat (see Koch 2006: 796–797 and Ó hÓgáin 2006: 265–266). Be-spelling formulas are typically composite in form, for example:

(8) [*tha*] *mi a' cur mar chroisean, is mar gheasan ort...*
 am beathach maol, carrach
 is mì-threubhaiche is mì-threòraiche na thu fhèin,
 a thoirt do chinn 's do mhuineil 's do choimhead-bheatha
 [recte: *do chaitheamh-bheatha*],
 mar am faigh thu dhomhsa claidheamh solais
 rìgh nan uinneagan daraich
 (*PTWH* I, 99)

'I lay crosses and spells on you...
that the bald, mangy creature –
even less gallant and powerful than yourself –
should take your head, your neck and your livelihood,
unless you get for me the Sword of Light of the King of the Oak Windows'

Such formulas are common in Gaelic oral narrative, and many go back as far as Old Irish, at least (Bruford 1966: 196).

Our penultimate category, DESCRIPTIONS AND TRANSITIONS, subsumes Lord's "settings and non-character actions". These formulas deal with temporal-spatial movement or provide miscellaneous descriptive details. Many composite formulas fall into this category, such as sailing, arming and battle runs (see Bruford 1966: 182–193). Two narrators had a version of the "pounding earth" formula, which we can place in this category: *dhèanadh iad bogan air a' chreagan agus creagan air a' bhogan, 's an t-àite bu lugha rachadh iad fodha gan glùinean, 's an t-àite bu mhotha rachadh iad fodha gan sùilean* ['they would make a bog of the rock and rock of the bog, and the shallowest they'd go down would be their knees and the deepest they'd go down would be their eyes'] (*PTWH* II, 171). We can also include the "superhuman speed" formula, used by three narrators, *bheireadh i air a' ghaoth luath Mhàirt a bhiteadh roimhpa, is cha bheireadh a' ghaoth luath Mhàirt oirre* ['she would catch the quick March wind that would be before her, and the quick March wind would not catch her'] (*PTWH* I, 100). Another common formula, employed when protagonists traverse liminalities between the real and supernatural, is the following, found in the tales of five narrators: e.g. *chunnaic i taigh beag solaisd fada uaithe 's ma b' fhada uaithe cha b' fhada a bha ise ga ruigheachd* ['she saw a wee house of light long away and if it was long away, she wasn't long reaching it'] (*PTWH* I, 144). Also prevelant is a formula expressing a quick transition between day and night: *ma bu mhoch a thàinig an latha bu mhoiche na sin a dhèiridh an gobha* ['if it is early that the day arrived it was earlier than that that the blacksmith rose'] (*PTWH* I, 506). This is, thus, the most variegated category, involving the narrator's attempts to paint vivid, dynamic scenes and transition between them.

Our final category is NOMINAL REFERENCE. Surprisingly, few "naming" formulas appeared consistently across the different narrators. In Gaelic oral tradition, names are notoriously variable (Bruford 1966: 169–170). This seems to be true of character reference in folktales, more generally, as opposed to the functions that they perform (Propp 1968: 20–21). Related to this, and echoing Lord (2000: 34), I found few epithets, and none that repeated across narrators. Some names were recognisable from other sources, such as the standard characters *Mac Rìgh Èireann* ['Son of the King of Ireland'] and *Cailleach nan Cearc* ['Hen-wife'], but most of them were idiosyncratic. Generally, they share the tendency of names, in the wider oral tradition, to be compounds featuring genitives and adjectival strings, often with alliteration. A larger sample would provide a more complete inventory. Until such is collected and analysed, the reader is referred to Bruford (1966: 168–171) for more information.

To summarise this section, the micro-functions of traditional formulas in Gaelic storytelling involve marking the boundaries of the register, character discourse and ideation, power dynamics, descriptions and transitions, and nominal reference. These are the core thematic and "register marking"[37] qualities of Gaelic storytelling observed in this sample. As argued above, in order for a communicative function to become lexicalised in a set or semi-set form, it must have had the opportunity to do so. What remains to be seen is whether these categories endure for a larger sample, and how they correlate with the motifs identified for Gaelic traditional narrative at large.

For example, is there a detectable correlation between a motif's frequency and its conventionalisation as a formula in the tradition? Furthermore, what structural relationships obtain between the formulas? Perhaps their sequential relations to one another will suggest story grammars (cf. Lord 2000: 35–36) that are distinct from those identified by Propp and other structuralists. Finally, what differences can be located between the formulas of different genres of storytelling? Much remains to be done on the subject of formulas and their micro-functions.

Conclusions

This paper was motivated by the need to take stock of a little-surveyed area and prepare the ground for further investigation. Few authors have dealt exclusively with the formulaic language of traditional prose as opposed to poetry, and relatively little has been written on the set language of Gaelic storytelling. From the examples provided, it appears that an identifiable phrasal lexicon can be located for the register of Gaelic traditional narrative, and that it was shared across the *Gàidhealtachd* until relatively recently.[38] This lexicon would have been rare in everyday conversation, but prevalent in storytelling domains. It is a case of niche language being preserved over an extended period.

In line with traditional storytelling formulas, more generally, these phrases carried several important macro-functions in Gaelic society – such as keying the larger cultural framework in which they played a part – although these are subordinate to the primary function of dealing efficiently (and artfully) with a recurrent communicative need. Five micro-functions were identified and there were indications that the formulas of Gaelic hero tales might have been influenced by historical literacy. Finally, a number of suggestions were made for future work.

To return to the theme of this volume, perhaps we ought to view the phenomenon of register variation as a continuum, with formulaic language at one end. Like registers themselves, formulas arise out of the exigencies and regular pathways of communication. Perhaps they are the most extreme, solidified aspects of contextualised language; crystals of speech formed under the pressure of *in-situ*, recurring communicative needs. What is clear is that the study of the formula has much to offer towards our understanding of linguistic variation, and, indeed, language itself.

Acknowledgements

I am indebted to Lillis Ó Laoire, Wilson McLeod and John Shaw for reading a draft of this essay and providing helpful comments and suggestions. Special thanks to Asif Agha for helping me to clarify how semantic constraints operate in templates, and to Frog, for suggesting various enhancements and additional sources. Any remaining deficiencies are my responsibility alone.

Notes

1. Although it was once widely assumed that all utterances generated by humans were theoretically possible, corpus linguistics has revealed this to be a fallacy (Wray 2002: 13).
2. Scottish Gaelic is currently spoken by 58,000 individuals (2011 census), the greatest density of whom live in the archipelago known as the Outer Hebrides. See Lamb (2008) for information on Gaelic sociolinguistics and register variation.
3. Bruford thought that it could take a lifetime (1966: 182; cf. Lord 2000: 50), but a modern corpus approach could expedite it significantly. See Bruford (1966: 182–209) for a useful summary of the formulas common in Gaelic folklore.
4. As a rule, far greater attention has been given to intertextual work in classical and epic verse than prose narrative of any kind (Bauman 1986: 78–79).
5. Much of the world's narrative traditions are prosimetric to some degree (Clover 1986: 27).
6. There are some notable exceptions, e.g. Kellogg & Scholes (1966); Lönnroth (1976) and Silverstein (1984). Most authors, however, have merely remarked that Oral-Formulaic Theory is potentially applicable to non-metrical narrative, without going much further than this (e.g. Hymes 1977: 438). My appreciation to Frog for these observations.
7. As a measure of its influence, it has spawned so many re-interpretations that some are contradictory (Rosenberg 1981: 444). For instance, contrast Gray's (1971: 292) notion of the formula – a verbal construction that repeats within a particular work – with that of O' Nolan (1971: 244), for whom it means repetition *between* works.
8. Lord later said that formulas probably originated in "simple narrative incantations" and that their metrical boundedness was likely to have been a late development (2000: 67).
9. Native conceptualisations of "meaningful units" betray similarly fuzzy boundaries. In Gaelic, the semantics of *facal* ['word'] can extend to structures larger than a single lexeme, as seen in the expression *seanfhacal* [lit. 'old-word'], which means 'proverb' (Ó Laoire 2004: 199). Foley's discussion (2002: 11–20) of the way that Yugoslavian *guslars* conceive of *rěc* ['word'] shows that this is not limited to Gaelic: for them, it can extend to scenes, motifs and entire speech acts. For additional parallels, see also Frog 2014b: 282–283 n.3; Foley, this volume; Stepanova, this volume.
10. An example of the latter is the English formula, "put NP on" (e.g. *he put it on for the crowd*; cf. *he put a show on for the crowd*). Here, *put* and *on* are closed, obligatory elements, but they are intersected by an open noun phrase.
11. Campbell exhorted his collectors to "give me exactly what [the narrators] give you as nearly as you can in your own words" (Thomson 1987: 34–35) and "write it down from dictation" (*ibid.*: 39). In this, he diverged from the practices of earlier collectors, such as the Grimms, who had improved their texts for stylistic ends.
12. Ó Laoire (2005: 43–87) discusses the infelicity of the English word *learnt* in this context. Irish tradition contrasts between the act of *tógail* ['assimilating and absorbing'] and that of *foghlaim* ['formal learning']. From my experience, the same distinction is maintained in Scottish Gaelic.
13. Although I do not know of a native Gaelic term for them, Irish uses *cóiriú catha* [lit. 'battle preparations'] and *cultacha gaisce* [lit. 'martial equipment']. Thanks to Lillis Ó Laoire for this information. (NB: these are not formal categories and seem merely to reference the motifs involved.)
14. However, as oral narrators generally called upon similar language each time the need for a particular run arose (Bruford 1966: 36; Zall 2010: 216), the chunks seem to cohere like atoms in a molecular structure, and are not entirely divisible. Although I am including them here as formulas, additional work is required to ascertain whether the constrains operating upon them in Gaelic are different in nature, degree

or both. For thoughts on the divergence between formulas and "runs" – which some authors term "multiforms" – see Honko (1998: 100–116).
15 *-adh* is the impersonal past suffix. It is often labelled inaccurately as a passive (see Lamb 2008: 242–244).
16 My appreciation to Asif Agha for this observation.
17 This phrase is rendered as the binding of the *five* narrows in Ireland – two wrists, two ankles and the waist.
18 Depending on the dialect and predilection of the narrator, there are a number of words for NEAR in Gaelic: e.g. *teann, goirid, faisg* (the commonest), *fagus* (more literary) and *dlùth*. For FAR, *fada* is the only real candidate.
19 Ong (2005: 35) gives a version of this notion when he says: "Heavy patterning and communal fixed formulas in oral cultures [...] determine the kind of thinking that can be done." This could be stated in a more accurate way, I believe, by replacing the word *oral* with "all", and *determine* with "facilitate".
20 The Gaelic romances were hero tales that circulated in manuscript in medieval and early modern Scotland and Ireland. They were written in a stylised, conservative form of the language known as Classical Gaelic, which served as a kind of high-prestige *lingua franca*, used by the intelligentsia and nobility.
21 Matters are complicated by the fact that it was normal practice at the time for most to consume writing aurally, by hearing it read out aloud from another person (Crosby 1936: 89).
22 As a word's frequency is a good predictor of its morphophonemic stability over time (Pagel et al. 2007; 2013; cf. Bybee 2006: 714–715), it seems reasonable to expect the same for formulas: antiquated morphology is one of their most cited features (Ross 1959: 10; Rutledge 1981 in Ong 2005: 62; Watkins 1992: 405–406; Wray 2002: 261).
23 On the use of verbal and visual memory in Gaelic storytellers, see MacDonald (1981).
24 In Pagel et al. (2013), some infrequent words, such as 'bark' (i.e. the outer layer of trees), were found to have remained stable over protracted periods, as well. Ostensibly, they avoided displacement by filling a semantic niche.
25 This refers to the Aarne-Thompson-Uther (ATU) folktale classification system (Uther 2004).
26 Akinnaso (1985: 340), following McDowell (1983), posits that the main function of obscure or obsolete words appearing in ritual language is to index the particular register in which they occur (cf. Bauman 1984: 21). However, as I discuss above, this is a secondary development: formulas only become capable of marking a register via the semiotics invested in them through use and association.
27 Lillis Ó Laoire suggests to me that *crua* can be interpreted here as vigorous, lively or tough as well. Additionally, he suggests that another function should be mentioned here, "the embodied pleasure of listening". Listeners and reciters alike derived aesthetic pleasure from the formulas as heightened, well-shaped language. See discussion of *cuma* ['appearance, shape'] in Ó Laoire (2005: 91 *et passim*).
28 A schema is an abstract, internalised knowledge structure providing an adaptable and anticipatory framework for organising knowledge (see Casson 1983; Rumelhart 1980: 34; Rubin 1995: 21–24).
29 The notion seems to have originated with Biebuyck and Okpewho (see Clover 1986: 23–24). They wanted to convey the idea that an *immanent* epic might exist for participants in an oral tradition, where different parts of an epic cycle represented a potential whole, although they had never been performed together.
30 A motif is "the smallest element in the tale having a power to persist in tradition" (Thompson 1977: 415).
31 These are the dividing lines indicated to me by the present sample. Further study may necessitate revision.
32 It was also common for storytellers to say at the end of tales, *mas e breug bhuams' e,*

's e breug thugams' e ['if it was a lie from me, it was a lie to me'], indicating a tentative dissociation with the story world. Turkish narrators convey a similar sense with the inferential particle -miş (Zeyrek 1993: 169).

33 There may be a tendency for them to be formulaic across human culture (Coulmas 1979: 245).

34 Illustrating the syntactic flexibility of some formulas, the same narrator fronts the elements of this formula in another tale: *greim chan ith mi, deoch chan òl mi, cadal cha tèid air mo shùil gus an ruig mi far a bheil iad* ['a bite I won't eat, a drink I won't drink, sleep won't come upon my eye until I reach them'] (*PTWH* II, 168). Examples very similar to the non-fronted version turn up elsewhere in the corpus, e.g. *chan ith mi biadh 's chan òl mi deoch, ars' an rìgh, gus am faic mi mo dhà mhac gan losgadh am màireach* ['I won't eat food, and I won't drink a drink, said the king, until I see my two sons burnt tomorrow'] (*PTWH* II, 201).

35 In Propp's terms, this would be an interdiction and interdiction violated sequence (1968: 26–27).

36 Typically, each sets off upon hearing of the elder sibling's demise.

37 As mentioned previously, the only clear cases of register marking amongst the formulas were those signifying beginnings and ends.

38 Many of the same formulas were used in Ireland, and further research could investigate the extent of verbal overlap between the two countries' traditions.

References

Sources

PTWH = Campbell, John Francis 1994 [1860, 1861]. *Popular Tales of the West Highlands* I–II. New edn. Edinburgh: Birlinn.

Lòchran an Anma: Leabhar-ùrnaigh Caitliceach. Catholic Church. Dùneideann: Sands, 1906.

Literature

Agha, Asif 2005. Voice, Footing, Enregisterment. *Journal of Linguistic Anthropology* 15(1): 38–59.

Akinnaso, F. Niyi 1985. On the Similarities between Spoken and Written Language. *Language and Speech* 28: 323–359.

Bauman, Richard 1984. *Verbal Art as Performance*. Prospect Heights: Waveland Press.

Bauman, Richard 1986. *Story, Performance and Event: Contextual Studies of Oral Narrative*. Cambridge Studies in Oral and Literate Culture 10. Cambridge: Cambridge University Press.

Bauman, Richard 2004. *A World of Others' Words: Cross-cultural Perspectives on Intertextuality*. Oxford: Blackwell.

Belcher, Stephen 2008. African Tales. In *The Greenwood Encyclopedia of Folktales and Fairy Tales*. Ed. Donald Haase. London: Greenwood Press. Pp. 12–20.

Bruford, Alan 1966. Gaelic Folk-Tales and Mediæval Romances: A Study of the Early Modern Irish 'Romantic Tales' and Their Oral Derivatives. *Béaloideas* 34: i–285.

Bruford, Alan 1979. Recitation or Re-creation? Examples from South Uist Storytelling. *Scottish Studies* 22: 27–44.

Bybee, Joan 2006. From Usage to Grammar: The Mind's Response to Repetition. *Language* 82(4): 711–733.
Campbell, John Francis 1872. *Leabhar na Feinne – Heroic Gaelic Ballads: Collected in Scotland Chiefly from 1512 to 1871.* London: Spottiswoode.
Casson, Ronald W. 1983. Schemata in Cognitive Anthropology. *Annual Review of Anthropology* 12: 429–462.
Clover, Carol J. 1986. The Long Prose Form. *Arkiv För Nordisk Filologi* 101: 10–39.
Coulmas, Florian 1979. On the Sociolinguistic Relevance of Routine Formulae. *Journal of Pragmatics* 3(3–4): 239–266.
Crosby, Ruth 1936. Oral Delivery in the Middle Ages. *Speculum* 11(1): 88–110.
Davies, Sionad 1992. Storytelling in Medieval Wales. *Oral Tradition* 7: 231–257.
Foley, John Miles 1988. *The Theory of Oral Composition: History and Methodology.* Bloomington: Indiana University Press.
Foley, John Miles 1991. *Immanent Art: From Structure to Meaning in Traditional Oral Epic.* Bloomington: Indiana University Press.
Foley, John Miles 1992. Word-Power, Performance, and Tradition. *Journal of American Folklore* 105(417): 275–301.
Foley, John Miles 2002. *How to Read an Oral Poem.* Urbana: University of Illinois Press.
Frog 2011. *Alvíssmál* and Orality I: Formula, Alliteration and Categories of Mythic Being. *Arkiv för Nordisk Filologi* 126: 17–71.
Frog 2014a. Mythological Names and *dróttkvætt* Formulae I: When is a Valkyrie like a Spear? *Metrica et Poetica* 1(1). Pp. 100–139.
Frog 2014b. Oral Poetry as Language Practice: A Perspective on Old Norse dróttkvætt Composition. In *Song and Emergent Poetics – Laulu ja runo – Песня и видоизменяющаяся поэтика.* Ed. Pekka Huttu-Hilttunen et al. Kuhmo: Juminkeko. Pp. 279–307
Gray, Bennison 1971. Repetition in Oral Literature. *The Journal of American Folklore* 84(333): 289–303.
Honko, Lauri 1998. *Textualising the Siri Epic.* FF Communications 264. Helsinki: Academia Scientiarum Fennica.
Hymes, Dell 1977. Discovering Oral Performance and Measured Verse in American Indian Narrative. *New Literary History*: 431–457.
Hymes, Dell 1994. Ethnopoetics, Oral Formulaic Theory, and Editing Texts. *Oral Tradition* 9(2): 330–370.
Jackson, Kenneth 1952. The Folktale in Gaelic Scotland. *The Proceedings of the Scottish Anthropological and Folklore Society* 4(3):132–139.
Kellogg, Robert, & Robert Scholes 1966. *The Nature of Narrative.* London: Oxford University Press.
Koch, John T. 2006. *Celtic Culture: A Historical Encyclopedia.* Santa Barbara, CA: ABC-CLIO.
Kuiper, Koenraad 2000. On the Linguistic Properties of Formulaic Speech. *Oral Tradition* 15(2): 279–305.
Lamb, William 2008. *Scottish Gaelic Speech and Writing: Register Variation in an Endangered Language.* Belfast: Cló Ollscoil na Banríona.
Lamb, William 2013. Recitation or Re-Creation? – A Reconsideration: Verbal Consistency in the Gaelic Storytelling of Duncan MacDonald. In *'A Guid Hairst': Collecting and Archiving Scottish Tradition.* Ed. Katherine Campbell, William Lamb, Neill Martin & Gary West. Maastricht: Shaker Verlag. Pp. 171–184.
Lönnroth, Lars 1976. *Njáls Saga: A Critical Introduction.* Berkeley: University of California Press.
Lord, Albert Bates 2000 [1960]. *The Singer of Tales.* Ed. with an introduction by Stephen A. Mitchell & Gregory Nagy. London: Harvard University Press.
MacDonald, Donald Archie 1981. Some Aspects of Visual and Verbal Memory in Gaelic Storytelling. *Arv: Scandanavian Yearbook of Folklore* 37: 117–124.

MacInnes, John 2006. The Panegyric Code in Gaelic Poetry and Its Historical Background. In *Dùthchas nan Gàidheal: Selected Essays of John MacInnes*. Ed. Michael Steven Newton. Edinburgh: Birlinn. Pp. 265–319.

MacNeil, Joe Neil 1987. *Sgeul gu Latha/ Tales Until Dawn: The World of a Cape Breton Gaelic Story-Teller*. Kingston: McGill-Queen's University Press.

McDowell, John H. 1983. The Semiotic Constitution of Kamsa Ritual Language. *Language in Society* 12(1): 23–46.

Ó Ceannabháin, Peadar (ed.) 2000. *Éamon a Búrc: Scéalta*. Baile Átha Cliath: An Clóchomhar.

Ó Duilearga, Séamus 1945. The Gaelic Story-Teller: With Some Notes on Gaelic Folk-Tales. *Proceedings of the British Academy* 31: 176–221.

Ó Laoire, Lillis 2004. The Right Words: Conflict and Resolution in an Oral Gaelic Song Text. *Oral Tradition* 19(2): 187–213.

Ó Laoire, Lillis 2005. *On a Rock in the Middle of the Ocean: Songs and Singers in Tory Island, Ireland*. Oxford: The Scarecrow Press, Inc.

Ó hÓgáin, Dáithí 2006. *The Lore of Ireland: An Encyclopaedia of Myth, Legend and Romance*. Woodbridge: The Boydell Press.

Ó Súilleabháin, Seán, & Reidar Thoralf Christiansen 1963. *The Types of the Irish Folktale*. FF Communications 188. Helsinki: Suomalainen Tiedeakatemia.

O' Nolan, Kevin 1971. The Use of Formula in Storytelling. *Béaloideas* 39/41: 233–250.

Ong, Walter J. 2005 [1982]. *Orality and Literacy: The Technologizing of the Word*. London: Routledge.

Pagel, Mark, Quentin D. Atkinson, Andreea S. Calude, & Andrew Meade 2013. Ultraconserved Words Point to Deep Language Ancestry across Eurasia. *Proceedings of the National Academy of Sciences of the United States of America* 110(21): 8471–8476.

Pagel, Mark, Quentin D. Atkinson & Andrew Meade 2007. Frequency of Word-Use Predicts Rates of Lexical Evolution throughout Indo-European History. *Nature* 449(7163): 717–720.

Parry, Milman 1930. Studies in the Epic Technique of Oral Verse-Making. *Harvard Studies in Classical Philology* 41: 73–147.

Propp, Vladímir. I. A. 1968. *Morphology of the Folktale*. Trans. Louis A. Wagner. American Folklore Society Bibliographical and Special Series. Austin: University of Texas Press.

Rosenberg, Bruce A. 1981. Oral Literature in the Middle Ages. In *Oral Traditional Literature: A Festschrift for Albert Bates Lord*. Ed. John Miles Foley. Columbus: Slavica Publishers. Pp. 440–450.

Ross, James 1959. Formulaic Composition in Gaelic Oral Literature. *Modern Philology* 57(1): 1–12.

Rubin, David C. 1995. *Memory in Oral Traditions: The Cognitive Psychology of Epic, Ballads, and Counting-Out Rhymes*. Oxford: Oxford University Press.

Rumelhart, David E. 1980. Schemata: The Building Blocks of Cognition. In *Theoretical Issues in Reading Comprehension*. Ed. Rand J. Spiro, Bertram C. Bruce & William F. Brewer. Hillsdale: Lawrence Erlbaum Associates. Pp. 33–58

Shaw, John 1999. The Ethnography of Speaking and Verbal Taxonomies: Some Applications to Gaelic. In *Celtic Connections: Proceedings of the 10th International Congress of Celtic Studies*. Ed. Ronald Black, William Gillies, Robert Mullally. Edinburgh: Tuckwell Press. Pp. 309–323.

Shaw, John William (ed.) 2007. *The Blue Mountains and Other Gaelic Stories from Cape Breton – Na Beanntaichean Gorma agus Sgeulachdan Eile à Ceap Breatainn*. Montréal & London: McGill-Queen's University Press.

Silverstein, Michael 1984. On the Pragmatic 'Poetry' of Prose: Parallelism, Repetition, and Cohesive Structure in the Time Course of Dyadic Conversation. In *Meaning,*

Form and Use in Context: Linguistic Applications. Ed. Deborah Schiffrin. Washington, D.C.: Georgetown University Press. Pp. 181–199.

Ternes, Elmar. 1982. The Grammatical Structure of the Celtic Languages. In *The Celtic Consciousness*. Ed. Robert O'Driscoll. Edinburgh: Canongate Publishing. Pp. 69–78.

Thompson, Frank G. 1987. John Francis Campbell. *Transactions of the Gaelic Society of Inverness* 54: 1–57.

Thompson, Stith 1977 [1946]. *The Folktale*. Berkeley: University of California Press.

Uther, Hans-Jörg 2004. *The Types of International Folktales: Animal Tales, Tales of Magic, Religious Tales, and Realistic Tales, With an Introduction*. Helsinki: Suomalainen Tiedeakatemia, Academia Scientiarum Fennica.

Watkins, Calvert 1992. The Comparison of Formulaic Sequences. In *Reconstructing Languages and Cultures*. Ed. Edgar Polomé. Berlin: Mouton. Pp. 391–418.

Wray, Alison 2002. *Formulaic Language and the Lexicon*. Cambridge: Cambridge University Press.

Wray, Alison 2008. *Formulaic Language: Pushing the Boundaries*. Oxford: Oxford University Press.

Wray, Alison 2013. Formulaic Language. *Language Teaching* 46(3): 316–334.

Zall, Carol S. 2010. Variation in Gaelic Storytelling. *Scottish Studies* 35: 210–244.

Zall, Carol S. 2013. Learning and Remembering Gaelic Stories. *Scottish Studies* 36: 125–139.

Zeyrek, Deniz 1993. Runs in Folktales and the Dynamics of Turkish Runs: A Case Study. *Asian Folklore Studies* 52(1): 161–175.

Margaret Bender

12. Shifting Linguistic Registers and the Nature of the Sacred in Cherokee

As we have learned from recent linguistic anthropology (see e.g. Agha 2000; 2005; 2011; Danielson 2006; Haugen & Philips 2010; Irvine 2011; Tetreault 2009), registers are meaningfully clustered indexicals that entail and presuppose social environments, roles, identities, and values. Speakers mobilize registers with many effects – entailing social environments, for example, imbuing physical environments with meaning, or projecting a specific self and its history. Register is therefore a key frame through which to explore how changing features of Cherokee religious language index changing theological and socio-spiritual alignments in the last two centuries. In particular, the dynamism and *portability* of register (see Mendoza-Denton 2011 on semiotic hitchhiking) make it a highly appropriate concept with which to think about the social meanings of patterned language use in a context of great historical and cultural volatility such as that of the 19th century Cherokee Nation.

In this chapter, I focus on exploring the evidence for changes in register associated with the language of spiritual contact and supplication in three sets of Cherokee language texts: (1) *The Swimmer Manuscript*, a set of nineteenth-century non-Christian medicinal texts from the Cherokee homeland in what is now North Carolina (Mooney & Olbrechts 1932); (2) a twentieth-century post-removal set of medicinal texts, held by a medicine man named Ade:lagti:ya who was also a Christian minister, published as *Notebook of a Cherokee Shaman* (Kilatrick & Kilpatrick 1970); and (3), The Book of John from The Cherokee New Testament. The first two are collections of medicinal texts (often described as notebooks containing "formulas"). These notebooks were the individual property of medicine men who used the texts they contained in healing ceremonies that included herbal treatment, physical manipulation, and bodily positioning of the patient/supplicant. The conditions treated would have included not only medical conditions as understood by western medicine (e.g. fever) but also spiritual conditions such as having dreamed of ghosts. This entire range of conditions was (and in many cases still is) understood as spiritual by Cherokee medicinal practitioners. The Book of John was translated into Cherokee and printed in the Cherokee syllabary in 1838 by Samuel Worcester, a white missionary, and Elias Boudinot, a Christian

Cherokee, and the full New Testament was published by the American Bible Society in 1860. Since that time the New Testament, and particularly the Book of John, has arguably served as the central text in Christian Cherokee life, culture and literacy. Cherokee Christians have used the Book of John for religious instruction individually and in groups, as a model for prayer and as a source of prayer texts.

As I indicated above, these three sets of texts were produced in a time of nearly comprehensive social upheaval for the Cherokees. The forced removal to Indian Territory resulting in the death of 25–30% of the Cherokee population took place in 1838. Missionization proceeded throughout the 19th and into the 20th centuries until nearly all Cherokees had converted to either the Baptist or Methodist faiths. And the U.S. Civilization Program encouraged and enforced changes in economy (toward private property and enterprise, away from collectivism), agriculture (away from traditional horticultural practices), and gender (away from matrilineal structure and female control of land and crops and toward patriarchy, patrilineal descent and neolocality).

It is reasonably safe to assume that the Swimmer Manuscript contains oral poetic forms that predate the invention of the Cherokee syllabary in the 1820s (Fogelson 1975). Therefore, in addition to representing language used in the Cherokees' pre-removal homeland, we can consider it to represent the oldest language of the three. Ade:lagti:ya's notebook at least partly represents language used in the post-removal context (as evidenced by social references) and the 20th century (as evidenced by references to World War I). The Book of John was translated into Cherokee from the King James English language version in the mid-19th century. It therefore falls between the two medical conditions in historical time, but of course represents a more recently introduced spiritual tradition. The triangulated comparison of the three collections allows us to explore the intersecting shifts in register that accompany Cherokee movement across the American landscape, from the 19th to the 20th centuries, and toward increasing dialogism between Cherokee medical-spiritual beliefs and practices and those of Christianity.

There are significant linguistic shifts between the two sets of texts. The later texts reveal a loosening of the indexicality that, in the earlier texts, aligns the patient's body with a specific, ordered cosmology manifest in the Southern Appalachian Cherokee homeland, a movement toward greater symbolic abstraction in healing language and an increasing sense that the forces of illness and health are not under the medicine man's immediate proximal control. However, the voice of the medicine man shifts over time and space away from, rather than toward, a relatively unitary, autonomous, declarative voice (which is also a performative voice), and toward a more relational one that presupposes the presence of relevant external agents.

I argue that these changes are textual manifestations of the enormous disruptions and trauma brought on by the removal from a homeland with deep cosmological importance. The evidence of this trauma in these texts comes not from fragmentation, loss of complexity, loss of verbal art, and so forth, but from the indexical and vocal shifts just described. But these texts do not merely reflect a changed social and historical reality. They also show us the enormously creative power of language which here resituates, reorients, and re-centers those who use it.

That is, these healing texts do not merely *depend on* the social, physical, and spiritual worlds in which they are created and performed to complete their meaning, but in turn imbue these social, physical and spiritual worlds with meaning. These actions together could be said to comprise the *indexical force* of the medicinal texts. The performance of these texts makes and remakes meaningful context out of potentially meaningless surroundings, and reflects a centralized location of the patient within this meaningful context. Although the medicinal texts from East and West share the ultimate objective of restoring the health and balance of the patient via the indexical assertion of his or her centrality, the nature of this center and the periphery it presupposes differ dramatically between the two collections. The older, pre-removal texts presuppose a horizontal center with the simultaneous geographical Cherokee homeland and cosmological Cherokee world as the periphery. The later medicinal texts index more of a vertical center in more spatially indeterminate and hence portable healing contexts. Furthermore, the nature of this indexical force is closely related to the voice of the medicine man, which must align through its own force and footing (following Goffman 1981; see also Levinson 1988) the medicine man's actions and words, the relevant contextual forces and entities, and the health and life course of the patient. With the Cherokee New Testament represented here by the Book of John, we enter new worlds of indexicality and voice, wherein the text is more linked to social than to geographic environments.

Levels of Register in the Three Sets of Texts

It should not be surprising that there are several layers of register operating here, only some of which can be addressed in this chapter and the separation of which is something of an artificial process. There are, for example, elements of register that pertain to the linguistic content of the texts: degree of archaic or otherwise specialized language, relative presence of euphemism or avoidance of direct reference, the presence and nature of repetition, deletion and insertion of segments and syllables and dialect as it affects these phenomena, the relative presence of grammatical voices and modes, motion- and position-related morphemes, and the nature of pronominal prefixing. (For a more detailed discussion of shifts in deictic morphemes and pronominal prefixing in Cherokee medicinal texts, see Bender 2013.) Then there are features specific to the *written* registers that emerge here, such as the use of handwriting vs. print, and style of each, writing implement and color, pages, binding, etc. There are the features of register that arise in the ritual performance or other reading of the texts such as the nature of performance co-requisites, understood animators or controllers of text, and communicative channels. This third set of features points to the fact that linguistic registers are generally linked to registers of conduct guiding or accompanying their use. In this case specifically, the use of sacred texts is concomitant with the performance of specific interactional routines which have their own register features. And finally, there are features pertaining to the distribution, circulation, and other semiotic uses of these texts such as the texts' understood uniqueness, ownership, and range of permissible use. These four layers of register move us from linguistic register as traditionally understood to something akin to commodity register as defined and illustrated by Agha (2011). The following four tables provide detail about the register variation across the three sets of texts in each of the four categories just discussed.

Table 1. Lexicogrammatical form and content

Linguistic Feature	Swimmer Manuscript	Ade:lagti:ya's Notebook	Cherokee New Testament
archaic or specialized vocabulary	frequent	less	no
Western (Oklahoma) dialect	yes	yes	yes
eupheism, reference avoidance	yes	yes	parables, polynyms
repetition	yes, emphasis on 4*	shift from 4 to 7**	unstructured?
epenthesis or deletion of segments or syllables	yes	less	no
declarative-performative voice	widespread	shift to imperative	shift to imperative
use of reportive mode for spirit-actors	widespread	less	used only to narrate actions of God by narrators other than Jesus or in negatives
locative (horizontal) morphemes	abundant	shift to lexemes focused on verticality	emphasis on lexemes related to verticality
Cherokee mythological-cosmological references	ubiquitous	fewer	absent
creator' stem -nehlanv:hi with subject-object pronouns	wide range	creator stem combined with two prefix options	creator stem combined with prefix u- to become proper name God
local toponymic references	frequent	replaced by Cherokee social references	both absent
references to medicinal plants	local pharmacopeia frequent, tobacco occasional	frequent references to tobacco	neither

* The number four is considered to be sacred in Cherokee cosmology. It is associated with the four cardinal directions and related qualities, colors, and cosmological lands inhabited by sacred beings. In Swimmer's medicinal texts, lines, groups of lines, or directed actions are often repeated (sometimes in modified form) four times.

** In the texts of Ade:lagti:ya, the number seven eclipses the number four as the central number structuring repetitions. Like four, seven is considered to be a sacred number in Cherokee cosmology, but whereas four represents the cosmological world in two dimensions, with two axes (north-south and east-west), the ordering number seven represents the cosmological world in three dimensions with three axes: north-south, east-west, zenith-center-nadir. Seven is also the number of Cherokee clans, reflecting the social as well as the cosmological order

Table 2. Production of text-artifacts

Literacy Feature	Swimmer	Ade:lagti:ya	Cherokee New Testament
how produced	written by hand	hand	printed
style	difficult, illegible handwriting	same, though neat and beautiful	standard printing with emphasis on clarity
materials	variety of colors and writing implements	same, though core of notebook is uniform	uniform black

Table 3. Manner of performance

Performance Feature	Swimmer	Ade:lagti:ya	New Testament
Contextual co-requisites	texts must be contextualized with locations and medical treatments	some texts have medical performance co-requisites but not location co-requisites	salvation experience likely co-requisite; populist Christian language ideology indicates no location co-requisites
Animator/controller	medicine man (third party) controls language	same	text initially controlled by preacher or Sunday school teacher; convert-supplicant comes to participate
Communicative channel	singing, speaking, whispering, thinking	speaking	preacher or Sunday school teacher reads aloud; convert reads silently, then in class, then in worship

Table 4. Circulation and distribution

Distributive or Circulatory Feature	Swimmer	Ade:lagti:ya	New Testament
uniqueness	though drawn on oral tradition, each text and collection unique	same	identical text
ownership	single owner, inheritance	same	widely distributed
use	highly limited and context-specific	same	frequent, widespread

Three Text Samples

Specific illustrations will allow us to appreciate some of these register variations as they come to life in particular texts. The following three text samples (one from each collection) have been chosen to give a sense of each genre and its associated linguistic register features. Key register features are in bold if they are specific elements of the ritual register and underlined if they occur in ordinary speech as well. The underlined and bolded items are then identified following the translation of each line. Free translations are those of the editors; in a few important cases, I have given morpheme-by-morpheme analysis.

Text Sample 1. Adapted from Mooney and Olbrechts 1932, Formula 20, pp. 196–197.

Title. *Hi?a ina:dv tanski:tskv nvwo:ti tihuti: igawe:sti*
'This is the medicine to give them to drink when they dream of snakes'
(mythological reference)

Line 1. ***Ske?** ha nogwo statvga:nika stiskaya disti:ga stita:wehi usv:hi distahlto-histi* (di-(distantive)/-st-(2D pronoun)/-ahltohis-(STAY)/-di (infinitive))
'**Ske**! Now you two little men staying far away in the Night Land have come to listen'
(formulaic interjection, mythological references, declarative-performative voice, distantive prefix/horizontal deictic))

Line 2. *Statsanvgigwv higese*
'Just for you two to adorn yourselves, that is what it is (reportive)'
(mythological reference, reportive mode)

Line 3. *U:hlske:dv hidunu:yhtanile:ʔi inatvgwv hige:seʔi*
'It is (reportive) just this snake that has put the important thing under him'
(reportive mode, circumlocution, mythological reference)

Line 4. *Aniski:nv u:nadvnvʔi hige:seʔi*
'Ghosts have said it (reportive)'
(cosmological reference, reportive mode)

Line 5. **skeʔ** *ha nogwo statvga:nika stiskaya disti:ga stita:wehi usv:hi distatltohisti*
(di-(distantive)/st-(2D pronoun)/-ahltohis-(STAY)/-di (infinitive))
'**Ske!** Now you two little men staying far away in the Night Land have come to listen'
(formulaic interjection, mythological references, declarative-performative voice, distantive prefix/horizontal deictic)

Line 6. *I:ga aye:hli u:lsgedv du:niksohvʔteʔi*
'In the middle of the day they have let the important thing down'
(circumlocution, reportive mode)

Line 7. *Stihyvstani:ga*
'You two have come to take it (the solid thing) away'
(circumlocution)

Line 8. *Stutsanvgigwv hige:seʔi*
'Just for your adornment it is (reportive)'
(mythological reference, reportive mode)

Line 9. *Uhsvhi ganeʔsa digvhnage da:ditohistv wvʔstiskwanigo:tani:ga* (wi-(translocative)/sdi-(2D pronoun)/-sgwanigotan- (PUT AWAY)/-i:ga (declarative-performative))
'You two have just come, as you pass by, to put it away over there in the black boxes kept in the Nightland'
(mythological references, declarative-performative voice, horizontal deictic morphemes)

Line 10. *Igv:wahlsto:tigwv*
'How little it is worth!'
(formulaic insult)

Text Sample 2. Adapted from Kilpatrick and Kilpatrick 1970 (Ade:lagti:ya), Formula 22 "To Help Oneself With", p. 107.

Line 1. **Kaʔ sge:ʔ** *tsu:sgvdv:ni:sdi gigage:ʔi galv:laʔdi tsa:hl(i)to:hi:sdi*
'**Now, listen**, Red Garter Snake, above in your resting place'
(formulaic interjections, mythological reference, lexicalized vertical deictic)

Line 2. *Hida:we:hiyu itsu:la igv:kti digoho:sda:ya,*
'You great [wizard], both sides of you are equally sharp'
(reference to Cherokee medical-spiritual expert)

Line 3. *Gohu:sdi ditsadawo:hiladi:sdi nige:sv:na*
'Nothing is to climb over you'

Line 4.   *U:sinu:liyu haʔtv:ga:ni:ga*
          'You have just come to hear very quickly'
          (declarative-performative voice)

Line 5.   *Hna:gwo: nv:no:hi tikso:ʔtani:ga*
          'Now you have just brought down the pathway'
          (declarative-performative voice)

Line 6.   *haʔ e:lo:hi haʔ na e:hi haʔ yv:wi tsvde:halu:*
          '**Ha!** Those who live – **ha!** – on earth – **ha!** – you block them.'
          (formulaic interjections, vertical spatial reference 'on earth')

Line 7.   *Diga:nsdaʔhlaʔni tsunda:ntoʔ diga:hilo:hiʔse:hi*
          'You bypasser of their souls in the Clan Districts'
          (Cherokee social reference)

Line 8.   *Tso:lv tsuksv:sdi hna:gwo: inisalada:ni:ga*
          'You and I have just come to hold up the tobacco smoke'
          (reference to medicinal tobacco, declarative-performative voice)

Line 9.   *Haʔ ge:dehalu:*
          '**Ha!** You block them over there.'
          (formulaic interjection)

Line 10. *Unihne:ʔsdi nige:sv:na*
          'They are not able to speak.'

Line 11. *Getsanuyv:seʔdi nige:sv:na*
          'They are not able to pass under you.'

Line 12. *Galv:laʔdi une:ga aʔdhohi:sdide:ga gvwatv:hwidv hatsv:siye:sge:sdi*
          'You will be walking around everywhere white has been reposed above'
          (lexical deictic, vertical)

Line 13. *Agayv:li tsuksv:sdi usaʔlaʔdv:ʔ gini:saʔla:de:sdi*
          'In the place where the old one holds up the smoke, you and I will hold it up'
          (double-voiced (Christian and traditional) reference to Cherokee spiritual being, reference to medicinal tobacco)

Text Sample 3. From John 1 and John 17.

Title: *Osdv kanohedv, Tsa:ni uwowelanv:hi, Ayadolvʔi I*
          'The Gospel of John, Chapter 1'

Line 1.   *Didalenisgv kanohedv ehe:ʔi*
          'In the beginning was the Word'
          (reportive mode)

Line 2.   *Ale nasgi kanohedv unehlanv:hi itsulaha aneheʔi*
          'And the Word was with God'
          (verb stem *–nehlanv:hi* combined with 3S prefix to create unambiguous proper name 'God', reportive mode)

Chapter 17

Line 3. *Nasgi hi?a nuwesv:gi Tsisa*
'These words spake Jesus'
(assertive mode)

Line 4. *Ale dusaladanv:gi digadoli galv:la?di widukahnanv:gi*
'and lifted up his eyes to Heaven'
(use of lexical vertical deictic as proper name 'Heaven', assertive mode)

Line 5. *hi?a nuwe:sv:gi*
'and said'
(assertive mode)

Line 6. *Edo:da, hnagwo uskwalvhv*
'Father, the hour has come'

Line 7. *Hilvgwoda tsetsi*
'Glorify (imperative) your son'
(imperative mode)

Although none of these sample texts captures the full range of linguistic register features associated with each collection, they do illustrate some of the key shifts and developments indicated in the summary tables. I will especially focus on linguistic features (Table 1) and performance features (Table 3), the latter of which can to some extent be extricated from the text itself. (For a foundational work on such relationships, see Silverstein 1993.) First, an interesting trend is exemplified here with regard to the reportive and assertive modes in the Cherokee past tense. The Cherokee past involves alternation between two possible verb suffixes: one of which indicates that the speaker does not have direct personal knowledge of the event described by the verb (the reportive, usually manifest as *-e?i* or *-ehi*) and one of which indicates that he or she does have such knowledge (the assertive, usually manifest as *-vgi* or *-vhi*). Swimmer's texts use the reportive several times (lines 2, 4, 5, 7, and 9) to describe events that, in the text, are projected to be taking place in the Cherokee cosmological surround, with which the medicine man is not in immediate contact. The action of ritually performing the texts is intended to calibrate the patient's physical surroundings in the Cherokee homeland with the cosmological world in such a way that the patient emerges from the treatment fully at the center of both worlds. Ade:lagti:ya's texts, on the other hand, were read and performed in the post-removal world where that calibration was no longer possible. This particular text contains no uses of the reportive past, drawing heavily instead on the immediate past declarative-performative suffix *-i:ga*. From the older medicinal texts to the newer, then, we see a shift from the narration of unseen but projected past cosmological events to a performative summoning of immediate spiritual events. In The Book of John, both the reportive and the assertive modes are used. The reportive is used to narrate the actions of God at the beginning of time (actions of which the text's posited author, John, has no direct experience) as in lines 1 and 2. The assertive is used to narrate the actions of Jesus (actions to which the Gospel is specifically intended to testify) as in lines 3–5. In the shift from medicinal text to Christian text, we note the use of the assertive and the reportive to fix the relative timeline of sacred events and to assert textual authority.

Second, the three samples demonstrate a shift in the cultural specificity and cultural nature of their worlds of reference. Swimmer's text brings to life a specific set of spiritual forces and events, relying on the help of the Two Little Men (creator figures associated with thunder and the west) and even making specific mention of their jewelry of snake bracelets. Ade:lagti:ya's text, by comparison, is more rooted in contemporaneous Cherokee social organization (the Clan districts, medicine men) and medicinal practice (e.g. the use of tobacco). The Book of John, of course, does not contain spiritual, social nor medicinal references that are specifically Cherokee. The point here is not that The New Testament could have been translated in such a way as to give it more cultural specificity, though that may be true, but rather just that as Cherokees began using Christian texts for healing and prayer, they were for the first time using sacred texts that required contextualization neither from the Cherokee homeland, nor from Cherokee cosmology, nor even from the Cherokee social world.

Third and finally, these three texts demonstrate a movement away from frequent and productive use of Cherokee's extremely rich system of horizontal deictic morphemes and toward a greater reliance on lexicalized expressions of verticality. In Swimmer's texts, we see four uses of Cherokee's horizontal deictic morphemes. The word *distatltohisti* ['you two are staying over there'] in which the distantive prefix *di-* indicates distance from the speaker, appears in lines 1 and 6. In line 10, the word *da:ditohistv* ['they are kept over there'] contains the translocative prefix *d-*, indicating that the items being kept are facing the speaker. Finally, the word *wvʔstiskwanigo:tani:ga* ['you two have just come by to put away'] contains the cislocative prefix *w-*, indicating that the action is moving away from the speaker. In Ade:lagti:ya's text, there is a shift in emphasis toward the lexicalization and verticalization of spatial relations – e.g. note the use of *e:lo:hi* ['earth'] (line 6) and *galv:laʔdi* ['above'] (line 1 and 12). In The Book of John, *galv:laʔdi* has become the translation of the proper place name, Heaven. The more vertical cosmic order indexed by Ade:lagti:ya's text may represent a shift toward compatibility with Christianity (remember that the text's possessor was both Christian and a traditional medicine man), but verticality is also a less problematic spiritual trope in the post-removal era than the horizontality that so powerfully allows Swimmer's texts to calibrate cosmic time and space with the immediate lived experience of the patient.

In the distinct deictic projections of these sacred texts (seen in the linguistic register as outlined in Table 1) we also see a model for the performative context and the related behavioral register (connected to the performance features in Table 3). Swimmer and Ade:lagti:ya would both have been performing these texts in the company of their patient-clients, but Swimmer's use of horizontal deictics to position the agents of disease and cure away from and facing toward the patient would have clearly reinforced the patient's position at the horizontal geo-cosmological center with the Cherokee geo-cosmological world extending out to the periphery. In many cases, this centering would have been reinforced by having the patient sequentially face the cardinal directions. The use of Ade:lagti:ya's texts and the *Cherokee New Testament* became performatively less context-dependent, being used in the post-removal Cherokee Nation and then globally (context-independently) respectively.

Taken together, the text collections as a whole and what we know about their use from the ethnohistorical record (as summarized in Tables 1 through 4) offer evidence of movement: toward the indexing of greater abstraction of (that is, decontextualization of) sacred forces, toward a higher degree of dialogism between human speaker and spiritual beings, toward a more clearly single-referent creator, toward a greater value placed on evidence and assertion, toward a greater uniformity of text, away from private distribution (or non-distribution, i.e. unique ownership) to an ideal of universal public dissemination, from a private triadic communicative encounter to highly public exchanges coupled with private dyadic ones. Though each of these shifts merits a full discussion in its own right, I have emphasized here the general trend in the linguistic features toward the decontextualizable – hence, toward the portable and universal.

A Reassertion of Limited Distribution via Literacy

Literacy in all its forms clearly participated in this shift toward textual portability. But when literacy technologies were taken up by Cherokee speakers in the production, consumption and circulation of sacred texts, there were some unexpected results. One goal of the Cherokee translation of the New Testament was to popularize access to Christian religion and its sacred scripture, and to indicate the generality of access to the spiritual world (and salvation in Christian terms). In the end, however, one of the cultural responses to this new technology was that literacy *itself* became a sacred register in order to preserve the status quo – that is, the Cherokee religious social order developed over generations in which spiritual access was a specialty requiring participation by a third party. Though Cherokee literacy was reportedly very widespread in the generation or two after the invention of the Cherokee syllabary, literacy gradually assumed the pattern of a carefully distributed resource and marker of spiritual maturity. That pattern of specialization has remained, in some segments of the Cherokee communicative community at least, until the latest generation ushered in a linguistic revitalization with a goal of widespread literacy.

References

Sources

The Cherokee New Testament. New York: American Bible Society, 1860.

Literature

Agha, Asif 2000. Register. *Journal of Linguistic Anthropology* 9(1–2): 216–219.
Agha, Asif 2005. Voice, Footing, Enregisterment. *Journal of Linguistic Anthropology* 15(1): 38–59.
Agha, Asif 2011. Commodity Registers. *Journal of Linguistic Anthropology* 21(1): 22–53.
Bender, Margaret 2013. Language Loss and Resilience in Cherokee Medicinal Texts. In *Trauma and Resilience in Southern History*. Ed. Ulrike Wiethaus & Anthony Parent. New York: Peter Lang. Pp. 91–107.
Fogelson, Raymond D. 1975. An Analysis of Cherokee Sorcery and Witchcraft. In *Four Centuries of Southern Indians*. Ed. Charles M. Hudson. Athens: University of Georgia Press. Pp. 113–131.
Goffman, Erving 1981. *Forms of Talk*. Philadelphia: University of Pennsylvania Press.
Haugen, Jason D., & Susan U. Philips. 2010. Tongan Chiefly Language: The Formation of an Honorific Speech Register. *Language in Society* 39: 589–616.
Irvine, Judith T. 2011. Leaky Registers and Eight-Hundred-Pound Gorillas. *Anthropological Quarterly* 84(1): 15–40.
Johnstone, Barbara, Jennifer Andrus & Andrew E. Danielson 2006. Mobility, Indexicality and the Enregisterment of "Pittsburghese". *Journal of English Linguistics* 34(2): 77–104.
Kilpatrick, Jack Frederick, & Anna Gritts Kilpatrick 1970. *Notebook of a Cherokee Shaman*. Washington, D.C.: Smithsonian Institution Press.
Levinson, Stephen C. 1988. Putting Linguistics on a Proper Footing: Explorations in Goffman's Concecepts of Participation. In *Erving Goffman: Exploring the Interaction Order*. Ed. P. Drew & A. Wooton. Boston: Northeastern University Press. Pp. 161–227.
Mendoza-Denton, Norma 2011. The Semiotic Hitchhiker's Guide to Creasky Voice: Circulation and Gendered Hardcore in a Chicana/o Gang Persona. *Journal of Linguistic Anthropology* 21(2): 261–280.
Mooney, James, & Frans M. Olbrechts (eds.) 1932. *The Swimmer Manuscript: Cherokee Sacred Formulas and Medicinal Prescriptions*. Washington, D.C.: Smithsonian Institution.
Silverstein, Michael 1993. Metapragmatic Discourse and Metapragmatic Function. In *Reflexive Language: Reported Speech and Metapragmatics*. Ed. John A. Lucy. Cambridge: Cambridge University Press. Pp. 33–58.
Tetreault, Chantal 2009. Cité Teens Entextualizing French TV Host Register: Crossing, Voicing, and Participation Frameworks. *Language in Society* 38: 201–231.

Eila Stepanova

13. The Register of Karelian Lamenters

This paper examines the lament genre of Karelian oral poetry and the speech registers distinctive to Karelian lamenters. Karelia is a territory situated on both sides of the Finnish–Russian border, extending from the Gulf of Finland to the White Sea. This large area is now populated by multiple ethnic groups, including Finns, Russians, Ukranians and Karelians. Until around the 1930s, the majority population was Karelian, with their own distinctive language, culture and ethnic identity. Today, however, Karelians have been largely assimilated to Russian or Finnish cultures. They are now a minority in the Republic of Karelia of the Russian Federation as well as in Finland. The Karelians are a Finnic linguistic-cultural group closely related to Finns, Ižorians and Vepsians, and more distantly to Estonians, Votes and Setos. Karelian laments belong to the broader Finnic lament tradition preserved primarily among Orthodox populations in the Russian Federation and in Estonia (see Map 1).

The Finnic lament tradition includes Karelian, Ižorian, Votic, Vepsian and Seto laments, which all share certain pan-regional features of verbal and non-verbal expression (or, organizational restrictions of speech and other behaviours common to lament performances across the region), while exhibiting variation in other features that indexically differentiate the context, setting or locale of each individual performance. It is important to point out that Finnic linguistic-cultural groups were not isolated, but rather have a long history of contact with each other as well as with Russians, Balts and Sámi peoples. These inter-group encounters have played an important role in shaping the oral traditions of this large, multi-cultural area, and not least in shaping traditional lament poetry. (See Stepanova E. 2011.)

Laments can be defined as sung poetry of varying degrees of improvisation, which nonetheless follows conventionalized rules of traditional verbal and non-verbal expression, most often performed by women in ritual contexts and potentially also on non-ritual grievous occasions. Karelian laments are here approached as women's sung improvised poetry with its own conventional organizational restrictions. Karelian laments were not learned by heart, but rather were created anew in each concrete situation: there are no fixed texts of laments, and different lamenters will give different performances in

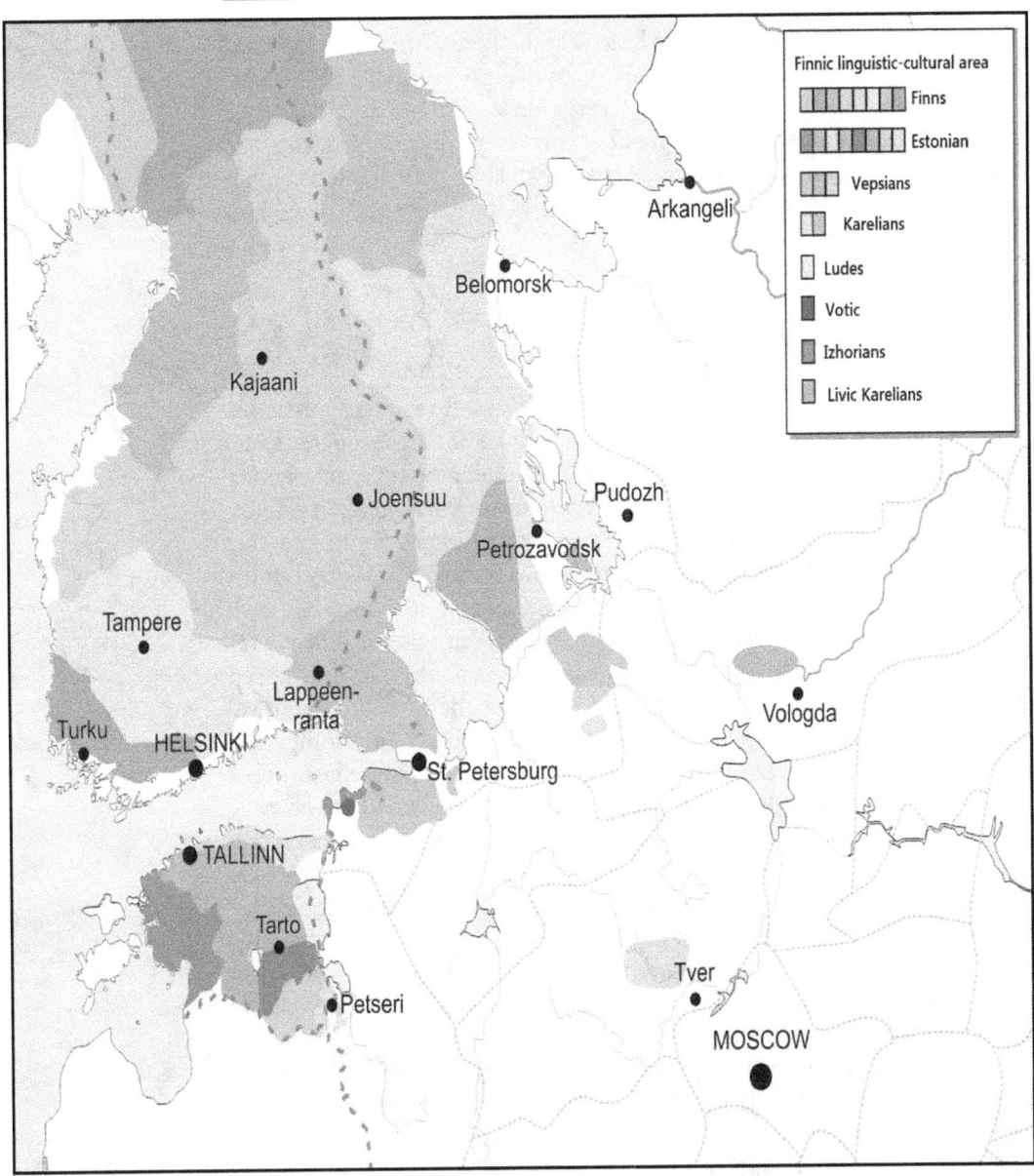

Map 1. Distribution of Finnic linguistic-cultural groups.

equivalent situations, and the same lamenter will give different performances on every occasion. However, all lamenters follow a conventionalized traditional register. Thus each lament exhibits features that index its membership in a common tradition, as well as being unique within the tradition.

This paper starts with a general discussion of the characteristics of oral poetry and of the concept of register, followed by a brief introduction to the Karelian lament tradition, and a review of the key features of the Karelian lament register. I then discuss variation within lament registers, as well as certain pan-regional features of these registers, which tend to be common to all Finnic lament traditions. Within one local or regional semiotic register of lament, I also differentiate the *core lexicon of this register* from its *situation-specific lexicon*. Differentiating these parts of the lexical register at the local level is significant for understanding variation in individual competence because some lamenters develop greater competence in certain areas of the situation-specific lexicon than others, even if all lamenters develop competence in the core register. My conclusion reviews the nature and function of the lament register in its social context.

Oral Poetry and Register

Oral poetry can be approached in a variety of ways. It may be approached through its formal features or content and composition or through its historical, cultural or traditional background. The different approaches often depend on the theoretical or academic background of the scholar. In folklore studies, oral poetry is understood in terms of sung performances, and, due to the influence of scholarship in Oral-Formulaic Theory, oral poetry is most often approached as not learned by heart but rather composed anew in each concrete situation. This is evident in the case of Karelian epic and lyric poetry (Kallio 2013; Harvilahti, this volume) and in the lament poetry discussed here (Stepanova E. 2014a). It is difficult to separate the verbal and musical features of genres of oral poetry, because both elements jointly comprise a whole performance. (See Feld & Fox 1994: 25–53; Banti & Giannattasio 2004: 290; Kallio 2013.) Nevertheless, oral poetry can be approached as *poetically organized discourse*, a type of discourse in which speech acquires certain constraints on formal organization through "meter, rhythm, morphosyntactic parallelism, assonance or other procedures" (Banti & Giannattasio 2004: 315).

Traditional lament poetry also has a register organization that differentiates it as a channel of cultural expression from ordinary speech and from other genres of folklore. Its distinguishing features include a highly specific and idiomatic lexicon. In linguistics and linguistic anthropology, registers are understood as different modes or models of speech behaviour associated with specific social situations. M. A. K. Halliday proposes that register varies according to three broad contextual parameters: field of discourse, tenor of discourse and mode of discourse (see e.g. Halliday 1978; Halliday & Hasan 1989; Shore 2012a; 2012b; Shore, this volume). According to Asif Agha (2007), registers represent cultural models of speech and action. These are not petrified models, but rather models which continuously develop within the interaction between people in different situations. (See Agha 2007; 2004: 23.) Within a particular society or community, one can find many registers for different social situations and practices. The members of the community are able to recognize a wide range of different registers, and most individuals cannot use all of them fluently. Thus a person's social identity forms in relation to the range of registers that he or she is able to use. (Agha 2004: 23–24.)

In ethnopoetics, registers are identified as "major speech styles associated with recurrent types of situations" (Hymes 1989: 440). The register of a particular genre of oral poetry, such as lament, can be approached from a corresponding point of view, as involving a distinctive linguistic repertoire (Agha 1999: 216). As an oral-poetic register, lament involves the language which a performer uses to perform lament, and which the audience uses to understand it. This includes a distinctive lexicon with poetic "words" in the sense of idiomatic formulaic verbal expressions (Foley 2002: 109–117, and this volume; cf. Harvilahti, this volume), as well as other linguistic and non-linguistic features. In the case I discuss here, the register is characterized by all of the features that index laments and lamenting. A lament register also connects oral poems to an oral tradition. (E.g. Foley 1995: 50, 210; Harvilahti 2003: 95.) However, some approaches to registers of oral poetry are more narrowly linguistic and closer to registers as defined by Halliday. Others are more inclusive. For example, linguistic anthropologist James M. Wilce defines the register of Karelian laments "both narrowly (as a set of expressions substituted for everyday expressions) and broadly (as a linguistic variety best understood in relation to its genre, voice, and participant structure characteristics)" (personal communication 7.2.2014; see also Wilce & Fenigsen, this volume). Whether a register of oral poetry is defined broadly or narrowly, we must bear in mind that, as John Miles Foley (2002: 91) puts it: "Just like different languages, oral poetries have their own sets of operating rules. We reduce them to a single simplistic model at our peril."

Scholars of oral poetry normally differentiate register and genre: researchers with a register-oriented approach often stress the verbal features of texts, whereas those studying genres emphasize the contextual factors of whole texts (Voutilainen 2012: 76). In folklore studies, the concept of register often refers to (poetic) linguistic forms used in certain genres and contexts for mediating meanings (e.g. Foley 1995). Kaarina Koski (2011: 324–325) introduces a new concept of "narrative registers", a term that refers to the variation of narrative structure across narrating situations according to the narrator's goals. Koski's narrative register is not limited to differences of linguistic or syntactic features, but involves broader narrative structures and strategies beneath the surface of verbalization (*ibid.*). The present discussion will not delve into questions of motifs and themes. Yet it is important to recognize that in discussions of registers of oral poetry, these features have also been included as elements of a register in the research literature (e.g. Foley 1995: 49–53; cf. Frog, this volume).

In my study, I distinguish the concepts of register and genre. Genre is a scholars' analytical tool, which was used in earlier folklore studies for the classification of folklore texts. In more recent work, rather than as a category for classification, genre has been understood in performance studies and linguistic anthropology as a principle for creating or generating performances and texts as well as for receiving and interpreting them. In this sense, a genre is a flexible framework that governs the production, reception and interpretation of expression. (Honko 1968; Ben Amos 1982; Briggs & Bauman 1992; Bauman 2000; Siikala & Siikala 2005: 88–90; Koski 2011: 49–53; Kallio 2013: 93–97; Kallio, this volume.) Alongside the concept of genre, concepts of style and register are also used in the literature in a variety of ways, depending on the researcher's theoretical approach, academic field and research interests (Heikkinen et al. 2012; cf. Frog 2011; 2016).

Karelian Lament

Karelian lament is easy to approach as a consistent and homogeneous genre, which stands apart from other genres of Karelian oral poetry. Finnic laments are forms of poetically organized discourse, whose verbal features are inseparable in practice from their non-verbal features (e.g., melody and paralinguistic features). Both types of features jointly give the lamenter the freedom to be creative within the traditional framework of rules, and thus to convey both traditional and personal meanings through her laments. Verbal and non-verbal features of laments are resources with which the lamenter can emphasize, intensify, highlight and specify the symbolic influence of her poetry. Put simply, lament could be called sung poetic language (see also Feld 1990: 241–266; Leino 1981) that a lamenter uses to create unique expressive utterances. At the same time, lament is tightly bound to its cultural context and cultural meanings (cf. Foley 1995), for which it provides a channel of cultural expression.

My discussion on Finnic lament poetry is based both on published lament texts (Stepanova & Koski 1976; Konkka & Konkka 1980; Virtaranta & Virtaranta 1999; Nenola 2002; Zaitseva & Zhukova 2012) as well as on the archival materials from institutions in Finland and in the Russian Federation. The largest published collection of Karelian lament poetry, from 1976 (Stepanova & Koski), contains 233 lament texts recorded from 69 lamenters from three different areas of what is now the Republic of Karelia (Russian Federation): Viena Karelia, in the North; Olonec Karelia, in the South; and Seesjärvi Karelia, the area between them. The laments selected for this publication were collected by Soviet researchers in 1928–1971 – over a period of only 43 years. I also use the results of my analysis of 98 laments collected in 1970–2001 from Praskovja Saveljeva (1913–2002), a talented lamenter from Seesjärvi Karelia, to provide a better view on individual use of the lament register. Important sources for understanding the lamenting as well as the meanings of the laments were interviews and comments of Karelian lamenters on the language of laments and lamenting practices. These I acquired from earlier publications (e.g. Lönnrot 1836; Paulaharju 1995 [1924]), published archival materials (e.g. Konkka & Konkka 1980), through listening to archival recordings collected in the Karelian Scientific Center as well as through conducting my own fieldwork in 1998 and 2007. As the basis for the comparison of different Finnic laments, I focused mainly on the published materials available (e.g. Nenola 2002; Zaitseva & Zhukova 2012).

The sources for lament poetry used in my study pose some interesting issues relevant to the study of register. One of the concerns involves how the archival sources were collected: some earlier data was written down by hand, often without proper contextual information, and sometimes it is not possible to be certain about how accurately laments were transcribed (especially taking into consideration their distinctive lexicon and manner of performance). The text-scripts of handwritten archival materials do not provide us with certain important features of the lament register, especially non-verbal ones. The same issue stands with earlier studies published in the late 1800s and early 1900s. However, beginning from the 1950s with the development of recording technology, researchers acquired a broad range of audio and later also video recordings. The result is that scholars today are also able to study, for example, the melodies of laments and the manners of performances of lamenters. These archival and published data are often primarily comprised of the text-scripts of laments and only rarely include some ethnographic data about the lamenting tradition, which is important for understanding lament practices and metapoetics. However, I have searched for the scarce ethnographic materials from different potential sources, interviewed senior fieldworkers (e.g. Aleksandra Stepanova, Nina Lavonen, Raisa Remshujeva) and have also conducted my own fieldwork in the Republic of Karelia. By gathering data, working in archives, close reading documented text-scripts of laments, listening to and transcribing lament poetry, and studying laments for 10 years, I have artificially internalized the lament register. Combining all these different types of sources has made it possible to approach the register of Finnic laments properly.

The main feature of Karelian and other Finnic laments is that their special poetic idiom is not easily comprehensible to the uninitiated listener because it is full of circumlocutions designed to avoid directly naming relatives, intimate people, certain objects and associated phenomena. (Nenola-Kallio 1982; Stepanova A. 1985; 2003; 2012; Stepanova E. 2011; 2012; 2014a.) Avoidance registers have been studied in a wide variety of languages in linguistic anthropology, including the languages of Australia (Haviland 1979; Dixon 1974) and Africa (Irvine & Gal 2000). They take a variety of culture-specific forms. In the Karelian case, avoidance registers are rooted in naming taboos, which include avoiding the names of deceased persons (Honko 1963: 128; Konkka 1975: 178). In addition to containing a lexical register of avoidance terms, the language and performance of Karelian laments also conforms to a variety of other linguistic conventions, such as alliteration, parallelism, and an abundance of plural, diminutive and possessive forms. Karelian laments are also performed with characteristic descending melodies, and accompanied by what Greg Urban (1988) describes as "icons of crying" that saliently express the grief-stricken feelings of the lamenter (discussed below). This poetry was not subject to a fixed meter. The primary organizational units were based on the rhythms of melodic phrases of varying length that were marked by a consistent pattern of alliteration. These units can be referred to as poetic "strings" (see Frog & Stepanova 2011: 197), which in some regions could be quite long while in others the structure of phrases could be shorter like lines of verse. A good example of Karelian lament is the beginning of the memorial lament performed at the grave by Maria Prohorova (born in 1905) from Seesjärvi Karelia, recorded in 1974 in the village of Muaselga. In this short example, we can observe all of the features of the lament register listed above.

Täššä i tytär, nuoresta aijoista,	Here is [my] daughter, [who] at a young age,
jätti kaksi kandamaista...	left behind two carried ones...

Oi, oi kukki Šura-rukka, tulin jo angeh da aivin abeudunun muamo-rukka, siuda näinägö lämbyminä, ľubiimoiloina kezäzinä vieľä enzikerrat kukkahista syndyzisťä kuonnuttamah. Tulin angeh da aivin abeudunun muamo-rukka siuda, alli-aigomazeni,	Oh flowery, poor Šura, [I] came bleak and very depressed poor mother, in these warm, beloved summers another time from flowery *syndyzet* (the otherworld) to get you up. [I] came, bleak and very depressed poor mother, my long-tailed-duck-made-one (daughter)
armahista syndyzisťä aigauttamah. Näinä lämbyminä kezäpäiväzinä... (Fon. 2061/5)	from dear *syndyzet* to wake you up On these warm summer days...

Maria Prohorova's lament was performed on the grave of her deceased daughter, who died young and left two orphaned children in the care of Prohorova. Following the conventional pattern of memorial laments, the lamenter begins by trying to wake up her daughter from the otherworld in order to talk to her. The use of lament for communication with the otherworld and its inhabitants is a typical function of this register. According to traditional beliefs, dead members of the family could not understand colloquial speech but could understand the language of laments (Stepanova A. 2003: 186). However, laments and lament language were also a medium of communication in other ritual contexts. In weddings, lamenters not only communicated with the otherworld and the powers inhabiting it; laments were also used for communication between the kin groups of the bride and of the groom, as well as within a kin group (between mother and daughter, for example), or between the bride and her friends in ritual dialogues. The lamenters were responsible for this ritual communication on behalf of different participants – even on behalf of the bride. In addition to ritual contexts, laments were also performed in non-ritual contexts for the communication of the lamenter's own sorrows, whether to other women, members of the family, deceased kin, supernatural powers or without any specific audience.

Karelian Lament Register

The Karelian lament genre contains a characteristic register as an essential part. The register is a cultural model of conduct (Agha 2007: 81–83) that includes distinctive features of verbal conduct – including a special lexicon, grammar, syntax, stylistic features, and melody – as well as forms of non-verbal communication, and the use of specific objects during the performance of the lament. These essential features are characteristic of all Finnic laments. (See more Honko 1963; Nenola-Kallio 1982; Konkka 1985; Stepanova A. 1985; 2012; Stepanova E. 2012; Sarv 2000.) All of the discursive features of the lament register can be observed in the short sample above.

Maria Prohorova uses circumlocutions, as required by the register, to avoid naming her deceased daughter directly, saying "my long-tailed-duck-made-one"; instead of using the personal pronoun 'I', she uses the circumlocution "bleak and very depressed poor mother"; and she uses the special circumlocution *syndyzet* ['origin.DIM.PL'] to avoid naming the location of deceased members of the family, the otherworld. The lexical register of Karelian laments contains over 100 semantic classes of circumlocutions for different nouns – e.g. mother, parents, husband, son, house, cow, grave, coffin, a bride's hair, etc. – and is thus consistent with other avoidance registers that exhibit lexical specialization in avoidance behaviour (Haviland 1979). Each group of circumlocutions has its own rules of lexical formation and variability, and contains dozens of synonymic avoidance expressions that are capable of satisfying different patterns of alliteration. The precise rules of formation are dependent on the dialect of the tradition. (Stepanova A. 1985; 2012.)

This system of circumlocutions is flexible and generative, which gives the lamenter freedom to produce new circumlocutions of her own, although these remain within the rules of the broader register. For example, a circumlocution for mother is made from a verb reflecting the actions of a mother toward her child such as *voalie* ['to cherish'], *lämmittiä* ['to warm'], *kylvettiä* ['to bathe'], *kantoa* ['to carry']. Deverbal nouns then provide basic circumlocutions: *voalija* ['cherisher'], *lämmittäjä* ['warmer'], *kylvettäjä* ['bather'], *kantaja* ['carrier']. These are core words for the circumlocution for mother. Usually, each of the core word will be used in diminutive form (.DIM) with a 1st person possessive suffix (.POSS): *voalijaiseni* ['cherisher.DIM.POSS']. The core word can then be complemented by different sorts of alliterating elements with great flexibility. In the following example, the potential for flexible expansion of the core word *kantaja* ['carrier'] is illustrated:

(1) *kandajazeni*   carrier.DIM.POSS

(2) *kalliz kandajazeni*   dear carrier.DIM.POSS

(3) *kumbane olet kallehilla ilmoilla piälä kandelija kalliz kandajazeni*   one who is into the dear.PL world.PL bringer dear carrier.DIM.POSS

(4) *kumbane olet kallehilla ilmoilla piälä kaheksien kuuhuzien kandelija kalliz kandajazeni*   one who is into the dear.PL world.PL for eight.PL months.DIM.PL bringer dear carrier.DIM.POSS

Rather than fixed formulaic expressions, the lexicon of the register is characterized by systems of alliterative vocabularies linked to different semantic classes of referent. Within the rules of formation characteristic of the particular class, such vocabulary would be generatively realized. Thus, this example of expansion reflects only a single possibility for how the core-word *kantaja* ['carrier'] might be used. The amount of conventional synonymic variation within a semantic class of circumlocution depends on how widely the avoided noun is used in lament poetry. Circumlocutions that are used in many different contexts (e.g. terms for 'mother', 'child', etc.) have significantly more variants than those used only in very specific situations (e.g. terms for 'dowry', 'soap' or 'gambling') (cf. Hainsworth 1968: 25).

The lexicon of laments also contains a broad range of verbs that are used to avoid the naming of certain actions described in laments. For example, verbs related to death and life are avoided: 'burying' is expressed as 'rolling' or 'concealing in the earth'; 'sending', 'placing' or 'wrapping to the *syndyzet* (otherworld)'; 'life' or 'living' is expressed through the metaphor of travelling (Stepanova E. 2015). Typical of the lament lexicon is the use of positive epithets for all close relatives, for the world of the dead and the world of the living, as well as for all objects and phenomena related to the close family, like *lämbyminä, l'ubiimoiloina kezäzinä* ['warm beloved summers'] and 'dear *syndyzet*'; negative epithets are correspondingly used for lamenter herself, such as 'bleak and very depressed', and for strangers including the husband's or the groom's family.

The grammar of the lament register is an important means of generating appropriate meanings and circumlocutions. The most outstanding grammatical peculiarity of the lament register is the use of plural forms even when only one object, phenomenon or process is in question. Regular use of plural in the place of a singular form is an element which shows the lamenter's stance and which guides or directs the interpretation of an audience (see also VISK § 1707; Agha 2007: 14). The singular is used when a lamenter tells about one concrete person; expressions for the pronoun 'I', for the lamenter's mother or her husband are always used in the singular. Use of the plural form reveals honorification in many registers around the globe (Silverstein 2010: 345; see also Wilce & Fenigsen, this volume).

Patterns in the use of certain features of the register are informed by culturally important models of interrelations within society. Such models of interrelations are reflected and constructed through the abundance of the diminutive form's use especially in connection with everyone and everything related to "one's own" kin and family, including especially the otherworld and deceased relatives. Possessive forms are also used in the register to differentiate persons, objects or phenomena belonging to "one's own" kin or to that of "others". In addition, the diminutive also shows a lamenter's extreme affection (VISK § 206; Silverstein 2001: 388–390) toward the worlds of the living and the dead as well as towards all relatives. This sort of social differentiation associated with language use is clearly evident in Maria Stafejeva's description of how she learned to lament:

(5) *Kuundelin da kuin se šanatten sinne pid'äy šanuo da ked'ä miksi pid'äy vel'ičaija.*
  Vielä pid'äy kaikkie malttoa ka.
  Omie pid'äy omalla i šanalla, vierahambie pid'äy vilummalla šanalla šanuo.
    (Fon. 1898/7.)

  I listened to how those words need to be said there [in laments] and how you
    need to call people.
  And on top of that, you have to understand everything.
  You call your own people with certain words, and strangers with colder words.

Affection in lament performance is not exclusive to verbal communication: it is also shown through kinesics (body language), haptics (touch) and proxemics (use of space). A lamenter tries to lean toward the object of her lament, to touch and embrace the object of lament. In contrast, diminutive suffixes are not used when referring to, for example, foreign places (including the home of a groom or husband): e.g. *igävät ikonattomat rannat* ['sad shores without icons'; i.e. non-Christian, those who do not have icons]; enemies: e.g. *ottamien okajannikat* ['cursed of taken-one.PL'; i.e. cursed strangers]; the groom's retinue: e.g. *viidojen alla vilizijät viidazvierit* ['in the thicket.PL bustling thicket-animal.PL']; or a heavy drinker: e.g. *kabakkavedzyien kannottelija* ['carrier of pub water.DIM.PL'; i.e. liquor]. The diminutive is a unique signifier communicating the attitude of the speaker toward the subject of speech and thus the communicated attitude changes into a contextual reality which affects how the communication will happen in the future (Silverstein 2001: 388–390).

Various kinds of repetition, including alliteration and semantic parallelism, are another of the prominent features of poetry in general (Jakobson 1987: 99) including oral poetry. These features are also characteristic of the lament register. Maria Prohorova, in the lament quoted above, as well as other lamenters try to maintain the same pattern of alliteration especially within a single circumlocution and more generally within the individual utterance or "poetic string" of a lament. Lamenters then repeat the content of a poetic string usually 2–3 times in parallel strings. Sometimes, however, when the theme of a string is particularly important to a lamenter, she might repeat the theme in up to 7–9 parallel strings. The passage below illustrates how a lamenter could maintain the same alliteration in one poetic string of a wedding lament. In this lament, the bride is telling her brother that it would be better for him to kill her than to let her marry:

(6) *Oi,   ottajazen'i   okluada,*
    Oh,   my takers'.DIM (parents')   riza [metal cover of an icon] (boy),

   olizit ottanun   oigeilla   olgapeellä   obladaittavat
   you would have taken   on-the-right.PL shoulder.PL   being-kept.PL

   oigeammat   oružaraudazet,   olizit
   right.COMP.PL gun-iron.DIM.PL (rifle), you would have

   ottajani   uul'ičalla   ostrel'innun.
   my taker (mother) in the yard   have shot [me].
       (Irinja Nikonova, born 1881, KA. 63/88)

The function and meaning of these types of repetition are aesthetic as well as formal and indexical. This is one string, the content of which is repeated in subsequent strings. There is also a parallel structure within the string (take the rifle + shoot me) as well as figura etymologica (e.g. *ottajazen'i – ottanun – ottajani*) while *o*-alliteration on thirteen out of the fourteen words creates a special audible sound harmony, a euphony. The repetition of sounds highlights the semantic connection between the words (Kantokorpi et al. 1990: 71), which reinforces the string as a united semantic unit within lament performances. When listening to a lament, the euphony brings the impression of very fluent and flowing performance, especially when the lamenter is competent. The major features of the lament register, such as parallelism, dominate in the melodic expression of laments as well (Niemi 2002: 697). As Heikki Laitinen and Jarkko Niemi have pointed out, the role of alliteration and its euphony, its harmony, are important from the point of view of the lament's tonal expression. These also affect how lament is orally transmitted and how it is received when hearing it. Euphony and harmony created by alliteration create a special soundscape of lament performance. (Laitinen 2003: 298–299; Niemi 2002: 697.)

Because laments are mostly performed in grievous occasions, their content is usually mournful and sad. Laments do not simply describe grief, but also perform emotions and make them audible. In interviews, lamenters stress that performing lament without performing the grief, without being in a depressed mood, is not lamenting, but singing (see more Stepanova E. 2014b). The performance of grief is characterized by what Gregory Urban (1988) refers to as icons of crying: (1) the "cry breaks", or breaks in voicing attributable to crying; (2) voiced inhalation; (3) a creaky voice; and (4) falsetto vowels. Icons of crying symbolically transmit an intense emotional participation in the ritual event, the lamenter's close connection to the object of the lament as well as the weakness and physical suffering of the lamenter in the situation of grief (Urban 1988; Tolbert 1990). All of these effects are communicated in the performance of lament in four complementary ways. They are audible through the icons of crying; they are semantically salient through verbal expressions (circumlocutions and themes of laments); they index relationships through diminutive and plural forms of reference; and they are kinesically expressed through body language, e.g. by leaning toward the object of the lament or by swinging back and forth while lamenting (Wilce 2005: 61). (Stepanova E. 2014a; 2014b.) The emotions of the lamenter and also of the audience have a crucial impact on the soundscape of laments, thus the performance as a whole is created with the melody and alliteration of the lament on the one hand, and with the sobbing and voiced inhalations of the icons of crying on the other (Rüütel & Remmel 1980: 179; Urban 1988; Niemi 2002: 697).

The formal features of laments or the rules of the register include a generative system of circumlocutions, the use of grammatical and stylistic features, a distinctive melody, and forms of non-verbal communication. All of these features are conventionally required of all lamenters, and together comprise the cultural model of conduct that we identify as the lament register.

Variation

The features listed above are shared across all local traditions of Karelian laments and are more generally common across all Finnic lament traditions. These features can therefore be described as a *pan-regional semiotic register* of Finnic laments. The pan-regional register also has locale-specific variant forms or *dialects*, which indexically differentiate locale-specific lament traditions from each other. Karelian lament traditions represent one of the dialects within the Finnic lament tradition (as do Ižorian laments, Votic laments, Seto laments). There are also sub-dialects within the Karelian lament tradition itself. This distinction is useful because the geographical distribution of Karelian sub-dialects of the Finnic lament register do not necessarily correspond to dialects of the Karelian language (Stepanova A. 1985: 16).

Within the semiotic register of Karelian laments, the lexicon can be divided into a core lexicon (which is essential to all lament performances) and a situation-specific lexicon (the different areas of which are characteristic of performances associated with particular social and ritual situations). The *core lexicon* consists of those elements which are employed in all ritual laments (funeral laments, wedding laments, military conscription laments) as well as in all non-ritual lament contexts. The elements of the core lexicon include circumlocutions for the ego of the lamenter, terms for familial relations, for this world and the otherworld, and for divine beings. The *situation-specific lexicon* consists of vocabulary items that are associated with specific themes, motifs or subjects that are conventional to certain situations of lamenting, but the situation-specific lexicon is not fundamental to all laments. Certain situations require a concentration of situation-specific terms. For example, the image of a coffin as an eternal home is specific to laments performed at a special stage of the funeral ritual. Similarly, the motif of the bride asking her friends to prepare her last bridal sauna is specific to laments performed at a special stage of wedding rituals. These images and motifs require the appropriate elements of the situation-specific lexicon, elements that are rarely used in any other context. However, other elements of the situation-specific lexicon may reflect, for example, aspects of secular life, such as food, drink, body-parts, feelings, time, modes of transportation, buildings, and so forth. (Stepanova A. 2012.) This principle of a distinction between a core lexicon and situation-specific lexicon is a feature of the pan-regional register of Finnic laments. In other words, every dialect of the Finnic lament tradition exhibits this division, although it may be realized in culturally and locally specific ways.

Although the lament register is a highly conventional system, each lamenter internalizes the lament register on the basis of her own experience, and uses it on the basis of her own competence. That competence is also shaped by her own experience and motivations. Every lamenter develops competence in the core lexicon of the register. Interestingly, if a lamenter knows the core lexicon and the other fundamentals of the register, then she can perform basic laments in any context or situation where she might need them. Back in the beginning of the 20th century, every Karelian woman was expected to be able to perform laments (Konkka 1985: 9). This was a basic competence for women in social life. Some women gained greater experience through participation in more varied social events and networks, and by listening to the laments of other (especially more experienced) women. Personal experiences and interests would result in some lamenters becoming competent in certain areas of the situation-specific lexicon as opposed to others. Thus, some lamenters were extremely competent in funeral ritual laments but not in wedding laments. In addition, exposure to a greater variety of idiolects and dialects of the tradition enabled some women to realize the potential that the register offered for creativity and expressivity as a resource (cf. Honko 2003: 61). This can provide such lamenters with greater ability to vary and innovate within the register (Stepanova E. 2012: esp. 280–281). This process was essential to the development of the lexicon in local dialects of the lament register (e.g. the lamenter Anni Lehtonen, on whom see Paulaharju 1995 [1924]). There is a great variety of idiolects of the lament register with the consequence that while every lament shares generic features with other laments that belong to this tradition, every lament is also unique within the tradition to which it belongs.

Conclusions

The register of Karelian laments consists of an intersecting and complementary system of verbal and non-verbal features in performance. In practice, its exclusive use by women leads this register, as a socially recognized metasemiotic entity, to be treated as an indexical of gender: all members of a community perceive it as a register characteristic of women. The historical development of the lexical register of laments also reveals the special role of women in the role of lamenter: the circumlocutions of this register always track kinship relationships through the mother (Nenola-Kallio 1982). Equally important is its interconnection to mythic knowledge: the lament register reveals, represents, uses and communicates knowledge about the mythic world and its actors and powers, and these representations are internalized in conjunction with the lexical register (Stepanova E. 2012). This mythic knowledge of laments is, of course, part of the broader belief systems and understandings of the mythic world in the particular cultural area to which the lamenter belongs. However, it is necessary to point out that the mythic world conventionally represented through laments could differ in key features from the mythic world presented through other genres of folklore such as epic and incantation, including genres from the same local community (Tarkka 2005; Stepanova E. 2012).

The register also indexes "lamenter" as social role: the lamenter is the intermediary between the community of this world and the community of the otherworld, but also between the in-group community of the lamenter and other communities in ritual contexts. She is a ritual specialist especially of rites of passage (Honko 1974). She is also an interpreter and expresser of feelings. The lament register is emotionally expressive: it is meant to express grief, both personal and collective. This is made audible through "icons of crying", its melody, epithets and even alliteration, all of which together index precisely the feelings of grief that it is characteristic for the register to express. The lament register is also an honorific register (Wilce & Fenigsen, this volume). Characteristics of its honorific quality are practices of name avoidance through circumlocutions, of deference and affection through plural forms and diminutives for addressees and referents, and the use of the third person rather than first person by the lamenter to refer to herself (*ibid.*). A key factor in the honorific nature of the register is its association with beliefs and understandings of the mythic world and what is necessary for communication with that world. Within the context of ritual performance, the lamenter verbalizes the events, activities and agents, and her own relationships to persons, in both the living community and the unseen world. In this way, she actualizes the events, making them known and real for the unseen community of the dead while simultaneously verbalizing the unseen mythic world and making it real for the living community. By using the lament register in performance, a lamenter actualizes her own identity, role or feelings, and the identity, role or feelings of the addressee of her laments, and thus concurrently realizes and actualizes the whole world surrounding the performance, both seen and unseen.

References

Sources

Fon. 2061/5, 1898/7 = Фонограммархив Института языка, литературы и истории Карельского научного центра Российской академии наук. Петрозаводск (Audio Archive of the Institute of Linguistics, Literature and History of the Karelian Research Centre of Russian Academy of Science, Petrozavodsk).

КА. 63/88 = Научный архив Карельского научного центра Российской академии наук. Петрозаводск (Scientific Archive of the Karelian Research Centre of Russian Academy of Science, Petrozavodsk).

Literature

Agha, Asif 1999. Register. *Journal of Linguistic Anthropology* 9(1–2): 216–221.
Agha, Asif 2004. Registers of Language. In *A Companion to Linguistic Anthropology*. Ed. Alessandro Duranti. Oxford: Blackwell Publishing. Pp. 23–45
Agha, Asif 2007. *Language and Social Relations*. Cambridge: Cambridge University Press.
Banti, Giorgio, & Francesco Giannattasio 2004. Poetry. In *A Companion to Linguistic Anthropology*. Ed. Alessandro Duranti. Oxford: Blackwell Publishing. Pp. 291–320.
Bauman, Richard 2000. Genre. *Journal of Linguistic Anthropology* 9(1–2): 84–88.
Ben Amos, Dan 1982. Perinnelajikäsitteet. In *Kertomusperinne: Kirjoituksia, proosaperinteen lajeista ja tutkimuksesta*. Helsinki: Suomalaisen Kirjallisuuden Seura. Pp. 11–28.
Briggs, Charles, & Richard Bauman 1992. Genre, Intertextuality, and Social Power. *Journal of Linguistic Anthropology* 2(2): 131–172.
Dixon, R. M. W. 1974. A Method of Semantic Description. In *Semantics: An Interdisciplinary Reader in Philosophy, Linguistics and Psychology*. Ed. Danny D. Steinberd & Leon A. Jakobovits. Cambridge: Cambridge University Press. Pp. 436–471.
Feld, Steven 1990. Wept Thoughts: The Voicing of Kaluli Memories. *Oral Tradition* 5(2–3): 241–266.
Feld, Steven, & Aaron A. Fox 1994. Music and Language. *Annual Review of Anthropology* 23: 25–53.

Foley, John Miles 1995. *The Singer of Tales in Performance*. Bloomington: Indiana University Press.

Foley, John Miles 2002. *How to Read an Oral Poem*. Urbana / Chicago: University of Illinois Press.

Frog 2011. Traditional Epic as Genre: Definition as a Foundation for Comparative Research. *RMN Newsletter* 3: 47–48.

Frog 2016 (forthcoming). 'Genres, Genres Everywhere, but Who Knows What to Think?': Toward a Semiotic Model for Typology. In *Genre – Text – Interpretation*. Ed. Kaarina Koski & Frog with Ulla Savolainen. Studia Fennica Folkloristica. Helsinki: Finnish Literature Society.

Frog & Eila Stepanova 2011. Alliteration in (Balto-) Finnic Languages. In *Alliteration in Culture*. Ed. Jonathan Roper. Houndmills: Palgrave MacMillan. Pp. 195–218.

Hainsworth, John Bryan 1968. *The Flexibility of the Homeric Formula*. Oxford: Claredon Press.

Halliday, Michael Alexander Kirkwood, & Ruqaiya Hasan 1989 [1985]. *Language, Context, and Text: Aspects of Language in a Social-Semiotic Perspective*. Oxford: Oxford University Press.

Halliday, Michael Alexander Kirkwood 1978. *Language as Social Semiotic: The Social Interpretation of Language and Meaning*. London: Edward Arnold.

Harvilahti, Lauri 2003. *The Holy Mountain: Studies on Upper Altay Oral Poetry*. FF Communications 282. Helsinki: Academia Scientiarum Fennica.

Haviland, John B. 1979. Guugu Yimidhirr Brother-in-Law Language. *Language and Society* 8(3): 365–393.

Heikkinen, Vesa, et al. (eds) 2012. *Genre-analyysi: Tekstitutkimuksen käsikirja*. Helsinki: Gaudeamus.

Honko, Lauri 1963. Itkuvirsirunous. In *Suomen kirjallisuus I: Kirjoittamaton kirjallisuus*. Ed. Matti Kuusi. Helsinki: Suomalaisen Kirjallisuuden Seura. Pp. 81–128.

Honko, Lauri 1968. Genre Analysis in Folkloristics and Comparative Religion. *Temenos: Studies in Comparative Religion* 3: 48–66.

Honko, Lauri 1974. Balto-Finnic Lament Poetry. In *Finnish Folkloristics 1*. Ed. Pentti Leino with Annikki Kaivola-Bregenhøj & Urpo Vento. Helsinki: Suomalaisen Kirjallisuuden Seura. Pp. 9–61.

Honko, Lauri 2003. *The Maiden's Death Song and The Great Wedding*. FF Communications 281. Helsinki: Academia Scientiarum Fennica.

Hymes, Dell 1989 [1974]. Ways of Speaking. In *Explorations in the Ethnography of Speaking*. Ed. Richard Bauman & Joel Sherzer. Cambridge: Cambridge University Press. Pp. 433–451.

Irvine, Judith, & Susan Gal 2000. Language Ideology and Linguistic Differentiation. In *Regimes of Language: Ideologies, Polities, and Identities*. Ed. P. V. Kroskrity. Santa Fe NM: School of American Research Press. Pp. 35–83.

Jakobson, Roman 1987 = Якобсон, Роман 1987. *Работы по поэтике*. Москва: Прогресс.

Kallio, Kati 2013. *Laulamisen tapoja: Esitysareena, rekisteri ja paikallinen laji länsi-inkeriläisessä kalevalamittaisessa runossa*. Tampere: Tammerprint.

Kantokorpi, Mervi, Pirjo Lyytikäinen & Auli Viikari 1990. *Runousopin perusteet*. Helsinki: Lahden Tutkimus- ja Koulutuskeskus, Helsingin Yliopisto.

Konkka, Unelma 1975 = Конкка, У. С. 1975. Табу слов и закон иносказания в карельских плачах. In *Проблемы фольклора*. Москва. Pp. 170–178.

Konkka, Unelma 1985. *Ikuinen ikävä: Karjalaisia riitti-itkuja*. Helsinki: Suomalaisen Kirjallisuuden Seura.

Konkka, Unelma & Aleksi Konkka 1980 = Конкка, У. С. & А. П. Конкка 1980. *Духовная культура сегозерских карел конца XIX–начала XX в*. Ленинград: Наука.

Koski, Kaarina 2011. *Kuoleman voimat: Kirkonväki suomalaisessa uskomusperinteessä*. Helsinki: Suomalaisen Kirjallisuuden Seura.

Laitinen, Heikki 2003. *Iski sieluihin salama: Kirjoituksia musiikista.* Ed. Hannu Tolvanen & Riitta-Liisa Joutsenlahti. Helsinki: Suomalaisen Kirjallisuuden Seura.

Leino, Pentti 1981. Itämerensuomalaisen itkuvirsikielen tutkimusongelmia. *Sananjalka* 23: 103–113.

Lönnrot, Elias 1836. Itkuvirsistä Venäjän Karjalasta. *Mehiläinen* 1836, syyskuu–lokakuu.

Nenola-Kallio, Aili 1982. *Studies in Ingrian Laments.* FF Communication 234. Helsinki: Academia Scientiarum Fennica.

Nenola, Aili 2002. *Inkerin itkuvirret – Ingrian Laments.* Helsinki: Suomalaisen Kirjallisuuden Seura.

Niemi, Jarkko 2002. Musical Structures of Ingrian Laments. In Nenola 2002: 708–728.

Paulaharju, Samuli 1924. *Syntymä, lapsuus ja kuolema: Vienan Karjalan tapoja ja uskomuksia.* Porvoo: Werner Söderström.

Rüütel, I., & M. Remmel 1980. = Рютель, И., М. Реммель 1980. Опыт нотации и исследования вепсских причитаний. In *Финно-угорский музыкальный фольклор и взаимосвязи с соседними культурами.* Ed. И. Рютель. Таллинн: Ээсти раамат. Pp. 169–193.

Sarv, Vaike 2000. *Setu itkukultuur.* Ars Musicae Popularis 14. Tallinn: Eesti Kirjandusmuuseumi Etnomusikoloogia Osakund.

Shore, Susanna 2012a. Kieli, kielenkäyttö ja kielenkäytön lajit systeemis-funktionaalisessa teoriassa. In *Genreanalyysi: Tekstilajitutkimuksen käsikirja.* Ed. V. Heikkinen, E. Voutilainen, P. Lauerma, U. Tiililä & M. Lounela. Helsinki: Gaudeamus. Pp. 131–157.

Shore, Susanna 2012b. Systeemis-funktionaalinen teoria tekstien tutkimisessa. In *Genreanalyysi: Tekstilajitutkimuksen käsikirja.* Ed. V. Heikkinen, E. Voutilainen, P. Lauerma, U. Tiililä & M. Lounela. Helsinki: Gaudeamus. Pp. 158–185.

Siikala, Anna-Leena 2000. Variation and Genre as Practice: Strategies for Reproducing Oral History in the Southern Cook Islands. In *Thick Corpus, Organic Variation and Textuality in Oral Tradition.* Ed. Lauri Honko. Helsinki: Suomalaisen Kirjallisuuden Seura. Pp. 215–242.

Siikala, Jukka, & Anna-Leena Siikala 2005. *Return to Culture: Oral Tradition and Society in the Southern Cook Islands.* Folklore Follows Communication 287. Helsinki: Academia Scientiarum Fennicae.

Silverstein, Michael 2001. The Limits of Awareness. In *Linguistic Anthropology: A Reader.* Ed. Alessandro Duranti. Oxford: Blackwell Publishers. Pp. 382–401.

Silverstein, Michael 2010. "Direct" and "Indirect" Communicative Acts in Semiotic Perspective. *Journal of Pragmatics* 42: 337–353.

Stepanova & Koski 1976 = Степанова, А. С., & Т. А. Коски 1976. *Карельские причитания.* Петрозаводск: Карелия.

Stepanova, A. 1985 = Степанова, А. С. 1985. *Метафорический мир карельских причитаний.* Ленинград: Наука.

Stepanova, A. 2003 = Степанова, А. С. 2003. *Карельские плачи: Специфика жанра.* Петрозаводск: Периодика.

Stepanova, Aleksandra 2012. *Karjalaisen itkuvirsikielen sanakirja.* Helsinki: Suomalaisen Kirjallisuuden Seura.

Stepanova, Eila 2011. Reflections of Belief Systems in Karelian and Lithuanian Laments: Shared Systems of Traditional Referentiality? *Archaeologia Baltica* 15: 128–143.

Stepanova, Eila 2012. Mythic Elements of Karelian Laments: The Case of *syndyzet* and *spuassuzet*. In *Mythic Discourses: Studies in Uralic Traditions.* Ed. Frog, Anna-Leena Siikala & Eila Stepanova. Helsinki: Suomalaisen Kirjallisuuden Seura. Pp. 257–287.

Stepanova, Eila 2014a. *Seesjärveläisten itkijöiden rekisterit: Tutkimus äänellä itkemisen käytänteistä, teemoista ja käsitteistä.* Kultaneito 14. Tampere: Suomen Kansantietouden Tutkijain Seura.

Stepanova, Eila 2014b. The Soundscape of Karelian Lament from the Seesjärvi Region. In *Song and Emergent Poetics – Laulu ja runo – Песня и видоизменяющаяся поэтика.*

Ed. Pekka Huttu-Hiltunen, Frog, Karina Lukin & Eila Stepanova. Runolaulu-Akatemian Julkaisuja 18. Kuhmo: Juminkeko. Pp. 173–181.

Stepanova, Eila 2015. Elämä on matka: Elämänkulun käsitteellistäminen karjalaisessa rituaalirunoudessa. *Elore* 2015(1), 1–16.

Tarkka, Lotte 2005. *Rajarahvaan laulu: Tutkimus Vuokkiniemen kalevalamittaisesta runokulttuurista 1821–1921*. Helsinki: Suomalaisen Kirjallisuuden Seura.

Tolbert, Elizabeth 1990. Women Cry with Words: Symbolization of Affect in the Karelian Lament. *Yearbook for Traditional Music* 22: 80–105.

Urban, Gregory 1988. Ritual Wailing in Amerindian Brazil. *American Anthropologist* 90: 385–400.

Virtaranta, Pertti, & Helmi Virtaranta 1999. *Ahavatuulien armoilla: Itkuvirsiä Aunuksesta*. Ed. Raija Koponen & Marja Torikka. Musical noatation Ilpo Saastamoinen. Vammala: Suomalais-Ugrilainen Seura.

VISK = *Ison suomen kieliopin verkkoversio*. Available at: http://kaino.kotus.fi/visk/etusivu.php.

Voutilainen, Eero 2012. Rekisteri. In *Genreanalyysi: Tekstilajitutkimuksen käsikirja*. Ed. V. Heikkinen, E. Voutilainen, P. Lauerma, U. Tiililä & M. Lounela. Helsinki: Gaudeamus. Pp. 70–76.

Wilce, James M. 2005. Traditional Laments and Postmodern Regrets: The Circulation of Discourse in Metacultural Context. *Journal of Linguistic Anthropology* 15(1): 60–71.

Wilce, James M. 2009. *Crying Shame: Metaculture, Modernity, and the Exaggerated Death of Lament*. Oxford: Wiley-Blackwell.

Zaitseva, Nina, & Olga Zhukova 2012. *Käte-ške käbedaks kägoihudeks*. Petrozavodsk: Juminkeko.

Performance and Poetics

V

"On Traditional Register in Oral Poetry" (pp. 277–306), comprised of previously published selections of John Miles Foley's works, is not included in the open access publication for reasons of copyright.

Lauri Harvilahti

15. Register in Oral Traditional Phraseology

Professor John Miles Foley was invited to the seminar "Register, Intersections of Language, Context and Communication" as a keynote-speaker. J. M. Foley passed away on 3 May 2012, in Columbia, Missouri, a couple of weeks before the seminar was to be held. As a duty to my long-time colleague and friend, I presented a paper on his theories on *register* in the field of oral narrative research at that event. That text serves as a basis for the present article, owing to which I will also preface discussion with a short obituary of John Miles Foley.

John Miles Foley in memoriam (1947–2012)

Professor Foley was the Director of The Center for Studies in Oral Tradition, and William H. Byler Chair in the Humanities, Curators' Professor of Classical Studies and English (University of Missouri). Professor Foley was a scholar of oral tradition of international repute and founder of the journal *Oral Tradition*. In 2005, he established a new center The Center for eResearch at the University of Missouri to serve as a campus and international focus for Internet research.

In his early *opus magnum*, the annotated bibliography *Oral-Formulaic Theory and Research* (1985), professor Foley mentions over 1800 monographs and articles from over 90 language areas. In his monographs *The Oral Theory of Composition* (1988), *Traditional Oral Epic: The Odyssey, Beowulf, and the Serbo-Croatian Return Song* (1990), *Immanent Art: From Structure to Meaning in Traditional Oral Epic* (1991) and *The Singer of Tales in Performance* (1995), Foley stresses the importance of the inherent features of a given tradition in comparing Ancient Greek, South Slavic and Old English epic poetry, presents an interpretative model, and suggests the factors to be borne in mind when comparing different oral literatures. Furthermore, his approach represents a shift away from the world of grammar-like structures and compositional device systems towards a new synthesis that we know by now as his Theory of Immanent Art, Traditional Referentiality and Word-Power.

During the last ten years of his life, John Miles Foley paid more and more attention to digital and internet studies, as he himself expressed, "to illustrate and explain the fundamental similarities and correspondences between humankind's oldest and newest thought-technologies: oral tradition and the Internet". The first book-length volume in this field of interest by Foley was *The Wedding of Mustajbey's Son Bećirbey* (2004) on Serbian Moslem epics that can be used together with an "E-companion", available at http://www.oraltradition.org. The last book that Foley was able to finalize is entitled *Oral Tradition and the Internet: Pathways of the Mind* that appeared in August 2012.

Due to the lifetime work of John Miles Foley, an offshoot of classical literature research, created by Milman Parry and Albert Lord and known widely as Oral-Formulaic Theory has expanded into a universal, internationally renowned interdisciplinary approach. John Miles Foley acted as a Guest Professor Fellow at the Centre of Excellence of the Nordic Centre for Medieval Studies (NCMS) during the period October 15 through November 25, 2006. During his stay in Finland (at the Finnish Literature Society and Department of Folklore Studies of the University of Helsinki), Sweden (at the University of Gothenburg), Norway (at the Centre of Medieval Studies of the University of Bergen), and Denmark (at the University of Odense) he carried out a demanding programme that included a total of ten lectures, consultations with doctoral students and post-doctoral researchers, seminars, workshops and master classes. The organizers of the conference "Register: Intersections of Language, Context and Communication" sincerely express condolences for the loss of Professor John Miles Foley.

Professor John Miles Foley had very close connections with the Finnish folkloristic institutes and the Department of English of the University of Helsinki. He was a corresponding member of the Finnish Literature Society and a Full Member of the Folklore Fellows organization.

Many of us have worked together with Professor Foley at the international training courses entitled Folklore Fellows Summer School in Finland in 1995, 1997, 1999 and for the last time in 2007 in Kuhmo, Finland and in Archangel Karelia, in the Russian territory. We also co-directed group discussions on international oral epics for the Folklore Fellows Summer School and a series of workshops in the field of study of the world's epics, organized by the late professor Lauri Honko. A number of Finnish scholars have undertaken many research projects, conferences, and publications together with Professor Foley.

In a cooperation between the Centre for the Study of Oral Tradition of Professor Foley, the Folklore Archives of the Finnish Literature Society, and the Institute of Ethnic Literatures of the Chinese Academy of Social Sciences, we had a plan (in 2011) to establish an International Society for Epic Research. The Society was established, posthumously, in Beijing in November 2012, on the initiative of Professor Chao Gejin, Professor Karl Reichl, and myself. One idea to honour the memory of John Miles Foley is to develop a versatile web-infrastructure that would be applicable to diverse epic traditions and frameworks, adaptable to the culture-specific features of individual epics and epic traditions.

Register

The central concept employed by John Miles Foley in examining the compositional art of epic singers is *register* in the meaning that Dell Hymes has given to the term: a "major speech style associated with recurrent types of situations". (Hymes 1989 in: Bauman & Scherzer)

The term was centrally defined in linguistics by M. A. K. Halliday (e.a. 1964). According to Halliday register can be accounted for according to three variables (1964: 90–92):

- Field of discourse (the sphere of language activities)
- Mode of discourse (spoken and written, with many layers of taxonomy such as rhetorical modes)
- Tenor of discourse (relations among the participants)

Register is the configuration of semantic resources that a member of a culture typically associates with certain types of situation. A register is recognizable as a particular selection of words and structures, but it is defined in terms of meanings. The meanings that are conveyed form the decisive factor determining the use of the register. It is not the conventional forms of expression, but the selection of meanings that constitutes the variety to which a text belongs (Halliday 1978: 111; 1989; Foley 1995: 50).

According to Foley, traditional oral phraseology functions in oral texts as a storage of idiomatic means of communication. The register plays an important role for the singer in producing oral epics, but it is equally important for the audience, for the process of reception. Traditional registers may survive in the post-oral (semi-literary and literary) texts, as well – in which case the reader, as an equivalent of the listener of the oral performances, has to be aware of these idiomatic devices in order to be able to decode the meanings of the narrative patterns.

Foley has examined registers in oral tradition using material from different genres and traditions, as for example in Homeric and South Slavic epics (Foley 1999: 65–88), in Serbian charms (Foley 1995: 110–115), in the Homeric hymns (1995: 150–175), in oral-derived texts (1995: 82–92), and a theoretical overview to the concept is available in the volume *The Singer of Tales in Performance* (1995: 49–53; Foley 2015, forthcoming.). I will concentrate here on Foley's research on South-Slavic epics, and provide the reader with some comparative examples from Finnic and Turkic oral poetry. As background material for this article, I have drawn on the most recent essay of John Miles Foley of which I am aware, "Oral Epic in Stolac: Collective Tradition and Individual Art" (2015, forthcoming). In this essay Foley has paid a great deal of attention to the singers' own cognitive units of utterance of the idiomatic and "proleptic" storytelling language that forms a network of inherent meanings. Like other languages, this storytelling language can, according to Foley, be divided into structural, morphological and lexical levels. He discerns a *pan-traditional language* of the six geographically defined areas in the Bosnia-Herzegovina region that he was dealing with in the essay (Novi Pazar, Bijelo

Polje, Kolašin, Gacko, Stolac, Bihać). Further, he discusses the *dialectal level* of the region (in the article: Stolac), and the *idiolectal level* of any individual singer of tales (Foley 2015, forthcoming; see also e.g. Foley 1995: 49–53). Although Foley's discussion centers on the *guslari* (sg. *guslar*), the singers of South-Slavic epics that used the plucked instrument called *gusle*, these levels and concepts are readily adaptable to many other oral poetry traditions in cultures around the world. As Foley puts it:

> The formulaic repertoires of the Stolac *guslari* illustrate this dynamic interaction of individual and tradition, consisting as they do of regional or dialectal phrases alongside personal or idiolectal equivalents. For example, consider the various avatars of an idea we could summarize as 'for a long time', a prominent adverbial phrase that appears very frequently in a wide variety of songs and song-types. An analysis of 14,000 lines from the recorded Stolac epic tradition uncovers a dialectal formula, *za nedjelju dana* 'for a week of days', that is employed by all three singers sampled: Bajgorić, Bašić, and Kukuruzović. But each of them has other options as well to express the same idea, options that are not shared with their comrades but that seem, on available evidence, to be idiolectal. For instance, Bajgorić alone uses the formula *dva bijela dana* 'two white days', while only Kukuruzović deploys the 'word'-synonyms *sedam godin' dana* 'seven years of days' and *cijo mjesec dana* 'a whole month of days'. (Foley 2015, forthcoming; see also Foley 1990: 191–192; Elmer 2009; 2010.)

As Foley has discussed, these formulas are examples of something that the South-Slavic singers called "words" (*reč* in Serbo-Croatian). He describes how the collectors Milman Parry and Albert Lord and Nikola Vujnović were asking the singers, how they called, for example, a verse like *U Stambolu, u krčmi bijeloj* ['In Istanbul, in the white tavern']. The singers answered that this is a *reč* ['word']. A crucial primary feature of the poetics of South-Slavic epics relevant understanding these poetic "words" is the *deseterac*, the decasyllable meter of the epics. The connection between the meter and these units of utterance can be illustrated by the following a short section of Nikola Vujnović's interview of Ibro Bašić on "What is a *reč*?" (Foley 2002: 16):

> NV: What is, let's say, a single *reč* in a song? Tell me a single *reč* from a song.
> IB: This is one, like this, let's say; this is a *reč*: 'Mujo of Kladuša arose early, / At the top of the slender, well-built tower' (*Podranijo od Kladuše Mujo, / Na vrh tanke načinjene kule*).
> NV: But these are poetic lines (*stihovi*).
> IB: Eh, that's how it goes with us (*kod nas*, implying the singers); it's otherwise with you, but that's how it's said with us.

Accordingly, the singer's own cognitive units of utterance and networks of inherent meanings are crucial: the 'words' (*reč*) of the idiomatic storytelling language. Regarding the plurality and variation in formulas such as the different ways of expressing "for a long time" above, Foley (2015, forthcoming) observes:

Parsed into their component lexical units, these formulas obviously diverge. But in terms of the South Slavic epic register, which yields actual articulated phrases only as products deriving from a rule-governed process, they are equivalent. The point is that all of these variants are pathways to the same traditional idea, generated in performance through the natural morphology of the register and empowered by the indexical force of traditional referentiality. The singers simply navigate these pathways in different ways.

In the following section, I present a case study of a formula that could be summarized as *it took a long time* from the Finnic epic singing tradition.

A Case Study of the Formula It Took a Long Time in Finnic Poetry

In the formulaic language of Kalevala-meter poetry, the most common combination for *it took a long time* is *viipyi/mäni viikko* ['passed/went a week']. Kalevala-meter poetry was a traditional oral-poetic form of the Finns, Karelians and Ingrians. This poetry is characterized by a verse structure of eight syllables with the trochaic meter employing typical poetic devices such as alliteration and assonance and rules for syntactic parallelism. Naturally, the performers were not consciously aware of the finer distinctions of the tradition that can be brought forward in systematic analysis, but they did observe the basic register of Kalevala-metric poetry: together these created a poetic culture observing a fairly uniform poetic system. The digitized corpus of *SKVR* (*Suomen Kansan Vanhat Runot* ['Old Songs of the Finnish People']) contains more than 87,000 variants and fragments of this poetry. It is easy to find the occurrences of the formula in this database by searching the word *viikko* ['week'], as shown in Figure 1. The challenge for the user is that he/she should know the primary features of Kalevala-metric poetry, including lexical and syntactic parallelism. For example, words such as *kuu* ['month'] or even *päivä* ['day'] or *yö* ['night'] could be used by the singer to express the passing of time in formulaic language. Dialectal variation should also be taken into consideration as well, which presents great difficulties because the corpus has not been lemmatized, and there are no vocabularies or indices in other languages, such as in English. In its present form, the database is not really very easy to use for a general audience. Nevertheless, the database can be effectively used for the examination of formulaic language as one learns to navigate it. In order to alleviate some of the complications, I will concentrate here on examples from the region of West Ingria, where the tradition was predominantly maintained by women. Discussion will then be expanded by looking at the corresponding formulaic expression in Estonian *regilaul*, which is a historically related variation on the common Finnic alliterative tetrameter.

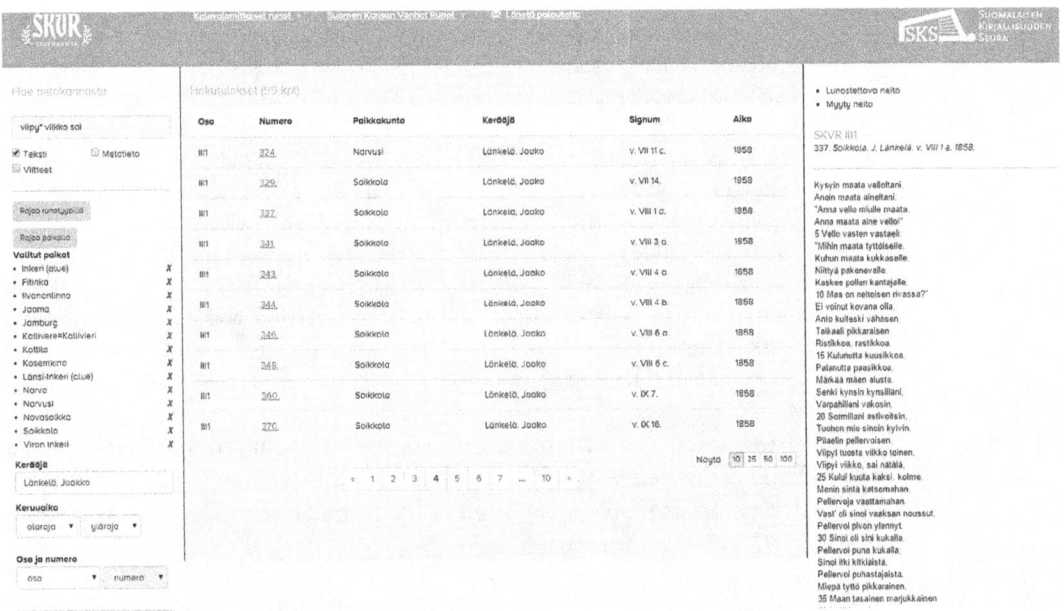

Figure 1. A screenshot from the SKVR corpus: searching for poems that contain the word viipyi ['a week'] among the collections from the region of Soikkola in the southern part of the Gulf of Finland. The results of the search are on the left, among which one poem (SKVR III 1192) was chosen to be presented (on the right).

A significant number of the themes of the songs performed by the female singers involved concrete or symbolic searching. An allegory of doom and longing is portrayed in these songs that I have called *the seeking poems*, and this allegory of searching for something that is lost, representing childhood and youth before the marrying age, lies at the core of the lyrical epic of Ingria (Harvilahti 1994: 91–98). The seeking episodes of variants from the mythologically inspired *The Origin of the World* (*Maailmansyntyruno*), *The Origin of the Kantele* (*Kantelen synty*) and *The Giant Oak* (*Iso tammi*) appear in the first person, which is a form of adaptation prompted by the regional poetic system. As a result, the poetic 'I' – the maiden – has an active role in the mythic poems, not only in the epic-lyric ones. In the introductory episode of *The Origin of the Kantele*, the poetic 'I' seeks her brother to fell a giant oak or orders her three brothers to kill a fighting elk; in some variants of *The Origin of the World*, she takes the place of the mythic swallow that lays the cosmic egg, thereby giving birth to the world. The poem *The Bartered Bride* tells about a girl who has been sold (married off) against her will. She has sown the seeds of "the blue" (i.e. corn-flower) and flax, and is waiting for the seeds to germinate. It takes a long time for the seeds to grow in the poor soil that she has received from her brother:

> *The Bartered Bride*, performed by a woman named Kati from the village of Väärnoja (*it took a long time* formula in italic font)
>
> *Viipyi tuosta viikko toin,*   Passed thereafter a week, another,
> *Viipyi viikko, sai netteeli,*   Passed a week, it took seven days,

Katoi kuuta kaksi, kolmet	Vanished months two, three
mäninpä siintä katsomaa,	I went to look at the corn-flower,
pellavasta vaattamaa.	to check the flax.
Jo sinoi sinikukalla,	The corn-flower was already blue,
pellavas punakukalla;	The flax was red;
sinoi itki kitkijäistä,	the corn-flower cried to be weeded,
pellavas puhastajaista.	the flax to be cleaned.
aloin miä kitkiä sinnooja,	I began to weed the flowers,
puhassella p[ellavasta]),	to clean the flax.
kitkin nurkan, k[itkin] toisen,	I weeded one corner, weeded another,
kitkin kolmatta vähhäisen,	weeded part of a third.
(SKVR III 1192, 35–48.)	

As the maiden was working in the field, she learns that she has been married off and cannot cultivate anymore, not even this poor soil of hers. However, let's turn now to look at variation of the formula that expresses the passing of time in texts from other singers.

The Bartered Bride, performed by a woman named Maaroi from the village of Tarinaisi

Viipyi tuosta viikko, toin,	Passed thereafter a week, another,
Katui viikkoa kaksi, kolmet	Vanished weeks, two, three
Sai tuosta moni netteelä	It took thereafter many seven-day cycles
(SKVR III 1193, 36–38.)	

The Bartered Bride, performed by a woman named Oiko from the village of Oussimäki

Mänipä tuosta viikko, toin	Went thereafter week, another
Kului kuuta kaksi, kolmet	Elapsed months two, three
(SKVR III 1195, 28–29.)	

The formula *it took a long time* may consist of two or three verses bound together according to the rules of parallelism, or (in some cases) it comprises only a single verse. There are many possibilities to verbalize the pattern by altering the lexical components, the morpho-syntactic structure, and there is also minor dialectal and idiolectal variation to be seen, just as in the South-Slavic examples presented by Foley. As in the South-Slavic examples, the variants in Ingria are generated by using the traditional "morphology" of the register.

In the countless versions of the seeking poems performed by Ingrian female singers, the same traditional idea has been modified over and over again for use in different co-texts, or rather in an intertextual network. This can be seen, for example, in a poem called *Messages from the War*, which tells about messages that take a long time to come from the battlefield. Another example is from a poem called *Presents of the Son-in-Law*, which describes the anxiety and fear of a mother who has not heard anything from her daughter after she has been married off, and then following the passage of time, she learns about her daughter's tragic, cannibalistic death, the parts of her body boiling in a pot or lying on a grill. In terms of subject matter, this provides us with three poems that are quite different from one another, which illustrates the flexibility of the formulaic language for use in different contexts:

The Bartered Bride, performed by a woman named Naastoi from the village of Säätinä

Viipy viikko, sai netelä	Passed a week, took a seven-days cycle
Kului kuuta kaksi	Elapsed two months
(SKVR III 1961, 23–24.)	

Messages from the War, also performed by Naastoi from the village of Säätinä

Tuosta viipyi viikko, toine	Passed thereafter week, another
Ja katoi kuuta kaksi	and vanished two months
(SKVR III 2275, 69–70.)	

Presents of the Son-in-Law, performed by Anni, the wife of Porisa in Kaipaala

Kulu yötä viisi, kuusi,	Elapsed nights, five, six,
Katosi kaheksan yötä	Vanished eight nights
(SKVR III 886, 31–32.)	

An equivalent to this formulaic pattern is also found in lyric epics of Estonian *regilaul* poetry. This poetry is in a language that is close to the Ingrian and other Finnic languages and dialects, and the tradition not only uses the same poetic devices, but also has close thematic relations. It presents surprisingly similar cases of formulaic variation, the use of the same type of pan-traditional register, as in the following Estonian version of the *Messages from the War* poem. The search has been made by using the Estonian equivalent of the Finnish on-line corpus (Eesti Regilaulude Andmebaas ['Estonian Runic Songs' Database']) as seen in Figure 2.

Sai siis nädal sai siis kaks,	It took a week, it took two,
Kolmandama koju ootama!	On the third waiting (for him) to come home!
(E 54321 (20), Tori Parish, Estonia, 1924, lines 8–9.)	

Using the terminology of Lauri Honko, the Estonian and Finnish lyric epics can been seen as exhibiting milieu-morphological adaptations of the *it took a long time* formula, situated in their respective "ecosystems" constituted of traditions shaped by social and natural environments (e.g. Honko 1998: 101–102 and *passim*). When dealing with South-Slavic epics, Foley refers to this kind of ecology or ecosystem on the basis of Lauri Honko's work – as those of us who attended the series of workshops Foley and Honko organized together very well know. The model of adaptation within a tradition "ecology" provides a valuable tool for considering variation across dialects of traditions.

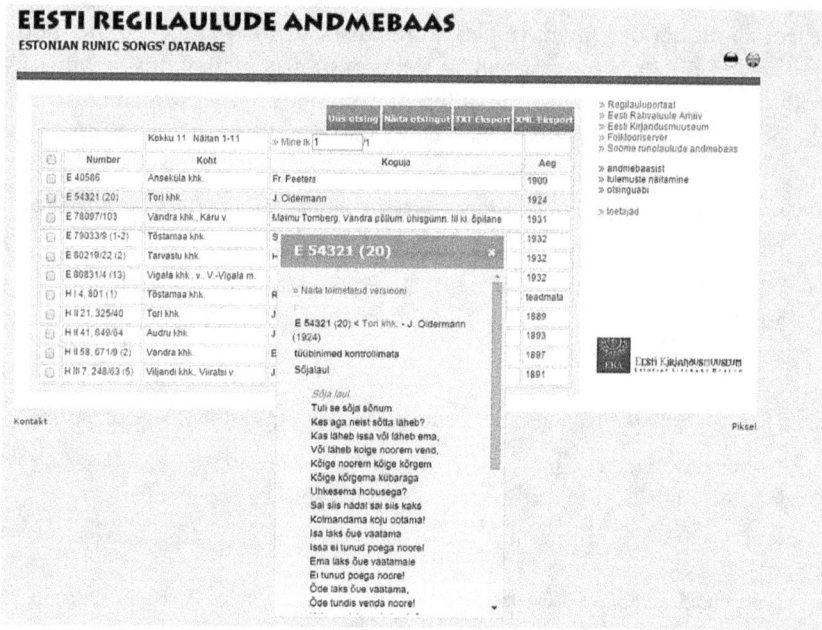

Figure 2. A screenshot from the Eesti Regilaulude Andmebaas corpus: results of a search for poems that contain the words "sai siis nädal" ['It took a week'] and "kaks" ['two']. The results of the search appear on the left, among which one poem (E 54321 (20)) was chosen to be presented (in the pop-up window).

The traditional registers function in oral texts as storage containers for idiomatic means of communication. A number of scholars have used the term "structure of expectation" (Ross 1975: 183–191, Siikala 1987: 99–100; van Dijk 1980) or "horizon of expectation" (Jauss 1982, Foley 1995: 49) to refer to the mental processes by which listeners recognise features of registers and genres and other expressive strategies within their own culture. It is thus possible to analyse the specific ethnocultural essence of traditions by making allowance for the narrative registers of the vernacular. In speaking of this, Dell Hymes uses the expression "co-variation of form and meaning" (Hymes 1985: 394), a concept launched by Roman Jakobson, as Dell Hymes himself told me in 1999, during a colloquium on epics that we headed with John Miles Foley and Lauri Honko in Turku, Finland.

Thematic Patterning and Story-Patterns

Another aspect of registers in traditional oral poetry that will be addressed here is something that Foley calls story-patterns:

> Within the epic subgenres of Wedding and Return, the two basic tale-types persist. Structurally, each one follows a recognizable latticework of events, with early narrative signals suggesting a story-map that will guide both performer and audience (and readers, if they know the tradition). For instance, whereas the prologue

Photograph of Elbek Kalkin, just about to begin the performance. When the listeners hear the first words, they will recognize that the song telling about Maaday-Kara and his son Köküdey Mergen will be performed. (Photo by Lauri Harvilahti, 1996.)

or *pripjev* to a song usually divulges nothing of the action to come (acting instead as a ritual "breakthrough into performance"[1]), the very first four-syllable increment of the main narrative can by itself subtend the particular subgenre of epic to follow. If a performance starts the main story with *I pocmili*, or 'And he cried out', the listener knows beyond doubt that a Return Song is in the offing. Why? Because that story-pattern conventionally begins with a captive shouting in prison, loudly enough to wake the ban's infant son and keep him from nursing. For that threatening situation the only possible relief is to send the captor's wife, the *banica*, to strike a bargain for the release of the offending prisoner. Thus signaled, and via an expressive economy that only the dedicated traditional register can support, the Odyssey-like tale begins. (Foley 2015, forthcoming.)

In the following, I will take an example from the Turkic Altay tradition, a song (*Maaday-Kara*) performed by the singer Elbek Kalkin in the traditional *kay* style, to the accompaniment of the instrument called a *topshuur*. In Altay epics, the singer, the *kayči*, signals the beginning of the performance with a specific introduction by playing the *topshuur*, starting to sing in *kay* style and using characteristic opening formulas.

Alïp jüzi kïzïl örtti,	The hero with a face like red flames,
Ak čïrailu ol albatï,	The people with white faces,
Altay tübin ödüp öskön,	At the bottom of the Altai multiplied,
Jaraš-čečen tildü aymak,	Eloquent, quick-witted people,
Jïltïs-čolmon köstü aymak	Morning-star-eyed people
Künniŋ közin pöktöy bergen	Covering the eye of the sun
Kün aldïnda jürbey kayttï.	Below the sun is living, it was told.
(*Maadai-Kara*, lines 1–7.)	

This famous epic has been translated into Russian in a bilingual edition (Surazakov 1973), a version of 7738 verses. Aleksej Kalkin's son Elbek was able to perform three variants from the introductory part of the epic on the same day.

The use of ethnocultural (idiomatic) strategies and registers explains the technique utilized in performing long epics. Skilled singers are able to form suppositions and expectations (hypotheses) concerning the songs' subject matter on the basis of clues provided by the traditional network of meanings. They are also able to condense the songs' subject matter, form (macro) propositions and to situate this knowledge in relation to the traditional overall structures with which the singers (and the listeners alike) are familiar. This is naturally only possible if the singer and listener share in common a sufficient amount of knowledge associated with the traditional genres to be performed. A similar process takes place in the reproduction of the poem. During the performance, the singer activates traditional verbalization processes, both generally encountered within that tradition and as a register, microstructural elements, lines and line clusters typical of that particular singer (Honko 1998: 62–65; Foley 1995: 51–52). Verses activated in the working memory, verbalized ideas, reactivate in turn new metonymic integers, which for their part are verbalized at the level of the metrical line.

Wallace Chafe (1986: 143–145) introduces the hypothesis that the limited length of the intonation entity and the working memory's restricted capacity are commensurate. The conclusion one can draw from this is that the speaker (or a singer) can retain in his/her memory one idea or intonation entity activated from a dormant state at a time. These research results are useful from the standpoint of research on epics. The intonation entity that can be found in an analysis of narrative production corresponds to the traditional poetic unit that we might call a poetic line or couplet, or, as the South Slavic singers call it, a "word" (*reč*). In any given line (or couplet) of meter there is one idea (or "word"), which either refers to an object or describes a situation/event. The length of the line or couplet, and supporting melodic phrases, normally does not exceed the limits of the working memory. One important thing is that parallel or alternating phrases, couplets or even enjambments or clusters of verses might be regarded in this sense as a single unit or "word". Since the capacity of working memory is limited, a person requires cognitive strategies by which these limitations can be circumvented. This explains the importance of parallelism and formulaic networks for the singers' memory. The formulaic diction, parallelism, thematic patterning and story-patterns together form the "art of memory" of the tradition (Harvilahti 2000: 57, 72; Reichl 1992: 269). As I have written elsewhere, the repetition of synonymic, analogous or antithetical words combined with the same morphosyntactic structure and poetic features creates a symmetric, parallel structure that functions as a very important mnemonic device (Harvilahti 1992: 92–95; 2003: 84–89). The more often the singer performs the same epic theme, the more fixed become not only the links between the superstructure, core subject matter and microlevel elements, but also the features characteristic of the singer's idiolect. This explains why singers develop their own idiosyncratic styles of singing despite the idiomatic registers of oral poetry (Harvilahti 1992: 147).

The variation of individual words, formulas, lines and line clusters makes up systems of elements that, as Foley mentions, "stand in relationships to their referents, with those referents being much larger and more complex than those to which the usual modes of textualization have access" (Foley 1995: 50), and "each metonymic integer [interchangeable word] functions as an index-point or node in a grand, untextualizable network of traditional associations" (Foley 1995: 54, cf. 65–66). The basic elements of cognition, which underlie the processes of traditional performances, rely on the collective tradition of the community, that is, on congruent features of the shared semantic knowledge.

Conclusion

Foley's impressive approach has provided completely new tools for understanding the nature of oral tradition. He also sought new strategies to make these phenomena approachable and accessible to individuals from modern cultures as well as reciprocally applying insights from these perspectives on oral traditions to culture manifesting on the internet. This is an example of Foley's work not only on register, but also to make it accessible to readers from outside the tradition.

In the following I will pay attention to Foley's book on Serbian Moslem epics *The Wedding of Mustajbey's Son Bećirbey* (2004). In this monograph, Foley presented for the first time a method that he developed in using the internet as a platform for multimedia solutions in the field of oral tradition research. For his monograph, Foley choose a version of the epic *The Wedding of Mustajbey's Son Bećirbey* performed by the South Slavic *guslar* Halil Bajgorić in 1935 to Milman Parry and Albert Lord in the village of Dabrica in Herzegovina. The performance was recorded on aluminium records with the aid of the native *guslar* and co-fieldworker Nikola Vujnović. The book can be used together with an "E-companion", available at http://www.oraltradition.org. The reader may listen to the sound-file and read the texts. This impressive approach gives tools of a digital age for understanding oral tradition.

The combination of a printed book and an e-volume includes an informative introduction, a biographical portrait of the singer, a synopsis of the epic, the original text of 1030 poetic lines as an accurate transcription of the acoustic recording, and the translation of the text into English. The translation intends to give an understanding of the recurrent phrases and scenes of the text, instead of trying to attain to a poetical quality. This method of scientific translation gives really convincing results. After the translation the volume continues with an impressive performance-based commentary. The commentary provides us with information about poetic and ethno-cultural peculiarities of the performance and, more especially, information about the singer's personal idiolect. The chapter *Nikola Vujnović resinging* describes the checking process of the transcription made in Cambridge by NikolaVujnović. Foley notes that being himself a singer, Nikola had made eliminations, substitutions and additions, or "hearings" for what Halil had originally sung. Nikola's own idiolect influenced him while making the transcription. The next chapter, *Apparatus Fabulosus* is an analytical idiomatic lexicon of the local tradition. The lexicon is based on performances by several singers from the Stolac region. The book includes further an ethno-musicological analysis of the *guslar's* music by Wakefield Foster. The core idea of the book and the E-companion is, as professor Foley himself has written, "to ask not only what the poems mean, but also, and more fundamentally how they mean".

During the subsequent years Foley developed a new approach for digital and internet-related research in his Center for E-Research. In his article "Oral Epic in Stolac", Foley compares the system of distributing and using the open source software with the shared, idiomatic authorship of the oral traditional poetry. In the same manner that open source software is shared and developed among users, the authorship of traditional oral epic is distributed as an "idiomatic code" across whole regions in different traditions rather than "owned" by any individual performer. In the case of Stolac (or, in this article, Ingria and the Altai region), any singer of tales is able to create and re-create his/her songs, keeping the register pan-traditional, dialectal and idiolectal. Thus, the term "distributed authorship" is used in Foley's last writings as an analogue taken from the lexicon of the digital software engineering. The term has been previously used in *The Museum of Verbal Art in Pathways Project*, which Foley led. The major purpose of the Pathways Project is to illustrate and explain the fundamental similarities and correspondences between oral tradition and the internet. Foley's impressive approach has given totally new tools for understanding the nature of oral tradition. The project as a whole presented a new model building up an interdisciplinary web-portal, research platform and interactive scientific forum for the research on oral traditions of the world. The work will be continued in new arenas of performance.

I conclude my article with a proverb by John Miles Foley from his last article:

Without a tradition there is no language; without a performer there is only silence.

Thinking about the life-time work of John Miles Foley, there will be new performers and the research tradition will continue at an international level.

NOTE

1   On which see Hymes 1975; 1981: 79–141.

References

Websites

Center for Studies in Oral Tradition. Available at: http://www.oraltradition.org. Last viewed December 16, 2013.
Eesti Regilaulude Andmebaas corpus of regilaul poetry. Available at: http://www.folklore.ee/regilaul/andmebaas/. Last viewed December 16, 2013.
The Museum of Verbal Art in Pathways Project www.pathwaysproject.org. Last viewed December 16, 2013.

The SKVR corpus of Kalevala-Metric Poetry. Available at: http://www.skvr.fi. Last viewed December 16, 2013.

Literature

Chafe, Wallace 1986. Beyond Bartlett. *Poetics* 15: 139–151.
van Dijk, Teun A. 1980. *Macrostructures: An Interdisciplinary Study of Global Structures in Discourse, Interaction, and Cognition*. New Jersey: Hillsdale.
Elmer, D. F. 2009. Presentation Formulas in South Slavic Epic Song. *Oral Tradition* 24: 41–59. Available at: http://journal.oraltradition.org/issues/24i/elmer.
Elmer, D. F. 2010. Kita and Kosmos: The Poetics of Ornamentation in Bosniac and Homeric Epic. *Journal of American Folklore* 123: 276–303.
Foley, J. M. 1990. *Traditional Oral Epic: The Odyssey, Beowulf, and the Serbo-Croatian Return Song*. Berkeley / Los Angeles: University of California Press.
Foley, J. M. 1995. *The Singer of Tales in Performance*. Bloomington IN: Indiana University Press.
Foley, J. M. 1999. *Homer's Traditional Art*. University Park, PA: Pennsylvania State University Press.
Foley, J. M. 2002. *How to Read an Oral Poem*. Urbana / Chicago: University of Illinois Press.
Foley, J. M. 2004. *The Wedding of Mustajbey's Son Bećirbey*. FF Communications 283. Helsinki: Academia Scientiarum Fennica.
Foley, J. M. 2015 (forthcoming). Oral Epic in Stolac: Collective Tradition and Individual Art, in Singers and Tales in the 21st Century. In *Legacies of Milman Parry and Albert Lord*. Ed. David Elmer & Peter McMurray. Publications of the Milman Parry Collection. Cambridge, MA: Harvard University Press.
Halliday M. (e.a.) 1964. *The Linguistic Sciences and Language Teaching*. London: Longmans.
Halliday: M. A. K. 1978. *Language as Social Semiotic: The Social Interpretation of Language and Meaning*. London: Edward Arnold.
Harvilahti, Lauri 1992. *Kertovan runon keinot: Inkeriläisen runoepiikan tuottamisesta*. Helsinki: Suomalaisen Kirjallisuuden Seura.
Harvilahti, Lauri 1994. The Ingrian Epic Poem and Its Models. In *Songs Beyond the Kalevala: Transformations of Oral Poetry*. Ed. Anna-Leena Siikala & Sinikka Vakimo. Studia Fennica Folkloristica 2. Helsinki: Finnish Literature Society. Pp. 91–112.
Harvilahti, Lauri 2000. Variation and Memory. In *Thick Corpus, Organic Variation and Textuality in Oral Tradition*. Ed. Lauri Honko. Studia Fennica Folkloristica 7. Helsinki: Finnish Literature Society. Pp. 57–75.
Harvilahti, Lauri, in collaboration with Zoja S. Kazagačeva 2003. *The Holy Mountain: Studies on Upper Altay Oral Poetry*. FF Communications 282. Helsinki: Academia Scientiarum Fennica.
Honko, Lauri 1998. *Textualizing the Siri Epic*. FF Communications 264: Helsinki: Academia Scientiarum Fennica.
Hymes, Dell 1975. Breakthrough into Performance. In *Folklore: Performance and Communication*. Ed. D. Ben-Amos & K. Goldstein. The Hague: Mouton. Pp. 11–74.
Hymes, Dell 1981. *"In Vain I Tried to Tell You": Essays in Native American Ethnopoetics*. Philadelphia: University of Pennsylvania Press.
Hymes, Dell 1985. Memory, and Selective Performance: Cultee's "Salmon's Myth" as Twice Told to Boas. *The Journal of American Folklore* 98(390): 391–434.
Hymes, Dell 1989. Ways of Speaking. In *Explorations in the Ethnography of Speaking*. 2nd edn. Ed. R. Bauman & J. Sherzer. Cambridge: Cambridge University Press. Pp. 433–551, 473–474.

Jauss, Hans Robert 1982. *Toward an Aesthetic of Reception.* Trans. Timothy Bahti. Theory and History of Literature 2. Minneapolis: University of Minnesota Press.

Reichl, Karl 1992. *Turkic Epic Poetry: Traditions, Forms, Poetic Structure.* New York / London: Garland.

Ross, Robert N. 1975. Ellipsis and the Structure of Expectation. San Jose State Occassional Papers in Linguistics 1. San Jose, CA: San Jose State University. Pp. 183–191.

Siikala, Anna-Leena 1987. Kertomus, kerronta, kulttuuri. In *Kieli, kertomus, kulttuuri.* Ed. T. Hoikkala. Helsinki: Gaudeamus. Pp. 98–117.

Siikala, Anna-Leena 1989. Myyttinen ajattelu ja loitsujen variaatio. In *Runon ja rajan teillä.* Ed. Seppo Knuuttila & Pekka Laaksonen. Kalevalaseuran vuosikirja 68. Helsinki: Suomalaisen Kirjallisuuden Seura. Pp. 65–81.

Surazakov S. S. 1973. *Maadaj-Kara: Altaj kaj čörčök* (zapis' teksta, perevod, priloženija). Moskva: Nauka.

Kati Kallio

16. Multimodal Register and Performance Arena in Ingrian Oral Poetry

I initially encountered problems when trying to interpret the attested variation in historical and locale-specific genres of West-Ingrian oral poetry. On the basis of earlier research on indigenous (emic, local) genres in various cultures, it seemed evident that no overarching classification could be found, but that each local system was flexible, and that local categories overlapped with one another. Despite this assumption, I was not able to explain the ways that the different poetic, musical and performative patterns and references to various performance situations were combined in the archival records until I considered combining the concepts of register, multimodality and performance arena. The basic idea of *register* as a situational style of communication, based on reflexive models of conduct that yield shared conventions within a speech community (Agha 2004; 2007) shows that even the most problematic Ingrian recordings may be analysed as natural results of the use of specific registers in atypical contexts, resulting in fractionally distinct variants. On the other hand, the concept of *multimodality* helps to grasp the meaning potentials of different textual, musical and performative features, which may either contradict or reinforce each other (Kress 2010; see also Finnegan 2002). In the context of Ingrian poetry, where the local genres and performance styles are highly defined and determined by the contexts of singing, the concept of *performance arena* (Foley 1995, and this volume; see also Sykäri 2011) is also a useful one. It denotes the typical situation of a use of a register, or a memory of that situation, which can be activated through the register itself by association. These theoretical frames help to explain the complex archival representations of Ingrian singing cultures.

The material of my research (Kallio 2013) that forms the base of this article consists of archival manuscripts and sound recordings collected from the Soikkola and Narvusi districts of West-Ingria from 1853 to 1938 by some thirty scholars and students. Ingria of the time was a multiethnic and multireligious area, situated between St. Petersburg and Estonia on the southern shore of the Baltic Sea. Three prominent Finnic groups, Votes, Izhorians and Ingrian-Finns, all sang Kalevala-metric poems in their own languages and in their own, partly shared ways. Kalevala-metric poetry was a mega-genre: epic, lyric, charms, ritual songs, mocking songs, lullabies and proverbs all used the same poetic idiom. In Ingria, the most prominent singers of these songs were women and girls. Theoretically, any Kalevala-metric poem may be sung with any melody, but in practice the melodies and ways of performing the poems were connected to situational local genres. In the context of Finnic Kalevala-metric poetry, Ingria is known for its exceptionally vast spectrum of different melodies and performance styles. The archival material that has been used here consists of roughly 5,500 poems, 500 musical notations and 170 short sound recordings.

Genre in Kalevala-Metric Poetry

For a folklorist, the concept of *genre* is more conventional than that of register. Genre was developed in early folklore research as a clear-cut taxonomic category, defined by the researcher for the needs of archives and comparative research. More recently, scholars have become interested in analysing local and indigenous models of the relationship between forms of communication and their meanings, and, thus, have redefined the concept as a more flexible and layered one. (See Ben-Amos 1992; Finnegan 1977: 15; Honko 1998: 24–29; see also Briggs & Bauman 1992.) Richard Bauman (1992: 54) notes that genre has been defined in quite diverse ways, "ultimately taking in everything that people have considered significant about folklore: form, function of effect, content, orientation to the world and the cosmos, truth value, tone, social distribution, and manner or context of use." At its best, the concept is taken as a tool for analysis, communication and scholarly comparison, and there, it also provides the means to move between abstract, theoretical structures and local practices (see Tarkka 2005: 67–70; see also Koski 2011: 49–53, 61–62; Tarkka 2013: 67–102.)

William Hanks (1987: 681) notes that the genres of oral tradition are better defined as stereotypical models of performance, and construal rather than as fixed features of "discourse structure":

> [Genres] can be defined as the historically specific conventions and ideals according to which authors can compose discourse and audiences receive it. In this view, genres consist of orienting frameworks, interpretive procedures, and sets of expectation that are not part of discourse structure, but of the ways actors relate to and use language. (Hanks 1987: 870; see also Bauman 1986.)

The forms, contents, appropriate settings and performance styles of a genre may vary depending on the tradition. Lauri Honko (1998: 75–88) describes how the same epic may be performed in very different ways and in very different contexts: in solo or group performances, in ritual or while working, with different melodies or speech, and in performances of very different length. In this case, it would be rather suitable to talk about the epic genre and its applications in different registers (or "enregistered styles", Agha 2007: 186) and performance arenas.

It was customary in earlier scholarship to classify the genres of Kalevala-metric poetry along the lines of classical western poetry as epic, lyric, ritual poems, proverbs and charms. Especially in Ingria, this led to difficulties. Most of the poems consisted of both epic and lyric features, others of lyric and ritual or proverbial features. When Väinö Salminen edited the Ingrian poetry for publication in the extensive volumes of *Suomen Kansan Vanhat Runot* ['The Ancient Poems of the Finnish People'], he had to add new categories and to confess in the preface that the system still did not work (Salminen 1915: 3; Kallio 2013: 97).

The perspective is very different in recent works, notably in that of Senni Timonen (2004: 84–195, 238–303). Timonen has analysed the ways the Ingrian singers themselves used and labelled their poems. In her discussion, the old labels given by the researchers are only an aid for scholarly communication and analysis. Her results are in line with modern approaches to oral genres: the local system was flexible and layered. Some poems or poetic themes were used only in one particular indigenous genre, while others could be used in a spectrum of genres. For the singers, the categories of epic and lyric were insignificant. Their genres were built on the typical singing situations and were highly context-dependent. It was common to start singing with a particular theme or poem that was explicitly connected to the performance context. The melodies were connected to the genres and singing contexts, not to any particular poems (see also Särg 2009). After the first contextual poem or theme, other poems were performed with the same melody. Timonen (2004: 156) notes that these other poems were still, in one way or another, adapted to the characteristics of a particular genre, singing context and habitus and mood of performers.

A more detailed study of the Ingrian performance practices (Kallio 2013) shows, that, indeed, not all the genres were built according to the same principles. In some ritual contexts, the local genre consisted of one poem or poetic cycle only, and no other themes or poems were added. In some genres, such as in dancing songs or lullabies, there were many optional melodies and opening formulas, and, particularly in lullabies, almost any Kalevala-metric poem could be used. In still other contexts, such as when all the village gathered to sing by the huge swing or when the girls were ritually walking to the seasonal bonfires, the case was exactly as defined by Timonen: the singers began with one poetic and one musical context-bound theme and kept the very same melody when continuing with a rich variety of different, thematically connected poems.

Multimodal Register

The concept of *register* has gained increasing popularity also in folkloristics. Here, the use of the concept is often based on the notion of the sociolinguist Dell Hymes (1989: 440), who described registers as "major speech styles associated with recurrent types of situation." Kaarina Koski (2011: 324) points out that folklore researchers using the concept of register often emphasise linguistic forms or stylistics, while those using genre tend to concentrate on the content, functions or uses of tradition. Some folklorists use both of the concepts. Koski (2011) herself uses the concept of genre to denote the typical content, and (linguistic) register to illustrate the features that are connected to linguistic, intentional or contextual features of a narrative. Lotte Tarkka (2005) takes register to depict the common poetic idiom (Kalevalameter), and genre to denote indigenous or practical genres based on different kinds of uses of the idiom, such as proverbs, charms and wedding songs. Eila Stepanova (2012) takes register to represent the communicative whole based on the traditional genre, communicative situation and the structure of participants. Lauri Harvilahti (2003: 78–81) shows the prose and verse forms of Altaic epic are dependent on the mode of performance, not on the epic entity itself. One register (or a mode or a way of performance) may be used to perform several genres (Harvilahti 2003: 101).

In linguistic anthropology, Asif Agha (2004; 2007) takes registers as socially constructed linguistic repertoires shared by a certain group of people, a speech community. These shared *ways of speaking*, to use the term of Dell Hymes (1989), change and vary in different historical contexts, yielding fractionally distinct models that differentiate persons and groups from each other (Agha 2007: 258). With Ingrian songs, this means that there is a need to take into account the local, ethnic and historical variation of what I will call the *ways of singing*. Agha (2004: 24) states that registers are associated both "with particular social practices and with persons who engage in such practices." In similar way, Anna-Leena Siikala (2000; 2012) has analysed different local Kalevala-metric song cultures in relation to central contexts and practices of performance as well as to the typical habitus of the performers. Indeed, the Ingrian registers of singing vary according to groups of typical performers. In weddings, for example, the unmarried girls had their own register, built on more melodic and textual variation than the other wedding registers (Kallio 2013: 306–312).

Agha (2004; 2007) stresses the recurrent, shared nature of registers. Nevertheless, this does not mean that all users would make similar interpretations. On the contrary: locale-specific differences are to be expected, based both on the differences of competence and on the different, sometimes competing interpretations of the registers among the users or among different sub-groups of users (e.g. Agha 2004: 24–25). This notion helps to explain instances, for example, where one Ingrian singer strongly emphasises one local genre, context of use and style of performance of a particular poem, while other singers of the same local community give descriptions that are nearly the opposite (Kallio 2013: 348–355). Agha (2004: 30) notes, that the possibilities of use of registers are always wider than what is explicitly being told by the users. The users usually talk about typical ways of using them, not about all possible applications and variations.

The concept of register is indispensable when analysing the Ingrian context-bound, flexible ways of singing. In my use, the term *local genre* refers to a register that is explicitly named and recognised by the singers themselves, while the term *register* provides possibilities to study additional implicit phenomena that are to be recognised only via analysing the uses and combinations of poems, melodies and styles of performance. John Miles Foley (1995: 8, 47–56, 79–82) uses the term of *performance arena* to refer to frames of interpretation based on the typical performance contexts and social settings. Here, performance arena and register are closely linked: particular performance contexts and ways of performance define each other. The concept of *performance arena* may be seen as the other half of the description of the register by Dell Hymes (1989: 440) above: the (stereo)typical, recurrent performance situation of a particular speech style. Like Venla Sykäri (2011: 61, 205–206), I consider that this recurrent performance situation may also appear as a mental reference only.

When analysing referentiality, Michael Silverstein (2005) discusses both references to single uses or performances and to conventional types of discourse. In the case of Ingrian archival material, we may primarily trace references of particular recorded performances to conventional registers, performance arenas and local genres. In Ingria, these referential ties may be linguistic or textual, but also kinaesthetic, vocal or musical: gestures, vocal styles, melodies, and movements. When communication is analysed as multimodal, the picture of the referential ties of discourse gets more and more complex. Meanings of non-linguistic features are seldom unambiguous, solid or easy to describe linguistically (Finnegan 2002; Harvilahti 1998: 200, 203; Tedlock & Tedlock 1985). Yet, via the concept of register, as used in linguistic anthropology, it is possible to conceptualise the ways the different non-linguistic features are associated with particular registers within a speech community, and thus how they are also associated with different areas of communication, central contents, performance arenas, and identities.

Social semiotics has lead a broad discussion on multimodality (Hodge & Kress 1988; Jewitt 2009; Kress 2010; van Leeuwen 1999), which, in some points, overlaps with what has been said about the concept of register. In a similar manner, the discussion has its roots in sociolinguistics (see Halliday 1978), and, later, in systematic-functional linguistics, where the linguistic meanings are taken as contextual, complex and formed in social practices. Instead of seeking solid, fixed meanings of codes or systems, social semiotics aims at analysing the semiotic (meaning-making) potentials or resources of different kinds of signs. The communicative meanings of a particular utterance are a sum total of various simultaneous features in different levels of communication. To understand the message means to make an overall interpretation of various simultaneous messages in different levels of communication that are modifying each other. For example, the tone of voice may reinforce, change or contradict the linguistic or kinaesthetic message. (Finnegan 2002: 235–239; Jewitt 2009; van Leeuwen 1999: 9.)

The tones of voice, emotions and various performative and musical features are universally understandable only to a limited extent from outside the tradition. Even though we typically recognise some basic emotions, such as happiness or sadness, in intercultural communication, the more subtle meanings and tones given to these emotions in particular situations are impossible to grasp without knowing the culture-specific patterns of communication. (See Johnstone & Scherer 2004; Knapp & Hall 2002.) Moreover, even the members of the same speech community have various interpretive competences and attitudes: a performance may enable various kinds of different, even contradictory interpretations also of emotions (see Agha 2004: 24; Finnegan 2002: 236–237). For example, in West-Ingrian singing culture, the sadness of a song emerged in various levels of performance. Of course, certain poems and poetic themes were explicitly sad, wrapping around the themes of loss, sadness and tears, such as the opening formula *La laulan surruisen verren, / surukkahan suita mööte* (SKVR III 588, 1–2) ['Let me sing a sad song, / a sad song along my mouth']. Some particular melodies and some refrains were also considered sad, and used with sad poetic themes in particular. The slow tempo of singing and slow movement, such as slow walking in a circle, or singing while standing still were likewise associated with the sadness of singing. Nevertheless, it was possible to combine happy or neutral poems with sad and slow melodies and, moreover, it was possible to sing sad and tragic poems with fast (and conventionally happy) dancing tunes, resulting in rather complex overall messages conveyed by the performance. (Kallio 2013: 348–355.) On the other hand, in the context of ritual poems, the slowness of tempo and movement did not stand for the sadness of the song, but rather for the ritual, serious and festive character of the performance (Kallio 2013: 220–316). The different features of song were usable in different contexts and in various combinations, and only in these combinations did they produce particular performance-connected meanings. The meaning of slowness, for example, depended on the context of singing and on the poems performed, both being basic elements of local genres. Indeed, as Frog (2013: 28) notes in discussing analysis of genres and registers, "the functions and/or significance of elements may vary across genres." The co-occurring parts of a multimodal message defined the situational meaning potentials of each other, and the message was the total sum of all the features involved (see also Finnegan 2002: 235).

Situational Registers in Ingrian Oral Poetry

In the Ingrian archival material, the public and ritual registers are easiest to recognise. They were recorded in abundant quantities and were performed in rather stable ways even in atypical recording contexts. These registers are of three types: *a*) some calendric festivals had particular ritual song registers; *b*) weddings consisted of a complex array of song and lament registers; and *c*) various kinds of dancing songs were connected to both of these contexts, but clearly separated from most ritual registers. In addition, there were other, less prominent registers: melodies connected to singing while standing still, working songs, lullabies, men's songs, various multi-purpose singing styles, poems and melodies etc. Nevertheless, these last registers are more difficult to define in the archival materials: it seems that they might have been more local, amorphous, versatile and diverse than the ritual, public registers. It seems also probable that the casual, everyday registers were not presented to the collectors with similar emphases on the ways of performance, or a similar amount of explanation about the typical contexts of singing, as were the heightened ones.

The most prominent calendric registers in West-Ingrian archival material are the bonfire songs (*kokkovirsi*) performed on Pentecost and Midsummer, songs for swinging (*liekkuvirsi*) performed on Easter and less ritually on other holy days during the summer, songs for St. Eliah and St. Peter (*Iilian virsi, Pedron virsi*) performed at the festivals of these saints (the 29th of June and the 20th of July, according to the Julian calendar), and the songs of *koljada* (*kiletoivirret*) during the Christmas period (*koljada* refers to the Slavic winter solstice with traditions of roaming around the village, singing and asking for hospitality).

The songs for the bonfire were sung by girls walking to or dancing by the seasonal bonfire: there was a particular opening theme and several local melody types, and all kinds of lyric and epic poetry was then sung to the same tune, all within the same register. The register of songs for swinging was similar, but the melody type was more stable. The whole village sang swinging songs on Easter, but only girls sang these songs on other festival days and on Sundays during the summer. The songs for Elijah and Peter (*Iilia* and *Pedro*) were nearly the same song except for the opening formulas addressing the particular saint. Both were performed as a part of the ritual drinking of beer which was intended to ensure enough rain to make the slash-and-burn crops sprout. No other poems were sung in this situation, which makes the register a particular one. The songs of *koljada* constituted a larger poetic cycle or drama in which youths walked from house to house, asking for food and beer, and dancing and singing the whole time. (Kallio 2013: 220–271.)

The most central and complex singing event in Ingrian culture was the wedding. Already the researchers of the early twentieth century claimed that almost every Ingrian oral poem was linked to the themes of the wedding poetry in one way or another, and in fact, that all kinds of Kalevala-metric poetry was also used during the ceremony, which lasted for several days, with some associated events occurring both before and after (Salminen 1917). The wedding ceremony included ritual wedding songs proper, lyric, lyrical epic, mocking songs, dancing songs and so on. Nevertheless, all of the various genres had their own places in the ritual, and they were not equally prominent (Kallio 2013: 274–316.) During the drinking at the end of the wedding, according to Väinö Salminen (1917: 30), all kinds of poems – "even the hymns from the Lutheran hymnal" – could be sung as a competition between the two families. Weddings marked a major social change in the life and the status of the bride: she was to leave her family and the group of unmarried girls in order to move to live with the family of the groom, which often meant moving to another village. For the two families, the wedding ceremony was about the negotiation and creation of a new mutual relationship. (Anttonen 1987; Ilomäki 1998.)

In the local system, the ritual wedding songs proper were typically called wedding poems (*pulmavirsi*). They consisted of various hierarchical sub-categories, such as bathing poems, poems of the bride, mocking poems and poems to make the bride sit (*kylvetysvirsi, morsiamen virsi, narrimisvirsi, istuttamisvirsi*) (Kallio 2013: 167–171). Some singers claimed all of these poems should be performed *yhellä sanalla* ['with one word'], that is to say, with song patterns of repeating only one poetic verse at a time. Indeed, all the wedding melodies proper proceed with the alteration of a lead singer performing one verse and a choir repeating it. In some registers of wedding song, the verse could include partial repetition, but one turn would in any case consist of only one new poetic verse. In the context of the quantity of various Ingrian song structures, this simplicity is remarkable. In Ingrian weddings, it was characteristic that the bride, groom and their parents did not sing poems. Instead, the bride and her female relatives were supposed to lament. The laments and Kalevala-metric poems were poetically, metrically and musically distinct registers, but, particularly in the wedding context, they were interconnected at many levels from phraseology to performative features. (Kallio 2013: 274–316.)

All in all, five distinct Kalevala-metric wedding registers proper can be distinguished in the West-Ingrian traditions. These registers were connected to certain poems, melodies, performance styles (tempo, movement, probably also voice quality), groups of singers and positions in the ritual. The most prominent ritual register was also the most simple both musically and stylistically. The most central wedding poems constituted a ritual dialog between the two families. These were sung with very simple and short, four- or six-beat melodies. Within this register, the most heightened poems were sung slowly while standing still or walking slowly in a circle, whereas thematically less prominent poems were sung faster, and sometimes danced to with rhythmic movements. It is not clear how great a difference the six- and four-beat melody types made within this register, whether they were totally interchangeable, made sub-registers of their own, or whether the differences of use were of local character. On the level of the whole region of Ingria, it is evident that musical registers varied by locality and ethnic group, indexically differentiating them from each other. There were local genres with similar contexts of use, poetic themes and performative features, but the melodies, refrains, poetic formulas and song structures typically represented different types in different localities. (Kallio 2013: 286–298.)

The girls of the village, the peer group of the bride, had their own register that consisted of the widest spectrum of poetic, musical and performative features of all the Ingrian ritual registers. It borrowed from the most central ritual wedding register, but also from laments, Kalevala-metric lyric and lyrical Russian melodies. With this register, the girls made the bride lament and created a dialogue with her laments, but also addressed the spokesman of the groom and gave advice to the groom. Many features of the register, the melodies in particular, were of very local character. (Kallio 2013: 306–312.)

In addition, there was a wedding register for singing while driving or walking from the bride's house to the home of the groom (often in another village), a register to thank the cook and a register to sing some lyrical epic connected to weddings in some non-heightened moments (the term 'lyrical epic' denotes personalized, often ballad-like poems that consist both of features that are typically associated with epic and of those that are associated with lyric poetry). In addition, the youths would sing all kinds of dancing songs outside the festive house, and there were also moments for different kinds of songs not belonging to any wedding registers proper. (Kallio 2013: 299–316.)

Versatile Uses of Wedding Registers

Ingrian wedding registers are a good example of the versatility of register models of conduct. The themes, melodies and performance styles of wedding songs were useable not only in weddings, but also outside of the most central performance arenas. This makes the interpretation of archival material more difficult: one has to decipher whether an instance of a poem or a melody exemplifies the primary register or is being applied in other performance arenas in occasion-specific ways, or whether some features of a particular register model have routinely become incorporated into one or more other registers. Our ability to answer such questions about registers depends on the availability of metapragmatic data, namely data that typify the kinds of act being performed through the usage (Agha 2007: 150–154). In the Ingrian archival data, the linear placement of an element within a song is an implicit metapragmatic cue in some cases. Descriptions of usage by singers provide explicit metapragmatic data in other cases. I illustrate both types of cases below.

As Senni Timonen (2004: 107–126, 153, 254) has shown, registers of wedding song were sometimes intertwined with bonfire songs and with some autobiographical songs. *Kokkovirsi*, the bonfire song, was sung when the girls were walking and dancing through the village to gather at the seasonal festive bonfire, and also while dancing at the bonfire itself. A particular poetic opening formula and characteristic melody types and refrains were typical of this local genre. Although all kinds of lyric and epic songs were used, their themes were typically connected to the experiences, dreams and fears of the young maidens. Marrying was one of their central dreams and fears, often represented in the poems connected to this local genre. Themes from the wedding songs proper were occasionally applied to songs for the bonfire in order to refer to this central locus of hopes and fears (Kallio 2013: 244–249). On the other hand, the opening themes and central formulas of bonfire songs were occasionally used in wedding songs, where they served as a symbol of the (past) community of girls. Typically, the opening themes of the song for the bonfire were embedded in the middle of some improvisational lyrical wedding poems. (Kallio 2013: 245–246.) This seems typical for the use of Ingrian song registers. When the central (opening) themes of one song register were embedded into some other register, they were not placed at the beginning of the song, but only in the middle of it. It seems that the opening verses were regarded as one of the most important signals of the register of the song (cf. Bauman 1977: 9–24). They could occasionally be used within other registers, but never in the opening position. In these cases, linear placement or position of elements within a song provides metapragmatic cues regarding the type of register to which a particular song primarily belongs.

The wedding songs were also used in autobiographical contexts. There, the ritual poems were treated rather freely, combining and moulding the themes, and merging them with various lyric and epic ones. (Salminen 1917: 20; Kallio 2013: 275; Timonen 2004: 153.) Unfortunately, there is very little information on the performance practices of these kinds of individual, personal songs. There probably were many possibilities and various choices of different genre-related melodies and performance styles. The assumption of rather free composition of autobiographical personal register helps to analyse one rare sound recorded song cycle, where the singer alternatively uses both the melodies and textual themes of wedding songs and of the bonfire songs. She sings the wedding poem with a melody for the bonfire and a poem for the bonfire with a wedding melody (SKSÄ A 301/43a–47a). In all the other archival sound recordings, the singers maintained the boundaries of ritual registers, using wedding melodies for the wedding poems proper. This leaves only a few interpretive options. A conventional genre-based interpretation would be that this particular singer was too nervous about the recording and got confused or was just very incompetent. Nevertheless, it is also possible that she was representing the autobiographical or other non-ritual ways of using and mixing these central ritual registers. In an autobiographical context, it was conventional to use and mould various lyric themes: this was, in fact, a central feature of the autobiographical register itself (see Timonen 2004: 161–195). This private register included various poetic themes: specific lyrical themes, features from ritual registers, and personal improvisation. Indeed, it is often difficult to conclude whether, in the recording situations, the singers presented improvisational lyrical wedding songs or autobiographical songs building on the wedding poetry, as the line between these is sometimes difficult to draw.

Further, wedding songs or other ritual songs were sometimes used even as lullabies or as private entertainment, and there, once again, not all the ritual register stereotypes were valid. In 1877, the Izhorian women Vöglä and Okkuli performed a cycle of songs to the Finnish scholar A. A. Borenius (SKS KRA e 193–199; SKVR III 591–598). Borenius was writing down both the poems and the first lines of the melodies. The recorded repertoire by Vöglä and Okkuli finely represents the most central Ingrian public song registers. The women started with a poem and melody belonging to the most central wedding register. Nevertheless, they told Borenius that with this 'same wedding melody [we] sing to children and other poems as well' (*Samalla pulmanootill lauletaan lapselleki ja muitaki versii*: SKS KRA Borenius 193). Such accounts constitute an explicit metapragmatic discourse about the uses of particular song elements, and the range of activities they enabled. After this first wedding song, the women sang a second one with another type of a central wedding melody, and then another melody belonging to the girl's wedding register. After that came one popular multi-purpose melody (*sitä noottii enemmikseen lauletaa* ['that melody we most often sing']: SKS KRA Borenius 196), another popular one with no specific remarks and then one very atypical swinging song (*leekutusvirsi*), which illustrates well the flexibility of the use of the registers and the effect of the singing context on the choice of register.

The swinging register was one of the most stable ritual registers. In this regard, it was similar to the most central wedding register. The swings were huge, made to seat from ten to fifteen adults, and swinging was a part of the ritual beginning of the summer season at Easter. In western Ingria, this register consisted of contextual opening formulas and themes, such as *La ka katson leekkuvani* ['Let me see my swing'], or *Leekkuvani keekkuvani* ['My swinger, my sawyer'], a simple one-line, four-beat melody and a lot of different epic and lyric poetic themes with which the song could continue. The poems were sung while swinging. (Kallio 2013: 236–243.) Now, the poem by Vöglä and Okkuli was a conventional swinging poem proper, but their five-beat melody was far from being a typical one (SKS KRA e 198). In order to explain this exceptional use of melody, we need to gather the little contextual information that is available. Borenius reports that a girl, still a child, was present and sometimes sang with the women. Here, it seems that the presence of the young girl affected the choice of register: the women used not the typical swinging melody, but one of the lullaby melodies. The verb *leekkua* ['to swing'] meant both to swing in the huge, ritual swing and to swing in a cradle. Accordingly, the women named their song not a swinging song, but *Leekutusnootti (jolla myöskin lapsia nukutetaan)* (SKS KRA Borenius 198) ['a song to make someone swing (that is also used while putting children to sleep)']; here the register name itself provides explicit metapragmatic data on the uses of the song. (See also Kallio 2013: 344–347; 2011.) They drew both from the ritual swinging songs and from private lullabies, and the result was a hybrid. It was a swinging poem used as a lullaby, or a lullaby making use of the swinging poem. Yet, as a text only, or without the contextual remarks on the manuscripts, it would be justifiable to interpret the song as a swinging song proper, with only some strange, very local or idiomatic exception of the melody type. These kinds of flexible, non-typical or transformative uses of the registers are important to take into account in analysis, although there is only rarely enough metapragmatic information in the archival material to properly explain all exceptional uses and combinations. It is probable that the autocommunicative, private and reminiscent uses of public registers have been common, although in the archives they are mostly present in the later materials, collected in the latter half of the 20th century. When the public Kalevala-metric singing was replaced with other genres and modes of performance, the private singing was still practiced, and it also assimilated features of public registers. (See Oras 2008.)

In addition to personal, private and improvisational contexts, the wedding registers were applicable in very festive and ritual-like performance arenas. The most ritual wedding themes and melodies were used to greet foreigners and guests. It is possible this style was traditional, or it might have developed as a result of modernisation, visiting fieldworkers and the emergence of stage-performances in the 1930s. Here, the themes of the wedding songs were moulded and added with newly created verses to salute and bid welcome to guests or foreigners, such as scholars, fieldworkers or even presidents (SKS KRA Enäjärvi-Haavio 912, 913; Kohtamäki VK 41:6; Salminen K. 73; SKSÄ A 507/8 a). Both the central opening formulas and the melodies of such welcome songs were borrowed from the most formal and ritual registers of wedding songs. All in all, the ceremonial wedding register, with its emphasis on heightened dialogue between the two families, appears proper indeed for such an encounter with strangers. In my interpretation, the wedding register was the most formal and respectful register that the singers had at their disposal, and precisely this valuation motivated its selection for use in such exceptional contexts.

Interpreting the Archival Material

All in all, the versatility of Ingrian wedding song registers illustrates well the factors that make the interpretation of registers in this kind of archival material a tricky task. Every instance of wedding themes or melodies requires considering whether this usage would represent a wedding song proper or whether it conforms to register stereotypes in some other private or public register or performance arena. Some registers that were based on the wedding registers proper, the autobiographical songs in particular, seem to have been local genres in themselves.

In Ingria, the recording situation itself was an atypical context for performing Kalevala-meter poetry, and this may have led to various adaptations and modifications of performance. There were several possibilities: the singer could try to represent some central register as accurately as possible, or she could try to do this only at some levels of performance (text, music, sound, movement), she could adjust the performed register to the recording context, or she could just use the features of some central registers to create or say something particular in the recording situation. This means that in order to understand the character of a particular performance, it is necessary to compare it to the larger corpus of other performances, and to analyse the typical and atypical, central and marginal ways of merging various components of performance that are associated with distinct registers, local categories and performance arenas. In recording situations, the nature of the performance arena becomes layered: both the immediate context of the recording situation and the typical cultural context of a particular performed text or melody affect what is being performed and in what way.

References

Sources

SKSÄ A 301/43a–47a. Finnish Literature Society, sound recordings by Armas Launis in 1907.
SKSÄ A 507/8 a. Finnish Literature Society, sound recordings by A. O. Väisänen, in 1931.
SKS KRA e 193–199. Finnish Literature Society, manuscripts by A. A. Borenius in 1877.
SKS KRA Enäjärvi-Haavio 912, 913. Finnish Literature Society, manuscripts by Elsa Enäjärvi-Haavio

SKS KRA Kohtamäki VK 41:6. Finnish Literature Society, manuscripts by Ilmari Kohtamäki
SKS KRA Salminen K. 73. Finnish Literature Society, manuscripts by Kaarina Salminen
SKVR III = *Suomen Kansan Vanhat Runot III*. Länsi-Inkerin Runot. Ed. Väinö Salminen. Helsinki: Suomalaisen Kirjallisuuden Seura, 1915.

Literature

Agha, Asif 2004. Registers of Language. In *A Companion to Linguistic Anthropology*. Ed. Alessandro Duranti. Malden: Blackwell. Pp. 23–45.
Agha, Asif 2007. *Language and Social Relations*. Cambridge: Cambridge University Press.
Anttonen, Pertti 1987. *Rituaalinen pilkka länsi-inkeriläisissä kylähäissä*. Unpublished master's thesis. S 351. University of Helsinki, Folklore studies.
Bauman, Richard 1977. *Verbal Art as Performance*. Illinois: Prospect Heights.
Bauman, Richard 1986. *Story, Performance and Event: Contextual Studies of Oral Narrative*. Cambridge: Cambridge University Press.
Bauman, Richard 1992. *Folklore, Cultural Performances, and Popular Entertainments: A Communications-Centered Handbook*. New York: Oxford University Press.
Ben-Amos, Dan 1992. *Do We Need Ideal Types (in Folklore)? – An Address to Lauri Honko*. Nordic Institute of Folklore. Papers 2. Turku: Nordic Institute of Folklore.
Briggs, Charles L., & Richard Bauman 1992. Genre, Intertextuality and Social Power. *Journal of Linguistic Anthropology* 2: 131–172.
Finnegan, Ruth 2002. *Communicating: The Multiple Modes of Human Interconnection*. London: Routledge.
Finnegan, Ruth 1977. *Oral Poetry: Its Nature, Significance and Social Context*. Cambridge: Cambridge University Press.
Foley, John Miles 1995. *The Singer of the Tales in Performance*. Bloomington / Indianapolis: Indiana University Press.
Frog 2013. Revisiting the Historical-Geographic Method(s). *RMN Newsletter* 7: 18–34.
Halliday M. A. K. 1978. *Language as Social Semiotic: The Social Interpretation of Language and Meaning*. London: Edward Arnold.
Hanks, William 1987. Discourse Genres in a Theory of Practice. *American Ethnologist* 14: 668–692.
Harvilahti, Lauri 2003. *The Holy Mountain: Studies on Upper Altay Oral Poetry*. Folklore Fellows' Communications 282. Helsinki: Academia Scientiarum Fennica.
Harvilahti, Lauri 1998. The Poetic "I" as an Allegory of Life. In *Epic. Oral and Written*. Eds. Lauri Honko, Jawaharlal Handoo & John Miles Foley. Mysore: Central Institute of Indian Languages. Pp. 193–206.
Hodge, Robert Ian Vere, & Gunther R. Kress 1988. *Social Semiotics*. Cambridge: Polity Press.
Honko, Lauri 1998. *Textualising the Siri Epic*. Folklore Follows' Communications 264. Helsinki: Academia Scientiarum Fennica.
Hymes, Dell 1989 [1974]. Ways of Speaking. In *Explorations in the Ethnography of Speaking*. Eds. Richard Bauman & Joel Sherzer. Cambridge: Cambridge University Press. Pp. 433–451.
Ilomäki, Henni 1998. The Image of Women in Ingrian Wedding Poetry. In *Gender and Folklore. Perspectives on Finnish and Karelian Culture*. Eds. Satu Apo, Aili Nenola & Laura Stark-Arola. Studia Fennica Folkloristica 4. Helsinki: Finnish Literature Society. Pp. 143–174.
Jewitt, Carey (ed.) 2009. *The Routledge Handbook of Multimodal Analysis*. London / New York: Routledge.

Johnstone, Tom, & Klaus R. Scherer 2004 [2000]. Vocal Communication of Emotion. In *Handbook of Emotions*. Eds. Michael Lewis & Jeannette M. Haviland-Jones. 2nd edn. New York: Guilford Press. Pp. 220–235.

Kallio, Kati 2011. Interperformative Relationships in Ingrian Oral Poetry. *Oral Tradition* 25(2): 391–427. Available at: http://journal.oraltradition.org/issues/25ii/kallio.

Kallio, Kati 2013. *Laulamisen tapoja: Esitysareena, rekisteri ja paikallinen laji länsi-inkeriläisessä kalevalamittaisessa runossa*. Tampere: [Kallio]. E-thesis available at: http://urn.fi/URN:ISBN:978-952-10-9566-5.

Knapp, Mark L., & Judith A. Hall 2002. *Nonverbal Communication in Human Interaction*. 5th edn. South Melbourne: Wadsworth / Thomson Learning.

Koski, Kaarina 2011. *Kuoleman voimat: Kirkonväki suomalaisessa uskomusperinteessä*. Suomalaisen Kirjallisuuden Seuran Toimituksia 1313. Helsinki: Suomalainen Kirjallisuuden Seura.

Kress, Günther 2010. *Multimodality: A Social Semiotic Approach to Contemporary Communication*. London: Routledge.

van Leeuwen, Theo 1999. *Speech, Music, Sound*. Basingstoke: Macmillan Press.

Oras, Janika 2008. *Viie 20. sajandi naise regilaulumaailm: Arhiivitekstid, kogemused ja mälestused*. Eesti Rahvaluule Arhiivi Toimetused 27. Tartu: Eesti Kirjandusmuuseumi Teaduskirjastus.

Salminen, Väinö 1915. Preface. In *Suomen Kansan Vanhat Runot III. Länsi-Inkerin Runot*. Ed. Väinö Salminen. Helsinki: SKS, 1915.

Salminen, Väinö 1917. *Länsi-Inkerin häärunot: synty- ja kehityshistoriaa*. Helsinki: Suomalainen Kirjallisuuden Seura.

Siikala, Anna-Leena 2000. Body, Performance, and Agency in Kalevala Rune-Singing. *Oral Tradition* 15(2): 225–278.

Siikala, Anna-Leena 2012. *Itämerensuomalaisten mytologia*. Suomalaisen Kirjallisuuden Seuran Toimituksia 1388. Helsinki: Suomalainen Kirjallisuuden Seura.

Silverstein, Michael 2005. Axes of Evals: Token versus Type Interdiscursivity. *Journal of Linguistic Anthropology* 15(1): 6–22.

SKVR III = *Suomen Kansan Vanhat Runot III. Länsi-Inkerin Runot*. Ed. Väinö Salminen. Helsinki: Suomalainen Kirjallisuuden Seura, 1915.

Stepanova, Eila 2012. Mythic Elements of Karelian Laments: The Case of *syndyzet* and *spuassuzet*. In *Mythic Discourses. Studies in Uralic Traditions*. Ed. Frog, Anna-Leena Siikala & Eila Stepanova. Studia Fennica Folkloristica 20. Helsinki: Finnish Literature Society. Pp. 257–287.

Sykäri, Venla 2011. *Words as Events: Cretan* mantinádes *in Performance and Composition*. Studia Fennica Folkloristica 18. Helsinki: Suomalainen Kirjallisuuden Seura.

Särg, Taive 2009. Context-Related Melodies in Oral Culture: An Attempt to Describe Words-and-Music Relationships in Local Singing Traditions. *Journal of Ethnology and Folkloristics* 3(1): 35–56. Available at: http://www.jef.ee/index.php/journal/article/view/20.

Tarkka, Lotte 2005. *Rajarahvaan laulu: Tutkimus Vuokkiniemen kalevalamittaisesta runokulttuurista 1821–1921*. Suomalaisen Kirjallisuuden Seuran Toimituksia 1033. Helsinki: Suomalainen Kirjallisuuden Seura.

Tarkka, Lotte 2013. *Songs of the Border People: Genre, Reflexivity, and Performance in Karelian Oral Poetry*. Folklore Fellows' Communications 305. Helsinki: Academia Scientiarum Fennica.

Tedlock, Barbara, & Dennis Tedlock 1985. Text and Textile: Language and Technology in the Arts of the Quiché Maya. *Journal of Anthropological Research* 41(2): 121–146.

Timonen, Senni 2004. *Minä, tila, tunne: Näkökulmia kalevalamittaiseen kansanlyriikkaan*. Suomalaisen Kirjallisuuden Seuran Toimituksia 963. Helsinki: Suomalainen Kirjallisuuden Seura.

Contributors

Asif Agha, University of Pennsylvania

Margaret Bender, Wake Forest University

Kapitolina Fedorova, European University at St. Petersburg

Janina Fenigsen, Northern Arizona University

John Miles Foley†, University of Missouri

Frog, University of Helsinki

Lauri Harvilahti, Finnish Literature Society (SKS)

Timo Kaartinen, University of Helsinki

Kati Kallio, Finnish Literature Society (SKS)

William Lamb, University of Edinburgh

Lian Malai Madsen, University of Copenhagen

Janus Spindler Møller, University of Copenhagen

Dorothy Noyes, The Ohio State University

Alejandro I. Paz, University of Toronto

Susanna Shore, University of Helsinki

Eila Stepanova, University of Helsinki

James M. Wilce, Northern Arizona University

# Index

Ancestors 46, 51, 167–168, 170–176, 179, 184, 194–195, 199–200, 205, 264
Ancestry 182, 184, 199, 216
Aoidos 284, 288, 294, 297
Arabic 28, 30–33, 46, 50, 55, 107–110, 113–118, 120–121, 126, 130–131, 134, 166, 175–176, 180, 184
Authority 18, 30, 45–46, 50, 92, 115, 130–131, 153, 165–170, 172, 174–175, 177–178, 180–183, 214, 255
Bilingual 17, 28–29, 33, 35, 109–113, 118, 120–121, 150–151, 159
Ceremonial register 46, 220; see also *Ritual register*, *Sacred*
Charm register 40, 278, 280, 282, 298–301, 309, 322, 324–325; see also *Incantation*
Cherokee 20, 247–256
Chinese 17, 34–35, 50, 140, 144–147
Circumlocution 45, 85, 87–88, 96, 187, 189, 193, 196–197, 201, 202–204, 206, 252, 263, 265–270
Communication 7, 13–15, 27–49, 63, 70, 77, 79, 82–84, 90, 92, 95, 108, 120, 125, 134, 138–147, 165–166, 171, 173, 176, 178, 182–184, 188, 190, 194–196, 203–204, 210, 225–227, 232–233, 235, 239–240, 249, 256, 264, 266–268, 270–271, 277–278, 280–282, 294, 297, 298, 309, 315, 322–326; *autocommunication* 332; *communicative channel* 249, 251; *communicative conduct* 13–16, 23, 27, 48
Danish 15, 17, 22, 28–33, 35–36, 39, 107–117, 120–121, 124, 126–127, 130–134
Decontextualization 256
Deictic 16, 42–44, 191, 229–230, 249, 251–255; *non-deictic* 43
Diatypic 60
Enregisterment 15, 18, 27–28, 30–36, 39, 41, 43–45, 47–49, 51, 90, 92, 107–110, 112, 116, 118–119, 121, 124–126, 131, 135, 150, 152, 155, 158–159, 189, 232, 323
Epic 16, 37, 42, 82–83, 87–90, 92–95, 97, 225, 234–235, 241, 242, 260, 270, 278, 280, 282–299, 302, 303, 307–312, 314–319, 322–325, 328–332; see also *Homeric*, *Kalevalaic poetry*, *Lyric poetry*, *South Slavic*
Estonian 19, 311, 314
Farsi 113
Field 63–66, 70, 72, 81, 260, 281, 309
Finnish 19, 83, 139, 187, 192, 195, 198, 201–202, 204, 205, 206, 258, 314
Foreigner talk 17, 34, 137–147
Formula 19, 37, 39–40, 42–43, 50, 81–82, 85–87, 89, 93–94, 97, 173–175, 178, 225–240, 247, 251–253, 261, 265, 278, 282–288, 290–291, 293, 295, 297, 299, 302, 303, 310–314, 316–317, 324, 327–330, 332
French 18, 47, 109, 111, 210–220
Gaelic 15, 19–21, 43, 225–240
Gender 20, 30, 41, 60, 139, 142–143, 150, 204, 248, 270
Genre 15–16, 36–41, 45, 47–48, 50, 51, 64, 66, 68–72, 73, 78–81, 83, 88–92, 94–96, 151, 165–166, 171, 176–179, 182–184, 188–190, 193, 197–198, 201, 204, 215, 234, 237, 240, 251, 258, 260–262, 264, 270, 277, 280, 282–283, 289, 295, 299, 301, 309, 315, 317, 322–333; *Bakhtinian speech genre* 64, 70, 79–81; *boundary genre* 166, 177; *genre family* 70; *genre-dependence* 16, 299; *macrogenre* 69–72; *subgenre* 188, 302, 315–316
German 29, 91, 109, 111, 139
Guslar 241, 278, 284–290, 292–294, 297, 301, 303, 310, 318–319

Hebrew 17, 28, 35–36, 150–159, 206
"Heroic I" 46, 170–171, 176, 182, 184
Heteroglossia 150–151, 159
History 46, 166–169, 171, 177, 192, 216–217, 256, 258; *disciplinary history* 79–80; *history of performances / practice* 38, 86, 88–90, 97, 109–111, 127, 147, 159, 182–183, 189, 194, 234–235, 247, 260, 270, 289–290, 311, 322, 325; *oral history* 166, 173–174, 176; *political history* 45, 210–220; *social history* 27–28, 31, 48, 150–151, 167, 180, 182–183, 248
Homer 284, 288–290, 293
Homeric 37, 50, 97, 225–226, 278, 282–284, 287–291, 294–295, 297, 302, 309
Homeric Hymns 278
Honorific register 45, 88, 158, 187–188, 190–195, 197–204, 205, 266, 270–271
Incantation 88–89, 241, 270; see also *Charm register*
Indexical 22, 27–49, 80–81, 90, 94–95, 124, 189, 195, 233, 247–249, 258, 277–278; *indexical force* 249, 311; *indexical significance* 15–16, 37, 45, 81, 94, 133–134, 152, 159, 191, 267; *indexical value* 16–18, 27–28, 31, 37, 39, 189; *indexical order* 125–126, 135, 203–204; *social indexical* 16–18, 27–41, 44–45, 48–49, 131, 268, 270, 329; *indexical selectivity* 33–36, 39–40, 46, 49; *indexical congruence* 31, 39–40; *indexical non-congruence* 49; *indexical effect* 15, 28, 46, 125, 195
Indonesian 46, 165–184
Ingrian 38–39, 313–314, 322–333
In-group 29, 35–36, 134, 270
Integer 21–22, 37, 82, 87, 89, 93–95, 278, 282, 302; *expressive integer* 37, 40, 298, 301; *metonymic integer* 21, 37, 42, 278, 280, 282–283, 298, 317–318; *structural integer* 37; *symbolic integer* 95; see also "Word"
Intonation 41, 56, 58, 154, 158, 317
Kalevalaic poetry 83, 86–89, 93–96, 234, 311, 322–333
Kalevala-meter 88, 97, 311
Karelian 15, 18, 20–22, 28, 41, 44, 51, 83, 86–88, 95, 187–189, 191–204, 258–271
Kenning 85–88, 95–96, 97, 98
Lament 15, 18, 20–22, 41, 44–45, 51, 86–88, 95–96, 187–204, 258–271, 280, 327, 329; *funerary lament* 44, 51, 187, 193–195, 197, 199, 263–264, 269; *wedding lament* 41, 96, 188, 193, 195, 205, 264, 267, 269
Languaging 17, 31, 107–110, 112–113

Latino 15, 17, 28, 35–36, 150–159
Lexical choice 21–22, 64–65, 86, 94
Linguistic register 16, 54–72, 77–78, 82, 88–89, 92–96, 97, 125, 166, 193, 249–251, 254–255, 325
Lyric poetry 79, 88, 95, 260, 280, 298–300, 312, 314, 322, 324, 328, 329–332
Malay 46, 166, 170, 175, 184
Melody 22, 28, 39–40, 206, 264, 268, 270, 298, 323–324, 328–333
Metafunctional 57–60, 64–65, 72
Metalinguistic 34, 37, 124, 131–132, 134, 140
Metapragmatic 17–18, 27, 29–33, 36, 39, 42, 44, 47, 50, 109, 112, 124–125, 133–135, 150, 153, 159, 165, 175, 177, 187–190, 201, 203, 330–332
Metasemiotic 15–17, 33, 40, 78, 91, 270
Metonymic 21, 37, 42, 44, 91, 98, 278, 280, 282–283, 298, 300–301, 317–318
Mode 47, 61, 63–66, 68, 70, 73, 81, 90, 178, 249–254, 260, 281–282, 298–299, 309, 325, 332
Monolingual 30, 33, 109, 121
Multilingual 16–17, 28, 31, 109, 115, 283
Multimodal register 82, 322, 324–327
Mythology 79, 94, 97–98, 168, 172, 178–179, 183, 194, 234, 250–252, 270–271, 312; *mythic knowledge* 270; *register of mythology* 97
Oral poetry 15, 18, 20–22, 37–38, 77–97, 258–261, 277–301, 309–318; see also *Epic, Kalevalaic poetry, Lament, Lyric poetry, Skaldic poetry, Wedding register, Wedding songs*
Oral-Formulaic Theory 21, 37, 81–82, 86, 93, 225, 260, 277, 308
Performance 15, 21–23, 28, 31, 36–45, 47, 50, 81–83, 95–96, 108, 113–114, 116, 118, 120–121, 129–130, 167, 172, 174, 178, 181–182, 188–191, 194–195, 198–199, 204, 206, 219–220, 249, 254–255, 258–264, 266–271, 277–285, 288, 290–292, 294–295, 298–301, 309, 316–319, 322–327, 329–333
Performance arena 37, 51, 91, 277–283, 298, 301, 322–323, 326, 330, 332–333
Performance register 21–22, 43, 96
Polylanguaging 31; see also *Languaging*
Polylingual 30, 114
Punjabi 33, 113, 131, 134
Regilaul (Estonian oral poetic form) 311, 314
Register – *term* 13–14, 37–38, 50, 54–56, 78–82, 188–189; *register boundary* 30,

33, 38; *register contrasts* 7, 16–17, 21, 33; *register differentiation* 15–17, 22, 27–28, 30–34, 36, 38, 41, 48–49, 77, 112, 138, 268, 325, 329; *register formation* 15–18, 29–30, 33, 36, 38, 41, 48, 49, 109; *register model* 14, 16, 18–19, 22–23, 27–29, 36, 38–40, 47–49, 78, 90, 109, 165, 171–172, 189, 264, 268, 330; *register name* 31–33, 126–127, 131, 187, 193, 199, 332; *register organization* 13, 23, 41, 48, 260; *register partial* 15–18, 41, 43, 45, 49, 50; *register studies* 19–22, 54–72, 92, 147

Repertoire 15, 19–20, 28, 30–34

Ritual register 251, 327, 329, 331–333; see also *Ceremonial register, Sacred*

Russian 15, 17, 34–36, 39, 138, 140–147, 205, 258, 329

Sacred 181, 190–194, 200, 204, 234, 249–250, 255–256

Semiotic 13–16, 22, 47–49, 51, 63, 67, 109–110, 125, 150, 188–189, 198, 250, 278, 326; *semiotic functions* 232–234; *semiotic co-text* 32; *higher-level / higher-order semiotic* 64, 67–68, 71; *semiotic system* 61, 64, 72, 73, 91; *semiotic range* 33, 210; *semiotic ideologies* 203; *semiotic partial* 16, 28, 36, 39; *semiotic process* 16, 48; see also *Register*

Semiotic register 18, 21–22, 27, 41, 44–45, 125, 189, 259, 268–270

Skaldic poetry 83–84, 87–89, 94–95

Somali 31, 107–108, 110, 113–116, 118–121

South Slavic 42, 95, 97, 278, 280, 282–301, 307, 309–311, 313–314, 317–318

Spanish 17, 28, 35–36, 49, 151–159, 160

Speech register 17, 22, 27, 48, 112, 258

Story-pattern 16, 42, 82, 93–94, 278, 283, 315–317

String (poetic unit) 263, 267

Style 16, 34–36, 38–38, 41, 44–45, 49, 50, 51, 55, 81, 125–126, 132–133, 159, 165–166, 215–217, 260–261, 281, 299, 309, 322–327, 330–332

Supernatural powers / beings 44, 51, 88, 194–196, 264

Systemic Functional Linguistics 54–72

Tenor 63–66, 70, 72, 81, 260, 281, 309

Theme 39, 82, 92–95, 261, 267–269, 299–300, 312, 317, 324, 327–333

Translanguaging 108; see also *Languaging*

Turkicism 294–296, 303

Turkmen 113

Urdu 33, 113, 131, 134

Valorization 17, 27–28, 31, 33, 36, 108, 117, 215, 232, 237

Variation 13–15, 20, 39, 50, 54, 60, 63–64, 66, 72, 77–80, 83, 85–87, 92, 96–97, 98, 125, 140, 150, 159, 173, 228, 230–231, 236, 240, 250–251, 258–261, 265, 268–270, 278, 293, 296, 300, 310–311, 313–315, 317, 322, 325; *co-variation* 39, 92, 315

Verbal art 22–23, 45–46, 48, 77, 82–83, 173, 184, 248, 279, 280, 282–284, 288; see also *Oral poetry*

Voicing 30, 34, 38, 44–46, 51, 116–117, 129–130, 134, 154, 158, 188–189, 206, 210, 249, 261, 268, 326, 329; *other-voicing* 34–35

Wedding register 329–333

Wedding songs 39–40, 88, 96, 325, 327–333

"Word" 21, 37, 87, 227, 241, 261, 278, 283–287, 289, 292–297, 301, 310, 317; see also *Integer*

Word-power 80–81, 87, 93, 277–279, 281, 298–299, 307

Written register 14, 18, 45–46, 54–56, 59, 62–63, 66–67, 70, 72, 89, 92, 97, 131, 165–167, 171–172, 175–178, 249, 286, 288–289, 295

Studia Fennica Ethnologica

Making and Breaking of Borders
Ethnological Interpretations, Presentations, Representations
Edited by Teppo Korhonen, Helena Ruotsala & Eeva Uusitalo
Studia Fennica Ethnologica 7
2003

Memories of My Town
The Identities of Town Dwellers and their Places in Three Finnish Towns
Edited by Anna-Maria Åström, Pirjo Korkiakangas & Pia Olsson
Studia Fennica Ethnologica 8
2004

Passages Westward
Edited by Maria Lähteenmäki & Hanna Snellman
Studia Fennica Ethnologica 9
2006

Defining Self
Essays on Emergent Identities in Russia Seventeenth to Nineteenth Centuries
Edited by Michael Branch
Studia Fennica Ethnologica 10
2009

Touching Things
Ethnological Aspects of Modern Material Culture
Edited by Pirjo Korkiakangas, Tiina-Riitta Lappi & Heli Niskanen
Studia Fennica Ethnologica 11
2009

Gendered Rural Spaces
Edited by Pia Olsson & Helena Ruotsala
Studia Fennica Ethnologica 12
2009

LAURA STARK
The Limits of Patriarchy
How Female Networks of Pilfering and Gossip Sparked the First Debates on Rural Gender Rights in the 19th-Century Finnish-Language Press
Studia Fennica Ethnologica 13
2011

Where is the Field?
The Experience of Migration Viewed through the Prism of Ethnographic Fieldwork
Edited by Laura Hirvi & Hanna Snellman
Studia Fennica Ethnologica 14
2012

LAURA HIRVI
Identities in Practice
A Trans-Atlantic Ethnography of Sikh Immigrants in Finland and in California
Studia Fennica Ethnologica 15
2013

EERIKA KOSKINEN-KOIVISTO
Her Own Worth
Negotiations of Subjectivity in the Life Narrative of a Female Labourer
Studia Fennica Ethnologica 16
2014

Studia Fennica Folkloristica

Creating Diversities
Folklore, Religion and the Politics of Heritage
Edited by Anna-Leena Siikala, Barbro Klein & Stein R. Mathisen
Studia Fennica Folkloristica 14
2004

PERTTI J. ANTTONEN
Tradition through Modernity
Postmodernism and the Nation-State in Folklore Scholarship
Studia Fennica Folkloristica 15
2005

Narrating, Doing, Experiencing
Nordic Folkloristic Perspectives
Edited by Annikki Kaivola-Bregenhøj, Barbro Klein & Ulf Palmenfelt
Studia Fennica Folkloristica 16
2006

MÍCHEÁL BRIODY
The Irish Folklore Commission 1935–1970
History, Ideology, Methodology
Studia Fennica Folkloristica 17
2007

VENLA SYKÄRI
Words as Events
Cretan Mantinádes in Performance and Composition
Studia Fennica Folkloristica 18
2011

Hidden Rituals and Public Performances
Traditions and Belonging among the Post-Soviet Khanty, Komi and Udmurts
Edited by Anna-Leena Siikala & Oleg Ulyashev
Studia Fennica Folkloristica 19
2011

Mythic Discourses
Studies in Uralic Traditions
Edited by Frog, Anna-Leena Siikala & Eila Stepanova
Studia Fennica Folkloristica 20
2012

Studia Fennica Historica

Medieval History Writing and Crusading Ideology
Edited by Tuomas M. S. Lehtonen & Kurt Villads Jensen with Janne Malkki and Katja Ritari
Studia Fennica Historica 9
2005

Moving in the USSR
Western Anomalies and Northern Wilderness
Edited by Pekka Hakamies
Studia Fennica Historica 10
2005

DEREK FEWSTER
Visions of Past Glory
Nationalism and the Construction of Early Finnish History
Studia Fennica Historica 11
2006

Modernisation in Russia since 1900
Edited by Markku Kangaspuro & Jeremy Smith
Studia Fennica Historica 12
2006

SEIJA-RIITTA LAAKSO
Across the Oceans
Development of Overseas Business Information Transmission 1815–1875
Studia Fennica Historica 13
2007

Industry and Modernism
Companies, Architecture and Identity in the Nordic and Baltic Countries during the High-Industrial Period
Edited by Anja Kervanto Nevanlinna
Studia Fennica Historica 14
2007

CHARLOTTA WOLFF
Noble Conceptions of Politics in Eighteenth-Century Sweden (ca 1740–1790)
Studia Fennica Historica 15
2008

Sport, Recreation and Green Space in the European City
Edited by Peter Clark, Marjaana Niemi & Jari Niemelä
Studia Fennica Historica 16
2009

Rhetorics of Nordic Democracy
Edited by Jussi Kurunmäki & Johan Strang
Studia Fennica Historica 17
2010

Fibula, Fabula, Fact
The Viking Age in Finland
Edited by Joonas Ahola and Frog with Clive Tolley
Studia Fennica Historica 18
2014

Novels, Histories, Novel Nations
Edited by Linda Kaljundi, Eneken Laanes & Ilona Pikkanen
Studia Fennica Historica 19
2015

JUKKA GRONOW & SERGEY ZHURAVLEV
Fashion Meets Socialism
Fashion Industry in the Soviet Union after the Second World War
Studia Fennica Historica 20
2015

Studia Fennica Anthropologica

On Foreign Ground
Moving between Countries and Categories
Edited by Minna Ruckenstein & Marie-Louise Karttunen
Studia Fennica Anthropologica 1
2007

Beyond the Horizon
Essays on Myth, History, Travel and Society
Edited by Clifford Sather & Timo Kaartinen
Studia Fennica Anthropologica 2
2008

Studia Fennica Linguistica

Minna Saarelma-Maunumaa
Edhina Ekogidho – Names as Links
The Encounter between African and European Anthroponymic Systems among the Ambo People in Namibia
Studia Fennica Linguistica 11
2003

Minimal Reference
The Use of Pronouns in Finnish and Estonian Discourse
Edited by Ritva Laury
Studia Fennica Linguistica 12
2005

Antti Leino
On Toponymic Constructions as an Alternative to Naming Patterns in Describing Finnish Lake Names
Studia Fennica Linguistica 13
2007

Talk in Interaction
Comparative Dimensions
Edited by Markku Haakana, Minna Laakso & Jan Lindström
Studia Fennica Linguistica 14
2009

Planning a New Standard Language
Finnic Minority Languages Meet the New Millennium
Edited by Helena Sulkala & Harri Mantila
Studia Fennica Linguistica 15
2010

Lotta Weckström
Representations of Finnishness in Sweden
Studia Fennica Linguistica 16
2011

Terhi Ainiala, Minna Saarelma & Paula Sjöblom
Names in Focus
An Introduction to Finnish Onomastics
Studia Fennica Linguistica 17
2012

Registers of Communication
Edited by Asif Agha & Frog
Studia Fennica Linguistica 18
2015

Studia Fennica Litteraria

Changing Scenes
Encounters between European and Finnish Fin de Siècle
Edited by Pirjo Lyytikäinen
Studia Fennica Litteraria 1
2003

Women's Voices
Female Authors and Feminist Criticism in the Finnish Literary Tradition
Edited by Lea Rojola & Päivi Lappalainen
Studia Fennica Litteraria 2
2007

Metaliterary Layers in Finnish Literature
Edited by Samuli Hägg, Erkki Sevänen & Risto Turunen
Studia Fennica Litteraria 3
2009

Aino Kallas
Negotiations with Modernity
Edited by Leena Kurvet-Käosaar & Lea Rojola
Studia Fennica Litteraria 4
2011

The Emergence of Finnish Book and Reading Culture in the 1700s
Edited by Cecilia af Forselles & Tuija Laine
Studia Fennica Litteraria 5
2011

Nodes of Contemporary Finnish Literature
Edited by Leena Kirstinä
Studia Fennica Litteraria 6
2012

White Field, Black Seeds
Nordic Literacy Practices in the Long Nineteenth Century
Edited by Anna Kuismin & M. J. Driscoll
Studia Fennica Litteraria 7
2013

Lieven Ameel
Helsinki in Early Twentieth-Century Literature
Urban Experiences in Finnish Prose Fiction 1890–1940
Studia Fennica Litteraria 8
2014

www.ingramcontent.com/pod-product-compliance
Lightning Source LLC
Chambersburg PA
CBHW080803020526
44114CB00046B/2765